Red Hat® Linux® 6 in Small Business

Red Hat® Linux® 6 in Small Business

Paul G. Sery

Eric Harper

M&T Books.
An imprint of IDG Books Worldwide, Inc.

Foster City, CA ◆ Chicago, IL ◆ Indianapolis, IN ◆ New York, NY

Red Hat® Linux® 6 in Small Business

Published by
M&T Books
An imprint of IDG Books Worldwide, Inc.
919 E. Hillsdale Blvd., Suite 400
Foster City, CA 94404
www.idgbooks.com (IDG Books Worldwide Web site)

Copyright © 1999 IDG Books Worldwide, Inc. All rights reserved. No part of this book, including interior design, cover design, and icons, may be reproduced or transmitted in any form, by any means (electronic, photocopying, recording, or otherwise) without the prior written permission of the publisher.

ISBN: 0-7645-3335-5

Printed in the United States of America

10 9 8 7 6 5 4 3 2 1

1B/RU/QZ/ZZ/FC

Distributed in the United States by IDG Books Worldwide, Inc.

Distributed by CDG Books Canada Inc. for Canada; by Transworld Publishers Limited in the United Kingdom; by IDG Norge Books for Norway; by IDG Sweden Books for Sweden; by IDG Books Australia Publishing Corporation Pty. Ltd. for Australia and New Zealand; by TransQuest Publishers Pte Ltd. for Singapore, Malaysia, Thailand, Indonesia, and Hong Kong; by Gotop Information Inc. for Taiwan; by ICG Muse, Inc. for Japan; by Intersoft for South Africa; by Eyrolles for France; by International Thomson Publishing for Germany, Austria and Switzerland; by Distribuidora Cuspide for Argentina; by Livraria Cultura for Brazil; by Ediciones ZETA S.C.R. Ltda. for Peru; by WS Computer Publishing Corporation, Inc., for the Philippines; by Contemporanea de Ediciones for Venezuela; by Express Computer Distributors for the Caribbean and West Indies; by Micronesia Media Distributor, Inc. for Micronesia; by Chips Computadoras S.A. de C.V. for Mexico; by Editorial Norma de Panama S.A. for Panama; by American Bookshops for Finland.

For general information on IDG Books Worldwide's books in the U.S., please call our Consumer Customer Service department at 800-762-2974. For reseller information, including discounts and premium sales, please call our Reseller Customer Service department at 800-434-3422.

For information on where to purchase IDG Books Worldwide's books outside the U.S., please contact our International Sales department at 317-596-5530 or fax 317-596-5692.

For consumer information on foreign language translations, please contact our Customer Service department at 800-434-3422, fax 317-596-5692, or e-mail rights@idgbooks.com.

For information on licensing foreign or domestic rights, please phone +1-650-655-3109.

For sales inquiries and special prices for bulk quantities, please contact our Sales department at 650-655-3200 or write to the address above.

For information on using IDG Books Worldwide's books in the classroom or for ordering examination copies, please contact our Educational Sales department at 800-434-2086 or fax 317-596-5499.

For press review copies, author interviews, or other publicity information, please contact our Public Relations department at 650-655-3000 or fax 650-655-3299.

For authorization to photocopy items for corporate, personal, or educational use, please contact Copyright Clearance Center, 222 Rosewood Drive, Danvers, MA 01923, or fax 978-750-4470.

Library of Congress Cataloging-in-Publication Data
Sery, Paul G.

   Red Hat Linux 6 in small business/Paul G. Sery, Eric Harper.

      p. cm.

   ISBN 0-7645-3335-5 (alk. paper)

   1. Linux. 2. Operating systems (Computers) 3. Small business--Data processing.

   I. Harper, Eric. II. Title.

QA76.76.063S469   1999

005.4'469--dc21   99-38069

                                                          CIP

> LIMIT OF LIABILITY/DISCLAIMER OF WARRANTY: THE PUBLISHER AND AUTHOR HAVE USED THEIR BEST EFFORTS IN PREPARING THIS BOOK. THE PUBLISHER AND AUTHOR MAKE NO REPRESENTATIONS OR WARRANTIES WITH RESPECT TO THE ACCURACY OR COMPLETENESS OF THE CONTENTS OF THIS BOOK AND SPECIFICALLY DISCLAIM ANY IMPLIED WARRANTIES OF MERCHANTABILITY OR FITNESS FOR A PARTICULAR PURPOSE. THERE ARE NO WARRANTIES WHICH EXTEND BEYOND THE DESCRIPTIONS CONTAINED IN THIS PARAGRAPH. NO WARRANTY MAY BE CREATED OR EXTENDED BY SALES REPRESENTATIVES OR WRITTEN SALES MATERIALS. THE ACCURACY AND COMPLETENESS OF THE INFORMATION PROVIDED HEREIN AND THE OPINIONS STATED HEREIN ARE NOT GUARANTEED OR WARRANTED TO PRODUCE ANY PARTICULAR RESULTS, AND THE ADVICE AND STRATEGIES CONTAINED HEREIN MAY NOT BE SUITABLE FOR EVERY INDIVIDUAL. NEITHER THE PUBLISHER NOR AUTHOR SHALL BE LIABLE FOR ANY LOSS OF PROFIT OR ANY OTHER COMMERCIAL DAMAGES, INCLUDING BUT NOT LIMITED TO SPECIAL, INCIDENTAL, CONSEQUENTIAL, OR OTHER DAMAGES. FULFILLMENT OF EACH COUPON OFFER IS THE RESPONSIBILITY OF THE OFFEROR.

Trademarks: All brand names and product names used in this book are trade names, service marks, trademarks, or registered trademarks of their respective owners. IDG Books Worldwide is not associated with any product or vendor mentioned in this book.

The image of the Linux penguin Tux was created by Larry Ewing (lewing@isc.tamu.edu) using the Gimp (http://www.gimp.org/), and was subsequently modified for use by IDG Books Worldwide on this book's cover by Tuomas Kuosmanen (tigert@gimp.org). Tuomas also used the Gimp for his work with Tux.

 is a registered trademark or trademark under exclusive license to IDG Books Worldwide, Inc. from International Data Group, Inc. in the United States and/or other countries.

 is a trademark of IDG Books Worldwide, Inc.

ABOUT IDG BOOKS WORLDWIDE

Welcome to the world of IDG Books Worldwide.

IDG Books Worldwide, Inc., is a subsidiary of International Data Group, the world's largest publisher of computer-related information and the leading global provider of information services on information technology. IDG was founded more than 30 years ago by Patrick J. McGovern and now employs more than 9,000 people worldwide. IDG publishes more than 290 computer publications in over 75 countries. More than 90 million people read one or more IDG publications each month.

Launched in 1990, IDG Books Worldwide is today the #1 publisher of best-selling computer books in the United States. We are proud to have received eight awards from the Computer Press Association in recognition of editorial excellence and three from Computer Currents' First Annual Readers' Choice Awards. Our best-selling ...*For Dummies*® series has more than 50 million copies in print with translations in 31 languages. IDG Books Worldwide, through a joint venture with IDG's Hi-Tech Beijing, became the first U.S. publisher to publish a computer book in the People's Republic of China. In record time, IDG Books Worldwide has become the first choice for millions of readers around the world who want to learn how to better manage their businesses.

Our mission is simple: Every one of our books is designed to bring extra value and skill-building instructions to the reader. Our books are written by experts who understand and care about our readers. The knowledge base of our editorial staff comes from years of experience in publishing, education, and journalism — experience we use to produce books to carry us into the new millennium. In short, we care about books, so we attract the best people. We devote special attention to details such as audience, interior design, use of icons, and illustrations. And because we use an efficient process of authoring, editing, and desktop publishing our books electronically, we can spend more time ensuring superior content and less time on the technicalities of making books.

You can count on our commitment to deliver high-quality books at competitive prices on topics you want to read about. At IDG Books Worldwide, we continue in the IDG tradition of delivering quality for more than 30 years. You'll find no better book on a subject than one from IDG Books Worldwide.

John Kilcullen
Chairman and CEO
IDG Books Worldwide, Inc.

Steven Berkowitz
President and Publisher
IDG Books Worldwide, Inc.

Eighth Annual
Computer Press
Awards ≥1992

Ninth Annual
Computer Press
Awards ≥1993

Tenth Annual
Computer Press
Awards ≥1994

Eleventh Annual
Computer Press
Awards ≥1995

IDG is the world's leading IT media, research and exposition company. Founded in 1964, IDG had 1997 revenues of $2.05 billion and has more than 9,000 employees worldwide. IDG offers the widest range of media options that reach IT buyers in 75 countries representing 95% of worldwide IT spending. IDG's diverse product and services portfolio spans six key areas including print publishing, online publishing, expositions and conferences, market research, education and training, and global marketing services. More than 90 million people read one or more of IDG's 290 magazines and newspapers, including IDG's leading global brands — Computerworld, PC World, Network World, Macworld and the Channel World family of publications. IDG Books Worldwide is one of the fastest-growing computer book publishers in the world, with more than 700 titles in 36 languages. The "...For Dummies®" series alone has more than 50 million copies in print. IDG offers online users the largest network of technology-specific Web sites around the world through IDG.net (http://www.idg.net), which comprises more than 225 targeted Web sites in 55 countries worldwide. International Data Corporation (IDC) is the world's largest provider of information technology data, analysis and consulting, with research centers in over 41 countries and more than 400 research analysts worldwide. IDG World Expo is a leading producer of more than 168 globally branded conferences and expositions in 35 countries including E3 (Electronic Entertainment Expo), Macworld Expo, ComNet, Windows World Expo, ICE (Internet Commerce Expo), Agenda, DEMO, and Spotlight. IDG's training subsidiary, ExecuTrain, is the world's largest computer training company, with more than 230 locations worldwide and 785 training courses. IDG Marketing Services helps industry-leading IT companies build international brand recognition by developing global integrated marketing programs via IDG's print, online and exposition products worldwide. Further information about the company can be found at www.idg.com.   1/24/99

Credits

ACQUISITIONS EDITOR
Laura Lewin

DEVELOPMENT EDITORS
Brian MacDonald
Terri Varveris

TECHNICAL EDITORS
Jim Knoble
Mohammed J. Kabir

COPY EDITOR
Julie M. Smith

PRODUCTION
York Graphic Services

PROOFREADING AND INDEXING
York Production Services

COVER ART
©TSM/George B. Diebold, 1999

About the Authors

Paul Sery is a UNIX systems administrator for Productive Data Systems, Inc., in support of Sandia National Laboratories in Albuquerque, New Mexico. He is a member of the Computer Service Unit, Special Projects, which specializes in managing and troubleshooting UNIX and Linux systems. Paul is the author of *LINUX Network Toolkit*, IDG Books Worldwide, 1998, and has a bachelors degree in Electrical Engineering from the University of New Mexico. When he is not beating his head against systems administration problems, Paul and his wife Lidia enjoy riding their tandem through the bosque in the Rio Grande valley. They also enjoy traveling throughout Mexico.

Eric Harper is the System Administrator at Allbee Green in Orem, Utah. His small business network includes Linux, NetWare, and Windows computers. He has written for *PC Magazine* and *LAN TIMES* magazine, and has authored several books on computer networking.

To my wife Lidia Maura Vazquez-Sery —PGS
To Tricia, Lauren, Nathan, and Alex —EBH

Preface

Your job is running a small business or office. And, since most small businesses don't have much of a budget, if any, for computer systems or dedicated technical personnel, we've created this book for you. It will help you build an inexpensive yet powerful network to support your operation, and run your new network in an efficient and safe manner.

Linux is very likely the ideal platform for running a small business, because it's both powerful and inexpensive. Linux is powerful because it's robust, efficient, multifunctional, and ships with a wealth of software. The Linux operating system and supporting software is inexpensive because it can be obtained for free or at a minimal charge from companies like Red Hat. This low cost is possible because Linux is published under the General Public License (GPL), which permits it to be used for profit or not, as long as the current developer places no restrictions on the next user or developer.

Linux can perform many functions. It can provide file and printer sharing within a network, or act as a Web or database server. You can use it as a router or firewall. And it's an excellent platform for a general-purpose workstation, providing office productivity tools and graphics capabilities.

Using Linux as a Personal Workstation

Several software companies are producing office productivity tools that allow a Linux computer to work as a general-purpose personal workstation. Manufacturers produce products like ApplixWare, StarOffice, and Corel WordPerfect. This software provides tradition functions like word processors, spreadsheets, and presentation graphics.

This book was mostly written using ApplixWare Words for Linux (the writing process took place on both a laptop and a regular PC, both running Linux of course). The evolution of these productivity tools places Linux firmly within the desktop world, and if you primarily use a computer to write, create spreadsheets, or to make slides, you can use Linux exclusively. There are more narrowly-focused Linux products available, and more being developed, so Linux is expanding its applications to serve an ever-wider range of areas.

Using Linux as a Windows File and Print Server

Until recently the primary use for Linux has been to provide services for other computers. In most cases this means to function as a file and print server to workstations. The Samba software system that comes with Red Hat Linux speaks the same "language" as Microsoft Windows. This means that you don't have to purchase any third-party software to provide Windows computers access to Linux files and printers.

Using Linux as an Web Server

Red Hat Linux also comes with the Apache Web server system. Apache (the name is derived from the phrase *a patchy system*) is the most widely used Web server software system in the world today. You can run your own intranet (within your own LAN) or Internet Web server with this system.

Using Linux as an Internet Gateway and Firewall Server

The Internet is the interconnection of all the world's computers and networks that speak the same language. That language is all the protocols – or rules – that tell the individual computers and networks how to find and interact with each other in a predictable, efficient, and reliable manner. The protocols (or language) are loosely referred to as TCP/IP.

The power of the Internet is such that most businesses want, and almost certainly need to be, connected to it. With the power comes the danger that of being exposed to crime, fraud, and abuse. Linux can readily act as both a gateway and firewall to the Internet. This means that your entire network or networks can be connected to the Internet via a Linux server via a phone or higher speed connection. That same server (or a separate machine) can also act as a firewall to provide protection from the potential dangers of the net.

Who Should Read This Book

This book is directed at the intermediate to advanced computer user—a person who has used computers for a long enough time to be comfortable with them and their quirks. The intermediate user is someone who understands the basic computer concepts such as directory trees and has some experience configuring important computer subsystems such as the network interface connector (NIC). The advanced user understands most concepts such as the Internet protocols and file systems and has installed an operating system such as Windows. The advanced user may have managed a network in some fashion and has experience troubleshooting computer problems.

No Linux or UNIX experience is required to use this book. The discussions and examples are organized in a linear form starting with the simple before moving to the more complex. New topics are discussed as they are introduced. However, this book is not intended to be a complete reference. The inexperienced Linux or UNIX user will most certainly want and need access to further resources. This need is addressed by pointing the reader to additional resources as needed. Much use is made of the on-line documentation found both on the companion CD-ROMs and the Internet.

Philosophy of this Book

This book takes the philosophy that the best way to learn something is by actually working with it. That is the impetus behind covering Linux installation in the first chapter. Once you have installed Linux, you can see how the system works by implementing the systems and examples as they are discussed in the book.

This book is also a tutorial describing how to put together the parts that are typically necessary to run a business. It aims at providing enough information to put each piece of the puzzle together to create a whole system. It really is a road map describing how to get from one place to another.

To do that, the basics such as installing Red Hat Linux and the basics of working with Linux are discussed in Part I, "Building and Using a Basic Linux Computer." Part II, "Managing Your Linux Network," covers the administration and management of individual Linux computers and networks. Part III, "Connecting Your Network to the Internet," describes linking your computers and network to the Internet. Finally, the workhorse applications necessary to run a business are introduced in the Part IV, "Getting Work Done."

This book does not intend to describe functions that can better be provided by others. For instance, as a person running a small business it is this book's view that it is better to pay an Internet Service Provider (ISP) to provide your Internet Web services rather than do it yourself (it probably makes sense to run your own intranet server, however). It makes more sense to pay someone else to take on the capital equipment and security risks in many cases. Trying to cover every subject is not possible or advisable in the context of running a small business.

This road map is a very directed one. It is not an atlas however. It describes a very popular route but not much of the surrounding scenery. This should suffice for most people who want to travel this route.

Anticipating Problems

The directed nature of this book precludes spending much time on all the topics that comprise the various systems. Therefore, we need to emphasize the topic of troubleshooting. If and when problems occur, you should be aware of the methods available for solving them.

Troubleshooting is as much an art as a science. The more you know about your computers and network, the better you'll be able to see the art. The innate knowledge that you build from working intimately with a complex system over time often helps you find a problem without being aware of how you came to the solution. However, you should keep in mind that certain methodologies work quite well even when you do not have much knowledge of a system.

The basic troubleshooting method is very simple: work backwards from the symptoms to the cause. If you eliminate simple causes of a problem first then you will eventually find the root cause. For instance, if your computer does not turn on, then you should first check to see if the power cord is connected before you start looking to see if the power supply is broken.

The chapters that deal with configuring hardware or software all contain troubleshooting information. Please keep in mind that they are not intended to be all-inclusive but are aimed at pointing you in the right direction.

Conventions Used in this Book

To help you distinguish the various types of commands (Linux, DOS), URLs, and file names that appear in this book, the following typographic conventions are used:

Windows menu instruction sequences are given as a connected sequence of menu names connected by arrows (→). Thus, the instructions "Click on the Start button, and then click on the Run menu" is stated as "select Start→Run".

DOS commands and their parameters are presented in uppercase, `monospace` fonts.

Linux commands and their parameters are presented in lowercase `monospace` fonts.

File names, and URLs are differentiated with lowercase, `monospace` font. (URL stands for Universal Resource Locator, and is usually in the form of the familiar Internet address: `http://www...`). All URLs used in this book are stored in the `bookmarks.html` file in the IDG directory on the companion CD-ROM. Commands that you should type are in **bold**.

When a file that is contained on the companion CD-ROM is listed, its entire path name is included. This includes the mount point for the CD-ROM (`/mnt/cdrom`). For instance, the Ethernet-HOWTO file is listed as `/mnt/cdrom/doc/HOWTO/Ethernet-HOWTO`.

When the installation, update, or removal of a Red Hat Package (RPM) is called for, the full name for the RPM file on the companion CD-ROM is not used. Instead the command substitutes the Linux asterisk (*) metacharacter for the version number part of the file. This works better in practice than having to specify the entire file name, and it also allows this book to more easily update the Red Hat distribution. Thus, the command `rpm -i /mnt/cdrom/RedHat/RPMS/smbfs*` is used instead of `rpm -i /mnt/cdrom/RedHat/RPMS/smbfs-2.0.1-4.i386.rpm`. See Chapter 8 for the discussion of the `rpm` command.

Acknowledgments

I want to thank my wife, Lidia, for her patience, support, and good advice, which made writing this book possible. Without her, I would not have been able to start, much less finish this project.

I'd also like to thank Eric Harper for conceiving this book. His insight saw the need to address the use of Linux in small businesses. There is a great need for the small business or organization to tap the potential that Linux provides. He got the project started and I am grateful that I was able to assist in its completion.

Laura Lewin managed the entire project and kept it running through all the problems that invariably occur with such projects.

The development editor, Brian MacDonald, worked tirelessly to keep the book on track. His advice and assistance was essential. Terry Varveris, Julie Smith, and Amy Barkat of IDG Books Worldwide all provided considerable help too.

Jim Knoble's technical knowledge was indispensable. His technical editing capability is enormous and I learned a great deal from his comments and advice. I also thank Mohammed Kabir for assisting with the technical edit.

I appreciate all the help that Sam B. Siegel of Knox Software provided me. Without his assistance, I would not have been able to include the Arkeia network backup software with the book.

Sally Mitchell of Applixware also helped me include the Applixware software with the book. Christopher Howell, also of Applixware, assisted me in some of the technical aspects of that software.

I'd also like to thank my colleagues at Special Projects who I depend heavily upon for advice and support in my job. In particular, Reg Olson and Ken Hatfield have helped me on innumerable occasions. I also appreciate Randy Ridley's advice on the discussion of Secure shell.

Finally, my employer, Sandia National Laboratories, encouraged me to take on this project. In particular, my manager, Tom Klitsner, was very enthusiastic in his encouragement which made combining work and writing easier to manage.

—Paul G. Sery

Thanks to the folks at Red Hat, Inc. for their work in bringing Linux to all businesses small and large. Special thanks go to the untiring staff at IDG Books Worldwide — Jim Sumser, Laura Lewin, Terri Varveris, and Brian MacDonald. They are the heroes of this project. Their patience and understanding prove they are the kind of publisher with whom every writer loves to work. And finally, thanks to my family — my wife, Tricia, and kids, Lauren, Nathan, and Alex — for not rolling your eyes when Dad said he wanted to do another book.

—Eric Harper

Contents at a Glance

Preface ix

Acknowledgments xiv

| Part I | Building and Using a Basic Linux Computer |

Chapter 1 Installing Red Hat Linux 3
Chapter 2 Navigating Linux 41
Chapter 3 Editing Files 65
Chapter 4 Configuring the X Window System 81
Chapter 5 Getting Help 95

| Part II | Managing Your Linux Network |

Chapter 6 Administering Your Linux Server 109
Chapter 7 Managing Your Network 147
Chapter 8 Sharing Files and Printers with Samba 173
Chapter 9 Sharing Printers 199
Chapter 10 Automating Network-wide Backups 207

| Part III | Connecting Your Network to the Internet |

Chapter 11 Connecting to the Internet 239
Chapter 12 Creating a Simple Firewall 265
Chapter 13 Configuring a Linux E-mail Server 291

| Part IV | Getting Work Done |

Chapter 14 Using Office Productivity Tools 309
Chapter 15 Configuring an Intranet Web Server 331

Appendix A: Using Secure Shell 343

Appendix B: What's on the CD-ROMs 357

Glossary 359

Index................................365

End User License Agreement 394

GNU General Public License 397

CD-ROM Installation Instructions............. 406

Contents

Preface ix

Acknowledgments xiv

Part 1   **Building and Using a Basic Linux Computer**

Chapter 1   **Installing Red Hat Linux** 3
    Basic System Requirements 3
    Introducing Linux Essentials 5
        Understanding the Linux operating system 5
        Using On-Line Documentation 8
    Preparing your Computer 8
        Understanding Partitions 9
        Understanding File Systems 9
        Using an Entire Disk for Linux 12
        Understanding LILO 12
    Installing Red Hat Linux 13
        Using the AUTOBOOT.BAT method 13
        Booting directly from the Red Hat CD-ROM 14
        Using the Red Hat Boot Floppy Disk 14
    Starting the Red Hat Installation Process 15
        Welcome to Red Hat Linux! 15
        Red Hat Linux 15
        Choose a Language 15
        Keyboard Type 15
        Installation Method 16
        Installation Paths 17
        Installation Class 17
        SCSI Configuration 19
        Disk Setup 19
        Active Swap Space 22
        Scanning 22
        Partitions to Format 23
        Components to Install 23
        Install Log 24
        Running 24
        Install Status 24
    Configuring Your New Linux Installation 24
        Probing Result 25
        Configure Mouse 25

Mouse Port 25
Network Configuration 25
Boot Protocol 25
Load Module 25
Module Options 26
Configure TCP/IP 26
Configure Network 27
Configure Time Zone 28
Configure Services 28
Configuring a Printer 29
Root Password 29
Authentication Configuration 30
Bootdisk 30
LILO Installation 30
Bootable Partitions 30
Choose a [Video] Card 31
Monitor Setup 31
Screen Configuration 31
Video Memory 32
Starting X 32
Done 32
Dealing with Installation Problems 33
Introducing Troubleshooting 33
Troubleshooting the Red Hat Installation Problems 33

Chapter 2 Navigating Linux 41
The Linux Shell 41
Virtual Consoles 43
The GNU Project 43
Listing Files and Directories 44
Using the List Command 45
Using pwd 47
Changing Directories 48
Managing Files, Permissions, and Ownership 48
File Handling 49
Changing Permission Modes 49
Changing the File Ownership 51
Changing the Group of a File 51
Copying Files 51
Moving Files 52
Removing Files 52
Making a Directory 53
Removing a Directory 53
Viewing Files 54
Concatenating a File 54
Displaying Pages of a File 54

	Using less 54
	Command Line Hints 54
	Changing Users 55
	Running Programs in the Background 55
	Running a Series of Commands 56
	Redirecting Command Output 56
	Connecting one Process to Another 57
	Process Commands 58
	Displaying the Process Table 58
	Signalling Processes 59
	Searching for Files 61
	Using find 61
	Using whereis 61
	Using which 62
	Using locate 62
	Using whatis 63
	Looking for Man Page Keywords 63
Chapter 3	**Editing Files** **65**
	Choosing an Editor 65
	Working with pico 66
	Starting pico 66
	Inserting Text and Moving Around 66
	Editing Text 67
	Making pico Your Default Editor 67
	Getting More Help with pico 68
	Working with joe 69
	Starting joe 69
	Working with Multiple Files 70
	Editing Text with joe 70
	More joe Options 71
	Making joe the Default Editor 71
	Working with vi 72
	Starting vi 72
	Inserting Text 72
	Navigating the Screen 73
	Deleting Text 75
	Undoing Changes 75
	Editing Text 76
	Searching for Text 77
	Saving and Exiting vi 77
	Getting More Help with vi 78
	Introducing emacs 78
	Checking Your Spelling 78

Contents

Chapter 4   **Configuring the X Window System** 81
        Understanding the X Window System 81
        Using the Mouseconfig Program 82
        Using Xconfigurator 82
            Xconfigurator AutoProbe 83
            Selecting Your Video Card 84
            Selecting Your Monitor 84
        Starting the X Window System 87
            X Display Manager 87
        Introducing the Enlightenment Window Manager 88
            Using the Start Menu 88
            Viewing an X Client on an X Server 89
        Troubleshooting Problems 91

Chapter 5   **Getting Help** 95
        Using Manual Pages 95
            Man Page Sections 96
            Man Page Organization 97
        The Linux Documentation Project 98
            FAQs 99
            HOWTOs 100
            mini-HOWTOs 100
            LDP Guides 100
        Getting Information from the Internet 101
            Using the Web 101
            Linux Newsgroups 102
            Linux Mailing Lists 103
        Finding Linux Publications 104
        Joining a Linux User Group 104

Part II   **Managing Your Linux Network**

Chapter 6   **Administering Your Linux Server** 109
        Introducing Systems Administration 110
            Understanding and Creating Policy 110
            Backing Up Your File Server 111
            Worrying about Security 112
            Providing Service to Your Customers 113
            Troubleshooting 113
        Understanding System Administration Essentials 114
            Introducing Control Panel and LinuxConf 114
            Making Simple Backups 116
            Managing User Accounts 125
        Introducing Computer Security 127
            Layering Your Security 128

	Training 131
	Backing Up Your Data 131
	Understanding the Red Hat Package Manager 132
	Installing an RPM Package 133
	Getting Information about an RPM Package 133
	Verifying RPM Packages 135
	Updating an RPM Package 135
	Removing an RPM Package 135
	Packages versus Tar Files 136
	Writing Scripts 136
	Subshells 138
	Automating Job Execution 139
	Monitoring Your System Logs 139
	Starting and Stopping Linux 140
	Troubleshooting 142
Chapter 7	**Managing Your Network 147**
	Understanding Network Administration 148
	Understanding and Creating Policy 148
	Worrying about Security 148
	Disaster Recovery 149
	Understanding TCP/IP Basics 149
	The OSI Network Layer Model 150
	Routing 151
	DNS 151
	Introducing paunchy.net 151
	The /etc/hosts Table 153
	Connecting to the Network 153
	Configuring Windows Computers 154
	Configuring Linux Network Parameters 156
	Using the Network Configurator 157
	Where the Scripts Are 161
	Modifying the Scripts Manually 163
	Network File System 163
	Network Information Service 164
	Introducing Network Usage and Security Policy 164
	Disaster Recovery 165
	Troubleshooting 166
	Make Simple Checks First 166
	Check Your Linux Computer 166
	Ping your Network 170
	Check your Windows Computer 171
	If you still have problems 171
Chapter 8	**Sharing Files and Printers with Samba 173**
	Understanding Samba 173
	Understanding the Samba Daemons 174

Contents

Samba Shares 174
smbd and nmbd 174
Starting and Stopping the Daemons 175
Exploring the Samba Configuration File 176
Understanding Global Settings 176
Understanding the [homes] Section 177
Understanding [printers] Shares 177
Understanding Authentication 178
Configuring Samba to Use Encrypted Passwords 178
Configuring Samba to Authenticate from an NT Server 180
Understanding Samba Permissions 180
Using the Samba Utilities 181
smbstatus 181
smbclient 181
nmblookup, testparm, and testprns 182
smbmount 182
Learning Samba by Example 183
Sharing your CD-ROM 183
Sharing Your /var/tmp Directory 185
Accessing Your Home Share 186
Using Macros 188
Introducing SWAT 190
Troubleshooting 191
Checking Your Network 192
Checking the Samba Daemons 192
Check the Lock Files 193
Checking the Samba Log Files 193
Checking the Samba Configuration 194

Chapter 9 **Sharing Printers** **199**
Introducing the LPD Daemon 199
The Printcap Configuration File 199
Print Filters 199
Configuring a Local Printer 200
Configuring a Remote Printer 202
Configuring a Samba Printer 203
Printing From a Windows Machine 204
Troubleshooting 205

Chapter 10 **Automating Network-wide Backups** **207**
Introducing Arkeia 208
Installing Arkeia on the Linux Server 209
Configuring the Arkeia Server 209
Server Administration 209
Drives management 210
Drivepack 210
Savepack 210

Contents   xxiii

	Pools Management 211
	Tapes Management 211
	Libraries Management 211
	The System 211
	Creating a Null Backup 212
	Using Real Backup Media 225
	Configuring a Zip Drive Backup 225
	Using a SCSI Tape Drive or Tape Library 229
	Configuring a Windows Client 230
	Restoring Data 231
	Troubleshooting 232

Part III   Connecting Your Network to the Internet

Chapter 11   Connecting to the Internet 239
Introducing Dial-Up Networking 239
Choosing an ISP 240
    High Speed Connections 241
    Obtaining Network Information 241
    Deciding on the Connection Type 241
Connecting to the Internet via a Dial-Up Connection 242
    Building a Dedicated Linux Gateway 242
    Setting up Your Modem 244
    Using the Network Configurator to Connect to the Internet 245
    Configuring a DNS server 248
    Using DIP to Connect to the Internet 250
    Connecting Automatically to the Internet with Diald 252
    Using DCTRL 257
    Controlling diald Manually 258
Troubleshooting 259
    Modem trouble 259
    Using the Control Panel to Connect to the Internet ... 259
    Using DIP to Connect to the Internet 259
    Connecting Automatically to the Internet with Diald 260
    Configuring Linux for Dialing In 262

Chapter 12   Creating a Simple Firewall 265
Introducing Firewalls 265
    IP Filtering Firewalls 266
    Proxying Firewalls 266
    ipchains 267
Creating a Filtering Firewall 268
    Building a Simple Filter 268
    Building a Working Filter 272
    Understanding IP masquerading 273
    Configure Linux Networking for Masquerading 275

Contents

		Automatically Starting Your Firewall 276
		Configuring Your Network for External Access 276
		Managing the Firewall 277
		Know your Enemies 277
		Know Their Tools and Methods 278
		Monitoring your Log Files 278
		Using NMAP to Test Your System 279
		Using Tripwire to Monitor Your System 283
		Using crack to Test Your Passwords 284
		Education is Your Firewall Too 286
		Troubleshooting 286
		IP Chains 287
		Masquerading 288
		DNS 289
	Chapter 13	**Configuring a Linux E-mail Server 291**
		Using the Netscape E-mail Client 291
		Configuring a Local E-mail Server 294
		Configuring the Netscape E-mail Client 295
		Configuring Sendmail for Local E-mail 296
		Configuring Sendmail for External Delivery 296
		Restart the Sendmail Daemon to Activate the Changes 297
		Installing imap 297
		Configuring Fetchmail for External Retrieval 298
		Troubleshooting 302
		Using the Netscape E-mail Client 303
		Fixing Problems with Local E-mail 303
		Fixing Problems with External Delivery 304
		Fixing Problems with External Retrieval 304
Part IV		**Getting Work Done**
	Chapter 14	**Using Office Productivity Tools 309**
		Introducing Applixware for Linux 309
		Installing Applixware 310
		Starting Applixware 311
		Using the Applixware Help System 311
		Using Applixware Words 313
		Introducing the Other Applications 315
		Introducing StarOffice 320
		Using Netscape Communicator 321
		Using Netscape Navigator 322
		Setting Up Secure Netscape Communication 322
		Configuring the Netscape E-mail Client 324
		More Linux Applications! 327
		Troubleshooting 327

	Applixware 327
	Postgres and Applixware Data 328
	Netscape Communicator 329
Chapter 15	**Configuring an Intranet Web Server** **331**
	Introducing the Apache Web Server 331
	Installing and Configuring the Apache Web Server 332
	Setting Up Simple Services 334
	Creating Your Own Intranet Web Page 334
	Adding Some Useful Information 336
	Introducing Advanced Intranet Web Pages 340
	Securing Your Server 340
	Troubleshooting 340
	Appendix A: Using Secure Shell **343**
	Appendix B: What's on the CD-ROMs **357**
	Glossary **359**
	Index **365**
	End-User License Agreement **394**
	GNU General Public License **397**
	CD-ROM Installation Instructions **406**

Part I

Building and Using a Basic Linux Computer

CHAPTER 1
Installing Red Hat Linux

CHAPTER 2
Navigating Linux

CHAPTER 3
Editing Files

CHAPTER 4
Configuring the X Window System

CHAPTER 5
Getting Help

Chapter 1

Installing Red Hat Linux

IN THIS CHAPTER

- Explore the basic requirements needed to install Red Hat Linux
- Get to know the basics of Linux
- Learn how to install Linux by itself or on the same disk as Windows
- Learn how to simplify the installation by preparing your computer
- Find out the basics of connecting Linux to a LAN
- Learn how to prepare for the installation
- Explore step by step installation instruction
- Understand basic troubleshooting techniques

INSTALLING RED HAT LINUX (www.redhat.com) is a generally straightforward, but not simple process. The process is definitely easier if one has a vanilla PC; and as long as you have a computer that has an IDE hard drive, an ATAPI CD-ROM and an SVGA capable monitor then you should not encounter many problems. The Red Hat installation system is fairly mature and can identify your hardware and install itself. It takes you step-by-step through the process using simple questions and answers.

If you have an unusual hardware configuration, or if you lack certain pieces like a CD-ROM, you can still install Linux. The method in that case is more complex and you have to work around some problems, but Red Hat does provide alternative installation paths. This book assumes that you are using a vanilla system but provides extra (though not exhaustive) information for those more unusual situations. And, in many cases where the very specific information is omitted, I've provided other resources for help or more information.

Basic System Requirements

The installation of Red Hat Linux requires the usual combination of an Intel 386 or greater CPU, 8 MB or more of memory, a floppy drive, at least 50MB of hard drive space, and a VGA video card and monitor. Installation is made much easier if you also have an ATAPI CD-ROM drive; the ATAPI type CD-ROM is automatically recognized by the installation process and precludes the need to load a specific driver for the CD-ROM. However, the Red Hat installation process includes drivers for CD-ROM drives with proprietary controllers.

Red Hat Linux provides distributions that run on Sun SPARC and Compaq (formerly Digital) Alpha systems. To use those platforms you must either purchase or download the appropriate distribution. You can download the distribution from the Red Hat FTP site (ftp://ftp.redhat.com) or one of its mirrors (http://www.redhat.com/mirrors.html). The Red Hat FTP site is often too busy to accept connections, so you might want to try a *mirror*. A mirror is an Internet connected computer that maintains a copy of the primary site files.

The Red Hat installation process works best when you have a local CD-ROM drive. If you don't have one, then you'll have to make provisions for accessing the Red Hat distribution. Typically that means accessing a Red Hat distribution CD-ROM which is mounted on another computer from across a local area network (LAN). For instance, I used a couple of Linux-based laptops for writing and testing this book and since neither has a CD-ROM attached to it, I installed Red Hat by mounting the remote CD-ROM drive over the network. I'll go into more detail later, but you should know that there's more than one way to do an installation.

This book assumes that you are connected to a LAN. The LAN is assumed to be a simple one without multiple subnets. Therefore, you do not need specialized routing within your LAN. If you do have multiple subnets with specialized routing, then it is assumed that you have the knowledge to manage the connection of your new Linux system. If you are not connected to a LAN, then you can skip the sections that deal with networking; you can always add networking later on.

Not all Ethernet network interface cards (NICs) are made equal. The Red Hat installation process carries many modules (a module is essentially a device driver that is loaded by the operating system only when needed) for recognizing various types of NICs. However, some NICs are not recognized easily; this is true of PCMCIA NICs too. Please consult the Ethernet HOWTO (/mnt/cdrom/doc/HOWTO/Ethernet-HOWTO) for detailed information if you have problems during the installation process.

The assumption of an existing network includes the necessary Ethernet infrastructure. The two most prevalent Ethernet media are twisted pair (10baseT or 100baseTX) and Thinnet (10base2). 10baseT works at 10 megabits per second (MB) while 10baseTX is rated at 100 MB. 10base2, on the other hand, works only at 10 MB. The twisted pair cables tend to look like regular phone cables while the Thinnet variety is similar to coaxial TV cables. You should be careful not to confuse the very common regular telephone cable with the proper types that are called category 3 and category 5. The difference doesn't usually present itself until you overload your network and start getting intermittent errors. The coaxial cable that is used for cable TV does not work with Ethernet networks because it has an impedance of 75 ohms rather than the necessary 50 ohms; the proper type is called RG52.

It is not the intention of this book to describe how to build a network. If you do not already have a network set up, then you should consult the Ethernet-HOWTO and the Networking-Overview-HOWTO in the /mnt/cdrom/doc/HOWTO directory on the CD-ROM included with this book, or in the resources listed in chapter 3. You might also consult the discussion on troubleshooting network problems at the end of this chapter to gain addition insight into how the networking functions work together.

Introducing Linux Essentials

This book aims to get you started with Linux as soon as possible and the goal of this chapter is to get Linux installed on your system quickly. However, there are several concepts and commands that are essential to this process. I'll indulge in a short digression at this point in order to point out what they are and what they mean.

Understanding the Linux operating system

The term *Linux* actually refers to several components and systems. First, it refers to the actual operating system—the Linux kernel—that connects the human user to the electronic computer. Second, it means the sum of the parts. That is, Linux is the *kernel,* plus the cooperating daemons (processes running constantly in the background that providebasic services), plus all of the user commands, plus all of the files that are installed on your Linux machine.

EXPLAINING THE LINUX KERNEL AND INIT

The Linux kernel is completely responsible for coordinating the interaction of user and system programs, which in the UNIX world are referred to as *processes,* using the physical resources of the computer. Thus, when a process wants to write to disk or read from a modem it must go through the kernel.

When you boot (power on or reset) your Linux computer, the first process that starts is the init process. It is the ultimate parent of all user and system processes, and it also performs some other housekeeping chores that are not discussed here. Later on, after you have constructed your Linux computer, you can see the process by running the `ps x` command (see the "Introducing Linux Commands" section in this chapter). The kernel is actually started by `init` and all other processes go through `init` as well.

EXPLAINING THE LINUX SHELL

When you work interactively on a Linux computer, you usually interact with a *shell*. The shell is just another process as far as Linux is concerned. Therefore, when you interact with the shell, the commands that you run are first intercepted by and then acted upon by the shell. (The shell prompt where you enter a command is referred to as the *command line*. It is similar to the DOS prompt.) The shell then interacts with the operating system—technically the *kernel*—to carry out whatever function you have called for, such as running another program.

The way that Linux works is quite different conceptually from the way of Microsoft. When you use DOS or Windows you are interacting directly—or mostly directly—with the OS. That's because the user interface, (either the DOS command line or the Windows GUI) is tightly bound to the underlying operating system. For instance, when you enter the DIR command, the DOS operating system interprets the command directly and then executes it.

The advantage of the Linux model is its flexibility and power. It is flexible because anyone can write a shell to fill a need. The default shell of Linux is the *Bourne Again Shell* (bash). It is based on the well-known *Bourne* shell (referred to as *sh*) from the UNIX crowd. There are several other shells available for Linux such as the C shell (csh) and the Korn shell (ksh). The power and flexibility comes from being able to use any number of commands and computer languages together within a shell. You can create simple or complex shell programs to perform almost any desired function.

UNDERSTANDING LINUX PARTITIONS AND FILE SYSTEMS

A big part of the Red Hat, or any other Linux distribution, installation process is configuring the hard drive for a file system(s). A file system is the way the kernel logically organizes a physical device, such as a hard drive, to store information in the form of a file or directory. A *partition* is the way that Linux (and many other operating systems, including DOS and Windows) divides a disk device in order to store a file system on it.

A Linux file system consists of low-level format entities called *inodes*. When a partition is formatted, inodes are written onto the disk and this can only be done during the format process. When a file or directory is created or modified, one or more inodes are used to describe the file or directory. The first inode contains the housekeeping information about the file and points to any additional inodes used for the file. The inodes also contain pointers to the data that comprises the file.

At a higher level, Red Hat Linux uses certain conventions to organize the way it stores system programs, configuration information, and user information. Red Hat uses, with slight variations, the *Linux File System Standard* (FSSTND) as its convention. For instance, Red Hat often wants to keep its log files in the /var/log directory. Please refer to http://www.pathname.com/fhs for more information.

UNDERSTANDING LINUX FILES

Linux uses the UNIX concept of describing almost everything as a file. Thus, Linux uses the file construction to interact with peripheral devices in the same way that it interacts with data stored in a file on a disk. Although Linux treats peripheral devices as a file, it doesn't treat network devices as files. A directory is also just another file as far as Linux is concerned, and, a directory file contains the names of the files that are associated with it.

INTRODUCING LINUX COMMANDS

Commands that are used, or are useful, in this chapter are listed in Table 1-1. A brief description and the DOS equivalents—if they exist—are shown too.

TABLE 1-1 BASIC LINUX COMMANDS

Command	Function	DOS Equivalent
ls	Lists the files in the current directory	DIR
cd	Change directory	CD
clear	Clears the current screen	CLS
cat	Display file contents	TYPE
fdisk	Partitions a disk	FDISK
ifconfig	Configure a network interface	IPCONFIG
lsmod	Lists modules in use by the kernel	
man	Displays information about a command	HELP
mkfs	Formats a partition with a file system	FORMAT
mount	Makes a file system known to the operating system	
netstat	Display networking information	NETSTAT
ps	Display process list	
route	Configure an IP route	ROUTE

These Linux commands are discussed in more detail in Chapter 2.

Using On-Line Documentation

This book makes use of numerous Linux resources. One of the best ones is the CD-ROM which includes many HOWTO documents on almost every subject; as well as many *Frequently Asked Questions* (FAQ) files that discuss questions that are asked, well, frequently.

You are advised in the section "Choose Components to Install" to select the Extra Documentation item. This installs many informational files into the /usr/doc directory. This book often refers to those documents and assumes that you do indeed install them. Most often a reference is made to the actual file such as /usr/doc/HOWTO/Ethernet-HOWTO. It is highly recommended that you choose to install the extra documentation. If you don't install it, then you can do so manually. Please refer to the first RPM installation example in chapter 6 for instructions for do that.

Preparing your Computer

You should know as much about your computer as possible before proceeding with the installation. The Red Hat installation process asks you about such things as what kind of monitor you have, how many hard drives, whether you have a local CD-ROM drive and what port your mouse is connected to. If you have a SCSI (small computer systems interface) adapter then it is best to know what manufacturer it comes from. The more information that you have the fewer guesses you will have to make.

If you are connected to a LAN, then you need to provide the installation process with your hostname, IP address, netmask, gateway address, domain name and *Domain Name Server* (DNS) IP address. It's possible, though, that you may be connected to a network that already provides *Dynamic Host Configuration Protocol* (DHCP) or *Bootp* services that automatically assign host IPs.

Public IP addresses

The Internet requires that every connected host (a computer, router, printer or any electronic device) has its own unique address. The address consists of four decimal numbers concatenated together with dots (.) or periods, such as 192.168.1.1.

Every IP address that is legally visible on the Internet needs to be registered with InterNIC. InterNIC is responsible for allocating addresses and domain names.

Understanding Partitions

A single disk can be divided into one or more partitions. To the operating system, a partition looks like a seperate disk. Using partitions allows you to divide a disk (or disks) into distinct parts. An operating system like Linux can then keep the files that comprise its various systems separate from each other. This practice makes for a more reliable and easily maintained system. For instance, you can create a partition for the operating system and its files, and another one for your users' home directories. You can then reinstall your entire operating system without touching your users' files and data. The separation creates a more easily managed system.

Linux uses the `fdisk` program to partition a disk. The Red Hat installation process uses either the `fdisk` program or its own Disk Druid to format a disk. DOS/Windows uses the `FDISK` program to parition a disk. Both the Linux and DOS versions have the same name and the same function, but they are different programs.

Understanding File Systems

A file system is an organizational structure that is written to a partition. The file system basically allows programs to read and write files and directories to a disk. Since a file system is laid on top of a partition, each file system must 'live' within its own partition.

Linux uses the `mkfs` program to format a disk partition; this process installs a file system onto the partition. DOS/Windows uses the `FORMAT` program to put a FAT or FAT32 file system on to a disk partition. The `mkfs` program can use the Linux standard ext2 file system or any of several other types of file systems, including a DOS one. Note that you can mount DOS file systems onto your Linux system.

When you boot your Linux computer, the operating system attaches—*mounts,* in Linux terminology—the root file system to its internal data structures. The root file system can be stored in memory, on a floppy or ZIP disk or, of course, on a hard drive. A Linux system can have just one file system—the root—or more than one. When you have multiple file systems, they are all mounted directly or indirectly to the root file system. If you look at them as the branches of a tree, you can see that they are all rooted to that one location.

USING THE DUAL BOOT METHOD

Linux can be installed on the same disk with other operating systems, including Microsoft Windows. The focus of this book, however, is an existing network consisting of Windows products so the discussion is oriented in that direction. If you are using other operating systems, however, you should be able to use this method with modifications.

 Linux uses the concept of partitions somewhat differently than Microsoft does. When you create a file partition under Linux, you divide a disk or disks into logically distinct areas just like under Windows/DOS. The partition is then formatted so that the operating system can read and write files to the disk. The difference is that the partition(s) must be mounted before Linux can use them. *Mounting* is the process where the Linux kernel is made aware of where it can access that particular file system. Under Windows/DOS the partition is intrinsically linked to the operating system.

If your computer is already running Windows and you have extra primary or extended partitions, then you can install Linux on one or more of those partitions.

If your computer has just one large partition running Windows then you can still install Linux along side it. However, you need to make room on the Windows partition for Linux by using the *First nondestructive Interactive Partition Splitting* (FIPS) program. FIPS reduces the space used by the Windows partition without destroying any data. The free space can then be used to create a Linux partition and install Linux. More information about FIPS can be found at on the Web at www.igd.fhg.de/~aschaefe/fips or at the Linux Documentation Project (LDP) at sunsite.unc.edu/LDP.

USING FIPS

You should prepare your disk before running *FIPS*. Because FIPS looks for unused sectors to reallocate, it is advisable to first check for, and mark as unusable, any bad sectors. ScanDisk is the Microsoft utility that provides that function. If you combine files that are physically scattered around the surface of the disk into one contiguous location, then you can free up more space for Linux to use. The process for doing this is as follows:

1. Back up any data or programs that you can not afford to lose. You should ideally back up your entire disk.

2. Run the ScanDisk tool by selecting Start → Programs → Accessories → System Tools → ScanDisk.

3. From the ScanDisk dialog box, select the Thorough and Automatically Fix Errors options. Then click the Start button to initiate the process. Be prepared to wait a long time if you have a large disk.

4. After ScanDisk is finished, go to the Disk Defragmenter utility by selecting Start → Programs → Accessories → System Tools → Disk Defragmenter. The Select a Drive dialog box appears. Select the appropriate drive and click OK. Back in the Disk Defragmenter dialog box, click the Start button. The disk is then defragmented. Again, this can take a long time.

FIPS works only with FAT and FAT32 file systems. FAT is also known as FAT16, and is used most often with DOS and Windows 95. Windows 98 defaults to the new FAT32 system, which allows long file names. Check to see which one resides on your computer. FIPS works only with FAT16 systems and FIPS20 with FAT32.

You can find out what kind of FAT partition your Windows computer is using as follows:

1. Open My Computer
2. Right click the C: drive
3. Select Properties

If File System: FAT32 is displayed, than you are using the newer file system and need to use FIPS20 instead of FIPS to repartition your disk.

Next, FIPS can not be run in a multitasking environment, so you need to shut down Windows and reboot into MS-DOS mode.

Once MS-DOS is started, run the FIPS program as follows:

1. Insert the CD-ROM (these instructions assume it is designated as the D: drive).

2. If you are using FAT16 then execute the following program:

   D:\DOSUTILS\FAT

   If you are using FAT32 then run the newer program as follows:

   D:\DOSUTILS\...\FIPS20

3. The initial screen shows you the version information along with a warning message. Press any key to continue. If you are running Windows you are shown a screen warning you that indeterminate results can occur if you continue. Proceed at your own risk.

4. The next screen shows your current partitions. Press any key to continue.

5. FIPS displays a summary of your disk parameters. You are given the option of saving a copy of your root and boot sector to a floppy. This is a very good thing to do as it allows you to restore the original hard disk partition information if you want to back out later on. Press Y. You are asked if a floppy is loaded. Insert a floppy disk and press Y. After the information has been written to the diskette, label it and put it in a safe place.

6. The next FIPS screen displays a simple partition table. The Old and New partitions are shown in megabytes along with the Cylinder number (a hard drive is divided into concentric cylinders). By pressing the left-arrow, right-arrow, up-arrow and down-arrow you can manipulate the sizes of

the partitions. Each keypress increments one partition while the other partition is decremented by the same amount.

Keep in mind that while Red Hat Linux can be installed on as little as 50MB, the size in practice is around 200MB. With that much space you can install the basic OS, networking, and a basic X Window system. With 300MB there should be enough space to use the computer as a workstation with enough space to save some of your work. With 500MB a couple or a few users can be accommodated. Your mileage may vary.

7. Once you have settled on a new disk organization, press the **Enter** key. You are prompted to continue or reedit. Press **C** to continue or **R** to go back and start over. You can also simply exit the process completely by pressing **Ctrl+C**.

8. Finally, FIPS displays what the new partition will look like and prompts you to write it to disk. Press Y to write it or N to exit without modifying the disk. Either way, FIPS returns you to the DOS prompt.

The FDISK program can be used to view the partitions if desired. You can also restore the old partitions by using the RESTORRB program.

Using an Entire Disk for Linux

If you want to load Linux onto an entire disk, then nothing needs to be done to it prior to running the Red Hat installation process. About halfway through the installation you are given the choice of using either the older, and more difficult, FDISK (the Linux version of fdisk works the same as the DOS one but it is a different program), or the Red Hat-developed Disk Druid, to install Linux partitions. The details of the process are discussed in the section "Installing Red Hat Linux."

The example installation in this chapter, and the examples used throughout this book assume that an entire disk is used. This is mainly because the focus of this book on business-related scenarios, most of which require a certain amount of horsepower. Using a dual-boot computer is a good way to experiment with and learn about Linux, but ultimately you should devote one or more computers solely to the function of providing services to your business.

Understanding LILO

Every PC is programmed through the BIOS to look at a certain locations on the floppy diskette or hard drive (or, for some newer systems, the CD-ROM) to get its initial boot information. The boot information consists of a very simple program called a *bootstrap loader* that starts the actual operating system; whether it be DOS, Windows, Linux or any other operating system. Under Linux, the bootstrap loader is called the LinuxLoader (LILO).

LILO allows you to start one or more operating systems. It allows you to set one as the default. More details of how to configure LILO is discussed in the section "Installing Red Hat Linux."

Installing Red Hat Linux

Completing the preparation in the previous sections should help you through the following installation process. The thing to keep in mind is that the average PC is a complex piece of machinery and there are many things that can go wrong to foil the process. Having done your homework helps greatly.

If you purchase the Red Hat box, you receive a manual that does a good job of describing both the installation and basic administrative process. That manual is included on the companion CD-ROM in HTML format in the directory /mnt/cdrom/doc/rhmanual/manual. At this point gaining access to it might be a problem since you have not installed Linux yet. However, if you have another computer with a Web browser and CD-ROM you should be able to view it.

You can get the installation process started via three different ways: A DOS program called AUTOBOOT.BAT, booting directly from the Red Hat distribution CD-ROM, or from a Red Hat boot floppy.

Using the AUTOBOOT.BAT method

The DOS program AUTOBOOT.BAT can be used if you are already running under Windows or DOS. If you have the companion CD-ROM already inserted as the D: drive, enter the following commands.

```
D:
CD \DOSUTILS
AUTOBOOT.BAT
```

A minimal Linux kernel is loaded into memory and started. You proceed as though you had used the more common boot floppy method. If you use autoboot.bat, then you should proceed from here and skip over the next section that describes how to use a boot floppy.

Booting directly from the Red Hat CD-ROM

If you have a fairly new PC, then you might be able to start the installation process directly from the Red Hat distribution CD-ROM. Enter the BIOS setup by rebooting your computer and by pressing the DEL key (some BIOSes use the Esc or F2 key). While the computer is checking the memory, you should see the memory check numbers incrementing during that time.

From the BIOS setup menu choose the ... menu (or similar message) and if you can toggle the drive bootup item to something like "boot from CD-ROM" then this method probably works. Select that method, insert the Red Hat CD-ROM and reboot your system. Your computer then boots from the CD-ROM and the installation process starts.

Using the Red Hat Boot Floppy Disk

You can create boot and supplemental disks by running the RAWRITE.EXE program found on the companion CD-ROM in the \DOSUTILS directory. If you are working from the D: (CD-ROM) prompt, type the following:

```
D:\>CD \IMAGES
D:\IMAGES>\DOSUTILS\RAWRITE.EXE
```

The program asks you for an input file name and the destination drive. To create the boot diskette enter boot.img and A:, and supp.img and A: for the supplemental diskette. Note that by changing to the directory where the boot.img and supp.img file are created you can simply enter their names when prompted rather then have to include the entire pathname.

The rescue.img file found along with boot.img and supp.img is used to create a disk that can be used to start Linux from the boot and rescue floppies alone. Use RAWRITE and enter supp.img when prompted for the input file. If, in the future, you can not start your Linux system then you can use the disk to get going and hopefully fix whatever the problem is. The file /mnt/cdrom/doc/rescue.txt on the companion CD-ROM contains further information on this subject.

Starting the Red Hat Installation Process

You can start the installation process by inserting the boot disk and rebooting the PC. The Red Hat installation process starts automatically. The following sections correspond to the Red Hat installation steps.

Welcome to Red Hat Linux!

You are presented with a `boot:` prompt. At this point, if you are experienced with Linux you can choose several different operations to perform. They are not within the scope of this book but are listed here.

- **Expert Mode:** Disables automatic probing of hardware — you are then responsible for entering the information yourself
- **Rescue Mode:** Use with the rescue disk to boot your computer
- **Kickstart Mode:** Use a script to automate the installation process
- **Kernel Parameter Options:** Supplies the kernel with information about unusual hardware

Press the **Return** key and your computer starts up the Linux operating system. A couple of pages of information are displayed. This information shows what Linux knows about your computer. For instance, if you look closely you see information about your memory, disks and other devices. This information is always displayed when you start Linux.

Red Hat Linux

Press any key to continue with the installation.

Choose a Language

Linux is international. Select the language that you wish to use and press **return**.

Keyboard Type

Select the your keyboard type. (You can modify your selection later by using the `kbdconfig` command.)

Installation Method

Red Hat provides for two different locations to install from. They are:

LOCAL CD-ROM

This is the most conceptually simple and reliable method. If you have a local CD-ROM drive then you can load Linux from the companion CD-ROM. The installation method is the one used in this book. This method does not require a supplemental disk.

HARD DRIVE

You can copy the Red Hat distribution to a local hard drive and use it to install your system. In that case it acts just like the Local CD-ROM method. This method does not require a supplemental disk.

When you choose this method, you are shown the Select Partition window with a menu of disk partitions. The Red Hat distribution must reside in one of the partitions. For instance, if you've copied the Red Hat distribution to the `/home/rh60` directory and `/home` sits on `/dev/hda5`, then you select `/dev/hda5` and enter **rh60** at the `Directory holding Red Hat` prompt.

This method requires you to enter the host network information as well as that of the server that you are accessing. In the case when you are using a DHCP or Bootp to retrieve your local IP address you need to know and enter the address of that server. If you do not have an InterNIC registered IP address(es) then you can use a public address. For instance, you can use one of the addresses used for the local networks in this book such as 192.168.1.1, or 192.168.1.2, etc. If you wish to use this method, please consult the *Red Hat Installation Guide* for additional information. The guide is in HTML format and can be found on the companion CD-ROM in the `/mnt/cdrom/doc/rhmanual/manual` directory. You need access to a Web browser and a CD-ROM drive to make use of it.

Using Other Installation Sources

The following three installation methods were formerly available under Red Hat 5.2. They are useful for installing Red Hat from a remote source over a network. You can still create a boot floppy with these capabilities if you download the `boot.img` from a Red Hat mirror.

- ◆ **NFS image:** If your computer is already connected to a network and there is also a *Network File System* (NFS) server attached then you can use it to install your system. This method is quite convenient when you have numerous installations to perform or when you have a machine without a CD-ROM drive.

Continued

> **Using Other Installation Sources** *(continued)*
>
> ◆ **FTP:** You can also install directly from an FTP server. The server can be a local computer on your network or one on the Internet. You need to supply the IP address of the FTP server and need have a network connection to that server. If you intend to use a Red Hat mirror - on the Internet - and only have a dial-up phone connection you should expect the installation to run over night. This method requires the supplemental disk.
>
> ◆ **SMB Image:** This method uses a Samba server on another machine to access the Red Hat installation files. Samba is a suite of programs which mimics the SMB protocol that Windows NT servers use. Thus, a Linux computer running Samba looks just like an NT server. You need to supply the local computer with all the network information of the remote server as well as the share name, user name, and password. A share corresponds to a directory or file name. This method requires the supplemental disk.
>
> If you use any of these methods, you will need to know the same host and server information that you need for installing from a hard drive.
>
> If you choose to install via a network, then you are asked if you require PCMCIA support. If you do not have a laptop then it is unlikely that you need this support. However, if you have a laptop with a PCMCIA Ethernet NIC and/or a PCMCIA CD-ROM then you need to load the appropriate module. If you answer yes, then your system is probed for PCMCIA devices. Please consult the *Red Hat Installation Guide* or the `/mnt/cdrom/doc/HOWTO/PCMCIA-HOWTO` file for more information on this subject.

Installation Paths

Red Hat provides two installation paths: install and upgrade. The *install* option writes over any existing operating system on the disk partition that you choose to use. An *upgrade* overwrites certain parts of an existing Red Hat installation but keeps the existing partitions.

Installation Class

If you choose to do a full install, then you are asked to choose between three types of disk partition organizations: *Server*, *Workstation*, and *Custom*. The first two write predefined partitions to your disk in anticipation of your computer working as either a server or a personal workstation.

CHOOSING THE SERVER CLASS INSTALLATION

The server class attempts to write the five partitions shown in Table 1-2 to your disk.

TABLE 1-2 THE RED HAT SERVER CLASS PARTITIONS

Partition	Description
/	The root partition. The mount point of all partitions
/boot	Contains the Linux kernel and extras needed for booting
/usr	Libraries and other static files. Also extra applications
/var	Variable files such as logs and temporary files
/home	User home directories

The root (/) and var (/var) file systems are made equal in size to each other. The usr (/usr) and home (/home) partitions are allocated the same space too. The boot (/boot) partition is only allocated enough space (about 25MB) to store the Linux kernel and associated files needed to boot the computer. The root and var are each given roughly 10 percent of the disk space as the usr and home partitions.

The setup program will install the software that is deemed necessary and helpful by Red Hat. Please refer to the rpmlist.server file on the companion CD-ROM for a list of those files. Once it has installed the software it continues with the installation as described in the section "Configuring Your New Linux Installation."

CHOOSING THE WORKSTATION CLASS INSTALLATION

The Workstation class attempts to write the two partitions shown in Table 1-3 to your disk.

TABLE 1-3 THE RED HAT WORKSTATION CLASS PARTITIONS

Partition	Description
/	The Root partition. In this case it contains everything
/boot	Contains the Linux kernel and extras needed for booting

The workstation mode makes two partitions out of the disk. The Root (/) partition uses the entire disk minus roughly 25M for the Boot (/boot) partition.

The installation proceeds and the software that is deemed necessary and helpful by Red Hat is installed on the system. Please refer to the `rpmlist.workstation` file in the IDG directory on the companion CD-ROM for a list of those files. Once it has installed the software it continues with the installation as described in the section "Configuring Your New Linux Installation."

CHOOSING THE CUSTOM CLASS

If you choose the custom method then proceed to the next step—SCSI Configuration.

SCSI Configuration

You are asked if you have any Small Computer System Interface (SCSI) devices. If you have a SCSI-based disks or other devices such as DAT tape drives, then you need to answer yes to this question. The Red Hat installation process attempts to detect the device or devices.

Inexpensive SCSI adapters, such as the ones that come with some ZIP drives, are often difficult to use. When it comes to SCSI adapters it is better to purchase the well-known name brands which you can find listed in the `/mnt/cdrom/doc/HOWTO/Hardware-HOWTO` file. (You can also consult the `http://www.cis.ohio-state.edu/hypertext/faq/usenet/scsi-faq/top.html` FAQ for more information.) Red Hat does a good job of recognizing such devices.

The use of SCSI devices is not germane to this book. Chapter 17 does mention the use of both stand-alone tape devices and robotic tape library (i.e., jukebox) but does not describe their actual use. Please refer to the *Red Hat Installation Guide* for more information.

Disk Setup

By choosing the Custom configuration you are given the choice of how to divide up your disk. This is much more important consideration under Linux than with DOS or Windows. Linux can be run on a single partition but this can create problems down the line.

There are different philosophies about how many and what sized partitions to use. The ones used in this book are based on the author's experience and best judgement. They are by no means the only or even the best way to do it. Use your best judgement and consult other literature for other viewpoints.

The suggested partitions for 1GB and 4GB disks are shown in Table 1-4. Please use your best judgement for smaller or larger sized disks.

TABLE 1-4 SUGGESTED DISK PARTITIONS

Partition	Size(1GB disk)	Size (4GB disk)	Function
/	50	50	The root of all mounted file systems.
/boot	50	50	Stores the kernel and supporting files.
/var	100	200	Used mostly for temporary files and logs.
/usr	300	400	Used for static, or mostly static, files and libraries.
/usr/local	200	1000	Store third party and custom software storage.
/home	100	2000	User home directories.
swap	Two or 2.5 times the RAM contained in your computer	Two or 2.5 times the RAM contained in your computer	Linux is a virtual memory operating system. If a process needs to be run but there is not enough memory to fit it into, then memory is freed up by moving (swapping) a chunk (page) of data or information from memory into the swap file. That chunk can later be reloaded into memory.

You have the choice of using the newer Disk Druid or fdisk. Fdisk is not a difficult program to use, but is not discussed here. Select Disk Druid.

If you are installing onto a very small disk, say 120MB–400MB, then you should consider creating just a single partition. The reasoning behind this is that some space needs to be left for padding on each file system, and using no more than 80 percent of any partition is considered to be good practice. For instance, if you divide a 200MB disk into several partitions then you stand a good chance of wasting 40MB. That much space can easily prevent you from installing all the components that you require for your needs.

Disk Druid displays a screen like that shown in Figure 1-1. In this case it shows the entire disk as available to your new installation.

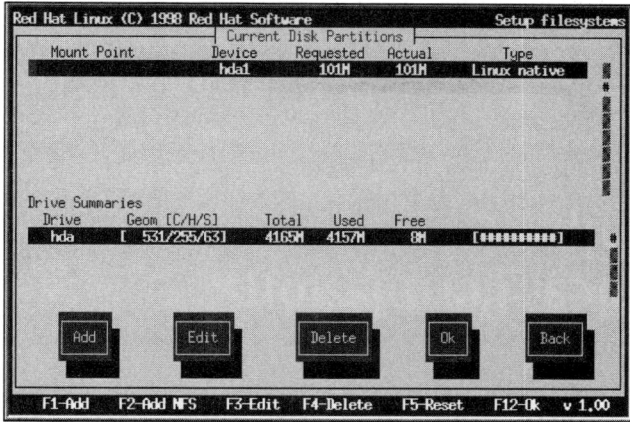

Figure 1-1: The Disk Druid GUI

The column headers are pretty much self-explanatory. The mount point is the place where each file system connects to the directory tree. For example, if the mount point for the file system on partition hda6 is /home, then hda6 will contain all the files and directories that 'live' beneath the /home directory.

You can alternatively add and then edit partitions until you have a file system that meets your need. First use the Add button to create your Root partition. Figure 1-2 shows the screen that results from adding that partition.

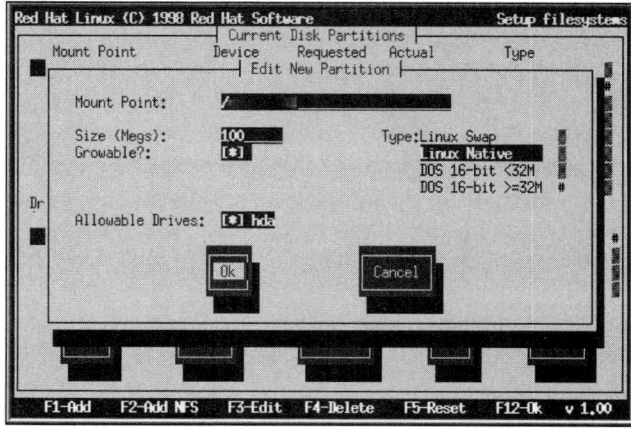

Figure 1-2: Add New Partition

Navigate through this screen and enter the mount point (/) and size. If you press the Space bar on the Growable option, then that option gets turned on. This means that Disk Druid expands the disk space for the particular partition using its own algorithm; every partition with this option toggled on adjusts its size dynamically until you quit Disk Druid. You also need to set the Type field to Linux Native. You can tab your way through each option continuously. Press OK when you are satisfied with the values and you return to the screen shown in Figure 1-1 but it contains the new partition.

Continue the previous two steps to create each new partition. Don't forget to create a swap partition (the swap partition does not have a mount point because Linux reads and writes directly to the disk). You can use the Delete button to remove any or all partitions. You can also use the Edit button to modify the existing partitions.

Linux is a demand-paged, virtual memory operating system. That means that it can "swap" out portions of memory, called pages, to disk when its memory is filled up. The place on disk where it stores the information is the Swap partition. A reasonable rule of thumb is to make the swap partition 2.5 times the size of the RAM in a computer (up to 128MB), if you have enough hard disk space available.

Once you've added all the partitions that you think you need, you can go back and edit any or all of the partitions. You should see the basic information about the partition that you can edit as you see fit.

Once you are satisfied with all your partitions, click the OK button. You are prompted to save the new partition table. Click OK and a status window called Running... is displayed.

Active Swap Space

Next, you are asked what partitions you want to use for swap space. You only have created one swap partition, so your only decision is whether you want to check for bad blocks while formatting the swap partition. It takes longer to do so, but creates a more reliable partition. It's reasonable to check for bad blocks the first time through. If you've repartitioned your disk in the near future it is probably not necessary to do so frequently.

Scanning

The system looks for packages to install.

Partitions to Format

You need to format the new partitions. A format is different from a partition. Formatting installs a file system on top of a partition. A file system is what the operating system mounts. Files and directories are placed on a file system. For instance, when you use the ls command, the information displayed are the files and directories that sit on top of a file system.

One advantage of using multiple file systems is that you do not have to format any or all of them when you are this point in the installation process. For instance, you can do a complete installation over an existing Linux system without destroying data or applications. If you have a separate /home file system for your user home directories, then you can choose not to format it at this point; the same goes for the /usr/local file system (or any file system) too. By formatting the / (root) and /usr file systems, for instance, you install a new operating system without touching the user data in /home or the extra applications loaded in /usr/local.

After you choose the partitions to format, the system scans for software to install.

Components to Install

This is the point where you get to choose what, if any, the Red Hat software packages that come with the distribution to install. By default, Red Hat installs the essential packages as well as a selection of other ones deemed popular or useful. In many cases, and especially while you are suffering through the initial learning curve, it is reasonable to accept the default. However, you should be aware that you do have a choice.

If you wish to modify the software selection then you can make general or more detailed choices. The general choices fall into categories such as the Extra Documentation component shown in Figure 1-3.

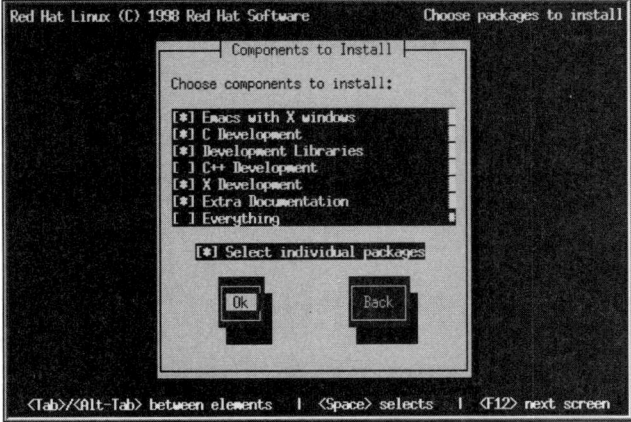

Figure 1-3: Components to install dialog box

You can also make more detailed selections if you choose the Select Individual packages option shown in Figure 1-4. (Red Hat uses its own creation called the Red Hat Package Manager (RPM) to store, install, remove, and get information about all the software that it uses. RPM is has become a very popular system because it is an efficient, convenient and reliable software distribution method. It is discussed in more detail in Chapter 5.) When dealing with individual packages RPM is what the installation process is using.

This book uses the HOWTO and FAQ documents that are included on the companion CD-ROM. It is highly recommended that you install that documentation during this installation process. It only takes a few megabytes of disk space and is well worth its weight. Go towards the bottom of the installation dialog box and click the Extra Documentation item to do so.

Once you finish selecting the software to install and press the OK button the software is copied onto your disk. A reasonably fast CD-ROM drive takes around 10 to 12 minutes to finish. A simple progress display is shown. It is reasonable accurate in estimating the time to go.

Install Log

You are told where you can view the installation log after the installation is completed. Click OK and the installation proceeds.

Running

The file systems are formatted.

Install Status

During the installation you are shown the Install Status window. This display shows each package as its being installed as well as the number of packages already installed. It also lets you see how many packages are left to go and the estimated time it will take to install them.

Configuring Your New Linux Installation

After the installation of the software is complete the process focuses on configuring your new Linux computer.

Probing Result

Red Hat probes your hardware and tries to find a mouse. If one is found, then a dialog box is displayed showing what port the mouse was found on. If one is not found, and you have a mouse attached, don't worry because you can enter the information manually in the next step.

Configure Mouse

Select the type of mouse that you have. If you don't know, then use your best judgement and make a guess. Keep in mind that you can reconfigure the mouse by running the `mouseconfig` program after the installation is complete.

Mouse Port

If you have a serial mouse, then you are prompted to enter the device file that controls it. For instance, if your mouse is connected to the first serial port (COM1: under DOS), then you should choose `/dev/ttyS0`.

Network Configuration

If you are, or expect to be connected to a network then choose Yes. But, you need to have an Ethernet adapter installed in your computer. If you don't have one installed, you can setup networking later using Network Configuration tool.

Boot Protocol

This book uses static IP addresses. Static addresses are assigned once (although they can be changed at any time by editing the appropriate configuration files or by using the Network Configurator described in Chapter 12) and do not change when you reboot the computer. Select this Static IP address option.

However, you can have another computer dynamically assign your Linux computer an IP address every time that it boots. Choose the Bootp or DHCP option if you want, and know how, to use that option.

Load Module

Remember that Red Hat Linux uses loadable modules to support various pieces of hardware. A loadable module is analogous to a Windows/DOS driver and is the software that allows the Linux kernel to interact with and understand hardware like Ethernet NICs. In this step you need to tell the installation program which Ethernet adapter you have installed.

Select the manufacturer and model of the NIC.

 **TIP** If you do not know the manufacturer and/or model of your NIC, then look for the manual. If you don't have the manual, then it is probably best to power down your system, unplug the power cord, open up the case, and look at the adapter. At worst, you can systematically select the NICs from the list until you find one that works.

Module Options

This step allows you to manually enter the interrupt and input/output (I/O) address information of your NIC or let the install program attempt to automatically find it. Linux may still have trouble with Plug 'n Play (PnP) hardware. If you are using a PnP Ethernet NIC, then turn it (PnP) off if you encounter problems. (To turn off PnP, you should first reboot your computer under DOS/Windows and then use the configuration program — 3c5x9cfg for 3Com NICs.) If you are installing Linux on a computer that only runs Linux then you don't lose anything by turning off PnP anyway.

Configure TCP/IP

This is where the host network information is entered. Figure 1-4 shows the *IP address, Netmask, Default Gateway,* and *Primary Namesever* entries. The *IP address* is the number address that every computer requires to use the TCP/IP protocol suite. The Netmask tells the host what kind of addressing scheme is used on the LAN. The Default Gateway refers to the computer that acts as the interface to the Internet. The Namesever entry is the IP address of the computer that translates the numeric IP address into the more familiar IP name.

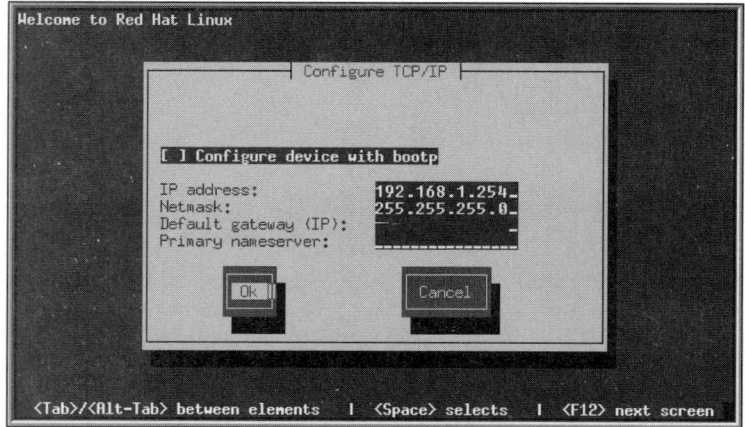

Figure 1-4: Entering the host IP address and other information

If you do not have an InterNIC registered—official—IP address then you can, and should use a public IP address. The most frequently used addresses are 192.168.1.X through 192.168.254.X where X can be any number between 1 and 254. These addresses should use the 255.255.255.0 netmask.

If you are installing your new Linux machine on an existing network that has a connection either to the Internet or another network, then you should enter the IP address of that connection as the Gateway. If your new Linux computer is going to be the gateway, then enter it's IP address there. Otherwise you can leave it blank and enter it later.

Configure Network

You enter the information about the rest of your network here. Figure 1-5 shows typical entries. The domain name is the alphanumeric name that you'll use when referring to your network. The next entry contains your host name followed by the domain name. Additional name servers fill out the dialog box.

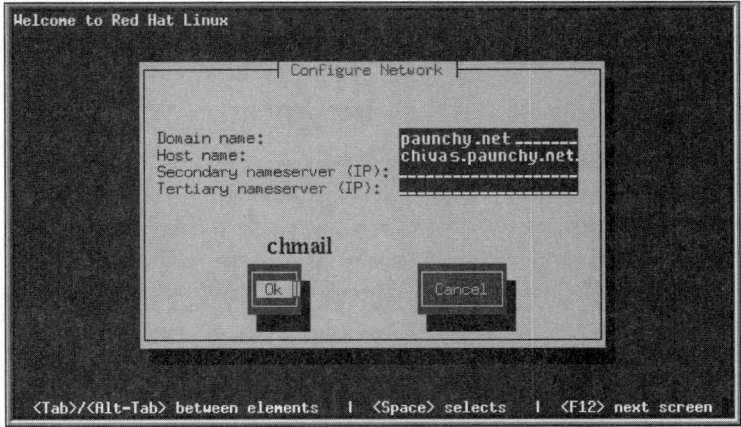

Figure 1-5: Continuing with the network information

If you have an InterNIC-registered domain name then you should use it. However, you can make up your own name as long as you use IP masquerading to connect to the Internet. Masquerading – which is also known as Network Address Translation (NAT) – converts your internal LAN IP addresses into the single IP address of your Internet gateway. If you are connecting to the Internet through a dial-up connection with your Internet Service Provider, then the address that your ISP assigns you will be the one that you masquerade. This topic is discussed in Chapter 9.

Configure Time Zone

Select your time zone.

Configure Services

This dialog box allows you to determine what daemons get started during the boot process. Daemons are programs which constantly run in the background and perform various system tasks (Linux is a true multiprocessing operating system and can easily run many processes at the same time). For instance, the heart of Samba, which provides NT like file and print services, consists of two daemons named `smbd` and `nmbd`.

The daemons listed in the dialog box are started or not started at boot time by toggling each box with the space bar. When toggled on an asterisk indicates that the daemon is to be started. Please take note that by minimizing the number of services that you run you maximize your security. By running fewer processes you remove places that a potential intruder can find a hole to squeeze through. This topic is discussed in more detail in later chapters.

Understanding the Red Hat start-up process

When Red Hat Linux is booted numerous processes called daemons are started. The specific daemons started are determined by the machine's run level. Linux uses *run levels* to define the basic functions that the computer provides. Each level has certain daemons associated with it. For instance, the default run level as defined by the Red Hat installation process is run level 3. When booted to run level 3 the system works with full networking services on a text-based interface. Run level 5 starts in the X Window System as the default interface.

Within each run level the method for determining what daemons or processes are started is by placing soft links in certain directories. A soft link is analogous to a pointer but is really a file with the name of another file in it. The directories that contain the soft links are the `/etc/rc.d/rc0.d`, `/etc/rc.d/rc1.d`, through `/etc/rc.d/rc5.d` directories. Each one, of course, corresponds to a run level. The run level is set in `/etc/inittab` file.

The soft links point to programs or scripts that do the actual starting of the daemons. Therefore, when a file in the `/etc/rc.d/rc5.d` directory gets executed, the script that it points to in `/etc/rc.d/init.d` gets executed and any commands that it want to run get run.

Configuring a Printer

You have three choices if you want to setup a printer: *Local, Remote lpd,* and *LAN Manager.* If you have a printer connected to your Linux machine then you can use this option. If you have a network printer—one connected directly to your LAN—then choose the second option. The last option is for accessing a printer that is controlled by an NT server or another Samba computer.

LOCAL PRINTERS

Choose the name of the printer queue and the spool directory. The print queue is the list of print jobs waiting to print. The spool directory is the place where Linux temporarily stores the print job while it prints. The default print queue on Linux systems is lp and the directory is /var/spool/lpd/lp.

The next prompt is for the physical device that the printer is attached to. The default is either /dev/lp0 or /dev/lp1 which are both equivalent to the Windows/DOS LPT1.

REMOTE LPD PRINTERS

Enter the IP address of the remote printer and its queue name. The default print queue on Linux system is lp.

LAN MANAGER PRINTER

Enter the network host name and IP address of the LAN Manger server. The share name as well as the user name and password associated with the share needs to be entered.

After the information for any of the three printer types has been input, the printer information has to be entered. Select your printer from the dialog box and click OK. Next select the paper size and resolution. Review the information and select OK to continue with the Linux installation or Back to reenter the information.

NETWARE

You are given the choice to choose a NetWare print server.

VERIFY PRINTER CONFIGURATION

After you have finished configuring your printer, you are shown a window with all the information that you have entered. Click OK to proceed to the next step.

Root Password

Enter your root password. The root user has privileges to do anything and is the most powerful user on a Linux computer.

When entering the password, the system checks the second one against the first and forces you to reenter it if they do not match. It is essential to the security of your Linux computer to use a proper password. Do not use a simple word, name or anything that can be easily guessed or associated with you. Instead, it is best to make up a simple phrase that is easy to remember but not found in any dictionary. Something like *car~lite* is appropriate. The idea is to be able to remember it and not have to write it down. The idea also is not to be able to find it in a dictionary where an automated program can find it. Please refer to Chapter 6 for more discussion.

Authentication Configuration

You are given the option of using the *Network Information System* (NIS) at this point. NIS allows you to use a single user account (with the same password) on one or more Linux/UNIX computers. This is a very useful system when you or your users work on more than one Linux/UNIX computers. However, NIS is not used in this book so leave it unselected.

The Red Hat installation system uses shadow passwords with MD5 checksums by default. The traditional Linux/UNIX system stores your encrypted passwords in the /etc/passwd file by default. That file must be world readable (any user can read but not write to that file) for a number of technical reasons. That makes it possible for a malicious person to copy the encrypted passwords and then run a password-cracking program and possibly discover your passwords. Shadow passwords stores the encrypted passwords in another file—/etc/shadow—which is not world readable. This system makes your Linux computer safer. *MD5* is an encryption method. Leave both items selected and click the OK button to proceed.

Bootdisk

Sometimes it is necessary to boot your computer from a floppy disk. If you choose to make a boot floppy at this time, a bootable floppy is made. Store it in an accessible and safe place for a rainy day.

LILO Installation

Remember that LILO is the program that configures the boot sector on your hard drive, and therefore allows it to know about the operating system(s) on it. Since this book assumes a drive dedicated to Linux, there is only one choice. However, if you are loading Linux onto a drive with another system on it—dual boot—then you can choose which one to be the default system here.

Bootable Partitions

In this example there are no other drives available to boot from. In some cases you might have, or want to have, Linux on another, non-primary drive and want to be able to boot from it. Enter the appropriate information into this dialog box in such cases.

Choose a [Video] Card

This is the first step in setting up the *X Window System* on your Linux computer; the X Window System is also referred to as X11 and X. You need to select what video adapter or card your computer has. If you do not know what it is you can select the generic SVGA driver that the installation system contains.

The system that runs to setup your X Window System is called *Xconfigurator*. It can be run as a stand-alone application after you have installed Red Hat Linux. You can also make use of the SuperProbe program that tries to discover what video adapter hardware you have installed. Both programs are described in more detail in Chapter 5.

Monitor Setup

After selecting your video adapter driver you need to tell X Window what monitor you have. Again, if you don't know what manufacturer and model it is you can choose from one of several generic settings. If you choose a generic monitor keep in mind that you almost always can get the 640 · 480 mode to work. If you start from the minimal setting you can try working your way up to a higher resolution. Use your best judgement.

It is possible to physically damage your video monitor by misconfiguring your X setup. Be very careful when manually configuring your system, especially concerning the Vertical Sync rate. If you do not know what values your monitor can take, then it is best not to configure it until you find what the values are. (You could conceivably cause damage by picking one of the predefined monitor settings that doesn't match your actual hardware.) Please beware!

Screen Configuration

The Xconfigurator wants to probe your video hardware. If the probe is successful then X Window is able to make the most efficient use of your video hardware. If it is not successful, then you can still choose manually from several generic settings. (In the unlikely case that your computer stops responding altogether, you should reboot your computer and restart the installation again. In that case don't probe your video hardware again.)

Video Memory

If you choose not to probe, then you need to manually enter the amount of memory on your video card. Select the amount and click OK.

CLOCKCHIP CONFIGURATION

It is generally best to select the No Clockchip Setting (recommended) option. If you have enough information about your video card, then you can select an appropriate setting, but if not, the No Clockchip Setting will still generally work.

SELECT VIDEO MODES

Select the resolution of your screen and the number of colors to be displayed.

Starting X

Once you configured every X setting, Xconfigurator tests your setup. If it is unsuccessful, then an error screen is displayed and you can optionally restart the configuration process again.

CAN YOU SEE THIS MESSAGE?

If your X configuration works, then you should see a small window asking you if you can see the message. You have 10 seconds to click the OK button. If you don't answer affirmatively, then the Xconfigurator assumes that the configuration has failed, displays an error message, and gives you the option of either going back or quitting.

AUTOMATICALLY START X?

You will be asked if you want X to start up automatically whenever you boot up your Linux computer. If you select yes, then you will be prompted for your user name and password every time that you want to log in. Otherwise, your Linux computer starts in a simple text-based console.

CONFIGURATION HAS BEEN WRITTEN

A simple informational screen is displayed. It shows you where the X configuration information has been stored. Click OK to continue.

Done

That's it. You're done. Click OK and you are prompted to remove the boot — or supplemental — floppy while the computer reboots. Remove your CD-ROM if it was used to start the installation process. It should come back up running Linux and you are on your way!

Dealing with Installation Problems

Troubleshooting problems is a fact of life for anyone who is running a computer or a network. Computers are complex devices and networking them together increases the complexity. It is necessary to systematically anticipate and deal with problems as much as possible.

The installation of Red Hat Linux can be problematic at times. Therefore, the topic of troubleshooting is introduced here in order to help you deal with the cases when the installation does not go smoothly.

Introducing Troubleshooting

Troubleshooting is more of an art then a science. It's an art because there are so many variables to deal with that it's impossible to quantify them all. It's a science because computers and networks are ultimately deterministic beings and every problem has an underlying reason or reasons for existing (even if they can not be readily identified).

The poor human who is responsible for dealing with problems must simply try and get a handle on what the particular problem is. The more one knows about a system the better one's mind can sort through all the variables and find a solution. The experienced administrator-troubleshooter is able to subconsciously sort through the evidence to find a pattern that points to a solution. If one uses the simple technique of eliminating the simplest causes *before* working through more complex ones, then troubleshooting becomes less of a mystery.

Troubleshooting the Red Hat Installation Problems

If you have encountered problems with the installation process then there are some common processes and tools to use in order to fix your problem.

INTRODUCING TOOLS

The Linux commands introduced in Table 1-1 can be useful in solving installation problems. You can make use of those commands by using the virtual consoles that Red Hat makes available to you during the installation process.

A virtual console is a separate interactive terminal session that you can access by pressing a key sequence. The installation process starts out and remains in console 1 unless you change to another one. You change consoles by pressing the Alt-F1 through Alt-F5 keystrokes. Table 1-5 describes the virtual console functions. You can switch back and forth between any of them by using the access code key combinations.

TABLE 1-5 VIRTUAL CONSOLE FUNCTIONS

Console	Access code	Function
1	Alt-F1	Primary installation screen. Displays dialog boxes and status.
2	Alt-F2	Interactive bash shell. Becomes active after the kernel is loaded. You have only a very limited number of commands to run from it. That is because it only has the programs available to it that come from the boot and/or supplemental disk.
3	Alt-F3	Installation log. Displays messages from installation processes These messages are the same ones that you would see if you ran the same program from an interactive shell session.
4	Alt-F4	System log. Displays messages from the kernel and other processes. These are the same messages that you would see when you view the system log (/var/log/messages for instance) from a running Linux system.
5	Alt-F5	Other messages. Any messages that don't get displayed in virtual console 3 or 4.

You can often track down the culprit by using the information displayed in virtual console 3 and 4. For instance, if the Red Hat installation process is not able to identify your Ethernet NIC, then you should see a message to the affect in one of those displays.

Two of the most common problems encountered during the installation process are when your CD-ROM drive or Ethernet NIC is not recognized. As mentioned previously, it is possible to determine when that happens by looking at virtual console 3 or 4 (sometimes a confusing message is displayed in the primary console too). If you determine that to be the cause then you can possibly go back and change the information that you provide the installation process or follow another path.

DIAGNOSING PROBLEMS AFTER THE INSTALLATION

Once you have successfully installed Red Hat Linux you still might encounter problems connecting to your network. If that is the case, then there are some possible problems shown in Table 1-6 that you should look at.

TABLE 1-6 COMMON POST CONFIGURATION PROBLEMS

Problem	Possible cause
Power doesn't come on	Power cable connected? Is the power turned on?
NIC connection fails	Network "wire" connected? Network wiring intact?
Module(s) not loaded	Loadable NIC module(s) available to Linux?
NIC misconfigured	Ethernet NIC has an IP?
IP routing misconfigured	IP route to your LAN okay?

The following sections describe possible solutions to the problems mentioned in Table 1-6.

CHECKING FOR SIMPLE SOLUTIONS

Very simple solutions can often be found to difficult problems. Keep in mind that a misbehaving Ethernet NIC, PCMCIA card or CD-ROM can often be attributed to a connector not being seated properly or a power supply cable not inserted fully. Check that the connectors are properly inserted both inside and outside your machine.

Sometimes older devices have built up dust or a little bit of corrosion on their connectors. Removing and reseating them can frequently clear up the problem

CHECKING YOUR NETWORK CONNECTIONS

Sometimes you have set up your network configuration correctly but the electrical signals are not getting to their destination. Infinite impedance—an air gap—gets you every time.

THINNET If you are using Thinnet (10base2 or coaxial cable) then you should know that it needs to be terminated at each end, with a 52 ohm terminator, and there can be no breaks in any of the cables or connectors. Thinnet uses radio frequency (RF) signals to carry the binary Ethernet signals and is what is called a waveguide. A *waveguide* is just that—a guide for waves. Think of a paper tube that you could speak through, and you've got the idea. If the waveguide is not terminated correctly, or there is a break within the wiring, then the electrical signal gets reflected back onto itself and becomes a jumbled mess.

With that in mind, you can check the terminations and make sure that they exist and are snugly connected. If you suspect a break in your wiring then it is best to try and systematically eliminate each segment as the culprit. That can be done by deliberately starting from a computer that you think, or know, is working correctly and connect it directly to another machine that is good. Work your way through the wiring until you find the bad connection(s).

TWISTED PAIR If you are using the telephone like cable that connects to a hub or a switch then you should start by checking the hub first (if possible). A hub can be either managed (expensive) or unmanaged (inexpensive). Most hubs have LED lights that display the status and use of each connection. If an LED is constantly on or nearly so, then you might have a NIC that is misbehaving. If you disconnect the cable that connects the suspect and your problems cease then that is a good indication that you have discovered the culprit. Use the manual that came with the device or consult the HOWTO on the CD and try to fix the device.

In the case where you do not have connectivity to the hub you should check the cable itself. The easiest way of doing that is to use a spare cable or borrow one from another device. Sometimes, you may find yourself in a situation where the wiring is buried in the building structure (in the walls) itself. In that case you'll have to use your best judgement to find an alternative way of testing the connection.

The hub or switch itself can be the problem too. If you are using a simple unmanaged hub, then you might have to find another hub in order to isolate the believed bad one. Managed hubs provide some additional troubleshooting capabilities, so consult its documentation for more information.

CHECKING YOUR NETWORKING MODULES

If you look closely at the information display while your new Linux machine boots you can see information about the NIC. Sometimes Linux can't properly configure the NIC because it does not have, or can not find, the correct module (driver) to load. If that is the case, then you can check the proc file system to make sure. The proc file system is not a physical disk or other device but a view into the internal structure of the kernel itself. If you list the contents of the (ls -l /proc) directory you see a bunch of numbered directories and others like /proc/net and /proc/devices. The numbered directories correspond to the process IDs (ps x) and contain the information about those processes. The other directories and files contain information about the subsystems that comprise your Linux computer.

Look at the contents of the networking devices by running the cat command on the various files. For instance, cat /proc/modules shows the modules that are loaded. If you have a 3Com 3c509, for instance, you should see the following.

```
3c509           2        1 (autoclean)
```

Chapter 1: Installing Red Hat Linux

In the case of examining modules please take note that the same information can be accomplished by running the `lsmod` command. The `lsmod` command access the /proc/modules file to get that information.

Other interesting /proc files to look at are shown in Table 1-7.

TABLE 1-7 INTERESTING AND INFORMATIVE PROC FILES AND DIRECTORIES

File	Function
/proc/devices	Peripheral devices that Linux is aware of
/proc/ioports	IO addresses corresponding to your hardware
/proc/interrupts	Interrupts (IRQs) corresponding to your hardware
/proc/modules	Modules that your kernel is using
/proc/meminfo	Information about your computer memory
/proc/net/dev	Network device information
/proc/net/arp	The Ethernet hardware addresses of computers on your network
/proc/scsi/scsi	SCSI information

Keep in mind that proc files and directories represent views of the internal kernel structures and data. If you list the directory (`ls -l /proc`), then you see that the /proc/kcore has the size of your total memory. If you display its contents, then each and every byte of memory is displayed to your screen. That is not interesting and can take a long time so avoid doing it.

CHECKING YOUR ETHERNET NIC INTERFACE

You configured your network during the installation process. It is possible that you did not enter the network information correctly. Your NIC has to have an IP address associated with it and it needs to be turned on. Use the `ifconfig eth0` command to display your current configuration. If it displays information like that below, then it probably is configured correctly.

```
eth0    Link encap:Ethernet  HWaddr 00:A0:24:2F:30:52
        inet addr:192.168.1.254  Bcast:192.168.1.255  Mask:255.255.255.0
        UP BROADCAST RUNNING PROMISC MULTICAST  MTU:1500  Metric:1
```

```
RX packets:0 errors:0 dropped:0 overruns:0 frame:0
TX packets:401 errors:0 dropped:0 overruns:0 carrier:0
collisions:0
Interrupt:10 Base address:0x280
```

The important information is the IP address, the netmask and the UP flag. The IP address must be the one that you specified and needs to match up with the addresses that you use on your LAN. If you use the public address 192.168.1.254, but your network uses another subnet like 198.59.1.X, then it is unlikely that your computers will be able to communicate without more advanced, proper routing which is out of the scope of this book. So you need to make sure that the proper addresses are being used. If you wish to reconfigure the IP address, then use the following command (substituting the actual address as necessary):

```
ifconfig 192.168.1.254 eth0
```

The subnet mask defines what range of IP addresses your computer expects to see on the local network. Class C subnets are used exclusively in this book and are the default of most computer networks being designed today. The class C subnet mask is 255.255.255.0 which means that the first three bytes of the four byte network address is devoted to defining the network address. The last byte—corresponding to the zero—defines the host address. Therefore, a class C network has 8 bits or 255 possible hosts. You can change the subnet mask by using the command:

```
ifconfig 192.168.1.254 netmask 255.255.255.0 eth0
```

Next, if the UP flag is not displayed then your interface is not turned on. You can turn it on by entering the following command:

```
ifconfig eth0 up
```

Please consult the ifconfig man page and /mnt/cdrom/doc/HOTWO/Ethernet-HOWTO for more information and insights. (The man command is the traditional method that Linux and UNIX uses for distributing information on commands and other information. Use of man is discussed in more detail in Chapter 3.)

CHECKING YOUR NETWORK ROUTING

The final configuration to check is to look at your network routing. Your system must have at least two routes in order to work. One is purely internal and based on the logical loopback (lo) interface. The other is necessary for accessing your local network and is based on your Ethernet NIC (most often eth0). The third, and optional, is your default route that directs all traffic that does not match up with a known network to an arbitrary interface. In a case where you have a simple network, such as in this book, the default route is used to get to the Internet. Use the following command to check your routes.

```
netstat -r -n
```

You should get the following result if you've set up the simple network described in the installation process.

```
Iface   MTU  Met  RX-OK RX-ERR RX-DRP RX-OVR  TX-OK TX-ERR TX-DRP TX-OVR Flags
lo      3584  0    495    0      0      0      495    0      0      0   BLRU
eth0    1500  0     20    0      0      0      454    0      0      0   BMRU
```

Remember that you were instructed not to configure the default route during the installation process unless your network already had a route to the Internet. Chapter 9 describes how to connect your Linux computer and your network to the Internet. This book assumes a network topology where a Linux server acts as the gateway to the Internet and therefore there is no connection at this point and a default route does not work within this context.

If you do not have either the loopback or Ethernet routes set up then use the following command to create one (Ethernet in this case).

```
route add -net 192.168.1.0 dev eth0
```

The second command creates a route that sends all network traffic with the network address of your LAN—192.168.1.X—to the Ethernet interface.

You can also remove routes as follows:

```
route del 192.168.1.0
```

USING THE RED HAT NETWORK UTILITIES

You can use the Control-Panel and LinuxConf utilities supplied with Red Hat Linux to attempt to do the actions discussed in this section. Those utilities are discussed in Chapters 9 and 10 in more detail.

Summary

This chapter covered the basics of installation Red Hat Linux. The installation is not an easy process, but can be made simpler by learning some essential topics and by making some basic preparations. When problems occur they can very often be solved by following basic troubleshooting techniques and knowing where the more common problem spots are.

- A description of the basic computer required to install Linux. Linux requires minimal hardware to create a usable workstation or server.

- A discussion of the basic components that make Linux work. Linux is the sum of its parts. The parts include the kernel, the daemons that provide basic system services, the user and system commands, the file systems. The GNU Project supplies many of the user and system commands. The X Window System provides the graphics.

- A description of the process of installing Linux by itself or along with Windows. The Red Hat installation process can be a pretty straightforward one, but you may occasionally run into difficulties. If you prepare your system and follow the process precisely, then it can be a good experience.

- A discussion of the process of dealing with problems encountered during the installation. If the installation process is not painless, then there are a number of things that you can do to finish the job. The basic process is called troubleshooting. If you systematically attempt to eliminate possible causes of a problem, then you can usually fix any problem.

Chapter 2

Navigating Linux

IN THIS CHAPTER

- Understand the GNU Project
- Learn about the Linux shell
- Learn how to list files and directories in Linux navigate the file structure of your new Linux server
- Get to know some of the most basic Linux commands line hints
- Learn how to manage, view, and search for files in Linux
- Learn the most basic arguments associated with these commands
- By the end of this chapter you will be able to get around in the Linux file system as easily as you have done in DOS or Windows 95

NOW THAT YOU have your Linux computer up and running, it's a good time to step back and learn—or relearn—some of the basics. This chapter expands on some of the Linux concepts and commands introduced in Chapter 1, while the next three chapters proceed to expand your Linux horizons by discussing the many resources available to you. You should view these chapters as the prelude to administering your Linux computer and network.

This book relies heavily on the use of the graphical X interface. However, it is often necessary and often helpful to use the *command line* (a synonym for the Shell prompt). When something goes wrong the command line is frequently the only way you can look at your system and run commands, and thus the only way to fix it. It's also a very good tool for understanding your system because it doesn't hide as much system data as a GUI does (remember, the purpose of a GUI is to hide as much as possible from you).

The Linux Shell

Now that your Linux machine is ready to go, you can start experimenting with it. There are quite a number of subjects to learn, but a good one to start with is the *shell*. The shell is the interface that you use to enter commands (and also just another program as far as Linux is concerned). If you're running the X Window System (please see Chapter 5 for more information), then the shell becomes a window that you interact with. Any number of shells and, thus, windows can be run at the same time. If you're not running X, then after you log in to your Linux machine the entire console is controlled by the shell, much like DOS.

The shell is also a powerful programming tool. The commands that you enter can be combined sequentially, on the same line, to perform a series of tasks, or entered in the form of a *script*. A script is a file that contains Shell directives and other programs to be executed and itself is executed like any program. Remember that a shell isn't an operating system in itself, but passes on instructions from you to the operating system. In fact, the shell is also called the *command interpreter.*

Shells operate differently in the DOS world. With DOS, you use the shell every time you type DIR to list the contents of a directory, type CD to change to another directory, or type COPY to copy a file from one location to another and, on a DOS machine, the shell is COMMAND.COM. If you're using DOS, you don't have the choice to use one shell over another. You have to work with whichever shell came with your operating system.

Well, Linux is different. Linux—and just about every version of UNIX—gives you a choice among many different shells. There's the Bourne shell (named after Stephen Bourne), the C shell (it borrows the syntax from the C programming language), the Korn shell (named after David Korn), and many others.

In your experience with Linux, you'll probably only use one or possibly two shells. People tend to learn one shell really well and stick with it. Of late, the shell chosen most often is bash. Bash stands for *Bourne Again Shell*. It's a derivative of the Bourne shell mentioned above, but also combines many of the good points from other shells.

Not coincidentally, your Red Hat Linux system defaults to the bash shell, and this book assumes it's in use. When you log in as a regular non-root user (such as paul), the default bash shell prompt looks as follows:

[paul@bart paul]$

The prompt shows your username and the computer that you are logged onto (paul@bart) and also shows which directory you're in. In this case, the second paul indicates that you're logged into your home directory because although the full directory name is /home/paul, only the last subdirectory in the full path is shown to keep the prompt from getting too long.

When you log on as root, a pound sign (#) is shown instead of a dollar sign ($), like this:

[root@bart /root]#

 It's redundant to say bash shell, but that's the common practice.

Virtual Consoles

Linux is a multi-user operating system (it is also a multi-tasking operating system, as explained in the section "Displaying the Process Table" later in this chapter). This means that more than one process can run at the same time. Linux also uses the concept of *virtual consoles*. By using key sequences, you can log on to several different sessions on the same computer. For instance, if you start a long process on one console (like backing up a part of your hard drive), you can switch to another console and do something else—like read your e-mail—from another session.

To switch between the virtual consoles, press the left Ctrl-Alt keys while you also press the function keys F1 through F6. For instance, press Ctrl-Left-Alt-F2 to switch to the second virtual console. The total number of consoles is set by the numbers of lines like that shown below that are in the /etc/inittab file.

```
# Run gettys in standard runlevels
1:12345:respawn:/sbin/mingetty tty1
```

When you switch to a new virtual console, Linux presents you with a completely new console, including a new login prompt. You can perform some tasks as user root while doing something completely different logged in under your own username.

The GNU Project

The term Linux was defined in Chapter 1 as meaning either the operating system—kernel—or the various parts that work with the kernel to provide a working computer. One of the major elements is the GNU software that comes with the Linux operating system.

GNU is a recursive acronym, which stands for *Gnu's Not UNIX*. This means that there are many programs and utilities that work alongside Linux to provide the functions necessary to run a computer (and therefore a business). Many of the commands discussed in this chapter and in the book as a whole, come from the GNU project. Richard Stallman started the GNU project and Linux would not exist as a viable operating system without his efforts.

> **The GNU General Public License (GPL)**
>
> Linux is distributed under the GNU General Public License (GPL). The Free Software Foundation developed the GPL as the key concept to its goal that software should be distributed freely. To that end, the GPL is designed to promote GNU's freedom to distribute its software.
>
> Distributing software under the GPL does not necessarily mean that that the software is free. For instance, you need to purchase Red Hat if you want their official distribution on the CD-ROM that comes with their manual. However, you can download that same software without paying for it from their Web site. The following highlights describe some of the features of GPL:
>
> - Software published under GPL in not in the public domain. It's copyrighted (some call it *copylefted*) to the author(s) and is protected by all international copyright laws. The author allows you to use it under the restrictions of the GPL.
>
> - GPL published software is not shareware. Shareware authors own the copyright to their software but ask you (without enforcing it) to pay after you start using their software.
>
> - GPL software can be distributed either free or for a fee. For instance, you can get Linux off the Internet for no charge or buy it from Red Hat for a fee. Both copies use GPL.
>
> - You can modify GPL software in any way that you want. If you want to distribute the software, then you must place it under the GPL.
>
> - GPL-based software must advertise that it is covered under the GPL.
>
> This is an ingenious mechanism. It enables the unhindered distribution of GPL software such as Linux and allows both individuals and companies to make money by enhancing the value of the basic Linux software. It also encourages people to work on GPL software purely for personal satisfaction. Finally, it prevents anyone form gaining a restrictive hold on GPL software.

Listing Files and Directories

The root user is added during the Linux installation process in Chapter 1. Because the process of adding regular users is not introduced until Chapter 6, the root user is used for the examples in this chapter. Root has total control of the Linux operating system and can be dangerous to operate. For instance, if you enter the command `rm -rf /`, you erase the entire disk (there is no undelete command under Linux). However, by using the following examples, which are not dangerous as stated, you won't risk as much. And remember, if you're following this tutorial verbatim, then you haven't installed anything of value other than the operating system.

The so-called learning curve is a cruel taskmaster. But taken step by step it isn't so bad. One of the biggest steps in the Linux learning curve is the process of installing Linux. Repeating that step at this stage is really quite useful. You have the process still fresh in your mind and by repeating it you can better cement the details, and get closer to seeing the overview. You also have the advantage of not having installed anything of value on your system (assuming that you have followed the line of the book).

Using the List Command

The `ls` command lists the files in a directory; it is equivalent to the `DIR` command of DOS, but more flexible. Enter the following command at your shell prompt:

```
ls
```

It writes out the file names of your current directory, which in this case is the root user home directory (`/root`). There is nothing displayed because the only files in that directory at this time are "hidden" files or files with their name prefaced with a dot or period (for instance, `.bashrc`). They won't be displayed without adding a command parameter to the `ls` command.

Linux, as with all versions of UNIX, is case sensitive. That means the text you type must appear exactly as described. `LS` is different than `ls`, for example. In fact, if you type `LS`, chances are you'll get an error message like this:
`bash: LS: command not found.`

Most commands that are provided along with Linux use parameters (also called *options* or *flags*). You can list the hidden files by using the following command:

```
ls -a
```

That command lists all the files in your current directory including hidden files. Now you should see something—at least `.bashrc`. Parameters must be prefaced with a dash (-) before the parameter.

Another command parameter is the one that produces a long format as shown:

```
ls -l -a
```

This command combines both the parameters to list all the files in the current directory and show information such as the ownership, permissions (who can read, write and execute a file) and file size.

You can enter the parameters separately or combine them

```
ls -la
```

to accomplish the same thing. Command parameters can usually be combined and listed after the initial dash (-).

If you want to see if a single file exists, or list that file's properties, type

```
ls -l .bashrc
```

The filename, in this case .bashrc, is called the command *argument*. An argument gives a command more specific information to consider. Sometimes arguments are required, as when copying files. Notice that the system displays the hidden file .bashrc even without the _a option. That's because you specified the filename as an argument.

The command parameter can include a directory name. Using a directory tells a command to work on that directory. For instance,

```
ls -l /
```

lists the files in the root (/) directory.

Metacharacters can also be used in the command argument. The following command lists all the files begining with the string sendmail in the /etc directory.

```
ls -l /etc/sendmail*
```

Metatcharacters are similar to DOS wildcards in some of the results that they produce, but are very different in their internal operations. The primary difference is that the Shell interprets—or in Linux terminology, *expands*—the metacharacter. When you type in the previous command, the shell sees the asterisk and expands it to match all the files in the /etc directory that begin with the string sendmail. Once the asterix is expanded the results are fed to the ls command. The ls command that gets executed looks as follows:

```
ls -l /etc/sendmail.cf /etc/sendmail.cw
```

The `ls` program never sees the asterix metacharacter. Under DOS, the `DIR` command sees the asterisk wildcard and acts as appropriate. The Linux process is more flexible as becomes clear when you start to using the shell to perform complex tasks.

The details of all of the information displayed in a long directory listing are discussed in the section "Managing File Permission" in this chapter.

Using pwd

You can list the current directory by typing:

pwd

The three letters *p w d* stand for print working directory. This command tells Linux to display (print) the current directory on the screen.

When you're browsing the root of a Linux file system, it's hard to tell the difference between a directory and a partition. Therefore, root directories and partitions cannot share the same name.

Linux versus DOS conventions

In the DOS world, drives have letters assigned to them_C:, A:, D:, and so on. The system represents the root directory of C: with a backslash (\) or C:\. If you had a DOCS directory on C:, that would be called C:\DOCS. A LETTERS directory under DOCS would look like this: C:\DOCS\LETTERS.

Linux shares some similarities with DOS, but it's also very different. The root of the Linux file is system is represented by a forward slash (/). Notice Linux does not use drive letters with a colon (:) like DOS does. When you installed Linux and set up the file system, you may have created other partitions on your hard drive besides the root partition. Instead of assigning a different drive letter like DOS does, Linux assigns a name to the partition like /home or /usr.

If you have a docs directory off the root (/) of a Linux machine, the system would represent it like this: /docs. A letters directory under docs would look like /docs/letters.

Changing Directories

As noted already, you can use `cd` to go to a different directory. Typing:

```
cd /usr
```

changes your current working directory to /usr. To verify this, type the following:

```
pwd
```

The `pwd` command verifies that you are in the /usr directory.

Managing Files, Permissions, and Ownership

Whenever you list the files in a directory with the `-l` command option, you see a long file listing with an output similar to this.

```
-rw-r--r--    1 root     root         2045 Aug  6  1998 DIR_COLORS
-rw-r--r--    1 root     root           17 Feb 27 11:21 HOSTNAME
-rw-r--r--    1 root     root         4741 Aug  3  1998 Muttrc
drwxr-xr-x   12 root     root         1024 Mar 15 22:19 X11
-rw-r--r--    1 root     root           10 Oct 15 18:11 adjtime
-rw-r--r--    1 root     root          732 Sep 21 18:54 aliases
-rw-r--r--    1 root     root        16384 Jan 18 13:16 aliases.db
-rw-------    1 root     root            1 Sep 10  1998 at.deny
-rw-r--r--    1 root     root          338 Dec  2 20:50 bashrc
...
lrwxrwxrwx    1 root     root           21 Jan 18 13:16 initrunlvl ->
../var/run/initrunlvl
...
drwxr-xr-x    2 root     root         1024 Jan 18 13:16 mail
```

Linux provides quite a bit of information about each file. The first column lists the permissions for the file. The second column shows the number of links. Next is the file owner's name followed by the file group's name. The fifth column tells you the size of the file, then the date and time the file or directory was either created or last modified. The last column is the name of the file itself.

File Handling

The first column of the long file listing (which lists the permissions for each file) is actually made up of ten different characters. The first character tells you what kind of file it is. Linux has many different file types, but the most common are:

- ‑ normal file
- d directory
- l symbolic link

You can see in the long file listing at the beginning of this section, most of entries are files. Now look at the remaining nine characters in the permissions column. Think of them as three groups of three. The first group displays the rights of the file's owner—which are read, write, or execute (represented by the letters r, w, and x). Each of the three slots in the group is reserved for one letter. That is, the first slot can only be either an r or a dash; the second can only be a w or a dash, and the third is either an x or a dash. The second group displays the rights of the file's group—once again using r, w, or x. And the third group displays the rights of everyone else with the prerequisite r, w, or x. The presence of a dash (-) means that no permission is granted.

The letters themselves are pretty self-explanatory:

- r The file can be read
- w The file or directory can be written to or deleted
- x The file can be executed. If the listing is a directory rather than a file, the x means it can be searched

You may have noticed that Linux filenames aren't limited to the 8-dot-3 format of DOS filenames. In fact, most Linux files don't consider the characters after a dot as an extension tying the file to a particular application. And you can use as many dots as you like in one filename.

Changing Permission Modes

Sometimes you need to change the rights of a file to give someone else access. To accomplish that, you need to use the chmod command. In order to change the permissions of a file, you have to be the owner of that file (see the next section for information on file ownership). In order to understand this command, you need to learn a few more codes. They are:

- u user who owns the file
- g group that owns the file
- o everyone else (easier to remember if you think of other)
- a all (u, g, and o)

Every Linux file has an owner, who is typically the creator of the file. Every owner (user) also belongs to at least one group. In Red Hat Linux, by default every user belongs to a group that has the same name as the username (which it creates when your account is created). When you create a user account with the name of *paul*, then that user's group name is also *paul*. User creation is covered in more detail in Chapter 6.

The chmod command uses a plus (+) or a minus (-) in conjunction with the previous codes to add or remove permissions. For example, suppose you create a shell script (something like a batch file in DOS) and you want to make it executable. To do so, type:

```
chmod u+x script
```

If you wanted to make it executable for the group as well, you could type:

```
chmod ug+x script
```

If you had a document that you wanted others to be able to read, but not necessarily execute, type:

```
chmod o+r shared.doc
```

If you want to combine permissions of a file—granting permissions to some users, removing them for others—you can separate the permissions options with a comma. For example, suppose you have a document you want to give everyone in the group the right to edit, and take away other's rights to view. Type:

```
chmod g+w,o-r shared.doc
```

You can use numbers in place of the + or - parameters to change permissions. Type:

```
chmod 777 shared.doc
```

This turns on read, write, and execute for all users. The first number corresponds to the file owner, the second to the group owner and the last to everyone. Please consult the man page for chmod for all the definitions.

You can recursively use chmod to change permissions on all the files within a directory tree by using the -R parameter. This example

chmod -R g+r /root

turns on the group write permission for every file in the root home directory and all of its subdirectories.

Changing the File Ownership

At some point you may want to change the ownership of a file. Maybe you've been working on a project and someone else is taking it over. Logically, they would set the new file permissions. Linux lets you change a file's ownership with the chown command using the syntax of chown newowner filename. You must be logged in as user root in order to use this command.

chown nobody /root/Xrootenv.0

This example changes the owner of the specified file to nobody, one of the standard users that Red Hat configures during the installation.

Changing the Group of a File

Like changing file ownership, you may want to change the group a file belongs to. When you create a new document, by default, Red Hat Linux assigns the group rights to the file using your username. But you're really part of a sales group, and everyone in that group needs access to the file. To change the ownership to sales, use the chgrp command. The syntax is chgrp newgroup filenames. For our example, type:

chgrp sales prospect.list

Copying Files

You can use the cp command to copy files in Linux. For example, if you want to turn the file project1 over to user lidia, your first step would be to copy the file to lidia's home directory. cp is the command to copy files in Linux. The format is cp *oldfile newfile*. So in this case, you would type:

cp project.file /home/lidia

After copying the file to lidia's directory, type the following to give Lidia ownership of the file:

chown lidia /home/ lidia/project.file

Now lidia has a copy of the file, which she owns, and you keep a copy that you own. Of course, another way to accomplish this same task is to have lidia copy the file to her own directory, allowing her to automatically own a copy of the file. The only caveat here is that lidia must have read access to the file in order to copy it.

Moving Files

If you don't want to keep your own copy and want to move the file to lidia's directory, you would use the `mv` command. The syntax is `mv filename newdirectory`. `mv` is also the command you use in Linux to rename a file. You would type `mv oldfilename newfilename`. In essence, what you're doing is moving the file to the same location and giving it a new name.

```
mv lidia lidia.txt
```

This example renames the file `lidia` to `lidia.txt`, but leaves the file where it is.

Removing Files

The `rm` command deletes files. The command

```
rm /tmp/xyz
```

deletes the file `xyz` in the temporary directory.

Two of the important options for this command are: `-r` and `-i`. The `-r` forces `rm` to work recursively; it removes every file that is specified within a directory tree. Thus, if you enter `rm -r /`, then you risk removing every file on your disk—please don't try this at home.

If you have copied a file and want to delete the original, or if you just don't need a file any more, you can remove it with the `rm` command and the `-i` option. It's used like `rm filename`. `rm` has a couple options you need to be familiar with. When you Type the following:

```
rm -i old.file
```

Linux prompts you to confirm the deletion and you should get used to employing this option. When you delete a file in Linux, it doesn't go into a trash can or recycling bin and wait for you to *really* delete it. Your only option may be to restore the file from a backup tape.

 You have to be careful, especially when logged in as user `root`. As a practice, you should never log in as user `root` for everyday tasks — only when you have to perform some system administration. And *always* think twice before deleting any file. It's a good idea to `ls` the file before you delete it. Sometimes that slows you down enough to catch a mistake before it's too late.

Making a Directory

Before long, you're going to want to create some directories, probably in your own user directory. To do so, use the `mkdir` command. For instance, if you're in your home directory and you type:

```
mkdir letters
```

Linux will create a subdirectory called `letters`. You can then copy and move files to this new location. Remember, if you want to give others the right to scan the directory, they must have executable rights (x).

Removing a Directory

Of course if you're creating directories, you're eventually going to want to delete some of them. Use the `rmdir` command to create directories. Type the following:

```
rmdir letters
```

This removes the letters subdirectory for you. There is one safety catch, however. The directory must be empty. If it's not, you see an error like this:

```
rmdir: letters: Directory not empty
```

and Linux will not remove it. Before you can delete this directory, you'll have to delete the files it contains first or use a recursive `rm` command.

```
rm -r letters
```

Viewing Files

Linux gives you quite a few ways to view a file. Viewing and editing files is discussed in detail in Chapter 4 but a quick discussion is given here for your convenience.

Concatenating a File

The cat command concatenates an entire file to your screen. For instance,

cat /etc/passwd

displays the contents of the password file to your screen. It works in much the same way as TYPE in the DOS world.

Displaying Pages of a File

If a file is too big to fit on the screen, then you can use more to display the file one page at a time. For example, type:

more /var/log/messages

More prompts you after it displays one screen worth of the file, and waits for your input. To continue one line at a time through the file, press Enter. To skip to the next page, press the Space bar. You can also go back a page at a time by pressing Ctrl-B or search for a string by press the slash (/) key. Pressing H displays a help screen. If you want to stop before the you've viewed the whole file, press Q to return to the command prompt.

Using less

The less command displays a file a page at a time like more. However it allows you to move backwards as well as forward:

less /var/log/messages

The man pages for less describe the differences in full.

Command Line Hints

Linux gives you many options when running programs. As mentioned earlier in this chapter, by default you can run up to six different virtual consoles (you can comfortably run up to 22 virtual consoles by modifying the /etc/inittab). So one process can run while you're doing another task. This section discusses some of the important Linux features such as running background processes, pipes and controlling processes.

Changing Users

Sometimes you may want to change to another user without logging off. Rather than switch to another console or logging out and logging in as another user, you can switch users by entering the command:

su

When you type su all by itself at the command line, Linux will attempt to log you in as root. After you enter the password, you have the same privileges as user root. To go back to your previous login account, type:

exit

Try adding a dash (-) as a parameter to the su command.

su -

With this parameter, once you correctly enter the root password you become the root user and also activate the root user's environment. A user's environment includes shell variables and aliases. A *shell variable* includes the pathname and shell type among other variables. The *pathname* tells the Shell to search through directories for commands and programs. The shell environment is displayed by entering the env command. The bash shell looks first to the /etc/bashrc and then the .bashrc file in the user's home directory.

If you want to log in as another user (besides root), type:

su username

You are prompted for the user password, and once correctly entered you *become* that user; you do not inherit the user's environment unless you include the dash. To go back to your previous login account, type:

exit

Running Programs in the Background

If you want to run an application that doesn't require much user interaction (like a backup for example), then you don't have to switch to a new virtual console. Just append an ampersand (&) to the command and the application runs in the background. For example, type:

updatedb &

This starts the `updatedb` program (explained later), but returns the prompt back to you so you can work on something else.

Running a Series of Commands

If you want to run a series of programs from one line, just separate the commands with a semicolon (;). For example, if you want to list your current processes, show the date, pause for ten seconds, then show who is currently logged on, you would type:

`ps; date; sleep 10; who`

`ps` shows the processes that you are using, `date` shows the date and time, `sleep` pauses the execution of the commands for 10 seconds, and `who` lists the users who are logged on to the computer. Each program is run as if you entered them on separate command lines.

If you want to run a series of commands in the background, enclose them in parentheses before adding the ampersand. For example:

`(ps; date; sleep 10; who) &`

This runs all four programs in the background and gives you your command prompt back.

Redirecting Command Output

Most Linux commands provide some sort of output for you to view. If you type `ls`, Linux displays a list of files. If you type `pwd`, Linux tells you your current directory. But sometimes the output of your commands flies by the screen faster than you can read it. You just read how to use the `more` and `less` commands to pause the output a page at a time. You can also save the output of a command to a file, then peruse the file at your leisure. To do this, use the greater-than sign (>) between the command and the filename.

For example, you can enter

`ls /usr/bin > ~/usrbin.list`

The filenames in the `/usr/bin` directory are inserted to a file called `usrbin.list` and put the file in your home directory. If the file `usrbin.list` already exists, then it is completely overwritten.

 The tilde combined with the forward slash (~/) is synonymous for your home directory.

If you use a double greater-than symbol (>),then the output file is appended rather than overwritten. For example, if you entered the following commands

```
ls /usr/local > ~/dir.list
ls /usr/bin > ~/dir.list
ls /usr/doc > ~/dir.list
```

The listings are appended to the same `dir.list` file.

Connecting one Process to Another

Being able to capture the output of a command is very useful, but Linux takes the approach one step farther. The output of one command can be used as the input of another. Just separate each command with the pipe character (|) which is also called the vertical bar.

SORTING STRINGS

One popular command you'll use with pipes is `sort`. The `sort` command is a Linux command used to sort lines of a text file in alphabetical order. If you had a file with order numbers and wanted Linux to sort the output for you, you would type:

```
cat orders | sort
```

The output may look something like this:

```
12345    carmine red     $245
34827    sky blue        $90
54234    orange          $130
83472    leafy green     $185
```

You can also use the `sort` command by itself. Type the following:

```
sort orders
```

This accomplishes the same result as the command above.

FILTERING STRINGS

Another very popular command used in conjunction with pipes is `grep`. The `grep` command finds the lines in files that contain a particular word or phrase. Consider the following:

```
ls -l /usr/doc | grep mtools
```

This command tells Linux to list (in long form) the files and directories in /usr/doc. However, maybe there are many entries in this directory, and you just want the entry that includes `mtools`. The `grep` command takes a look at the output of the file list, finds the entry you're looking for and displays it:

```
drwxr-xr-x   2 root      root         1024 Sep 28 04:13 mtools-3.8
```

You can use `grep` by itself to search a file for the text you're looking for. For example, if you were using the `orders` file discussed earlier and wanted the orders for green products, you could type:

```
grep green orders
```

This tells Linux to search the file `orders` for any lines that contain the phrase *green*. Grep prints out:

```
83472    leafy green    $185
```

Process Commands

The following sections describe the use of two important system commands: `ps` and `kill`. `ps` is used to display the process table. `kill` sends signals to processes, but the signals do not necessarily stop—kill—the process.

Displaying the Process Table

Linux is a multitasking, as well as a multiuser operating system. Multitasking means that more than one process can run at the same time. Actually, each process is given a time slot by the kernel—roughly 20/1000 seconds or 20 milliseconds—and, thus, effectively is running at the same time.

There are numerous processes running in the background all the time (other than the ones you've set in motion yourself). They're called *daemons* and are generally system processes that run in the background all the time. Functions such as printing are run in the form of a daemon so that your print jobs are immediately processed when you submit them.

The kernel keeps track of all processes by maintaining a *Process Table*. You can view it by logging on as root and typing the following:

```
ps
```

then, you see a few process table entries with five columns of information.

```
PID TTY STAT TIME COMMAND
430   1 S    0:00 -bash
```

```
  432     2 S    0:00 /sbin/mingetty tty2
  433     3 S    0:00 /sbin/mingetty tty3
  434     4 S    0:00 /sbin/mingetty tty4
  435     5 S    0:00 /sbin/mingetty tty5
  437     6 S    0:00 /sbin/mingetty tty6
29026    p1 R    0:00 ps
```

The first entry shows the bash shell process that is controlling the root user login. The next five processes are the daemons that control the virtual consoles. The last entry is the ps command that was typed to produce the listing.

The first column displays the numeric process ID (PID). This is a unique number assigned to each new process launched. The TTY column number gives the terminal ID that the process associated with. In this case, the root user is running on default virtual terminal one (Alt-F1). The stat column gives you status information for each process. S is for a sleeping process and R is for a runnable process.

The Time column shows how much time, in minutes and seconds, the process has run. It looks deceiving because although, in this case, root has been logged in for a of couple hours, the value is 0:00. However, this number refers to how much processing time this process has required from the operating system so even though the root has been logged in for quite some time, it has not required very much CPU time.

The command column displays the command or process that is associated with the PID.

The previous display only shows the processes owned by the user executing the ps command. If you want to look at all the processes, type:

```
ps x
```

The x parameter displays all the processes currently being run. You can display processes that don't have a connecting terminal—system daemons for instance—by including the a parameter.

The ps command by itself displays only those processes owned by the user entering the command.

The ps auxwww command shows which user owns each process, the entire command line used to start the process and a wide-wide-wide display, which is used to display all the extra information this command generates.

Signalling Processes

The kill command has a confusing name. It can remove—or *kill*—a process, but that is only one of its functions. It is also used to send signals to processes. One of the most common ones is the HUP signal that tells a process to reread its configuration file. The command:

```
kill -HUP pid
```

is the same as

```
kill -1 pid
```

Please refer to the `man 7 signal` file for information on all the signals.
You can stop a process by sending the KILL signal to a process.

```
kill -9 pid
```

or

```
kill -KILL pid
```

The -9 signal is a synonym for KILL. Both perform the same function of stopping (in this case killing) the process(es).

You can send signals to more than one process by including multiple pids on the command line.

```
kill -9 pid1 pid2 pid3 ...
```

Circumventing Locked up Processes

If the application has locked up your console, switch to another virtual console and log in, so that you can kill the job. You can only kill your own jobs. If the hung application belongs to someone else, you may have to log in as user `root`. All of the warnings I've given you about executing commands as `root` are still in effect, so be careful. First, type

```
ps auxwww | more
```

and when you come to the program that has locked up, note the process ID. If you know the name of the application, you can save yourself the hassle of sorting through rows and rows of jobs by typing:

```
ps auxwww | grep appname
```

When you have the process ID, type:

```
kill pid
```

where the `pid` is the process ID you identified. Use `ps` to make sure the program is really dead. If it isn't, you may have to be unmerciful. Sometimes applications just won't die easily. If that's the case, type:

```
kill -9 pid
```

Once the process is dead, you can exit from the virtual console you're in, and go back to the screen where all this grief started.

Searching for Files

As you can see, Linux uses a lot of files. It has many programs and commands, a few of which you're now familiar with, and many configuration files.

With all these files, sometimes it's difficult to locate what you're looking for. Linux has configuration files which you only need to peruse or edit once in a blue moon, and it's easy to forget where to find everything.

Linux provides several support tools to help you find what you're looking for. This final section discusses some of those tools so you can get familiar with them.

Using find

The program find searches any location specified for any filename specified. It has many other options (too many to mention here) that let you narrow the search criteria several different ways. The basic syntax for using this command is find path parameters. start searching at the path you specify, then follow subdirectories thereafter. So, if you wanted to find a file called hangman and you knew it was somewhere under /usr, you would type:

```
find /usr -name hangman
```

The name expression is just one of the possible parameters. You can look for files based on many divisions, such as permissions with the -perm option, files owned by specific users with the -user option or based on time of modification with the -mtime option. It's only drawback is that if you're searching through a large directory, like /usr, it can take a while to complete the search.

Using whereis

If you know the name of a file or command, then another useful tool is whereis. To use whereis to find the xclock file, type:

```
whereis xclock
```

and you are shown where the file resides:

```
xclock: /usr/X11R6/bin/xclock /usr/bin/X11/xclock
```

Two files show up because X11 is a symbolic link to the X11R6 directory where xclock is stored. The whereis command finds files very quickly, but that's because it doesn't search your whole hard drive. Specific directories are hard-coded into the program. If a file exists outside those directories, whereis won't find it.

Using which

The `which` command searches for one or more commands in the directories defined in your shell's PATH variable. For instance, when you login as the regular user iamme your default PATH should be as follows:

PATH=/usr/bin:/usr/local/bin:/bin:/usr/bin:/usr/X11R6/bin:/home/iamme /bin

If you want to search for the command xclock, then enter the command `which xclock`, and you get the following answer:

/usr/X11R6/bin/xclock

Since /usr/X11R6/bin is defined in your PATH variable, `which` finds it. If a command is not found in your path list, then you need to use `whereis`, `find`, or `locate` to discover the file's location.

Using locate

The `locate` command combines some benefits from both `find` and `whereis`. It can search every location on your hard drive, and it works very quickly. This is possible because it builds it's own database of file locations. To build the database, type the following while logged in as `root`:

updatedb

 Red Hat Linux runs `updatedb` every night at around 1 a.m. local time.

Once that database is built, using `update` couldn't be easier. Type:

locate xclock

and it will return the following text:

/usr/X11R6/bin/xclock
/usr/X11R6/man/man1/xclock.1x

The only caveat is that you have to run `update` fairly regularly to keep its database of files current.

Using whatis

The `whatis` command isn't exactly a way to find files. It's more of a tool to help you find out what a file does. As with `locate` you need to first make a `whatis` database. To do this, type the following while logged in as root.

`makewhatis`

After the database has been built, `whatis` gives you a quick summary derived from the command's manual page. Type the following at the command line prompt:

`whatis xclock`

and `whatis` it returns the following information:

`xclock (1x)           - analog / digital clock for X`

As with the `locate` database, you have to run `makewhatis` fairly regularly to keep it current. Red Hat Linux runs the `makewhatis` periodically on a weekly basis.

Looking for Man Page Keywords

You can look for a command or file by submitting a keyword to the apropos command. The `apropos` command uses the whatis database—configured as a default by Red Hat—to find files based on keywords you specify. For example, if you can't remember the name of the program `xclock` but you know that it's related to the word *clock*, then type:

`apropos clock`

It returns the man page entries that include the *clock* keyword. The `whatis` database maintains the keywords:

```
adjtimex (2)          - tune kernel clock
alarm (2)             - set an alarm clock for delivery of a signal
clock (3)             - Determine processor time
clock (8)             - query and set the hardware clock (RTC)
clock (n)             - Obtain and manipulate time
setclock (8)          - sets the hardware clock from the system clock
asclock (1x)          - the AfterStep clock
rclock (ouR CLOCK) (1) - clock and appointment reminder for X11
xclock (1x)           - analog / digital clock for X
```

You can produces many pages of output by searching on words like file. It's useful to pipe the output of `apropos`—or find or any number of commands—to a filter such as grep. For instance, if you want to change the permissions on a file but can't remember the name of the command, then you can enter a pipe line like the following:

```
apropos file |grep permission
```

Only three lines are returned out of many pages and it's obvious that `chmod` is the command that you are looking for.

Summary

This chapter provides you with the basic tools for navigating a Linux computer. Use this chapter as a simple reference to get familiar with the commands and concepts discussed here. Probably ten percent of Linux's commands account for ninety percent of what you typically do at the command line. This chapter represents that ten percent.

- The Linux shell, unlike the DOS shell, allows you to use many different shells.
- Linux is a multi-user operating system that allows you to switch among various consoles to perform multiple tasks simultaneously.
- Commands like `ls`, `pwd` and `cd` are used to help you list files and directories. Knowledge of these commands help jump start your system administration learning experience.
- The various commands that are used to manage, view, and search for files are described. These commands simplify your naviagition through the file systems and are necessary to manage your Linux system.
- Command line hints to are shown. The tasks discussed are ones that are used to perform many of the necessary and common functions necessary for system administration.

So now you have a good introduction to using Linux, you're ready to move on. And if you still feel completely lost, have no fear. Chapter 5 is titled "Getting Help."

Chapter 3

Editing Files

IN THIS CHAPTER

- ◆ Choosing an Editor
- ◆ Working with pico
- ◆ Working with joe
- ◆ Working with vi
- ◆ Introducing emacs
- ◆ Checking your spelling

BEFORE LONG, YOU'RE going to need to edit text files when working with Linux. Probably the most common file you'll work with is a text file. Many of the systems that comprise Linux are configured via text files–the startup, shutdown scripts (/etc/rc.d) are all text files. The networking system and X Window System and many others all use text files too. Editing those files can be a significant job if you administer your own network.

There are also many types of text-based files other than system configuration ones. Letters, shopping lists, reports, and e-mail messages, among other examples, consist of mostly text information. The recent development of full-featured word processors largely negates the necessity of doing big jobs with text editors, but you still need a quick and consistent method for modifying configuration and other files.

Choosing an Editor

There are several text editors available for Linux. A text editor, unlike a word processor, works on simple text files. Some, like *vi* (*Vi*sual editor), have been around for many years. Others are recent entries, like the *Emacs* editor, which provides powerful document editing features.

The best text editor is probably the one that you're most familiar with. Familiarity and muscle memory mean much more than the features do. However, before you develop that muscle memory you should look over the available editors.

Working with pico

Unlike the venerable vi editor, pico provides an online help system. It also provides an informational display (one line of text) across the bottom of your screen. Like the other text editors, however, it requires you to use key combinations to perform editing and movement functions.

Starting pico

To load pico and start editing a file, just type:

pico *filename*

You can also type **pico** by itself, and either load a file manually or just start typing and specify a filename when it's time to save. You see a white bar across the top of the screen with the file name (if you specified one). Along the bottom you see the commands you need to enter to perform some of the most common tasks.

This list along the bottom is what makes pico so easy to use. It's not that its commands are easier to learn or remember than other editors, but with that key along the bottom, you have a constant reminder. Of course, the trade-off is that that key takes up screen space. (Once you learn the commands you can start pico without the key as shown in the following sentences.)

Inserting Text and Moving Around

All you have to do to insert text with pico is to start typing. It automatically wraps words for you when you reach the end of a line, and if you make a mistake, use the arrow keys to navigate to the right place and the backspace key will erase your errors. Incidentally, the delete key works the same as the backspace key. (Although pico has a startup option to change that too—read on for instructions.)

One nice feature of this editor is that you don't have to take your hands off the alpha keys to move around. Almost every command consists of a holding down the Control key while you press another key. In pico, the Control key is annotated by the caret, "^". Therefore, Ctrl-X is written ^X. And the control keys are not case sensitive—Ctrl-K is the same as Ctrl-k.

You can use control keys to navigate around your text. For example,

Ctrl-F   moves the cursor forward one character

Ctrl-B   moves the cursor backward one character

Ctrl-P   moves the cursor up to the previous line

Ctrl-N   moves it down to the next line

Ctrl-A   takes you to the beginning of a line

Ctrl-E   takes you to the end of a line

Ctrl-V   moves forward one whole page of text

Ctrl-Y   sequence moves backward a page

If you're editing a long file and want to know where you are, press Ctrl-C. pico tells you what line you're on plus how many total lines are in the file.

You can also search for text strings. Press Ctrl-W and pico will ask you what text you want to search for.

Editing Text

Unless everything you type comes out perfectly the first time, chances are, you'll have to do some editing of your files. As mentioned, the backspace and delete keys delete characters one at a time. Pico also has some variations for deleting text. Ctrl-D deletes whatever character is at the cursor's position. If you want to move a whole block of text around, move your cursor to the beginning of the block and press Ctrl-^ (Ctrl-Shift-6) to mark the beginning of a block of text. As you move the cursor over and down, pico highlights the text from that beginning point. Pressing Ctrl-K cuts the text and holds it in a buffer. Move the cursor to the location that you want the paste the text to and press Ctrl-U. To deselect the highlighted text, press Ctrl-^ again.

If you want to check the spelling of your document, type Ctrl-T. Sometimes while editing text and inserting characters in a line, a line or two can get out of alignment. If this happens, go the paragraph and press Ctrl-J. Incidentally, if you press Ctrl-J, then change your mind, pressing Ctrl-U undoes the alignment, but only immediately after reformatting the paragraph. Once you move the cursor after press the Ctrl+J sequence, then Ctrl-U does not undo the reformat.

Sometimes you may want to insert a completely separate file into the one your editing. To do this, press Ctrl-R and pico will prompt you for the name of file you want to insert. If you can't remember the name or the directory the file is in, press Ctrl-T and pico presents a file browser you can use to navigate your file system until you target the file you need.

To save your file, press Ctrl-O; you can do that at any time. To exit pico (and save your file if it has changed) press Ctrl-X.

Making pico Your Default Editor

Red Hat automatically makes vi your default editor. Until you get familiar with vi, you may want to change you default editor to pico. You do this by setting the $EDITOR environment variable. As the root operator, edit the /etc/bashrc file to change the default operator for everyone on the system.

Look for an entry in this file that starts with EDITOR=. If it doesn't exist (it probably doesn't yet), insert the following line:

```
EDITOR=/usr/bin/pico
```

Next, look for a line that starts with export and make sure it contains the word *EDITOR*. Now save the file. To activate the change, type

```
# source /etc/profile
```

This changes the default editor for everyone on the system. If you only want to change the default editor for one or two users, follow the instructions above on the .bash_profile file in that user's home directory.

Getting More Help with pico

Fort more information, view the pico man page. It tells you about using the editor, and different startup options as well. For example, by typing

```
pico -d
```

the delete key works like you're used to (deleting forward from the cursor), rather than working like the backspace key. Typing

```
pico -m
```

enables mouse functionality (only works from within an X Window System). Type

```
pico -x
```

and pico starts without the key menu at the bottom of the screen. You can press Ctrl-G to bring it back momentarily. And typing

```
pico -w
```

disables the automatic word wrap, which is useful when working with some of the configuration files on Linux which have extremely long lines.

Linux also has some pico documentation available in /usr/doc/pine-4.04/ directory. Pico is a companion program to the Pine mail reader (pine is not discussed in this book, but is a useful non-graphical program for reading and writing mail). In fact, pico is short for *Pine Composer*.

Last but not least, by pressing Ctrl-G from within pico, you get help for the commands and features, most of which can be found in this discussion.

Working with joe

The joe editor got its name from its author—Joseph H. Allen. J-O-E is actually an acronym that stands for *Joe's Own Editor*. It comes in five different versions—joe, rjoe, jpico, jmacs, and jstar. Joe is its own personality; rjoe is a restricted version of joe. The restriction is that you can only edit files specified on the command line.

Each of the other versions is actually joe pretending to be a different editor. jpico, for example, is joe acting like pico. That means that all the commands that work with pico, work the same way with jpico. Jmacs is joe acting like the Emacs editor, and jstar is joe acting like WordStar. Only the basic version of joe is described in this section.

Starting joe

Like other text editors, you can start joe with a blank file or start editing a current file. To edit a current file, type:

`joe filename`

If you type joe by itself, it start working on a new a file. If joe is already running and you want to load in a file, press Ctrl-K, E and joe prompts for a filename. If you want a list of files, at the filename prompt, press your Tab key. In fact, any time joe prompts for a filename you can press the tab key to get a list of files in the current directory.

All you need to do to start working is to start typing. Like pico, joe is a non-modal editor (moded means modes which are described in the section on vi). Use the arrow keys to move around, or if you prefer, you can use control keys as with pico.

Ctrl-B	moves the cursor left
Ctrl-F	moves the cursor right
Ctrl-P	moves the cursor up one line
Ctrl-N	moves the cursor down one line
Ctrl-Z	moves to the previous word
Ctrl-X	moves to the next word
Ctrl-A	moves the cursor to the beginning of a line
Ctrl-E	moves the cursor to the end of a line
Ctrl-U	moves to the previous screen
Ctrl-V	moves to the next screen

Some of the key sequences in joe are a little more complex. There is a whole sequence of commands that start with Ctrl-K. For example, press Ctrl-K, then press U to move to the top of a file. Ctrl-K, V moves to the end of a file. If you press Ctrl-K, L joe asks for a specific line number to which you want to move.

Working with Multiple Files

One feature joe has over pico is the ability to open multiple editing screens simultaneously. Press Ctrl-K, O to split the screen in half. Now you have two windows—or views—to the same file. To move your cursor to the lower window, press Ctrl-K, N. To move back to the upper window, press Ctrl-K, P. This can be useful if you are editing a long file and want to look at two separate sections simultaneously. Changes and additions you make in one window are automatically reflected in the other window, so don't think you're working on two different versions of the same file.

But you may want to edit two completely different files. To load a new file in the current window, press Ctrl-K, E and joe will ask you to enter a filename.

When you first split the screen into two windows, joe makes them equal size. If you want to change the relative size of the windows, either press Ctrl-K, G to make the current window bigger (making the other window proportionately smaller), or press Ctrl-K, T to make the current window smaller (making the other window proportionately bigger).

You can keep splitting windows and opening new files as long as there's room on the screen. If you want to keep all of your files open, yet see the file you're currently editing full screen, press Ctrl-K, I. To go back to the multi-screen view, press Ctrl-K, I again. To close a window, press Ctrl-C. If the file has changed, joe will prompt you to save it.

Editing Text with joe

To delete a character to the left of the cursor, you can press either the bBackspace or dDelete key. They act the same in joe.

Ctrl-D	Deletes the character directly under the cursor
Ctrl-Y	Deletes a line of text
Ctrl-J	Deletes the rest of the line, starting from where your cursor sits
Ctrl-W	Deletes a whole word
Ctrl-_	Undoes your last entry

If you want to block a whole chunk of text to delete and/or move, joe lets you do that as well. First, put the cursor at the beginning of the block. Press Ctrl-K, B. (B for Begin.) Then move your cursor to the end of the text you want to block. Press Ctrl-K, K. If you want to delete the block of text, press Ctrl-K, Y. If you want to move it, move the cursor to where you want the block of text to go, then press Ctrl-K, M.

Joe has a built-in spell checker. For this command (and a few others in joe) you'll need to use the Escape key. You can hit the Escape key, release it and then hit the next key. You can also hold the Escape key down while you hit another key. To check the spelling of your document, press Esc-L. If you don't want to go through the whole file, you can press Esc-N to check the word.

If you have a whole other file you want to insert into your current file, press Ctrl-K, R and joe prompts you for the filename. Don't forget to use the Tab key for a list of files if you need it.

To access joe's search feature, press Ctrl-K, F and you'll be presented with some search options. Press Enter to start a forward search. If you press I (instead of F) then it ignores case as you search and, if you press B (instead of B), then you it searches backwards. If you know you're looking for the *n*th occurrence of the text, enter a number.

Joe moves the cursor to the text for which you are searching. If there are multiple instances of the text you're looking for, pressing Ctrl-L takes you to the next occurrence.

To save your file, press the Ctrl-K, D key sequence. If you want to save and exit, press Ctrl-K, X. If you don't want to save your changes, press Ctrl-C. Joe asks you to verify that you want to quit without saving—y for yes, n for no, or Ctrl-C again to cancel.

More joe Options

For online help when working with joe, pressing Ctrl-K, H brings up a help screen. There's actually more than one help screen. Press Esc-. to scroll forward through them, and Esc- to scroll backward. To close the help menu, press Ctrl-K, H again.

To set some of joe's options (like word wrap and margins), press Ctrl-T. To learn more about joe's features and options, check the man page. joe has many more search options than discussed here and many formatting tools useful for programmers. It also has some environment variables and options that you can set in joe's configuration file. That file is /usr/lib/joe/joerc which you can edit and change for all users on the system. Or you can copy that file to $HOME/.joerc to make settings for specific users. The file itself explains the options you can set.

Making joe the Default Editor

If you want to make joe the default editor, you'll have to set the $EDITOR environment variable. As the root operator, edit the /etc/bashrc file to change the default editor for everyone on the system.

Look for an entry in this file that starts with EDITOR=. If it doesn't exist, insert the following line:

```
EDITOR=/usr/bin/joe
```

Next, look for a line that starts with `export` and make sure it contains the word EDITOR. Now save the file. To activate the change, type:

`# source /etc/profile`

This changes the default editor for everyone on the system. If you only want to change the default editor for one or two users, follow the instructions above on the .bash_profile file in that user's home directory instead of `/etc/profile`.

Working with vi

Learning vi can be invaluable for you as a system administrator. vi doesn't try to do everything, but instead follows the model of many Unix applications. For example, it doesn't include a spell checker, but you can use a separate spell checker to check your spelling in documents created with vi. It doesn't format your text very well, but Linux has several text formatters you can use (but which are not discussed in this book).

But vi has many other features that pico and joe don't have. It does take some getting used to, no doubt about that and its commands can seem complex and cryptic. However, it is the defacto text editor in the Linux and UNIX world and deserves consideration

Starting vi

Start vi and it immediately opens a file. Type:

`vi filename`

If the file exists, you can begin editing it. Otherwise you are placed in vi's welcome screen (the place to open or create a files). If the filename you specify doesn't already exist, vi is ready to create it for you. If you type vi on its own without specifying a filename, it loads, and waits for you to enter new file information.

If you are working on a new file, the screen may look pretty confusing. Every blank line is represented by a tilde (~) along the left-hand side of the screen. On the bottom of the screen is a line, called the status line, that tells you the name of the file you're working on.

Inserting Text

Unlike pico and joe, you can't just start typing new text with vi. Before you can insert text, you have to go into edit mode.

VI MODES

At any given time, vi is in one of its two modes of operation. These modes are *command mode* and *insert mode*. When you start vi, it enters command mode. So most of the standard keys on your keyboard won't add text; they perform editing functions.

Why modes? Working with modes can actually be very efficient. Consider all the keystrokes you had to type in joe. There was Ctrl-this then that and Esc-something else. With vi, when you're in command mode, most of the commands are one keystroke. Also in vi, case matters. Typing a and A in command mode does two different things.

SWITCHING MODES

To go from command to insert mode enter one of the commands shown in Table 3-1.

TABLE 3-1 COMMAND TO INSERT MODE COMMANDS

Command	What It Does
i	begins inserting text at the current cursor location
I	begins inserting text at the beginning of the current line
o	inserts a blank line below the current line
O	inserts a blank line above the current line
a	begins inserting text after the current cursor location
A	begins inserting text after the last character in the current line

Once you hit the keystroke entering one of those commands, you can begin typing and entering text. You have made the transition from command mode to insert mode. To return to command mode, hit the Esc key. In fact, if you're not sure what mode you're in, you can press the Esc key. If you're in insert mode, it will switch you to command mode. If you're already in command mode, vi will beep at you, but there's no harm done.

Navigating the Screen

While you're in insert mode, you can use the arrow keys to move around, and the PageUp and PageDown keys work predictably. But while in command mode, you can move around and your hands never have to leave the alpha keys on the keyboard. Look at the Table 3-2 for a list of navigation keys.

TABLE 3-2 CURSOR MOVEMENT COMMANDS

Command	What It Does
h	moves the cursor one space to the left
l	moves the cursor one space to the right
j	moves the cursor down one line
k	moves the cursor up one line
H	moves the cursor to the top line of the screen
L	moves the cursor to the bottom line of the screen
w	moves to the beginning of the next word
b	moves to the beginning of the current word or the beginning of the previous word
e	moves to the end of the current word or the end of the next word
Ctrl-u	scrolls up half a screen
Ctrl-d	scrolls down half a screen
Ctrl-b	scrolls back one full screen
Ctrl-f	scrolls forward one full screen
$	moves the cursor to the end of the current line
^	moves the cursor to the beginning of the current line

Some times your files can get quite large and even moving with Page Up and Page Down takes too long. If that's the case, you can use vi to jump to a specific line number. To find out your current line number, press Ctrl-g. vi tells you what line you're on, how many total lines there are in the file and, by percentage, how far along you are in the file.

If you press a line number then G, vi takes you to that line number. Pressing G without a line number takes you to the end of your document. If you want to go to the beginning of your file, press **1G**. That will essentially take you to line number 1.

Deleting Text

To delete the character directly above the cursor, press x while in command mode. If you want to delete a number of characters at once, move the cursor into position and type

nx

where *n* is the number of characters you want to delete. Sometimes it's easier to just delete the whole word. To do that, you can type:

dw

This deletes a word from the point where the cursor sits to the end of the word. If you want to delete several words, type

*n*dw

where *n* is the number of words you wish to delete. vi also has a command to delete all of the text from the cursor to the end of the line. Type:

d$

    To delete a whole line of text, type:

dd

    If you want to delete multiple lines of text, type

*n*dd

where *n* indicates the number of lines to delete.

Undoing Changes

To undo changes, make sure you're in command mode and type **u**. To undo several changes on the same line, type a capital U. If you change your mind again and want to redo the commands you just undid, press Ctrl-R.

Editing Text

Another command that goes along with the delete commands you just learned is the `put` command. When you delete a character, word, or even line of text, vi stores the text in a buffer in case you want it back. Put is the command that gets it back.

To retrieve text you've just deleted, move your cursor to the spot just before where you want it to go. That means if you're replacing a whole line of text, place the cursor to the line above where the deleted line should go. If you're replace a word of deleted text, place the cursor in the space in front of where you want the word inserted. Once you have the cursor in the right spot, press p, and vi will replace the deleted text where you need it.

Often you delete a character only to replace it with something else. In vi, that's considered a huge waste of time. That's because there's a command specifically for replacing text.

To use it, simply position the cursor over the character you want to replace and press

`r, new character`

and vi will delete the character and replace it with the character you specify.

Of course, sometimes a word has more problems than just one character. vi has a separate command for that problem too. For example, you have a line of text that reads

`The rojmdu in Spain stays mainly on the plain.`

Obviously that second word has a problem. You could use the r command three times to replace the o, j, and m separately, then delete the d and u, but that would waste keystrokes and time. Instead, move the cursor under the o in *rojmdu* and type:

`cw, ain`

When you type `cw` vi deletes the rest of the word and places you in insert mode.

One last editing command to remember is s. This is a command you can use to substitute one word for another. To use it, go to the line where you want the substitution to take place and type the following (notice the colon—several vi commands use the colon):

`:s/old/new`

and press Enter. This will only change the first occurrence on the line. To change every occurrence on a line, type:

`:s/old/new/g`

and press Enter. This changes all occurrences on the line. To change every occurrence of a word between two lines, type

`:#,#s/old/new/g`

where #,# are the numbers of the two lines. To change every occurrence of a word in the entire file, type

`:%s/old/new/g`

Searching for Text

Occasionally in large text files you want to search for a specific word or phrase that would take too long by browsing the entire file. To search for a word or phrase in vi, type

`/search phrase`

When you press Enter, vi takes you to the first occurrence of the file that comes after your cursor position. To search for the next occurrence, press n. To search backwards for the next occurrence (which would be the previous occurrence) press N.

If you know you want to search backwards from your current position, you don't have to keep pressing N, you can start the search in the backwards direction. Just type

`?search phrase`

and you are be searching backwards. When you type n it looks for the previous occurrences and N takes you in the forward direction again.

Saving and Exiting vi

When you're through working on your file, type

`:q`

and press Enter. If it's a new file or if you've made any changes to the file, vi warns you that you haven't saved yet and would lose all your changes. To save your file, type

`:w`

To save and exit in one fell swoop, type

`:wq`

vi provides another way to save and exit. Type

`ZZ`

However, if you want to quit without saving any changes, type

`:q!`

but be careful. All your changes will be lost forever. But if you feel like you've screwed up an important configuration file, this can be a good way to bail out without saving your edits.

Getting More Help with vi

Quite a bit of information has been given about vi, but there is more available. Fortunately there is a plethora of information available for vi. In fact, entire books have been written on this application alone. In addition to the vi man page there is some more documentation found in the `/usr/doc/vim-common-5.3/ directory`. That includes a tutorial that takes about 25 to 30 minutes to complete.

Introducing emacs

emacs is an editor with powerful formatting capabilities. Since this book introduces and uses the ApplixWare Words word processor, the use of emacs is not described.

Many Linux users find that they need no other editor or word processor other than emacs. However, it takes a fair amount of time to learn and it is left up to you to investigate it. A graphical version — Xemacs — is also available for the X Window System.

Checking Your Spelling

You can check the spelling in a text file. There are several Linux programs that check the words found in computerized dictionaries against those found in the text file. The most common programs are *spell* and *ispell*. The `spell` program sends the words that it thinks are misspelled to the standard output. The `ispell` program is interactive and works from a menu. The syntax is:

`ispell filename`

Spell and ispell are installed as part of the default Red Hat installation. If you want to use the additional language dictionaries, then you need to install the appropriate dictionary. Please refer to the /usr/doc/HOWTO documents that refer to the languages for more information.

Summary

This chapter describes several of the Linux based editors available to you. The more widely used text editors are discussed at length. emacs is introduced but not described because it sits between the simple text editors and the full-fledged word processors.

- The text editor pico is described. It provides an intermediate alternative between vi and emacs.

- The text editor joe is described. It also provides an intermediate alternative between vi and emacs.

- The text editor vi is described. This is the old workhorse of the Linux and UNIX world. It's not pretty but gets the job done. It is the most universally available editor.

- Emacs is a powerful document processing text editor. It is also available for X Window. It is not described in this book but introduced to inform the reader.

- Simple spell checking is described. International dictionaries are available under Linux that make spell checking your text documents possible.

Chapter 4

Configuring the X Window System

IN THIS CHAPTER

- Understanding the X Window System
- Using Xconfigurator
- Introducing the Gnome/Enlightenment window manager
- Using the X Client and X Server across a network

THE X WINDOW SYSTEM is the graphical system used by Linux and is based on a client-server model. It is also network ready. That means that a process can be run on one computer and viewed either on the same computer or on another one on the network. It is a powerful system.

Understanding the X Window System

The X Window System is also called X Window or simply X. This is the default graphical system that Red Hat (and most Linux distributions) use to provide a Graphical User Interface (GUI). It provides much the same function as the Microsoft Windows GUI. (Actually, X combined with a window manager provides the same function.) The X Window System differs from Windows in that is not tied directly to the computer that it runs on. Therefore, you can be sitting at one computer and graphically view data from another computer.

X is based on a client-server model. That means that there is both a client part and a server part to X. The terminology can be confusing at times and deserves some attention.

The client half of X refers to the X-based programs that provide a specific function. *Xclock,* for instance, is an X client and displays a graphical clock. The X server is the software that translates the graphics of an X client into the pixels (or dots on a screen) that are shown on your monitor. For instance, xclock sends the clock image to the X Server that displays the image. The fact that the server and the client are separate means that the output of xclock—or any X client—can be shown on the same computer or a different one. This is a big advantage over Windows.

Using the Mouseconfig Program

Mouseconfig is another menu driven program that assists you in configuring your mouse. It's important that you know which device your mouse is connected to (in the Windows arena it is referred to as the port that your mouse is connected to). If you have a serial mouse, then the device most often used is either /dev/cua0 (/dev/ttyS0 is the same device) for the first port or else /dev/cua1 (/dev/ttyS1 is the same device) and you should select the appropriate menu item. If you have a PS/2 mouse then select from the PS/2 mice listed.

Start the program by logging on as root and entering the following command line:

```
/usr/bin/mouseconfig
```

You are presented with a screen listing of the mice that the program knows about. Select the appropriate mouse as listed in the menu. If you do not know what your mouse is, or if it is not listed, then select from among the generic or Microsoft-compatible ones.

Using Xconfigurator

The *Xconfigurator* program was introduced in Chapter 1. It's run by the Red Hat installation process automatically unless you did not install the X Window System. Xconfigurator is used to set what video adapter hardware and monitor type is used by X Window.

> ### Finding your Video Hardware with SuperProbe
>
> It is best that you know what video hardware that you have before starting Xconfigurator. To find out, you can either open up your computer or run the *SuperProbe* program. SuperProbe looks at the hardware on your computer and tries to determine what it is. If successful, then you can use that information for configuring X Window with Xconfigurator.
>
> Log on as root and enter /usr/bin/X11/SuperProbe (case is important) from the command line. The first screen warns you that your computer might hang (fail to interact with you) and that the program will start in 5 seconds. The delay gives you a chance to quit SuperProbe by pressing the Ctrl-C keys. A successful result looks like this:
>
> ```
> First video: Super-VGA
>         Chipset: Cirrus CL-GD5428 (Port Probed)
>         Memory:  1024 Kbytes
>         RAMDAC:  Cirrus Logic Built-in 15/16/24-bit DAC
>                  (with 6-bit wide lookup tables (or in 6-bit
> mode))
> ```
>
> This result shows a Cirrus video chipset that is found in the list of cards supported by Xconfigurator. Select the Cirrus Logic GD542x L-GD5420/2/4/6/8/9 and click OK. The next screen deals with setting up your monitor.

You can, of course, run Xconfigurator yourself in order to configure X Window for the first time or to reconfigure it after the initial Red Hat installation process. You can run it interactively from the command line or use it in conjunction with the Kickstart mode. *Kickstart* is a method for automating the Red Hat installation process by providing it with a script to follow, but, since it is an advanced feature, it's not covered in this book.

In interactive mode, Xconfigurator runs a simple menu-based system. Log on as root and enter the /usr/bin/X11/Xcofigurator command. You are presented with a greeting screen. Click on the Ok button.

Xconfigurator AutoProbe

Xconfigurator attempts to automatically probe your video hardware. Most PCI video cards can be discovered. Older ones like ISA or VESA local bus (VLB) video cards are discovered far less frequently. If the probe is successful, then you are presented with type of video adapter that is found. Click Ok and control is passed to the monitor selection process described in section Selecting Your Monitor.

Selecting Your Video Card

If the automatic probing fails to find your video hardware, then you are prompted to select your video hardware card as shown in Figure 4-1.

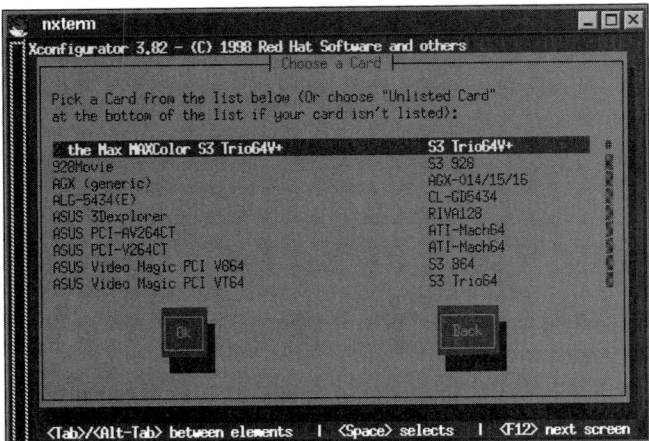

Figure 4-1: Select your video adapter hardware

If you know what your video card is, then highlight and select it. The tab, left-arrow and right-arrows move the cursor between the video card menu and the OK and Back keys.

If you do not know what your card is, then you have several options. First, you can open up your machine and look at the card or find your computer manuals. Second, you can run the SuperProbe program—as described in this chapter—from another window. It attempts to discover what your card is by reading the information contained in its chip. If it finds your video hardware then you can use that information. If it does not find your hardware, then you can use the Xconfigurator generic settings.

Selecting Your Monitor

If you find your monitor among the supported monitors as shown in Figure 4-2, then select it. Otherwise you can select from the Custom, Generic Monitor or Generic Multisync settings.

Chapter 4: Configuring the X Window System

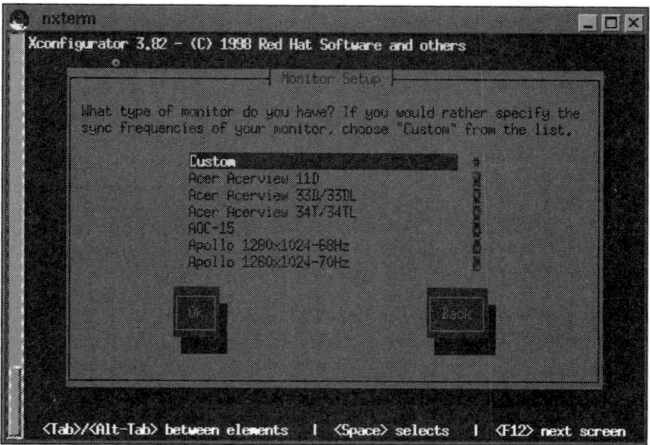

Figure 4-2: The Xconfigurator Monitor Setup screen

USING THE CUSTOM MENU

If you select the custom menu, then you have the option of the following standard types of monitors:

```
Standard VGA, 640x480 @ 60 Hz
Super VGA,    800x600 @ 56 Hz
8514 Compatible, 1024x768 @ 87
Super VGA, 1024x768 @ 87 Hz
```

The standard VGA setting is a nearly universal one. It works in most cases but is of minimal use. However, most hardware from recent years—say 1995—works with Super VGA mode. It is the one that this book is being written in; it's not great but can get the job done. You should be confident that you have the appropriate monitor if you wish to use the last two modes (8514 or Super VGA at 1024 · 768).

After selecting the monitor type you are asked to select the refresh rate. That parameter defines how many times per second the screen is rewritten.

 There is always a small risk that you could damage your monitor if you drive it at the wrong (too high) resolution and refresh rate. Please refer to the XFree86-Video-Timings-HOWTO in the `/usr/doc` directory (`rpm -i/mnt/cdrom/RedHat/RPMS/documentation.rpm`).

GENERIC MONITOR

Select this option if you have a monitor that supports only one resolution and refresh rate. Follow the instructions listed in the section Generic Multisync Monitor.

GENERIC MULTISYNC MONITOR

If you are using a Multisync monitor (one that can change between two or more resolution and refresh rates) then use the Multisync monitor. If you do not have Multisync or are in doubt, then select the simple generic monitor setting.

In either case you will be prompted as to whether or not you want to probe your monitor. If you select to probe and are successful, than the internal information is used to provide you with one or more possible settings—starting with the maximum resolution—that can be supported by your equipment.

If you do not have the system probe itself, then you are first prompted for the amount of memory that your card has and then your clockchip set type. If you don't know your video card clockchip type then select No Clockchip Setting (recommended). It's problematic, of course, to guess at the amount memory, but you can always start with the minimum and work your way up to the actual amount by running Xconfigurator and testing each setting. It's not pretty but it works.

Once you have finished with the Probe or Do Not Probe process you still have to select the resolution to run your video card and monitor. You can actually select more than one setting. (If you do select more than one setting, then you can manually toggle between the settings by press the Ctrl-Alt-+ and Ctrl-Alt- (Control-Alt-Minus) keys). Select OK and the settings are saved to the /etc/X11/XF86Config file.

TIP You can edit and even create the X Window configuration file by hand. Use your favorite editor and the appropriate HOWTOs to wind your way through this quite difficult system.

After selecting the video adapter and monitor, save the settings by clicking the OK button. The Xconfigurator tests your settings for you. If it can start X using your settings, then you are prompted to click on the Yes button. You have 10 seconds to do so. (If your settings do not work then you are given the option of going back and reconfiguring your system.) After that, you are asked if you want X to start up automatically when you boot up your computer. Choose your option. Xconfigurator saves the settings to the /etc/X11/XF86Config file. You can now start X Window.

Starting the X Window System

Once you have configured X you can start it by entering the following command.

```
startx
```

If your X configuration is correct, then it will start up. Since you are already logged in, you are presented with the Enlightenment window manager. Enlightenment is a sophisticated system that allows you to configure any aspect of the window manager. A sample screen is shown in Figure 4-3.

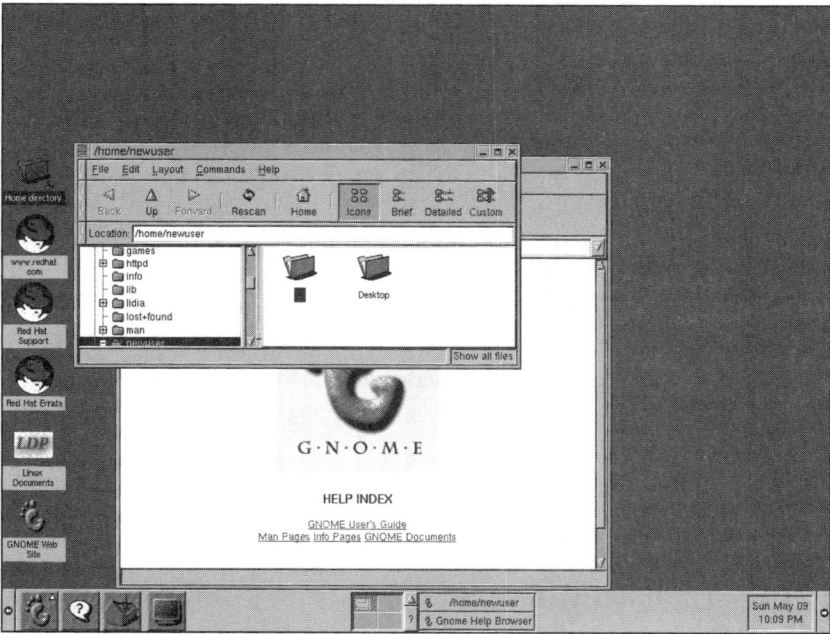

Figure 4-3: The Enlightenment Window Manager

X Display Manager

If you choose to have X start up automatically when you boot the machine by using xdm, then you are prompted to enter your user name and password from a graphical window. Once you login, then you are automatically placed in the Gnome/Enlightenment window manager that runs under X.

If you have any problems starting X then consult the section Troubleshooting Problems. (Note that you can switch to a virtual console by using the Ctrl+Alt+Fn key sequences.)

Introducing the Enlightenment Window Manager

When you start X after installing Red Hat, the default window manager Enlightenment is started. This is the software that gives your desktop its look and feel. Enlightenment allows you to configure every aspect of the interface. You can access the Enlightenment configuration menu by clicking both mouse keys at once on the desktop background. A general menu pops up and you can then click on Enlightenment configuration menu.

GNOME (GNU Network Object Model Environment) provides applications and utilities for the X environment and includes applications like a calendar and a file manager. When you start up X, the Gnome help screen window appears. It provides a good tutorial and reference about GNOME. You can also refer to http://www.gnome.org for more information.

Several other window managers run on Linux. The KDE, tvm, lesstif-wm, fvwm95, and AfterStep are all included with the Red Hat distribution. You can install them during the installation process or anytime afterwards, manually.

Using the Start Menu

The little Gnome footprint (similar in purpose to the Windows Start button) in the lower, left corner of the screen, provides access to many applications and utilities. Click on the footprint and the menu shown in Figure 4-4 is activated. The menu is self-explanatory: click on the applications folder and choose an application from the submenu.

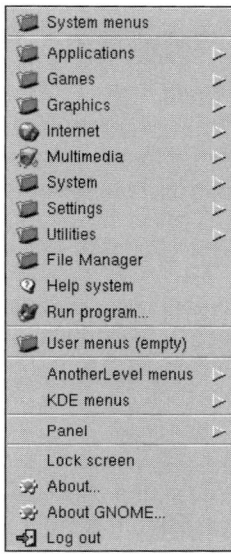

Figure 4-4: The Gnome/Enlightenment Start menu

The horizontal menu bar along the bottom of the screen provides access to commonly used functions. For instance, an icon for Netscape is included by default because Netscape itself was installed by default. You can add applications to this menu by clicking on the Gnome start button and clicking on Panel->Add new launcher. A window is displayed where you can enter the name of the icon and the location of the program to launch. For instance, to start the `diald` control program `dctrl`, you enter `/usr/bin/dctrl`. You can specify one of the generic Gnome icons or use one that you've provided yourself.

Viewing an X Client on an X Server

Recall that the X Window System is made of two parts: the X Client and X Server. The client and server can run on a single computer or on separate computers connected via a network. The following discussion briefly describes how to graphically view a remote process.

USING AN X CLIENT AND X SERVER ON THE SAME COMPUTER

First, display an X Client on your own X Server. Your X Server is the system that you started by running the startx program.

NOTE The terminology is somewhat confusing because the term server generally implies a computer that runs services for you while you are its client. In the case of X, the term *X Server* defines the software that takes care of displaying the graphical information generated by the X Client. Thus, when you start up X (literally the program /usr/bin/X11/X) you are starting up the X Server. The programs you run are all clients of that server.

You need to give permission to the X Clients to display on your X Server, so from a command line run the following program:

```
xhost +
```

This gives permission to any X Client on any network that has access to your X Server to display on your computer. This can be a security hazard so in the future use the more specific command like `xhost + somehost` to allow specific hosts or networks display access. Please refer to the man page on `xhost` for more information.

CAUTION Using `xhost` can still present a security problem if you are displaying sensitive information on a computer that is used by multiple people. That's because any user who can log onto that computer can connect to the X server. On the other hand, if you are the only person to work on a computer (your personal workstation, for instance) then using `xhost` should not be a problem. However, if you are sharing a computer with others and work with sensitive information, use the `xauth` program rather than `xhost`. Please consult the `xauth` man page for more help.

Next, from a command line on your computer display the simple graphical clock by entering the command:

```
xclock -display :0
```

You should see the clock displayed. You've now allowed X client access to your local display and have run the X Client and told it to send its display to your local X Server. The :0 stands for the first display at the default network location.

Chapter 4: Configuring the X Window System

DISPLAYING AN X CLIENT ON A REMOTE X SERVER

Once your local X Server has been told to display X Clients with the xhost command, you can expand the display variable to send the graphical information from an X Client running on a remote machine. If you are connected to a network that has another computer running X Window, then enter the following command from that machine (note that commercial products like Exceed give Windows machines the capability to do just that):

```
xclock -display chivas.paunchy.net:0.0
```

This command displays the graphical clock on the Linux machine with the network address of `chivas.paunchy.net` (that is the IP 192.168.1.254 that was used for the Red Hat installation described in Chapter 1). Note that in the typical case where a computer has just one physical monitor, the `0.` syntax is the same as `0.0`. The second `0` means the first display or monitor attached to the X Server and can, in most cases, be abbreviated from `0.0` to just `0`. It's confusing at first.

If you are sitting at the console of the remote machine then the clock is displayed on chivas. However, if you telnet to chivas from the remote machine and reverse the process, then you'll see the Xclock displayed on your machine. After you experiment with the system, it should become clear who is the server and who is the client.

Troubleshooting Problems

First, it should be pointed out that the Xconfigurator is a good troubleshooting tool in itself. If it can not properly start up X, then it allows you to quit or attempt to reconfigure.

If you have problems getting X Window started, then there are a few places to look at. First check that Xconfigurator has your correct video and monitor hardware information. Remember, SuperProbe can detect many types of video adapters. The `/cat/pci` file contains information about your video adapter if it is a PCI device (`cat /cat/pci | grep -i vga`).

If you've entered the correct information and you still can't get the display to work, then you have misconfigured the video adapter, the monitor, or both. If you are trying to specify a specific video driver, then you can try using a generic VGA adapter. Log in as root, mount the CD-ROM and install the XFree86-SVGA RPM (`rpm -ivh /mnt/cdrom/RedHat/RPMS/XFree86-SVGA*`). Rerun Xconfigurator as described in "Using Xconfigurator" earlier in this chapter.

In this case select the Unlisted card item which is at the very end of the Choose a Card menu. That puts you in the Pick a Server menu. From that menu, click SVGA.

After selecting SVGA you will see the Monitor Setup menu. Select the first item in the menu (the custom monitor) and click OK. For troubleshooting purposes it's best to choose the 640 · 480 setting, which should work on every VGA monitor. Pick the 50-70 vertical sync range. Skip the probing in the Screen Configuration window, and select the amount of video memory; if you don't know, select an amount that's reasonable. For a very old video card, you should probably select a lower amount of memory. Next, select the No Clockchip Setting in the Clockchip Configuration window. In the Probe for Clocks window, select the Skip choice. Next, select the 640 · 480 value and click OK. If you click OK in the Start X window, Xconfigurator will try to start X. If you are asked if you see the prompt then Xconfigurator has successfully set up your system.

If you successfully configure X but it still fails to start, then you need to look at the output from `startx`. Sometimes the information displayed from `startx` overflows the scrollback buffer and you cannot see all of the information. In that case, you can use the following command to both display and store the information:

```
startx 2>&1 | tee startx.log
```

The `2>&1` sequence sends the output of both the standard output and error to the pipe. The `tee` command splits the information coming out of the pipe and sends it to both the console and the startx.log file. You can then examine the log file at your leisure.

Typical error messages are due to misconfigured or non-existent monitor resolution modes, chip sets, etc. Please consult the `/usr/doc/HOWTO/XFree86-HOWTO` and `/usr/doc/HOWTO/XFree86-Video-Timings-HOWTO` documents as well as the `http://www.xfree86.org` web site for more information and insights into troubleshooting your X Window System. (If you have not installed the extra documentation—an option during the Red Hat installation process—then you can do so now by mounting the companion CD-ROM and entering the command:

```
rpm -ivh /mnt/cdrom/RedHat/RPMS/XFree86-doc*
```

The HOWTO and other documentation is installed in the `/usr/doc` directory.

Summary

This chapter discussed the basic theory of the X Window System. It also introduced the essentials for configuring the X Window System and the Gnome/Enlightenment window manager. The X Window System combined with a window manager provides a graphical system that works the same as Microsoft Windows in many ways, but is more powerful. It's more powerful because it can work across a network as well as on a single machine.

Chapter 4: Configuring the X Window System

- Basic X Window System theory is discussed. The X Window System is based on the client-server model. The client and server can be run on the same computer or across a network.

- How to configure the X Window System for your computer is covered. The Xconfigurator makes the configuration of X reasonably easy.

- How to use the mouseconfig program to configure your mouse is covered.

- How to configure the Gnome/Enlightenment window manager for your computer is discussed. The Gnome/Enlightenment window manager is the default of the Red Hat distribution. You can configure its operation by editing a configuration file.

- How to view an X client on a remote X server is covered. Instructions are given for viewing an Xclient from across a network.

- How to troubleshoot common problems is discussed. Some hints are given for fixing a broken X Window System.

Chapter 5

Getting Help

IN THIS CHAPTER

- ◆ Get help with Linux commands using manual pages
- ◆ Learn about the Linux Documentation Project (LDP) and how to find the FAQs, HOWTOs, mini-HOWTOs, and books written on Linux
- ◆ Find information on the Internet about Linux, Linux products, and support issues
- ◆ Learn about Linux publications, both printed magazines and online e-zines
- ◆ Find a local Linux User Group and enjoy the benefits of finding other users who live locally

THIS CHAPTER COVERS the many Linux resources that are available to you. Because Linux was initially developed over the Internet, many interactive information sources have been developed through it. For instance, the *Linux Documentation Project* documents many, if not all, of the systems that make up Linux. Newsgroups, such as Usenet, provide interactive sources for problem-solving and answering questions.

You may be surprised at the number of options available for a "free" operating system when it comes to support. It's no wonder the Linux user community won *InfoWorld's* Best Technical Support award in the magazine's 1997 Product Of The Year competition. In this chapter you'll learn why it won.

Using Manual Pages

In Chapter 2, you learned many of the important Linux commands as well as some options and arguments for those commands. By no means were all the commands or all the options for the commands mentioned. But help is never to far away, because Linux has a built-in method for providing information for just about every aspect of your system, called the manual pages. Usually called *man pages* for short, manual pages tell you almost everything you wanted to know about a Linux command, program, or feature. This section will teach you how to use `man` pages to learn more about Linux commands.

To get help for a command, just type

`man command`

and Linux will provide pages and pages of information about that command. If you type

`man man`

and you can see the manual page for the `man` command.

Since manual documents are usually several pages long, Linux uses `less` to display them. This keeps them from running off the screen and provides all of the viewing and searching options you get from `less`. To quit viewing a man page, type Q. To search the text in a `man` page, type a forward slash (/), followed by the word you're looking for. Less takes you to the next occurrence. If you want to search backwards, then use the question mark (?).

If you don't know which command you want, you can use the `-k` option. For example, type

`man -k editor`

and Linux will print a list of commands that match they keyword you entered. It searches the `whatis` database for the commands. In fact, if you've tried using `apropos` this should all look very familiar. (See Chapter 2 for information on `apropos`.) Of course the value of using the `-k` option is dependent on updating the `whatis` database regularly.

Man Page Sections

`Man` pages are mostly stored in the `/usr/man` directory on your Linux computer and additional `man` pages can be found in `/usr/X11R6/man`. When you look in that directory you'll notice numerous subdirectories titled `man1`, `man2`, `man3`, etc. The actual manual files are in these subdirectories.

Notice the `whatis` file also in this directory. This is the database file you create with the `makewhatis` command (see Chapter 2). When used with the `-k` option, `man` uses this database to provide general information on commands.

Each directory holds `man` pages pertaining to a specific help section:

- `man1`: commands
- `man2`: system calls
- `man3`: library calls
- `man4`: devices
- `man5`: files formats and conventions
- `man6`: games
- `man7`: macro packages and layouts
- `man8`: system management
- `man9`: kernel routines
- `mann`: new documentation (may be moved)
- `mano`: old documentation (kept for a grace period)
- `manl`: local documentation (relevant to your own particular system

When you type `man command` Linux starts with first `man` page section and marches through each successive one until it finds a match. Some commands, programs, or features actually have several `man` pages. To see all the `man` pages, use the `-a` option. For example,

`man -a man`

provides information about the `man` command (from `man1`). But it also displays information on creating a `man` page from `man7`. In the case where you know that you want the manual page from `man7` you can specify the section number. Typing

`man 7 man`

for example will display only the `man` entry from `man7`.

Man Page Organization

Each manual page is organized with several headings These headings are described in Table 5-1. Although not every `man` page will have every heading, most pages have most headings.

TABLE 5-1 MANUAL PAGE ORGANIZATION

Heading	Description
NAME	name of command and one line description (incidentally, the only required section of a man page)
SYNOPSIS	short overview of program options
DESCRIPTION	more detailed explanation of the program
OPTIONS	description of any command options
FILES	lists any files the program uses
ENVIRONMENT	any environment variables that affect the program
DIAGNOSTICS	overview of error messages the program is likely to generate
BUGS	known limitations or problems
AUTHOR	name (and sometimes e-mail address) of the program's author
SEE ALSO	list of related manual pages

Linux commands, features, and functions are written by many different people. Because of this, some are written better than others and some are often out of date. Also, some man pages may be written for people with a working knowledge of Unix, while others provide more basic information. But whatever your level of knowledge, manual pages are a great source of help as you familiarize yourself with the operating system.

The Linux Documentation Project

You might think that a free operating system wouldn't offer you the luxury of good documentation. Nothing could be further from the truth. Some argue Linux has the best documentation and support of any other software products. In fact, in February 1998, *InfoWorld* granted their Best Technical Support Award to the Linux user community as a whole. "As something you can download for free, of course, Linux doesn't necessarily come with the support of a commercial entity," *InfoWorld* columnist Ed Foster wrote. "But that's exactly why many readers said they like it." The support Linux users receive from their peers via Usenet, Web pages, and IRC, he explained, often surpasses anything offered by commercial software vendors.

It all starts with the *Linux Documentation Project* (LDP). This section describes the LDP and how you can use it to get answers to questions about setting up particular components, configuration details, and the way to use Linux for specific tasks.

Like many aspects of Linux, the LDP is a collection of efforts. Its goal is to provide good, reliable documents for the Linux operating system. If you want to know how to make Linux work in particular environment or for a particular purpose, chances are it's covered in the LDP. Anyone interested can contribute to the project.

 Although there are many contributors, the project is coordinated to keep people from duplicating efforts. Contributors are encouraged to announce their plans for a new document so that no one starts working on a project in progress somewhere else.

You can get documents from the LDP from many sources. The main web site is `http://metalab.unc.edu/LDP/` although many other mirrors can be found all over the world. If you don't have Internet access yet, you'll find a copy of the LDP documents on the CD-ROM included in this book.

If you selected the Extra Documentation, as I suggested, or installed everything during the Red Hat installation process in the Chapter 1, then you already have much of the LDP on your Linux machine. Check the `/usr/doc` directory for the HOWTO and FAQ document files.

FAQs

If you've spent any time on the Internet, you're probably familiar with the acronym FAQ. It stands for Frequently Asked Questions and provides answers for those common questions that just about everyone has asked before.

Authors have written FAQs on many subjects in Linux, including hardware support and common problem solving. As you probably know, before you ask anyone for help on the Internet, it's a good idea to look through the FAQs that cover the subject of your question. It's not that Linux users don't want to be helpful to new users, it's just that they get tired of answering the same questions over and over.

FAQs are an excellent place for new users of Linux to start because they don't assume much Linux knowledge. Robert Kiesling wrote an excellent general Linux FAQ that is available at `http://metalab.unc.edu/LDP/FAQ/Linux-FAQ.html`. If you installed the extra documentation, you can find it at `/usr/doc/FAQ/html/Linux-FAQ.html` which is in HTML format.

You can find a couple FAQs written specifically for Red Hat Linux users. Although not part of the LDP, these FAQs can provide helpful information for users of the Red Hat distribution.

The first is the official Red Hat Linux Support FAQ available at `http://www.redhat.com/knowledgebase/kb/cache/1.html`.

Another good source for Linux users is `www.linux.org`. It contains a wide range of information about Linux.

HOWTOs

Next to FAQs, HOWTOs are the heart of the LDP. HOWTOs are documents that describe how to use or configure a certain aspect of the Linux operating system. They cover a wide range of topics such as bash shell configuration, PCMCIA support, and using Linux with your 3Com Palm Organizer. HOWTOs are somewhat like FAQs, but they're not in question and answer format (although many HOWTOs include a FAQ section).

HOWTOs are available in many different formats including plain text, HTML, and PostScript. They are also translated in many different languages. The LDP has HOWTO documents in everything from Chinese to Slovenian.

In addition to the regular HOWTO documents, the LDP has a couple of Special HOWTOs. The only distinction is that they rely on figures which make them unavailable for regular HOWTO formats.

And finally, there are HOWTOs that are technically part of the LDP, but are no longer being maintained by an author. It may be the last place you should look, but it might also be the only place to find what you're looking for. Check out the unmaintained HOWTOs — especially if you're working with old hardware.

mini-HOWTOs

In addition to the HOWTO documents, the LDP also has documents on short, specific subjects. These are called mini-HOWTOs and are only available in plain text and HTML formats in the `/usr/doc/HOWTO/mini` directory.

In all actuality, the line separating HOWTOs and mini-HOWTOs seems to be blurring, so if you're looking for instructions on a particular topic, be sure to check both document collections.

LDP Guides

In addition to the HOWTOs, mini-HOWTOs, and FAQs, some authors have published full-fledged books under the LDP. They are called Guides and they cover topics for both beginners and experts. You can access them at `http://www.linux.org/help/projectguide.html`.

As of this writing, there are eight Guides available: *Installation and Getting Started Guide, The Linux Kernel, The Linux Kernel Hackers' Guide, The Linux Kernel Module Programming Guide, The Linux Network Administrators' Guide, The Linux Programmer's Guide, The Linux System Administrators' Guide,* and *The Linux Users' Guide.* Many of these guides are out of date but still make fine references.

Getting Information from the Internet

As previously mentioned, you can browse the information of the LDP from several Web sites in HTML or plain text format. But that's not the only source of Linux information you'll find on the Internet. This section will show you other Internet locations you can visit, not just for help, but for Linux news as well.

 Linux certainly could never have gained the momentum it now enjoys without the existence of the Internet. So the Internet is really the natural source for keeping up to date on Linux information. It is the single network that keeps Linux developers and users together.

In fact, you'll typically get better support for Linux over the Internet than the commercial UNIX help lines offer. The free flow of information and ideas provides an unmatched resource for an operating system like Linux. Bugs are discovered and fixed, drivers are written, and help is dispersed far better and faster than via the Internet than any other mechanism. A vast pool of talent is tapped in to fix and push forward the software and people are using their own time and resources to produce much of the value that Linux offers. The motive is to produce a quality product—personal pride and satisfaction drives Linux software to extremely high level of quality.

That's one of the reasons that Linux is so stable while at the same time advancing at such a fast rate. There are a large number of people to work on a large number of projects and ideas. The code is going to be seen and evaluated by their peers and thus must in general be elegant as well as functional. (Because people with all levels of experience contribute to Linux, sometimes it takes repeated peer review to produce a good product.) Public interest and passion for the operating system is also what fuels the support you'll find on the Internet for Linux.

Using the Web

The Internet has an abundance of Linux Web sites, each with its own emphasis. One good place to start is the Linux homepage:

http://www.linux.org

But that's only the beginning.

LINUX NEWS

The purpose of some of the sites is to "spread the word" about Linux. They exist to educate people on the virtues of Linux and to debunk some of the mysteries associated with it. One reason Linux is gaining mind share in the computer industry is because of sites like these. These are the places to go to find out what has been written in the industry about Linux. Some examples are:

- Slashdot: `http://slashdot.org`
- Linux Daily News: `http://lwn.net`
- Linux Today: `http://www.linuxtoday.com`

INFORMATION SITES

Some sites are informational. They are resources for those seeking answers to questions. I've already mentioned the home site of the LDP and the Red Hat Linux User's FAQ, but there are others. For example,

`http://www.redhat.com/support/docs/hardware.html`

provides the latest hardware compatibility lists for that particular distribution of Linux. If you're using a distribution other than the Red Hat 6.0 that's provided with this book, check their sites for the latest compatibility lists. If you want to checkout support for Linux on laptops, check out the Linux Laptop page:

`http://www.cs.utexas.edu/users/kharker/linux-laptop`

LINUX APPLICATIONS

If you think the idea of a free operating system is appealing, how about free software? Numerous sites exist with free Linux software for you to download. Most are organized by category so finding what you need is fairly simple. Check out the following to get started:

`http://www.linuxapps.com`
`http://www.xnet.com:80/~blatura/linapps.shtml`
`http://freshmeat.net`

Linux Newsgroups

Although some Web sites have discussion forums, most of the time it's one-way communication—you searching for information. What if you have a question that isn't a FAQ or it's not covered at any site you can think of? A good place to turn is newsgroups.

Quite a few Linux specific newsgroups have popped up over the last few years. I've included some in this table. The topic of your question should fit somewhere in here.

comp.os.linux.advocacy	comp.os.linux.alpha
comp.os.linux.development	comp.os.linux.hardware
comp.os.linux.m68k	comp.os.linux.misc
comp.os.linux.networking	comp.os.linux.portable
comp.os.linux.powerpc	comp.os.linux.setup
comp.os.linux.x	linux.redhat
linux.redhat.install	linux.redhat.misc
linux.redhat.ppp	

Of course, if you've ever spent much time in newsgroups, you know to lay low for a while until you get a feel for the group. Each newsgroup has it's own personality and rules and almost every one has a FAQ specifically for that newsgroup. It's good form to read the FAQ before posting a question. A group's archive is also a good place to check first. Most newsgroups have archives available so you can search to see if your question has been answered recently. Other readers don't appreciate re-hashing over a question that was just covered a week ago.

It's a good idea to get familiar with a group or two *before* you have a problem. Some newsgroups have far too many messages a day to read each and every one, but scanning the headers and following a thread or two that captures your interest will give you a good lay of the land.

Linux Mailing Lists

Another option, similar to newsgroups, is mailing lists. Mailing lists send messages directly to your e-mail inbox. If you send a question to a mailing list, every subscriber will receive your question via e-mail and they can either respond to the whole list or to you personally. If they respond to the list, then everyone will see the response in their e-mail. If they respond to you personally (called responding "backchannel"), you're the only one who will get the message.

You can find several mailing lists that deal with Linux. The rules of etiquette that apply to newsgroups also apply to mailing lists. Make sure you hang out for a while and get feel for the group before you post a message. Read the list's FAQ. And if you're new, check the archives before asking a question.

Red Hat manages several mailing lists that you can check out at:

http://www.redhat.com/support

Every mailing list is different, so there's really no way to predict how many messages you'll get in your mailbox any given day. If you subscribe to two or three lists, you may start getting hundreds of messages a day in your e-mail's inbox. A good idea for new users is to subscribe to the mailing list in digest format. A digest will take all the lists messages, combine them into one e-mail a day, and send it to you. That way you're only getting one message a day (even though it might be quite large).

Finding Linux Publications

Since Linux is getting more popular, more publications focusing on the OS are cropping up. The most popular paper magazine is *Linux Journal* published by Specialized Systems Consultants, Inc. It's a monthly magazine that covers a wide range of topics for developers, system administrators, and end users alike.

A sister publication to *Linux Journal* is *Linux Gazette*. This is an electronic monthly magazine found on the Internet at:

http://www.linuxgazette.com

It's also published by Specialized Systems Consultants, Inc. and has several how-to type articles. It also contains a section titled Help Wanted. This isn't for classified ads—it's for people to ask questions and give ideas for articles, among other things.

Some other electronic magazines are:

http://www.linuxworld.com
http://ext2.org
http://www.linuxfocus.org

Joining a Linux User Group

As you can see, the Internet is a great tool for getting Linux information. But you can't beat face-to-face communication with other users. If you would like to meet other people who work with Linux and can help with problems or just give advice, look into joining a local Linux user group.

Linux user groups (LUGs) are very important to the Linux movement. After all, there's no "Linux Corporate Headquarters," no "home office," or "regional office" for that matter. Users rely on LUGs for that "real person" contact that's so important.

User groups are certainly not new to Linux. They're not even new to computers, although computer user groups helped propel the development of the personal computer. Many hobbyists from ham radio operators to model train enthusiasts get together to share ideas, get help, and tout their own knowledge. The difference with a LUG is that Linux isn't just a hobby. The user group can give you real solutions for your business.

LUGs typically get together monthly. Meeting topics can run the gamut from trading shareware to writing device drivers. Sometimes they'll invite a vendor in to demonstrate their new Linux solution. Sometimes the meetings are more social and provide a way for friends with a common interest to get together.

Some LUGs have their own newsletters, web sites, and mailing lists. These are especially helpful because if you post a question, and someone has an answer, you might even be able to go to their office and have them show you how to solve your problem.

To find out more about LUGs, check out the User Group HOWTO document in the LDP. To see if there's one near you, check out:

```
http://www.linux.org/users/index.html
```

If you can't find one close by, consider starting your own LUG. The guidelines for doing so are outlined in the User Group HOWTO document mentioned above. You never know. You might just be the catalyst your area needs for Linux to gain popularity and support.

Summary

There are many places to go to learn more about Linux. It's a common miscon-ception that Linux lacks the support mechanisms of other operating systems. Nothing could be further from the truth. On the contrary, Linux users have myriad places to go for information and help. The Internet is probably the main source of support, but don't discount published works like magazines and books. Even virtual face to face communication is available through user groups. If you've got a question, you'll get an answer if you're willing to hunt a little.

- ◆ A discussion of manual pages is featured. Man pages are the traditional method of storing infomation about Linux. They can be accessed easily via the man command.

- ◆ An introduction to the Linux Documentation Project is covered. This is the global effort to pull together all the important Linux documents — FAQs, HOWTOs, and so on — into a coherent, ongoing collection.

- ◆ A description of obtaining information from the Internet is shown. The Internet was the incubator for Linux and now provides many different sources of information and help for the user.

- ◆ A discussion of using Linux publications is given. There are numerous magazines that are both traditional paper-based and online. These provide another useful resource.

- Linux User Groups (LUGS) are discussed. Geographically linked people form user groups to meet and share the Linux experience.

Part II

Managing Your Linux Network

CHAPTER 6
Administering Your Linux Server

CHAPTER 7
Managing Your Network

CHAPTER 8
Sharing Files and Printers with Samba

CHAPTER 9
Sharing Printers

CHAPTER 10
Automating Network-wide Backups

Chapter 6

Administering Your Linux Server

IN THIS CHAPTER

- Understanding systems administration from the top down
- Describing systems administration fundamentals
- Managing user accounts
- Backing up your Linux server
- Using the Red Hat Package Manager
- Using the Linux Configuration Tool
- Writing scripts
- Automating repetitive jobs
- Understanding system log files
- Starting and stopping a Linux computer

MANAGING A COMPUTER SYSTEM is a difficult and complex job. The sheer number of topics that you have to master requires a large effort over a long time, and the fact that running your business is your main focus makes it even more difficult to find the time. However, the more that your business depends on computers, the more important it is that you take the time to learn. Computers and networks must be managed correctly to prevent problems and disasters, and this is necessary to make your systems run productively.

This chapter is designed to introduce you to the philosophy of administration and the details needed to do the most important jobs. The focus of this chapter is on managing a Linux server, but the next chapter focuses on networking issues. However, some topics such as security are symbiotic to both, and are discussed in both chapters.

Once you have a good overview of systems administration, the job will seem less daunting and you can be sure that you are not missing anything important. This chapter is oriented to management issues specific to the operation of a Linux server and leaves network-oriented topics to Chapter 7.

Introducing Systems Administration

Your goal for administering a Linux server should be to make it work as efficiently and safely as possible. Any type of computer system—and Linux is no exception—will always take a lot of effort to run efficiently and reliably. However, by following the guidelines described in this chapter, you can run your system, instead of letting your system run you.

The term *Systems Administration* often includes many, if not all, of the functions of Network Administration. The terms can often be used interchangeably. For the purposes of this book they are treated separately in order to help break this amorphous subject into more manageable and easily understood chunks.

This goal certainly requires a lot of work to reach. However, the more that you concentrate on creating a structure that encourages your computer and network to run smoothly, the less work you'll have to do in the future.

The ideal working structure is a computer that has a recent operating system with all the latest updates (patches) installed. Its file system should be well thought out and consistent with only the necessary daemons running and the minimum system software installed. All application software should be installed correctly and its documentation kept in one place. The partitions themselves should be no more than 80 percent full. Minimalism is good when dealing with computers.

The list goes on and on, but you get the idea. The use of a consistent logic in the design your systems create a more easily managed computer, because trouble very often occurs at the intersection of two elements. If you have more hardware or software than you really need, you're forcing more systems than necessary to interact with each other. More interactions lead to more complexity and complexity very often spells trouble.

Understanding and Creating Policy

Seldom does one get to create the structure that is necessary for creating the ideal, or even reasonable, computer environment. Perhaps if you are starting your business from scratch and have the time and money to create a good computer model, then you can engineer a good environment. However, in the more common situation where you don't have the time or money (or else inherit an existing system) then your situation is more problematic; and you'll probably have your hands full just making sure your system is up and running.

You should have goals, however, and if you don't try to set and reach them, then you will never have anything close to a smoothly running system. They are often useful in setting base lines to work from. Whatever your situation is, if you can imagine the structure that you want to ideally operate from, then you will be better off in the long run.

The policies that you set now are your tools for freeing yourself from the control of the computers. Whether you're the sole proprietor and have a mental list, or the VP in charge of a significant number of people and use written policies, they are important to think about. The following list outlines several categories of everyday computer system administration that you might consider.

- Backups: How, when, why, and what kind of backups are performed. Your needs will depend on what your normal tasks are. Use your best judgment.
- Security: Protect your computer(s) from unauthorized access.
- Servicing your customers: Adding, deleting modifying accounts and other customer related services.
- Troubleshooting: Finding problems that occur and fixing them.

If you set your own policies and follow them, then you've made a consistent structure for your system. You need to balance ease of use for you and your users along with the extra work that such structures require. It's a balancing act just like everything else in your operation. Judgement is key.

It's very common to inherit a computer system, which means you'll inherit whatever the current structure is, if any. However, if there are no clear guidelines, your own practices can become new policy. For instance, if you always perform backups on Friday nights, after a while that's when people will expect backups to be performed. If you put it into writing, it will almost certainly become the defacto policy. Whenever possible *write it down*.

Backing Up Your File Server

This is the single most important job to do. This is such an important topic that it's included in this section with other generalities. If you have consistent, reliable backups you'll be okay no matter what else goes wrong. Consistency and liabilities are key.

Consistency is essential because, face it, the day to day grind of backups makes it easy to get lazy. It's just a matter of time, (or bad luck) before you'll need the one file, or file system that you didn't back up (just that one time) and all of a sudden you are out of a job, or a customer, or whatever.

Reliability is essential, because even if you got the one file or directory on tape, it could be worthless if your backups are not reliable.

How does one obtain consistency and reliability? Experience helps. Brute force dedication does too. However, both those qualities can be difficult to obtain and you should remember that the computer is your ally. The solution is to use the best equipment that you can possibly afford and then automate the processes. The details of making backups are discussed in this chapter and Chapter 10 (Chapter 10 introduces the commercial network-based client server backup software Arkeia).

Worrying about Security

One of the big headaches of computer administration is security. It's your responsibility to keep your computers safe from unauthorized access and abuse.

This book does not intend to attempt to cover the topic in depth. There's enough information on the subject of security to fill the entire book. But hopefully you'll learn how to lay down a strong foundation of philosophy and build a sturdy house to get you started safely. From that point, you can go on to learn as much as you think necessary to match the dangers that your particular business faces.

First, there is no silver bullet when it comes to security. These hackers will not be stopped by one type of firewall or one type of password encryption and you should view security as an amorphous and evolving animal. Your best protection is your own paranoia, which should be tempered by knowledge and as you gain it, experience. The following ideas or policies should help focus your paranoia into good protection.

Use layered security. You don't want your entire system to fail because of one breach. Therefore, use a firewall, use good passwords, monitor your system and be aware that all of your protective mechanisms are only as good as the people who manage them.

Educate yourself and your employees. The Internet is a great resource and you should keep track of security-oriented newsgroups and Web sites. There are numerous professional groups such as USENIX (www.usenix.org) and SANS (www.sans.org) which provide professional (and tax deductible) conferences on system administration and security topics. These conferences are probably the best way to cement knowledge that you've gained on the job, because professionals boil down the essential topics into half or full day tutorials which will help you with the basics.

The knowledge or experience level of the people attempting to break into your system can vary. Some *crackers* (the hackers are the good guys in this book, after all, hackers created Linux) are very sophisticated; while others, such as the ones referred to as *script kiddies* or *kiddiescripters,* don't necessarily have in-depth knowledge of computers and networks. They simply run sophisticated, publicly available programs that gather information and attack your system. Therefore, having *too* much paranoia and awe can be detrimental to your role as security administrator because it prevents you from reasonably scouting your opposition.

The education of your employees or whoever works on your systems is also essential. Sometimes just knowing why it's important to set up good passwords or to log out when you are not present helps people do the right thing. The better that everyone understands their role and responsibility, the more secure your systems will be.

Security should not be treated as an isolated subject and it should permeate every facet of systems administration including the way you install and configure your computer. The more processes and software that you have on your computer the more potential chinks in the your security armor. Every element of your computer has security aspects to it.

After some study, security shouldn't be much of a mystery. You should have a healthy fear of the dangers, but also be aware that potential damage can be handled in most cases. With the help of this book, you should be able to put your system into a reasonably secure state. From there you can read and study from the many security information sources and move forward with the knowledge that you have a reasonably safe system.

Providing Service to Your Customers

Running a small business can mean many things and you may or may not have customers of your own in your role as system administrator. If you're the sole proprietor, then all you have to do is keep your system running for yourself. But, if you function as a system administrator, a large part of your time will be spent with the people who use your system.

In that case, there's a range of services that you need to think about. One is managing the user login accounts and their environments and another is managing the application software that they use. You also have to worry about what your employees should and should not be able to do. There should be guidelines for the users to interact with each other – remember, threatening or vulgar email in particular requires that definite policies are in place and enforced.

Troubleshooting

Troubleshooting is one of the constants of systems administration. Your goal in setting up your computers should be to maximize usability while minimizing problems and most of the chapters in this book contain some troubleshooting information about a specific topic.

But there are some general troubleshooting models that can guide you when you're trying to solve problems. Basically, you should try to isolate the problem and then systematically work your way to the root cause. It's a simple and sensible concept but it's often difficult to use in practice because the many parts that make up a computer and a network clutter the landscape. The trick is to find the pattern within the camouflage.

Locating the root cause of a problem is more of an art than a science. Ultimately, there is always a simple cause and the gremlin is never magical but can always be explained scientifically (a misconfigured program, a loose connector, a paper jam). The art comes mostly from learning how your particular computers and networks work and interact with each other. The larger your own knowledge base of concepts, facts, and tips, and the greater your ability to solve problem.

The troubleshooting tips and suggestions in this chapter intended to help aid you. But this is not a complete guide to all potential problems (that would take several books and still not scratch the surface); it's a starting point. Combine what you learn here with your experience and knowledge of your network to solve your problems.

Understanding System Administration Essentials

Philosophy needs to be put into practice. There are several functions essential to the day-to-day operation of a Linux server or workstation.

This book makes use of both the command line (Shell) and X Window GUI-based system administration tools. It is important to keep in mind that the more that you know about the underlying administrative functions, the better you are able to work on your system. If you never use anything but an administrative GUI like LinuxConf, then you will never have a good feel for the ways your system is being manipulated. On the other hand, system administration is probably not your main concern and getting the job done is more important on a day-to-day basis than having full knowledge of the particulars. To that end, I discuss both methods whenever possible or practical.

Introducing Control Panel and LinuxConf

Red Hat Linux provides some useful tools devoted to systems administration. The X Window based control panel and Linuxconf cover many administrative functions. Table 6-1 shows the functions that they cover.

TABLE 6-1 CONTROL PANEL AND LINUXCONF FUNCTIONS

Utility	Name	Function
Control Panel	Run Level Editor	Configures which services are started or stopped in various runlevels
Control Panel	Time & Date	Changes time and date
Control Panel	Printer Configuration	Configures local, remote, and Samba printers
Control Panel	Network Configuration	Configures network functions
Control Panel	Modem Configuration	Creates a soft link to a modem
Control Panel	Kernel Daemon Configuration	Manually loads and unloads modules into the kernel
Control Panel	System Configuration	Starts LinuxConf
Control Panel	Package Management	Adds and deletes RPM packages
LinuxConf	Network management	Configures network functions
LinuxConf	User management	Adds, deletes, and modifies user accounts
LinuxConf	File System management	Manages Linux, NFS, and swap file systems
LinuxConf	Boot Mode	Configures LILO
LinuxConf	Control panel	Manages system functions such as shutdown
LinuxConf	Control files	Configures system and application configuration files
LinuxConf	Logs	Manages various system and log files

When you login as root and run X, you can access the ControlPanel, shown in Figure 6-1, by clicking on the Enlightenment window manager and selecting Start → Programs → Administration → Control Panel. You must be logged in as root to perform most of the functions, however.

Figure 6-1: ControlPanel Window

LinuxConf is a new system and its functions should grow with time. For now, it's useful for configuring several of the important Linux systems administration functions. LinuxConf is a GUI that ties together the Red Hat administrative utilities in one place. There is some overlap in functions between LinuxConf and control panel. You can use any of the overlapping functions as you see fit.

You can run LinuxConf from the command line, an xterm window, or a virtual console. Enter the command `LinuxConf` from a command line and you get a simple menu-based window. Use the Config menu item to select the LinuxConf program and the Control menu item to enter the Control Panel system. Use the cursor keys to navigate through either system.

Making Simple Backups

Backing up your file systems is the single most important function that you can do. Nearly every problem can be overcome to some extent if you have good back ups. The other functions of administration are important, of course, but some day you'll need your backups and you can't manage your user accounts or perform other tasks if you can't get your data back.

In this book, the backup function is divided into both local and network parts. Local backups are explained in this chapter and network backups are described in Chapter 10. They are separated because once you start managing a network and need to backup its individual machines, using separate backups does not work well in the long term.

To perform a local backup you need a storage device. If you are an author and are writing a medium-sized book, you may not need much more than a floppy disk or two to backup your manuscript. If you are running a sole proprietorship, a ZIP (100MB), Jaz (1GB) drive, or even use a writable CD-ROM could fit the bill. However, once your data grows above a 100MB (or 1GB if you use a Jaz drive) or so, then you need to graduate to a *Digital Audio Tape* (DAT) device.

Typically, tape drives are used because they have a reasonable amount of storage and are reasonably inexpensive. A 4mm DAT drive typically stores between 2 to 5GB of data. If you go to 8mm then those numbers increase somewhat.

This book focuses on using a IDE based ZIP drive; a device which is connected to the hard disk controller just like a hard drive or an ATAPI CD-ROM drive. They are inexpensive (approximately $100), are reasonably reliable, and store enough data for a small operation (100MB). They are also much easier to install and configure than the more robust DAT drives.

USING TAR TO SAVE TO A DISK

There are several commands that you can use to perform the backups. One of the most popular (and oldest) mechanisms is the *Tape Archive* (*tar*) program. It's flexible, nearly universal among Linux/UNIX systems, and it works quite well. Before practicing a backup to tape, try the following command:

```
tar cvf etc.tar /etc
```

Using a DAT drive

After installing the storage device (please consult the manufacturer and Linux documentation for more information) you can practice using it. The following command provides information about both the device and the tape in it. Login as root, insert a tape and then enter the command:

```
mt -f /dev/st0 status
```

This command controls the magnetic device and returns the status as shown below. The -f parameter specifies the file to operate on, which in this case is the device file connected to the DAT drive on the SCSI bus.

If you use the command mt -f /dev/rt0 rewind the tape rewinds.

The c parameter specifies that you are copying the files from the specified directory (/etc); while the v specifies that tar operates in a verbose mode (displaying the files being copied). The f declares the destination file to copy to (in this case the device file corresponds to the actual file etc.tar). If you list the files in your current directory you see the etc.tar file. It contains the archive and you can view the contents by using the tell (t) parameter as follows:

```
tar tvf etc.tar
```

You see a long listing of the /etc files and directories that were stored to the tar file. Note that the files found in the etc.tar file do not contain a leading slash. If a leading slash were included it would be referring to the root directory (/) and would also peg any restorations—called *extractions*—to that directory. Because the tar file does not include the leading slash, any extractions are done from your current directory. Therefore, if you are in the root user's home directory - /root - and restore from that archive, then an etc directory is created within the /root directory. Make sure that you are in that directory (use the cd /root command to make sure) and enter the command:

```
tar xvf etc.tar
```

There should be a new mirror image directory of the /etc directory in root's home directory (/root/etc). Next, delete that directory (rm -rf /root/etc) and try extracting an individual file by using:

```
tar xvf etc.tar etc/hosts
```

The full file name as tar knows it - etc/hosts - must be specified. List the directory and you see the etc directory again. The hosts file has also been extracted within the etc directory. Erase that directory (rm -rf /root/etc) again and this time extract an entire directory.

```
tar xvf etc.tar etc/X11
```

All the files and directories within what was the /etc/X11 are extracted to /root/etc.

USING TAR TO SAVE TO A ZIP DRIVE

The previous examples described how to use tar to save to a disk. The disk was used because it is simpler than tape to use. The following examples perform the same functions but make use of the tape drive.

 The following examples can be used for any other storage device that you have attached to your system. Substitute the appropriate device file for the tape device. For instance, if you want to use a floppy disk instead of a Zip disk, then use /dev/fd0 instead of /dev/hdd (or whatever the Zip device file is).

When Zip disks are shipped, they come formatted for the DOS file system. Linux recognizes and can mount DOS formatted disks. You can also reformat a Zip (or floppy) with the native ext2 Linux file system. The main advantage of reformatting with ext2 is that you can use long file names. However, retaining the DOS format means that you can use the Zip disk on Windows-based computers. This book reformats the Zip disk with ext2 in order to show you how the process works. If you wish to use DOS, then skip the instructions for formatting the Zip disk, and make sure that you use short filenames (8 characters for the file name and 3 for the suffix).

FORMATTING A ZIP DISK First you need to determine what device file is associated with your Zip drive. The Linux dmesg log (/var/log/dmesg) contains the messages displayed during the boot process. This information contains the devices that Linux discovers as it starts up. Login as root and enter the command. (Recall that the grep command filters the output of the pipe for a text string. The -i parameter tells grep to ignore the case of the characters.)

```
cat /var/log/dmesg | grep -i zip
```

If you have an IDE based Zip drive, then you should see something like the following message:

```
hdb: IOMEGA ZIP 100 ATAPI, ATAPI FLOPPY drive
```

The hdb indicates the device file that the Zip drive attached to.

> ### IDE Devices
>
> Modern PCs support up to four IDE devices on the system board (also called the motherboard). You can connect any IDE device, such as a disk drive, ATAPI CD-ROM, or Zip drive, by plugging them into the two IDE cable connectors on the system board; one or two IDE devices are supported on each cable. Under DOS the devices show up as the C:, D:, E:, or F: drives. Under Linux they appear as the /dev/hda, /dev/hdb, /dev/hdc and /dev/hdd files. To check this, login as root and enter the command:
>
> ```
> dmesg |grep -i hd
> ```
>
> A typical system looks as follows:
>
> ```
> hda: WDC AC21600H, 1549MB w/128kB Cache, CHS=3148/16/63, DMA
> hdb: IOMEGA ZIP 100 ATAPI, ATAPI FLOPPY drive
> hdd: 20DY, ATAPI CDROM drive
> ```
>
> This system contains a 1.5 GB hard drive and a Zip drive on the first IDE bus. The ATAPI CD-ROM sits on the second IDE bus and is the only device on it; there is room for another IDE device, such as a second hard drive, on this system.
>
> PCs require one of the two IDE devices on each connector to be a master and the other, if it exists, to be a slave. Typically, you want the Linux hard drive to be the master and whatever the second device to be the slave. The reason is that the device that you most often boot from should be the master and that is typically the hard drive. Most modern devices have a jumper (the small slab-like device that fits over the in-line metal pins) to select the master/slave settings. See your device manual for more information.

It is convenient to create a mount directory for the Zip drive as follows:

```
mkdir /mnt/zip
```

Mount the Zip drive by entering the command:

```
mount /dev/hdb /mnt/zip
```

Verify that it is mounted:

```
df
```

You should see the Zip drive mounted along with the normal file systems.

If you want to create the ext2 (default Linux) file system on the Zip disk and do not have any information stored on it, then unmount the drive and use the make file system command as follows:

```
umount /mnt/zip
mk2efs /dev/hdb
```

Remount the disk, run the `df` command and it appears like your other file systems:

USING TAR TO SAVE TO THE ZIP DISK The same basic commands discussed previously are used to save to the Zip disk, DAT, or any similarly attached storage device. Enter the following commands to make sure that your current working directory is /root, that the Zip disk is mounted, and to save the contents of the /etc directory to a tar file on the Zip disk:

```
mount /dev/hdb /mnt/zip
tar cvf /mnt/zip/etc.tar /etc
```

You can look at the contents of the archive as follows:

```
tar tvf /mnt/zip/etc.tar
```

Retrieving an archived file or directory is basically the same as before:

```
tar xvf /mnt/zip/etc.tar etc/hosts
```

or,

```
tar xvf /mnt/zip/etc.tar etc/X11
```

The `host` file or the `X11` directory are restored to the /root/etc directory just like before. The difference is that the archive that they are stored in now exists on a removable media.

COMPRESSING TAR ARCHIVES

The `tar` program includes the ability to compress and uncompress the data that it stores. It can use a couple of different compression formats, but Zip is the most commonly used. When the `-z` parameter is used, `tar` uses the `gzip` program to compress or uncompress the data as it copies, lists, or extracts the archive. (The `gzip` program uses the Lempel-Ziv coding (LZ77) format. The `gzip` program can be used independently to compress or uncompress any file.) The previous archive commands would use compression if the `z` parameter is included. For instance,

```
tar cvzf /mnt/zip/etc.tgz /etc
```

saves a compressed archive to the Zip disk. The `tgz` suffix is a standard suffix that indicates that the file is a `tar` archive and is `gzip` compressed.

MAKING INCREMENTAL TAR ARCHIVES

You do not want to continually make full archives because it takes up too much space and is time-consuming. By using the update feature of `tar` you can only copy files that are have been created or changed since the last full backup. The following command updates the tar archive with files that have been created or modified since you created the original `etc.tar` archive.

```
tar -uvf /mnt/zip/etc.tgz /etc
```

There are many ways that you can perform incremental backups. You are encouraged to read the `tar` man page for more hints. However, a reasonable schedule is shown in Table 6-2.

TABLE 6-2 A SIMPLE BACKUP SCHEDULE

Day of the month	Type	Description
1	Full	Full backup once/month w/ fresh Zip disk. Current disk stored offsite
2-14	Incremental	Daily incremental backup referenced to the Full backup
15	Full	Full backup. All successive incremental to be pegged to it
16-last day of month	Incremental	Daily incremental backups pegged to the Mid

This schedule really just gives you a feel for the things you should consider concerning backups. The mid-month full backup is used to prevent too many incrementals from building up. Otherwise, in the worst case scenario, you would have to sort through 29-30 incremental backups to find your data. By doing a full backup in the middle of the month, you can reduce that number to a maximum of 14.

It is advisable to store a reasonable amount of your data off-site. That means you should store the disks need to recover from a disaster such as a fire in a different place. That place could be another office, your home, a safety deposit box or wherever makes sense based on the value of your data.

The frequency of your full backup should reflect the value and turnover of your specific data. If your business is financial services, then you probably need to take more precautions than if your business is writing books. Use your best judgment.

KEEPING RECORDS

If you're only responsible for backing up the data that you create yourself, then the records that you keep can be minimal. However, once you start performing backup services for other people and organizations, or when your own data becomes too large to handle, then you have to keep good records.

In most cases, a simple paper log should suffice. Table 6-3 shows a simple form. Dates from 3/4 through 3/14 are omitted for brevity.

TABLE 6-3 BACKUP LOG FORM

Date	Disk label	Machine	FS	Description
3/1	chivas-101	chivas	All	Full backup of all file systems (chiva-100 offsite)
3/2	chivas-101	chivas	/home	incremental backup of home directories
3/3	chivas-101	chivas	/home	incremental backup of home directories
3/15	chivas-102	chivas	All	Full backup of all the file systems

This list shows that the machine chivas has overlapping backups through the middle of March, 1999. The overlap is because the full backup done on 3/15 includes most, if not all, of the data contained on the chivas-101 disk. It also shows that the previous Zip disk in sequence has been removed to an off-site location. Your situation might require more or less information but the idea is to document what you have and where you have it.

VERIFYING YOUR BACKUPS

The integrity of your backups should be tested periodically. The frequency and detail of your checks should match the comfort level that you wish to achieve. The method that you use can vary too, but a simple test is to restore part, or all, of a backup to a temporary location. You should then randomly sample the files and directories to verify that you can read the data and that it appears to be what you expect. For instance, if you login as root, and change to the generic temporary directory /var/tmp, then you can extract all or part of a backup to that directory and check it, like this:

```
cd /var/tmp
tar xvf /mnt/zip/etc.tar
```

A more sophisticated method is to use the `tar -diff` option to compare a recently created backup to the file system(s) that it archived. The `tar` program uses the `-d` option to compare an archive with a file system (the `df` option works as well). Enter the following commands to compare the archive that you just made to the actual /etc directory.

```
cd /
tar df /root/etc.tar etc
```

If you have not made any changes within the /etc directory then the previous command should not return any results. Next, modify the /etc/smb.conf file by using the `touch` command (if the file exists, then `touch` updates its time stamp, otherwise, it creates a file without any contents) and run the comparison again as follows

```
touch /etc/smb.conf
tar df /root/etc.tar etc
```

This time there is a difference and you see the difference displayed as follows:

```
etc/smb.conf: Mod time differs
```

This is by no means a complete verification but it is a simple test that should increase your confidence in your backups. Note that the difference function does not work if the tar archive is compressed.

DATA RETRIEVAL

Keep in mind that you might have to look through every incremental archive that you have in order to find the file or directories that you need. Therefore, the longer that you go between full backups, the longer and more difficult it is to restore data. However, the more full backups that you create, the more disks you need. Balancing your needs with the administrative overhead is key to creating a successful backup strategy.

> **BRU 2000**
>
> BRU 2000 is a GUI-based interactive and semi-automatic backup and retrieval system, and is a commercial product that can be found at www.estinc.com. You can use it to manually backup the computer that it is run on and it can also be programmed to perform backups at specified times or specific file systems. It can also be used over a network. One of its good features is its ability to hide the details involved with making backups and also it also assists in retrieving specific files and directories without sorting through a myriad of disks or tapes. It is not discussed at length in this book because the Arkeia backup system, discussed in Chapter 10, provides a higher level of service. However, it might make sense for you depending on your needs.

The difficulties involved with backing up data are quite intense. For that reason, Chapter 10 discusses the automatic, network-based Arkeia backup software. It automates the process of both the storage and retrieval of data. It keeps records of what's backed up, from where, when it was backed up, and where it is currently. It's not the only automated backup system, but at this point it appears to be one of the price/performance leaders in the Linux world.

Managing User Accounts

User login accounts are controlled by three files: /etc/passwd, /etc/shadow, and /etc/group. The passwd file contains the user name, (an encrypted password if you choose not to use shadow passwords); the user and group numeric id (which are the same by default under Red Hat); the user home directory; a field for general information about the user; the user account home directory; and the type of shell used. The shadow password file contains the user name, encrypted password, and access information about the account (note that system login accounts have no encrypted passwords because they can not be logged into and thus do not have passwords). The group file contains the user name, a numeric group identifier, and zero or more user names that belong to the group (it can also contain a group password but that is rarely used); additional user names are separated by commas.

The passwd file can be edited by hand to add and modify users. It is generally okay to manually modify an existing user account but better to use either the useradd, userdel, and usermod command line programs or the LinuxConf GUI to add and delete users.

CREATING USER ACCOUNTS WITH USERADD
That's a fairly difficult process and can be done better by using the LinuxConf or useradd program. Enter the following to add the new user paul.

```
useradd paul
```

If you examine the /etc/passwd, /etc/shadow and /etc/group files you see that the user paul has been added. Red Hat starts users with the user and group ids of 500. The home directory /home/paul has been created and the skeleton files copied over. Everything has the correct ownership.

RED HAT GROUPS
Red Hat creates a group for every new user. If you add the user paul, then the numeric user id might be 500. The group id for the group paul is set to 500 too. This method allows all of a user's files to be private unless the user wishes to share them. In that case, you add another user's or group's name to the user's group in the /etc/group file.

For instance, if you want to allow lidia and aida to access paul's files, then edit the following line for the user paul in the /etc/group file.

```
paul:x:500
```

and add the users lidia and aida:

```
paul:x:500:lidia:aida
```

This allows both of those users to access paul's files. The caveat is that lidia and aida can only access files with the group permissions that allow access. For instance, the following file

```
-rw-rw-r--   1 paul     paul          312 Mar 31 20:36 Xrootenv.0
```

belongs to paul and the group paul. The group access is read and write, so lidia and aida can both read and write to that file.

CREATING AND MODIFYING ACCOUNTS WITH LINUXCONF
You can create user accounts with the LinuxConf program. Initially, you must be root to run LinuxConf. It can run as a text based menu by starting LinuxConf from the command line. If you are running X Window, then activate it by clicking on the Start → Programs → Adminstration → Control Panel. When the Control-panel window is displayed (as shown in Figure 6-1), scroll down the menu items and click on the System Configuration button (the button name is displayed when the cursor is placed on the button).

Scroll down the menu and click on the User accounts menu. The User accounts menu is then shown in the right half of the window. Click the add button and you should see the screen shown in Figure 6-2.

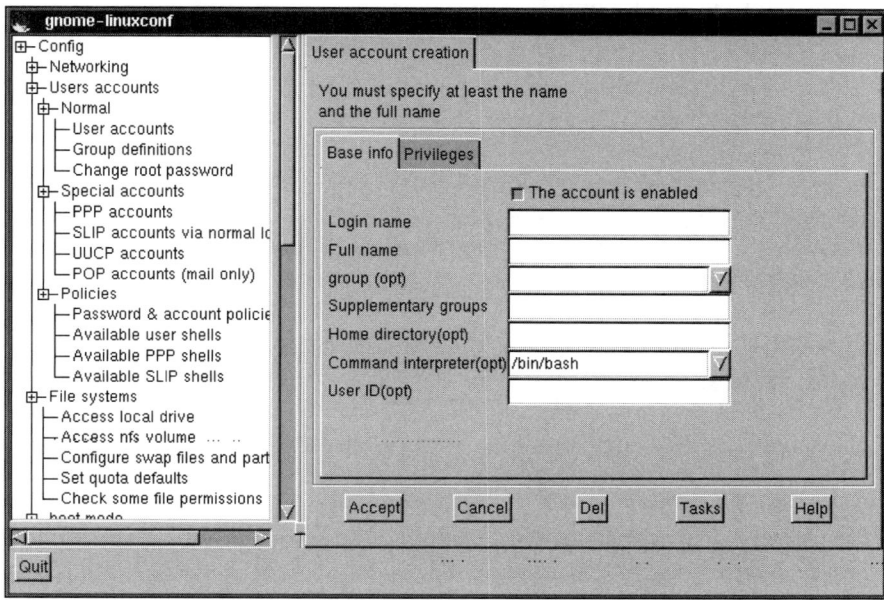

Figure 6-2: The User account creation window

Enter the information such as the new user's real name and username. Generally you want to allow LinuxConf to create the user's home directory, so leave that item blank. Once you are satisfied with the user account information click on the Accept button. You are prompted for the new user account password.

You generally want to allow the user to select the password—please refer to the section entitled Selecting Good Passwords — but you don't want to leave the account without one in the meantime. Therefore, select a temporary password that's active until the user changes it; use your best judgment in determining the method for informing the user of the temporary password.

Introducing Computer Security

Making both your computers and network secure (as discussed in Chapters 7, 11, and 12) is a complex and, at times, confusing process. There are numerous directions that you can be attacked from and the methods and types of attacks are also numerous and ever-changing.

Computer security is the process of protecting yourself against the known threats and educating yourself in order to anticipate and react to the new ones. There are many types of threats and tools to protect against them and it is difficult to learn them all. Given enough time and effort you can become well-educated about the overall threat to your computer system. However, while you are learning the overall process there are several steps that you can take to protect your system. The following sections describe the basic steps.

Layering Your Security

In order to protect against both the known and unknown threats, you need to layer your security. Trust no single mechanism or tool. There is no firewall, or encryption technique that is foolproof. The more locks, fences and walls that you put up the safer that you will be.

EXTERNAL SECURITY

All the normal methods are useful here. Lock your doors, limit access to your server room, allow access only to authorized personnel, log out when you are not present at your computer, and whatever other procedures make sense for your operation.

Another thing that should be mentioned is that the less information that you reveal about your computer operations, the less a potential cracker can use against you. For instance, if you are running a mail order business, then it is probably better not to advertise your operation on the front of your building. A big sign exclaiming www.mailordercoishere.com might just perk some cracker's interest in you.

More subtly, however, is the need to keep important information from any potential crackers. A system's information is the cracker's number one tool for breaking in. The more a cracker knows about your system, the greater the range of security holes that can be found and used against you.

INTERNAL SECURITY

Internal security measures consist of all the normal measures, such as using good passwords. The policies that you set up also are important for your internal security. Letting employees know what is and is not permitted helps improve security. For instance, maybe you've decided that use of your Internet connection to download pornography is strictly forbidden, while on the other hand, casual use of your Internet connection is generally an OK thing as long as work is being done. Make sure that everyone on staff is aware of these guidelines.

You should require that your employees or volunteers should always log off, or set screen locks on, their systems when they are not present for more than a minute or two. This is inconvenient but the best passwords are worthless if you don't use them correctly.

Just as you don't want to leave unnecessary information lying around operation from the outside, you need to consider that much computer crime occurs on the

PASSWORDS

Your passwords are the single most important security system that you possess and maintaining good passwords is an important function of an administrator. This is a combination of managing human factors and technical ones.

It is necessary to balance the ease of remembering your password against the probability of it being cracked. Under Linux, when you create a password, the text string that you enter is encrypted. The encrypted password is then placed in the password field of the /etc/passwd file. There are programs—such as crack—that encrypt the words and phrases found in various dictionaries and then compare the result against the encrypted password. When a match is found so is the password.

The existence of cracking program means that you should not use any word that can be found in any dictionary in the world. On the other hand, you should probably not use completely random strings of text either. (It might be necessary for you to do so depending on your circumstances.) If your password is so complex that you can not remember it, then you are more likely to write it down, making it easier for someone to obtain it.

The compromise is to create easily remembered phrases that are not found in any dictionary and can not easily be guessed. Combine words into some semi meaningful phrase. For instance, *radio* and *road* becomes radi~road; the inclusion of a non-alphanumeric character further helps. The password should be at least eight characters long.

UNDERSTANDING SHADOW PASSWORDS

Password security is further enhanced by using shadow passwords. Starting with Red Hat 6.0, shadow passwords are installed by default during installation (although you have the option of not using them). There are numerous Linux programs that use the /etc/passwd file. For instance, the ls command accesses that file. Generally programs that need to know information like user names require access to the passwd file.

This presents a problem for password security because the passwd file must be readable by everyone. That means that anyone who has access to your Linux machine can copy the passwd file to another location and run a crack program on your passwords. The solution is to copy the encrypted passwords to another file that only is readable by root. This makes your passwords safer but also makes choosing a good, difficult-to-guess root password essential. Only two or three trusted people at most should know the password. If you have to write down the password so that it can be found in an emergency, then store it in a safe, locked place.

> If you did not choose to use shadow passwords during the installation, then you can convert to them by running the pwconv program. Login as root and execute pwconv. Look at the /etc/passwd file and you'll see that the encrypted passwords have been replaced by a lower case x. If you look in the new /etc/shadow file, then you see that the passwords have been transferred into it. You can revert back to non-shadow passwords by using the pwunconv program.

SCREEN LOCKS

Installing and more importantly using screen locks is an easy and effective way of preventing unauthorized use of a computer. If you are using a Linux computer, then please refer to Chapter 5 for the instructions for installing screen locks. Once installed, you start a lock by clicking on the Start->Lock Screen/Screen Saver menu. You are presented with a menu of Locks/Screen Savers from which to choose. Once in place, you can stop the lock by entering your user name or root password.

Red Hat Linux does not install the screen lock/savers by default. To add them, login as root, mount the companion CD-ROM and enter the following commands.

```
rpm -ivh /mnt/cdrom/RedHat/RPMS/fortune-mod*
rpm -ivh /mnt/cdrom/RedHat/RPMS/xlockmore*
rpm -ivh /mnt/cdrom/RedHat/RPMS/xscreensaver*
```

Click on the Start->Lock Screen/Screen Saver. The XLock window is displayed and you are given the option to either use a screen save or a lock. If you choose the screen saver, then it displays your choice of screen saver. If you choose the lock, then you can only reopen your X Window display by entering your user password or the root password.

SETTING SECURITY POLICY

Devising a security policy is an essential part of protecting your security. If you have people using your computer systems, then clear dos and don'ts should be established. People should be made responsible for their actions.

One simple but effective security rule is when a user should log off from a workstation. All the security procedures and systems in the world do not protect you if anyone can simply sit down at a workstation and gain access to it. One rule of thumb is to log off or turn on a screen lock (if you are using X Window) when you leave your workstation for more than a minute or two. You certainly want to lock your system when you leave for a long period like for lunch or when you go home. On the other hand, logging off too frequently can inhibit your efficiency.

It is left up to you to devise a strategy that matches the level of security required by your business or organization. A coffee shop requires different rules than a technical consulting service. Once you establish your rules, then write them down. Require people to sign a consent form with the rules clearly displayed, to get an account for instance.

It is advisable to include a warning in your login message. It should read something like *Unauthorized use of this computer is prohibited*. You can include the message in the `/etc/motd` file. The contents of that file are displayed every time someone logs in. Consult your lawyer for the correct legal language and consequences of your message.

Training

The more that you can do to train the people using your system the better everyone is. Training can take many forms. At a minimum it is advisable to show a new person how to log in to the computer and tell him or her what your security policy is. Once again, use your judgment and keep in mind that you are saving yourself time and frustration by spending some time showing your users the ropes.

Backing Up Your Data

Your data backups are an important security tool. If your computer security is breached, then if you have valid backups, then you can recover your system. However, the big question is how to know for sure that your backups are not corrupted or compromised.

That question is very difficult to answer. The best way is to verify your initial system and data installation with the *tripwire* program. Tripwire creates a checksum of each file; the checksum is analogous to a fingerprint. The tripwire checksum database can be stored on a read-only storage such as a writable CD-ROM. With the checksum database, your restored data can be checked against the database. Tripwire is described in Chapter 12.

Tripwire can be run periodically to create a fingerprint of all the system files. That means that you have checksums to compare your current system files with known good ones. Some system files, like the ones found in `/bin`, `/sbin`, `/usr/bin`, etc. should never change. System configuration files like ones found in `/etc/rc.d/init.d` should only change when a system administrator performs the modification. Any files that you suspect might be a Trojan Horse should and can be checked via Tripwire. Tripwire is a powerful tool but is only as good as you are observant.

Unfortunately, there is no good way to verify that there aren't any unauthorized files contained within your backup. If you have a Tripwire checksum to some known good point then you can always use that backup. You can always reinstall your operating system after a breach; this is recommended, as it will eliminate any Trojan Horses and such

After an intrusion, the only certain method for eliminating intruders is to reformat all of your partitions with mke2fs and reinstall Linux. If you have information that you want to keep, then only reformat the system related partitions such as /, /usr, /var and possibly /usr/local. You must use your best judgment.

Once you have restored your system, then it is critical to find the most current updates for your operating system. This is necessary because when a security hole is found it can often be immediately found on the Internet. Patches soon follow but you need to be quick in order to keep ahead of the bad guys. For instance, check the Red Hat mirror page (www.redhat.com/mirrors.html) and find a location that stores updates. Download and install the updates with RPM.

Understanding the Red Hat Package Manager

The primary function that has set the Red Hat Linux distribution apart from the others is the Red Hat Package Manager (RPM). All the software that was installed during the Red Hat installation process is stored in RPM form. The /mnt/cdrom/RedHat/RPMS contains all of the RPM packages. You can also install, update or de-install software. As of this writing this is the most popular system for installing, modifying and transporting Linux software.

The concept of package management has been around for quite a while, with all the major UNIX vendors supplying their own systems. The idea is to distribute software in a single package and have a package manager do the work of installing, or de-installing and managing the individual files rather than having a human do it. The Linux world has benefited greatly from this system that greatly simplifies the distribution and use of software.

 The Debian distribution uses its own system package manager for software distribution. It is considered by some in the industry to have superior features to RPM.

The following sections describe the use of the RPM.

Installing an RPM Package

When you installed your Red Hat Linux system in Chapter 1, all the software that was copied to your disk came from RPM packages. When you want to add additional software from the companion CD-ROM or a Red Hat mirror (http://www.redhat.com/mirrors.html) you can do so by using the rpm command. If you want to add the HTML based HOWTO documents, then login as root, mount the CD-ROM and the package as follows:

```
mount -r -t iso9660 /dev/hdc /mnt/cdrom
rpm -ivh /mnt/cdrom/RedHat/RPMS/howto-html*
```

The i parameter tells rpm to install the RPM package, the v tells it to be verbose and the h creates a simple progress meter. Once completed you can view the documents with your browser.

Sometimes it's necessary to force the installation of a package. Sometimes the RPM database that keeps track of installed packages can become corrupted and refuse to install a package for you. The following command will force the installation of a package.

```
rpm -ivh -force /mnt/cdrom/RedHat/RPMS/
```

Getting Information about an RPM Package

Having installed the HTML HOWTO documents you can find out information about the files and the package by using the RPM query function. The command

```
rpm -qi howto-html
```

returns the information about the RPM package and a short description of its function.

```
Name        : howto                       Relocations: (not relocateable)
Version     : 6.0                              Vendor: Red Hat Software
Release     : 4                            Build Date: Mon Mar 29 21:44:10 1999
Install date: Fri Apr 30 16:45:59 1999     Build Host: porky.devel.redhat.com
Group       : Documentation                Source RPM: howto-6.0-4.src.rpm
Size        : 11370265                        License: distributable
Packager    : Red Hat Software <http://developer.redhat.com/bugzilla>
URL         : ftp://sunsite.unc.edu/pub/Linux/docs/HOWTO
Summary     : HOWTO documents from the Linux Documentation Project.
Description :
Linux HOWTOs are detailed documents which describe a specific aspect of
configuring or using Linux.  Linux HOWTOs are a great source of
```

```
practical information about your system.  The latest versions of these
documents are located at http://sunsite.unc.edu/linux.

Install the howto package if you'd like to be able to access the Linux
HOWTO documentation from your own system.
```

You can find out what files are in the package and where they live by using the query listing function:

```
rpm -qpl howto-html
```

This returns a long list of HOWTO files that sit in the /usr/doc/HOWTO/other-formats/html directory.

Later, you can check the state of the installed files by using:

```
rpm -qls howto-html
```

Any files that have been changed are listed as *changed* or *not installed*. Otherwise, they are listed as *normal*.

The all option -a is another useful query function that lists every RPM package installed on your system. The following command lists all of your installed packages

```
rpm -qa
```

If you pipe the output to the grep command you can find a specific package or packages:

```
rpm -qa | grep -i howto
```

You can determine what RPM package that a file belongs to as follows:

```
rpm -qf `rpm -qla |grep -I bash` | more
```

You can find out information about an uninstalled package as follows:

```
rpm -qpi /mnt/cdrom/RedHat/RPMS/zsh*
```

This displays the description of the RPM zsh. You can substitute various other options like the file listing l option with the i option to gain other information about the package. There are more options that are listed in the man page.

If you want to see what packages an installed package depends on, then use the command.

```
rpm -qR kernel
```

It shows that the `kernel` package requires the `initscripts` package.

Verifying RPM Packages

The RPM can be used to verify information about installed packages and their files. This is a very useful system administration tool. For instance, if you are in doubt about the Samba configuration file, then you can run the command:

```
rpm -V samba
```

The Samba RPM package keeps a checksum and compares the state of the installed files against it. The command returns

```
S.5....T c /etc/smb.conf
```

which means that the `smb.conf` file has been changed. Please consult the RPM man page for information about the meaning of the result.

Updating an RPM Package

When you obtain a newer version of a Linux package you may want to update the existing software, and the update function is a way of doing so. To upgrade Samba, for instance, simply enter the command:

```
rpm -U samba*
```

Sometimes RPM balks at installing or upgrading a package. Typically, RPM looks at an installed package and decides that you are not allowed to install the same, or older package, over it. It also does not want you upgrade the package with the same package. You can over ride RPM and force it to install or upgrade a package. Use the —force parameter to make RPM install or upgrade.

```
rpm -U —force samba*
```

Removing an RPM Package

You can remove a package by using the erase function (-e):

```
rpm -e samba
```

This removes the Samba software. Sometimes, other package files occupy the same directories of the package that you want to delete. In those cases, you get messages saying that the particular directory could not be deleted. That is just a warning and the package will generally be removed.

Packages versus Tar Files

Until the advent of the RPM and Debian package managers, Linux software was distributed via tar archives (sometimes referred to as *tarballs*). The tar mechanism is the same one that is used to perform system backups, as described in this chapter. The system is sufficient if your software does not change often. However, when you need to upgrade or change software, or work with complex software systems, it becomes quite difficult to work with. Systems like RPM greatly simplify working with system and application software.

Some software is still distributed exclusively via tar archives. Use the commands described in the backup section to use tar distributions and read any documentation that comes with such software. It is best to install tar archives into a common location so that you do not lose track of them. The /usr/local directory tree is generally considered to be the best location.

Writing Scripts

Linux provides the powerful feature of writing scripts. A script can perform almost any job that you can do manually as well as things that you can not do manually. A script is just a text file that contains shell commands and system commands. This section provides some simple examples to give you a flavor of what scripts can do.

A simple script to list the contents of the companion CD-ROM is show below:

```
#!/bin/sh
ls /mnt/cdrom/RedHat/RPMS/*.rpm
```

The first line tells the Shell to use the Bash shell (/bin/bash) to interpret the script commands and primitives. The second line lists all the RPM package files on the CD-ROM and is the same command that you can easily enter yourself. To create and execute the script login as root and use your favorite editor to create a file—call it list_cd.sh for instance—and add the two lines. To execute the script use the change mode command (chmod) to turn on the execute bit:

```
chmod +x /root/list_cd.sh
```

To run it:

```
/root/list_cd.sh
```

All the files in the RPM directory should be displayed to your screen.

Now, mount the CD-ROM (mount /mnt/cdrom). You can easily add a pipe line to filter out certain types of RPM files using the `grep` filter:

```
#!/bin/bash
ls /mnt/cdrom/RedHat/RPMS/*.rpm  | grep samba
```

Execute it as shown before and it lists all the Samba related RPM package files on the CD-ROM.

You can add more functionality by using the *back quotes* (`` ` ``, also called *back tics* or *grave accents*) to feed the results of the previous pipe line to the input of the RPM command. The function of the back quotes is to execute the command(s) within the tics as a separate operation and send the results to another command(s). Thus, the following script

```
#!/bin/bash
rpm -qpl `ls /mnt/cdrom/RedHat/RPMS/* | grep samba`
```

has the effect of listing all the files that belong to the Samba RPM package. The `rpm` parameters tell it list all the files in each package file that it sees. The result is that each file in all the Samba RPM packages are listed out.

Sometimes, for instance, you need to find a file (or files) that is contained in an RPM package but you do not know what the package is. In such a case, you can use the Bash Shell commands to sequentially cycle through the RPM files on the CD-ROM. Lets say, you want to make your Linux computer into a DNS server (which uses the `named` program; see Chapter 11) but don't know what RPM package carries it. The following script provides a simple (and somewhat crude) method for finding the RPM package.

```
#!/bin/bash
RPM=`ls /mnt/cdrom/RedHat/RPMS/*.rpm`
for X in `ls /mnt/cdrom/RedHat/RPMS/*.rpm` ;  do
   echo "$X"
   rpm -qpl $X|grep -i named
done
```

The first line tells the shell to use the bash shell. This is often redundant, but ensures that the script runs correctly no matter what shell that you run it from.

The `for` line sets up a loop. The back tics (`` ` ``) execute the command or commands in between them. The result is that the `RPMS` directory on the CD-ROM is listed. That creates a list. A loop is set up that sets the variable X to each item—RPM package —in that list.

The `echo` command sends the value of the variable to the standard output.

The `rpm` command queries the package pointed to by the X variable and lists each file in the package. The output is sent to the pipe (|). The `grep` command filters out the string named.

The `done` command specifies the end of the loop.

This script (call it `list_pkg` and store it in the `/root` directory) lists all packages. It lists the files in question within the clutter of the RPM packages. You should pipe its output to the `more` filter so the named files don't run past you. With a little more logic, you can make this script only show the package in question.

```
/root/list_pkg | more
```

Subshells

A subshell is designated by commands within parenthesis. (Technically, commands that are contained within two backquotes are also run in a subshell, but the details are beyond the scope of this book.) The current shell that it is executed from creates a new shell to run the command or commands. The new shell runs with the environment of the current shell. It gets its input and delivers its output to that shell.

A common use for subshells is the transfer of files and directories from one location to another. If you have a large number of files to transfer - especially if they contain a large number of sub directories, then the following command demonstrates the use of subshells.

```
tar cf - /usr | (cd /home/sysbak ;  tar xf - )
```

The first command in the pipe line copies the files and directories from the `/usr` directory to the pipeline (the `f -` sequence specifies that the output be sent to the pipe). The subshell contains two commands. The first one changes the working directory of the subshell to the `/home/sysbak` directory (it must be already created for this example to work). The second `tar` command extracts the contents of the pipeline, which in this case is the stream of data from the first `tar` command, into the current directory. The commands in the subshell run in their own environment and do not affect the environment of the parent shell; all communication is handled via the pipe.

```
1458  p2  S    0:00 -bash
1479  p2  D    0:00 tar cf - /usr
1480  p2  S    0:00 -bash
1481  p2  S    0:00 tar xf -
```

This output was produced by running the `ps x` command. The first Bash shell process is the parent of process 1479 which is the first `tar` command in the pipeline. Process 1480 is the bash subshell which is the parent of the second `tar` command in the pipeline process 1481; the process for the `cd /root` command is not shown because it executes very quickly in is not shown when the `ps x` command is executed.

Please consult the `man` pages for the bash, csh, and sh shells for more information.

Automating Job Execution

You can schedule one time or repetitive jobs by using `at` and `cron`. The `at` daemon schedules a job on a one-time basis. Cron provides for scheduling jobs by the minute, hour, day, day of the week, and monthly.

The `/etc/crontab` file controls the `crond` daemon. The `crond` daemon looks at this file once per minute and executes a command or script when one is scheduled. The `man` page for `cron`, `crontab`, and `at` describe how the system works. (The commands `man cron`, `man crontab`, `man 5 crontab` and `man at` give you access to those documents. Note that by including the section number 5 you will get the `crontab man` page that refers to the format of its configuration.)

Monitoring Your System Logs

An important administration job is to monitor the log files that Linux keeps. The log files are kept in the `/var/log` directory. The most important file is `messages`. This is the file that the `syslogd` daemon writes many of its messages to. Syslogd is responsible for tracking general system and error information. (This is important on Linux systems because there are many processes that run in the background and don't display their output to any terminal or window.) It is configured by the `/etc/syslog.conf` file. Part of it is displayed below:

```
# Log all kernel messages to the console.
# Logging much else clutters up the screen.
#kern.*                                            /dev/console
# Log anything (except mail) of level info or higher.
# Don't log private authentication messages!
*.info;mail.none;authpriv.none                     /var/log/messages
# The authpriv file has restricted access.
authpriv.*                                         /var/log/secure
# Log all the mail messages in one place.
mail.*                                             /var/log/maillog
# Everybody gets emergency messages, plus log them on another
# machine.
*.emerg                                            *
```

The first field specifies the type of service. For instance, messages that the Linux kernel produces are specified in the first line. The suffix—the asterisk—on that first line, says that any kernel message is to be recorded. The number signs (#) indicate a comment. Note that the configuration directive—kern.*—specifies that all messages from and about the kernel should be logged. However, it is commented out and so syslogd does not log such messages.

The second field describes where to send the information. The first rule specifies that all kernel messages are to be sent to the /dev/console device. When you are running X, the xconsole program is used as the console window that Red Hat defines for X Window and all kernel messages are sent there; if you are working from the actual console, then those messages are sent to the first virtual screen.

The most widely used log file is the messages file. The second rule defines what types of information is sent to that file. The Red Hat default is to send information messages, certain mail information but personal login information is not sent.

You can define multiple places to send one type of information. For instance, you could add a duplicate *.info rule that sends its output to the /dev/console device.

The information recorded in the messages file can add up quickly. It is up to you to be dedicated enough to keep track of it. You can also devise filters to find specific information about your system. For example, if you want to check the /var/log/messages to find all the times the useradd program has been used recently then run the command:

```
grep -i /var/log/messages
```

Red Hat configures the logrotate program by default. As configured, it rotates the files in /var/log every week. It keeps four weeks worth of files. logrotate is configured by the /etc/logrotate.conf file and is started by cron. Please refer to the man logrotate document for more information.

Starting and Stopping Linux

When a PC is powered up, it looks to the master boot record (MBR) on its first hard drive. The MBR is located on the first sector and cylinder of a hard drive. During the last part of the Red Hat installation process described in chapter 1 you installed a LILO boot system on your MBR. LILO puts information on what operating system(s) are installed and where they can be found. The installation described in chapter 1 uses the entire disk for Linux. By default, LILO installs the boot information for

Linux in that case. However, LILO can also boot Windows, MS-DOS and other operating systems. Please consult the lilo `man` page, the LILO User's Guide (located in `/usr/doc/lilo-*/doc`) and the `/usr/doc/HOWTO/BootPrompt-HOWTO` for further information.

When you power up your computer LILO loads itself and displays the LILO boot prompt. Once LILO has recieved the name of the kernel to boot and any additional parameters, it loads the kernel into memory. The kernel is stored in compressed form and needs to be uncompressed. Once uncompressed, it initializes itself and loads any built-in drivers.

Once the kernel is started it starts the `/sbin/init` process which reads the `/etc/inittab` configuration file to determine what it needs to do. The `init` process starts all of the scripts for the specified run-level. Once completed, you can use your Linux computer.

The run level that your system is set for determines what system processes are to run. For instance, the default Red Hat run level is 3. That run level is mapped to the `/etc/rc.d/rc3.d` directory which contains soft links to the scripts to start. Run level 3 starts up the standard system and networking daemons but does not start X Window. Run level 5, however, includes most everything that 3 does but starts X Window. (You can change the run level by modifying the number on the `id:5:initdefault:` line in `/etc/inittab` file.)

There are also a couple of scripts `rc.sysinit` and `rc.local` in the `/etc/rc.d` directory that perform general system initialization tasks. You can use the `rc.local` file to start processes of your own too. Once all of the scripts have been started, your Linux computer is started.

Correctly stopping a Linux computer is important. Linux temporarily stores data slated to be written to disk in memory. For instance, when this chapter's text (using ApplixWare Words) is saved to disk, the Linux kernel first stores (buffers) the information in memory. When the kernel is ready to save it to disk, it does so. However, there is a lag between the time the Save button is clicked and the time that these words are permanently saved to disk.

The upshot is that if the computer power is turned off suddenly then the buffer is not properly saved to disk. This can result in the loss of data and also a corrupted disk. The disk can almost always be restored to proper operation by using the File System Check (`fsck`) utility. Part of the normal Linux start-up process is to run `fsck` on any file systems that were not shutdown properly. (Linux periodically runs `fsck` as a precaution after about a dozen reboots.)

> ### Stopping Linux Properly
>
> You should not simply turn off the power to a Linux computer. The file systems are buffered in memory, and if they are not properly written to disk first, then data is lost and damage to your file system can occur.
>
> The proper method for shutting down Linux is to run the shutdown program from a text console after logging out of X.
>
> `shutdown -h now "chivas is being shut down for maintenance."`
>
> The above command tells the system to halt (`-h`), to start the process immediately (`now`) and the quoted message is sent to all users. You can exchange the halt for a reboot (`-r`), and extend the time to reboot by replacing now with the number of seconds.
>
> Once the message "System halted" is displayed, then you can safely power off your computer.

Troubleshooting

Linux computer system administration is often spread over many topics. Troubleshooting is often a matter of knowing what subsystem is not working. The following tips are intended to help point you in the right direction.

One of the best troubleshooting tools is the system logger `syslogd`. For instance, If you are having problems then you might be able to determine what is happening by looking at the `/var/log/messages` log file.

LinuxConf and Control Panel can be used to reconfigure misbehaving systems. For instance, if a user can not log on, then you can either manually examine the `/etc/passwd`, `/etc/shadow`, `/etc/group` files and make sure that the user home directory exists and is properly configured. Or, you can use the configuration GUIs to examine and reconfigure the problem account, if necessary.

Always make backups in order to recover from trouble. No matter what goes wrong with your computer, you can recover to some extent if you have backups. For instance, if you lose a disk completely, then troubleshooting the problem is accomplished by simply restoring the data to the original or some other working disk.

Use the `fsck` command to recover from disk problems. Sometimes, after an improper shutdown, the default fsck is not adequate. In such cases, you are prompted to enter the root password. Once entered, the system is put into single user mode; that is a minimal system that is similar to Windows Safe Mode. At that point you run `fsck` manually and are prompted by `fsck` to make fixes.

Displaying the contents of `/var/log/dmesg` displays important system information. This command replays the Linux system start-up information—the same that is displayed on your console. Sometimes you need to know what disk is connected to what device file (`/dev/hda` for instance), what serial ports you have, and so on. This information is often necessary to the solution of a problem. For instance, you are trying to mount a CD-ROM. By knowing what device it is connected, you might find out that you have been giving the mount command the wrong device file.

The `proc` file system is also another valuable repository of system information. The `/proc` file system is a virtual file system. The files in that directory structure are really view ports into the kernel. The kernel contains various tables and other structures with the internal configuration information of the Linux computer. The `proc` file system gives the system administrator a view of that information.

For instance, enter the command `cat /proc/cpuinfo` and you see the information on your CPU (for instance, Pentium, Cyrix, AmD).

```
processor       : 0
cpu             : 586
model           : 6x86
vendor_id       : CyrixInstead
stepping        : 2.7, core/bus clock ratio: 2x
fdiv_bug        : no
hlt_bug         : no
f00f_bug        : no
fpu             : yes
fpu_exception   : yes
cpuid           : yes
wp              : yes
flags           : fpu
bogomips        : 133.53
```

Even more useful information is stored in the `devices`, `interrupts`, `ioports`, pci and `filesystems` files.

The RPM command allows you to check the integrity of your packages. You can check the status of an installed package can sometimes help solve a problem. Or, if a package has a configuration file that is hopelessly mixed up, then you can replace the file. RPM is also a good resource of information about packages.

Understanding the Linux start-up and shutdown process can help track down problems. If your computer does not start up, then you can usually get it running again. First, try rebooting and when presented with the Lilo prompt enter **linux 1**, which will start Linux in single user mode. That starts a minimal system and is equivalent to the Windows safe mode. If that doesn't work and you have a boot floppy disk, then try booting from it.

Making a boot floppy is an option during the Red Hat installation process. If you did not make one during the Red Hat installation process, then you can do so by logging in as root and mounting the companion CD-ROM (mount /mnt/cdrom). You need two floppy disks - one to boot a minimal kernel (the boot disk) and the other to load a minimal file system (the rescue disk). There is a detailed explanation of the process in the /mnt/cdrom/doc/rescue.txt file on the CD-ROM.

Insert the first into the drive and run the command:

```
dd if=/mnt/cdrom/images/boot.img of=/dev/fd0 bs=1440
```

Insert the second disk and run the command:

```
dd if=/mnt/cdrom/images/rescue.img of=/dev/fd0 bs=1440
```

Insert the first disk again and reboot your computer. Enter rescue at the boot: prompt in the Welcome to Red Hat Linux! window. The kernel is loaded from the boot disk and you are prompted for the rescue disk. Insert the rescue disk and press the Return key.

A simple Linux system is loaded and you are automatically made into root user. You have a limited number of commands to use (see the /bin, /usr/sbin, and the normal command directories). You can mount your normal root file system for instance as follows.

```
mount /dev/hda1 /mnt
```

You can then access your existing Linux system by working from the /mnt file system. Depending on what your problem is, you can often fix it from this limited system.

Summary

This chapter introduces you to the basics of systems administration. One should look at this job from both the top down and from the bottom up. If you try to maintain an overview of systems administration, then you can keep ahead of problems to some extent rather than always reacting. The low level view is necessary so that you can configure and modify your system. Put them together and you are able to maintain an efficient and reliable system.

- ◆ System Administration philosophy is introduced. Having an overview of what systems administration is and setting out goals for your system ultimately simply your job and make for a more reliable computer system.

- The general areas of system administration are set out in general terms. Understanding the high level topics is essential for performing the low level jobs.

- The Red Hat Control Panel and LinuxConf system administration systems provide a consistent method for performing the most common jobs.

- Making backups is the most important job you can perform as a system administrator. You can recover from almost any problem or disaster if you have good backups and know where to find them. Simple Tape Archive (tar) backups are described.

- Managing user accounts is a simple but important administrative function. Manual, command line and LinuxConf methods for adding, deleting and modifying user accounts are described.

- The Red Hat Package Manager—RPM—greatly simplifies the modification and transport of Linux software. Simple examples are given for adding, updating, deleting and looking at RPM based software.

- The concept of writing scripts is introduced. Scripts are important method for automating repetitive jobs. They were introduced as a concept in Chapters 1 and 2 and are expanded upon in this chapter.

- Using at and cron automation systems is introduced. The at system is used to schedule one time jobs while cron controls repetitive ones.

- Using log files to enhance security and for troubleshooting purposes is introduced. Log file can record a wealth of information about what is going on within your Linux computer. The information can be used to keep an eye on unauthorized or suspicious use of your computer. It can also be use for to track down problems.

- Starting and stopping a Linux computer is discussed. It is important to understand the Linux start-up and shutdown process. That knowledge helps you prevent damaging your file systems and assists in the start-up of your computer if you have problems.

Chapter 7

Managing Your Network

IN THIS CHAPTER

- ◆ Introducing network administration fundamentals
- ◆ Introducing TCP/IP protocols
- ◆ Defining a model network
- ◆ Connecting to the network
- ◆ Configuring Windows 95 and Windows 98 computers
- ◆ Configuring Linux computers
- ◆ Introducing network security
- ◆ Introducing NFS and NIS

NETWORKING IS AN ESSENTIAL part of computing today. The interconnection of computers, printers, and other devices make the modern office a highly productive environment. Connecting your private network to the world's interconnected computers via the Internet provides you with an amazing extra dimension of resources. This chapter describes the administration of your local area network (LAN). (The process of securely connecting to the Internet is left for Chapters 11 and 12 in Part III.)

Managing your network is a full time job. The technologies that you need to master in order to manage your system are numerous, and remember, you also have to manage the people who use your network. And, the process of networking computers further complicates the security considerations that you have to juggle. This chapter distills the general topics of network administration into a manageable overview, and discusses the networking technologies that are used in general terms, using concrete examples.

… Part II: Managing Your Linux Network

Understanding Network Administration

Network administration is the close cousin of system administration. The former looks at managing the network media, protocols and the configuration of the individual parts, while the latter deals with managing the internal workings of each part. However, in a small business or organization, generally only one person, or a small number of people, end up managing the whole system.

The principles of network and systems administration are the same. You want an efficient, trouble-free, and secure operation. To that end, the place to start your trek is with the governing policies that ultimately determine how and why the administration is performed.

Understanding and Creating Policy

Your network policies are similar to the computer policies as described in Chapter 6. The following lists several categories of computer system administration that you might consider.

- **Connections:** When, why and how new network connections are made
- **Network:** What people can and can't do on your LAN and the Internet
- **Email:** What is considered acceptable and unacceptable use of email
- **Liability:** What people are responsible for
- **Disaster Recovery:** Who, what, when and how to recover from a catastrophe

If you can set your own policies and follow them, then you lay a consistent structure on top of your system. You need to balance ease of use for you and your users along with the friction that such a structure requires. It's a balancing act just like everything else in your operation. Judgement is key.

Worrying about Security

The concerns of network security are the same as that of systems security. Keep the bad guys out. Your goal is to devise a coherent, layered system. No one part or layer is to be completed depended on. Each layer should compliment the other.

For instance, the fact that you devised a good password system in Chapter 6 should be complemented by the construction of a good firewall (see Chapter 11). The firewall should be supplemented by regularly scanning your system, taking fingerprints of your files, and monitoring the system logs. If your firewall is a good one, then with a little luck, the sanctity your passwords should never be tested. But luck is not to be counted on and therefore, your passwords are protected by your firewall and your firewall is protected ultimately by your skill and dedication as an administrator.

To restate a point made in Chapter 6, this book does not intend to cover the topic of security in great depth. The intention is to provide you with a solid starting point. The security concerns mentioned in this chapter should provide you with an overview of what the areas are that you need to be concerned about. The firewall described in Chapter 11 should protect your internal network from the worst of what the Internet can throw at you. From there you need to continue to educate yourself and use your judgement to increase your protection.

Disaster Recovery

Recovering from any conceivable problem or disaster should be one of your constant concerns. The more useful computers and networks become, the more you and your operation will need to depend on them. With that dependency comes the risk of losing everything that you have worked for. Therefore, it is essential that you make plans for the worst and in doing so prevent it from happening.

The disaster recovery plans that you make are determined by the value of your business and the types of risk that you face on a daily basis. Consider the time frame that you must recover in, the equipment that you require, and the value of your operation.

For instance, an author who works alone has a different time frame than, say, a small catalog company. The author might work on monthly deadlines, and therefore an hour or a day of down time is not disastrous. But the catalog company will most certainly lose customers when its network is down for even a few minutes. Neither the author nor the financial planner can afford to lose data but even one byte of lost data could spell disaster for one but only an inconvenience for the other.

Therefore, you must make a judgement on who depends on you and what and how long it will take to get back on your feet. Like everything else, it is a judgement of dollars versus time — dollars versus equipment.

Understanding TCP/IP Basics

Your Linux computer contains most of the protocols that make the Internet possible and the term *TCP/IP* is a shorthand way of referring to this. These protocols are the rules that govern how each computer and network are to communicate with each other. The computer running IP in Turkey speaks the same language as the IP-based computer in Mexico; and the common language allows them to almost instantaneously speak to each other. The more important protocols of the TCP/IP suite are discussed in subsequent sections.

The Internet Protocols not only govern communication over the worldwide Internet but also on your own private network—the type described in this book. If your LAN uses Linux or Windows with TCP/IP installed, then you are using the same protocols to communicate with the computer in the next room as with the computer in Turkey. IP scales from the LAN to the Internet.

The OSI Network Layer Model

Many operations need to occur every time one computer speaks to another. The protocols that govern networking communication are hierarchical in nature, which means that there are several layers that deal with different aspects of networks. One layer works with the hardware while another specifies how the OS works with the hardware.

The International Standards Organization (ISO) developed the Open Systems Interconnect (OSI) networking model. The model specifies how the various protocols interact with each other. The OSI model is divided into seven layers, but for the purpose of this book I've simplified it to four layers. Figure 7-1 shows the simplified model.

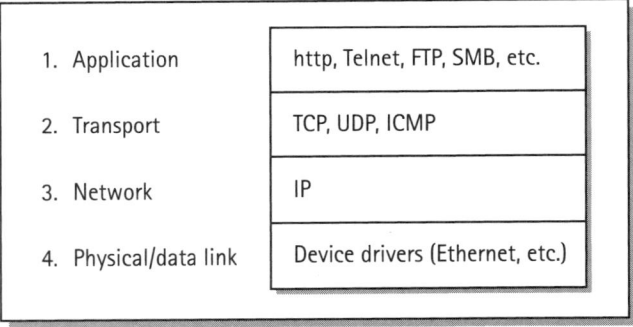

Figure 7-1: The simplified 4 layer OSI networking model

The layers are briefly explained in the following sections.

THE APPLICATION LAYER

The application layer describes how the programs are to interact with a network. When you design an application like a Web browser or Telnet, you don't want to worry about the details of how Ethernet works or how a packet of data gets from point A to point B. Therefore, you make use of the high-level functions defined by the application layer.

THE TRANSPORT LAYER
This layer provides the high-level networking functions used by the application layer. These functions, or hooks, are used by the application layer programs to gain access to the networking functions provided by the operating system.

Also, this layer contains the *Transport Control Protocol* (TCP), *User Datagram Protocol* (UDP), and the *Internet Control Message Protocol* (ICMP) protocols. These protocols provide different levels of handshaking that determine how information is sent across a LAN or the Internet.

THE NETWORK LAYER
This is the layer that is responsible for routing information across a network or the Internet. It bundles the packets from the Transport layer into IP packets and is responsible for making sure that the IP packets arrive at their intended location.

THE PHYSICAL/DATA LINK LAYER
This layer deals with the hardware. It defines both the type of wiring used, as well as how the Ethernet NIC processes the electrical signals that it receives. It is responsible for decoding the modulated signal into a stream of binary bits. An Ethernet NIC can recognize when a bit stream is addressed to it.

Routing

Routing is the process of directing IP packets from one network to another or between machines on a network. Any TCP/IP based computer that wants to send information to a network other than it's own must use routing to direct the IP packets.

DNS

Domain Name Service is the system that converts IP names into their numeric equivalent. For instance, when you direct your browser to `www.swcp.com`, that name must be converted to a unique numeric IP address that identifies the server. DNS performs that function (a DNS server is configured on the Linux server in Chapter 11).

Introducing paunchy.net

The network map shown in Figure 7-2 describes a fictitious network that is used from here on in this book. It is a simple LAN with five computers. It is connected to the Internet via the Linux server chivas; and the other computers are workstations. The connection is described more thoroughly in Chapter 11.

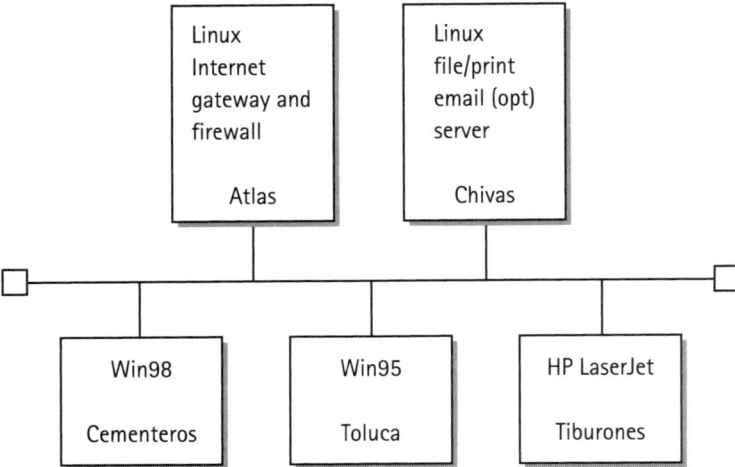

Figure 7-2: The paunchy.net network

Paunchy.net (named after a friend's dog in Albuquerque, NM) contains both the Linux server and clients. It supports both Windows 95 and Windows 98 computers. In this chapter the Linux server provides all the services. You can add Windows NT clients into the network, but the examples assume that there are no Windows NT servers. The examples were not tested with NT severs in the mix.

Table 7-1 displays that important network information for the computers on this model network. This book makes use of these values for all of the remaining examples. You can build your network using this model explicitly or as a template.

TABLE 7-1 NETWORK INFORMATION FOR MACHINES USED IN THIS MODEL NETWORK

Name	IP address	function
Chivas	192.168.1.254	Linux file, print and email(optional) server
Atlas	192.168.1.250	Linux Internet Gateway and Firewall
Cementeros	192.168.1.2	Windows 98 workstation
Toluca	192.168.1.3	Windows 95 workstation
Tiburones	192.168.1.200	LaserJet 5 printer

The /etc/hosts Table

When you installed Linux in Chapter 1 you were prompted to enter network information for the computer. Part of that process was entering the network name, alias and IP address into the /etc/hosts table.

The /etc/hosts table must contain the information on the local Linux computer, but optionally can contain the names and addresses of other network devices (computers, printers, and so on). If you intend to use DNS, then the information entered into the /etc/hosts table is redundant. Without DNS you should enter all of the names, aliases, and IP addresses of the computers and printers on your network into this file.

A sample /etc/hosts file with all of the devices described in Table 7-2 is shown below.

```
127.0.0.1        localhost             localhost.localdomain
192.168.1.254    chivas.paunchy.net    chivas      #file/print/email(optional) server
192.168.1.250    atlas.paunchy.net     atlas       #Internet gateway/firewall
192.168.1.2      cementeros.paunchy.net cementeros # Windows 98
192.168.1.3      toluca.paunchy.net    toluca      # Windows 95
192.168.1.200    tiburones                         #printer
```

This file (or one like it with whatever your network names and addresses are) should be placed on every Linux computer on your network unless you are using DNS. You can manually edit the /etc/hosts file or use the netcfg program, described in the section "Using the Network Configurator" later in this chapter, to do so.

Connecting to the Network

If you have never configured a network, then you should consults other sources of information. The HOWTO documents included on the Red Hat CD-ROM are a good starting place. Look at the Ethernet-HOWTO, Hardware-HOWTO, Intranet-Server-HOWTO, NET-3-HOWTO, Networking-Overview-HOWTO and the Unix-Internet-Fundamentals-HOWTO in the /usr/doc/HOWTO directory for more information. If you haven't installed the HOWTO RPM yet, then log in as root, mount the CD-ROM and enter the rpm -ivh /mnt/cdrom/RedHat/RPMS/howto-6* command to install it.

I assume you're using simple 10MB Ethernet on your network and you'll need to have an Ethernet NIC for both your Linux and Windows machines. It does not matter what Ethernet media (wiring) that you are using as long as all of your NICs can be connected together. You could also use coaxial or twisted-pair cabling.

The advantage of coaxial, which is also known as Thinnet and 10base2, is that it does not require any extra electronic devices. You can connect all your NICs together by running a 52ohm coaxial cable to each one, but both ends of the segment need to be terminated with 52ohm terminators. The disadvantage is that the wiring can be unmanageable once your network grows beyond a dozen or so machines. The entire network will be disabled if any of the cables breaks or if either end is not terminated correctly; Thinnet is not capable of handling greater that 10 megabit (MB) per second data rates.

The advantage of twisted-pair, which is also called 10baseT (10Mb), is that it is easy to connect and disconnect NICs once you have wired your office or building. It makes use of phone connectors and allows you to plug in and out as you desire. It's also capable of handling up to 100 megabits-per-second data rates (you must use category 5 twisted-pair cables for 100 MB (100baseT and 100baseTX) systems while category 3 twisted-pair cable suffices for 10baseT). The disadvantage is that you need to purchase an Ethernet hub or switch.

The primary difference between a hub and a switch is that the hub transmits all Ethernet packets (or frames) to all the NICs connected to it. If you load up your LAN too much, then all of your connected machines see all of the traffic and the response time is greatly diminished. A switch permits the segregation of traffic and effectively increases the bandwidth available to each machine. For instance, packets from machine A destined for machine B do not get relayed to machine C if A and B are on a different switch (also called a collision domain) than C.

Ethernet hubs can be either *managed* or *unmanaged*. Unmanaged hubs do not require any configuration and are less expensive than managed ones—unmanaged hubs with five ports now cost well under $100. Managed ones allow you to control their operation and 4 or 5-port 100baseTX hubs can now be found at around $100.

Configuring Windows Computers

This section describes the basic network settings necessary for a Windows 95 or Windows 98 computer to connect to the network. Keep in mind that Windows 98 uses password encryption by default, while older versions of Windows 95 use plain text passwords, which can be more easily intercepted as they travel across the network.

The following information is for a Windows 95 computer, but configuring a Windows 98 system is similar.

Open the Network GUI by clicking Start → Settings → Control Panel and then double click the Network icon. You should see the window similar to the one displayed in Figure 7-3. The following paragraphs describe the parameters that need to be specified. (The examples require that you use the Client for Microsoft Networks and the Microsoft TCP/IP protocol.)

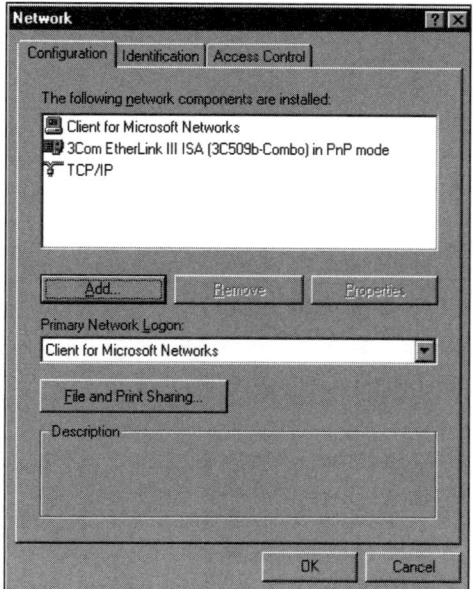

Figure 7-3: The Windows Network GUI

You can specify the name of your machine by clicking on the Identification tab in the Network window and then entering a name in the computer name field. Make sure that the computer name you choose corresponds to a name and IP address in the /etc/hosts table on your Linux server; optionally, with the name in the DNS tables if you are using that system on your Linux server.

Click the Configuration tab in the Network window. Next, click on Client for Microsoft Network, then click the Properties button. Next click on Log onto Windows NT domain checkbox and enter the Windows NT domain name. This book assumes you're using the MYGROUP domain name because it corresponds to the Samba default. You can use any name that you want to, but keep in mind that you may have problems browsing the Linux server if the names do not match. Click OK to return to the Network dialog box.

Tell Windows what Ethernet NIC to use. From the Network window, click on Add → Adapter and then click the Add button. From the Select Network adapters click on the manufacturer and model of your NIC.

You also need to specify the TCP/IP Protocol properties: IP address, the subnet mask, DNS and gateway address. From the Network window, click on the Configuration tab. Next, click the TCP/IP Protocol in the list, and then click the Properties button. There are several tabs that correspond to the properties that must be set. The IP address is from the public class C address space 192.168.1. The DNS server is the Linux server first and your ISP—if you have one—second. The gateway is also your Linux server. The values for these entries are shown in Table 7-2:

TABLE 7-2 WINDOWS NETWORK PARAMETERS

Property	Value	Description
IP address	192.168.1.2	Windows computer IP address
Subnet mask	255.255.255.0	Standard class C subnet mask
DNS	192.168.1.250	Linux server acts as primary DNS server
Gateway	192.168.1.250	Linux server acts as gateway to the Internet
NT Domain	MYGROUP	Samba defaults to this group
Ethernet NIC	3Com 3C509	Ethernet NIC manufacturer and model (ISA card)

Please note that the IP addresses for the DNS and Gateway reflect the computers that perform these functions in the model `paunchy.net` network. You can, of course, change these to point to any computer that provide these functions on your own network. I mention this because many people will want to combine the file/print server with DNS and the Internet gateway. If you do so, then make sure that you modify these parameters appropriately.

Configuring Linux Network Parameters

The Red Hat installation process prompted you to enter your networking parameters. If you entered them correctly, then your system probably should not need any more configuration. However, you might need to configure your Linux network at some point—if you modify your network, for instance—so this section provides information on how to do so.

Red Hat Linux provides several methods for modifying network parameters. You can manually edit the various configuration files and if you're interested in learning the workings of Linux networking and how it's configured than the manual method is recommended. There is no substitute for wrenching the nuts and bolts in order to learn how things actually work from the ground up. However, you're also running a business and probably don't have time to spend on the minute details.

Chapter 7: Managing Your Network 157

Therefore, the next few sections describe how to use the Red Hat GUI's to manage the networking. The last section describes where the important files are and you can feel free to experiment if you're interested.

Please take note that the following examples do not include a default route. A *default route* defines the path that all network communication takes when there is no explicit route to follow and is commonly used to direct network traffic to the Internet via the gateway. If you set up a default route, then it will interfere with the PPP connection described in Chapter 11. The examples in Chapters 11 and 12 use the PPP connection via the phone system as the default route to the Internet. If you are experienced with routing, then you can modify the routes as you desire. However, the examples in this book require that you follow them exactly if they are to work as you expect them to.

Using the Network Configurator

The Network Configurator (`netcfg`) GUI can be started from the Control-Panel or from the command line. Click Start → Programs → Adminstration → Control Panel and the Control Panel window is displayed. Click on the Network Configuration button which is the fourth one from the top and the Network Configurator (`netcfg`) opens as shown in Figure 7-4.

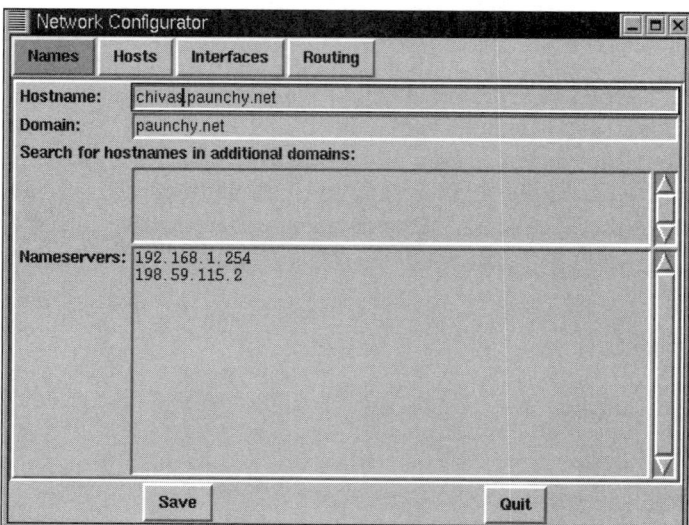

Figure 7-4: The Network Configurator Names window

The initial screen, or the Names tab, shows the computer names and DNS name servers that your system is aware of (the information is stored in the /etc/resolv.conf file). At this point, you have not set up and DNS services. Chapter 11 deals with configuring your own local DNS server and also connecting to external servers. Thus, for now, leave the Names window blank.

Click on the Hosts tab and you get the screen shown in Figure 7-5.

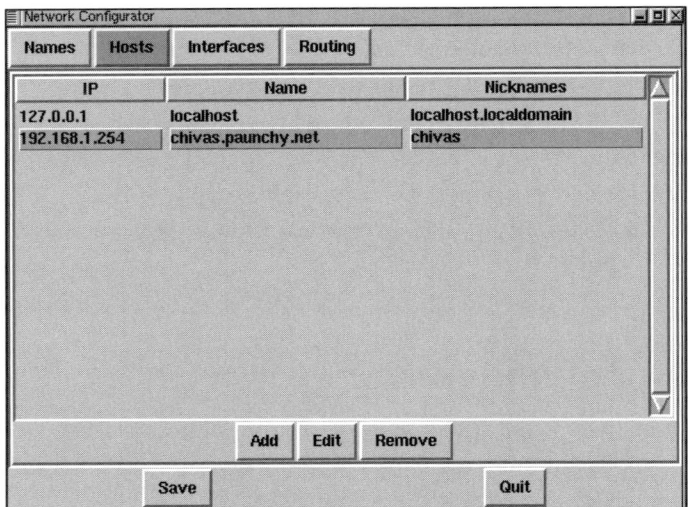

Figure 7-5: The Network Configurator Hosts window

Here you see the localhost and chivas.paunchy.net entries. The localhost is an internal, logical network connection (the *loopback* network) and should always be present. The chivas entry was entered during the Red Hat installation process (see Figure 1-6). If you have connected any of the other machines described in the section "Introducing paunchy.net", then you should enter their names by clicking on the Host tab in the Network Configurator window. To add another entry to the /etc/hosts table, click on the Add button and the "Edit /etc/hosts" window appears. Next, enter the IP address, network name and nickname (alias) as shown in Figure 7-6.

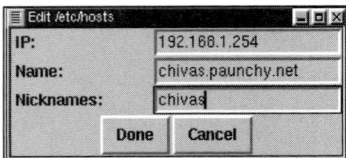

Figure 7-6: The Edit /etc/hosts window

Chapter 7: Managing Your Network

Click the Done button and the Save button and the values are saved to the /etc/hosts file and displayed in the Network Configurator Names window.

Click on the Network Configurator Interfaces tab and Interfaces window is displayed as shown in Figure 7-7.

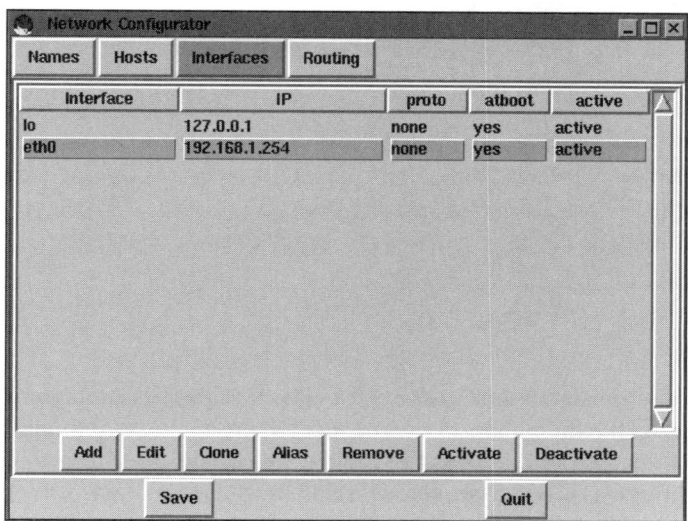

Figure 7-7: The Network Configurator Interfaces window

The loopback interface lo is shown along with the Ethernet NIC eth0. The localhost is added by default when the networking packages are installed. The Red Hat installation process prompted you to configure an Ethernet interface too. In the case that you want to add a NIC for the first time, or want to reconfigure an existing one, or you want to add an additional interface (in the case the you want to build a Linux router, for instance), then click on the Add button. The Choose Interface Type window, shown in Figure 7-8, is opened.

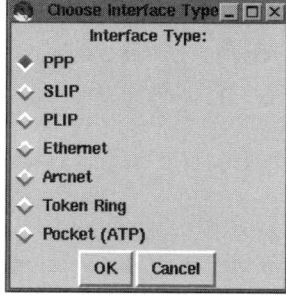

Figure 7-8: The Choose Interface Type window

Part II: Managing Your Linux Network

You have seven interfaces choices to pick from. Click on the Ethernet radio button and then click on the OK button. Figure 7-9 shows the Edit Ethernet/Bus Interface window.

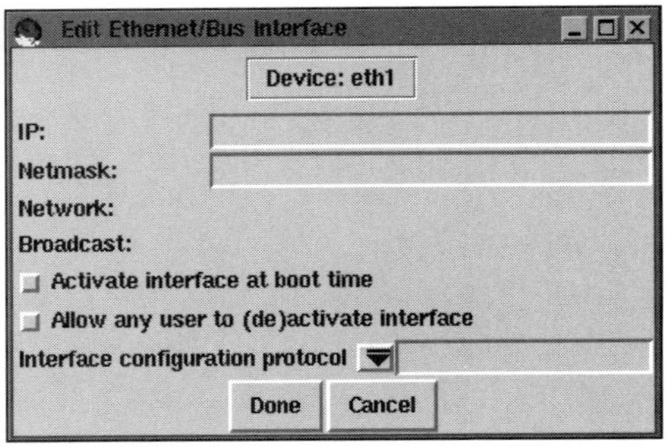

Figure 7-9: The Edit Ethernet/Bus Interface window

Add the IP address and the netmask sets itself to a class C mask. (Assuming that you use a class C address like the public 192.168.1.*nnn* (where *nnn* is any number between 1 and 254) that is used in this book, then the netmask sets itself to correct 255.255.255.0 value. There is no reason that a small business or organization should use anything but a class C network address.

> **NOTE** IP addresses are divided into three classes: A, B, and C. The classes define which parts of the network address correspond to the network, and which correspond to the local host. Each of the four parts of a network address (separated by the periods) represents eight bits. Class A address use the first eight bits for the network address, leaving the last 24 bits for the local hosts, which means you can define up to 16 million host addresses. Class B divides the 32 bits in half, leaving 16 bits for the local hosts, or up to 65 thousand host addresses. Finally, class C addresses use only the last 8 bits for the local hosts, which means you can define up to 254 hosts. Class C addresses dominates the landscape today and the small network will never need to use anything else. It is nearly impossible to have the InterNIC assign any other class today anyway.

You should also click on the Activate interface at boot time checkbox, and the Interface configuration protocol button should be set to "none." You may optionally click the Allow any user to (de)activate interface checkbox if you wish to allow non root users to start and stop the interface. It is probably best not to set this option because there shouldn't be many instances where the interface needs to be toggled on or off and therefore, it's best to leave that function to the root user.

Click the Done button and then the Save current configuration dialog button and the new interface should show up in the Network Configurator Interfaces window. Click the Activate button and the NIC should go online. If it doesn't, please consult the Troubleshooting section later in this chapter. It describes the manual, command-line methods for configuring networking interfaces.

Finally, click on the Routing tab and the window shown in Figure 7-10 is displayed.

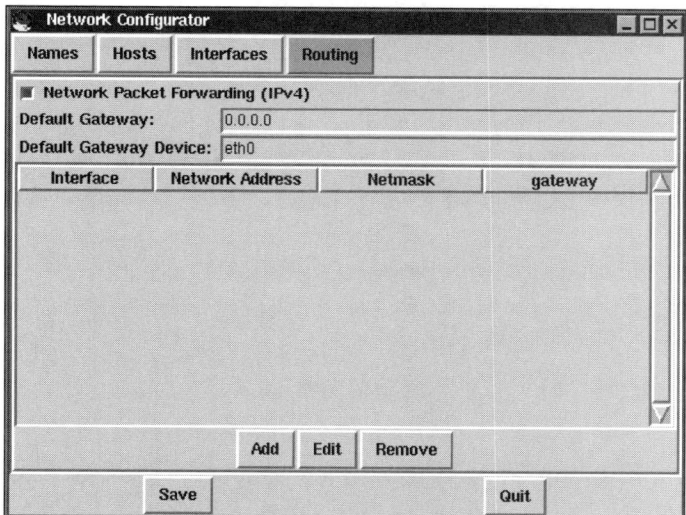

Figure 7-10: The Network Configurator Routing window

There should not be any routes set up at this time. Recall that the Red Hat installation process prompts for a default route, but the instructions in Chapter 1 deliberately did not provide one. That's because in Chapter 11, a single default route is configured to create a dial-up gateway to your ISP and, thus the Internet. Any default route that is configured now will interfere with the dial-up connection.

Click the Save and then the Quit button and you'll exit from the Network Configurator.

Where the Scripts Are

The Network Configurator GUI modifies the scripts and configuration files that actually control Linux networking. However, it's essential to know where those scripts exist and what they do, in order to understand Linux networking.

When a Linux computer starts up, it executes various scripts that start up services. The scripts that execute are determined by the run level set in the

`/etc/inittab` file. Most of the run levels include networking among those services.

The start-up scripts are found in the `/etc/rc.d` directories. The directories are `rc1.d`, through `rc6.d`. They include soft links to the actual scripts that live in the `/etc/rc.d/init.d` directory. The network script, in that directory, is used to start and stop (and restart) Linux networking.

You can restart your network, for instance, by running the script as follows:

```
/etc/rc.d/init.d/network restart
```

Stopping and starting the network is done by using stop and start as the parameter.

If you look inside the `/etc/rc.d/init.d/network` script, then you see a reference to the `/etc/sysconfig/network-scripts` directory. There is an important file and directory in this location. The `network` file contains the basic information about the Linux host name, network, IP address and domain name and such. The following is the network file used for this computer.

```
NETWORKING=yes
FORWARD_IPV4=no
HOSTNAME=chivas.paunchy.net
DOMAINNAME=paunchy.com
GATEWAY=0.0.0.0
GATEWAYDEV=eth0
```

It also shows where the default gateway is; in this case none exists. This book uses a PPP connection to the Internet. When the PPP connection is established over the phone, it becomes the gateway and you should modify the parameter appropriately. Please also note that you should have IP forwarding turned off FORWARD_IPV4=no unless the computer is acting as an Internet gateway.

The directory, `/etc/sysconfig/network-scripts` contains many small configuration files. When you use the Linuxconf or netcfg utilities to configure your network parameters, the files in this directory get modified. For instance, look in the ifcfg-eth0 file as shown below.

```
DEVICE=eth0
IPADDR=192.168.1.254
NETMASK=255.255.255.0
NETWORK=192.168.1.0
BROADCAST=192.168.1.255
ONBOOT=yes
BOOTPROTO=none
```

This file contains the information used to configure your Ethernet NIC. If you use the `ifconfig eth0` command, then you see that this information has been used to configure it. Similar files contain the information about the loopback device, and other networking systems.

There are several general purpose networking configuration files found in the `/etc` directory. They are `hosts`, `inetd.conf`, `resolv.conf`, and `nsswitch.conf`. Table 7-3 briefly describes each file's function.

TABLE 7-3 SOME GENERAL PURPOSE LINUX NETWORK CONFIGURATION FILES

Fil	Location	Description
hosts	/etc	Stores host names and IP addresses
inetd.conf	/etc	Execution information for on-demand system services
resolv.conf	/etc	Contains the DNS server addresses
services	/etc	Contains the names and port number of network services
nsswitch.conf	/etc	Stores the sequence that the OS looks for network services

Modifying the Scripts Manually

The experienced network administrator can modify any of these configuration files or scripts by hand. You can use any text editor described in Chapter 2. Just be aware that the scripts and files are often interrelated with each other and modifying one can change another's behavior. You can view the `man` pages of these to gain more understanding of the services.

Network File System

The Network File System (NFS) is a system used to share files and directories across a network. It is similar to Samba (as discussed in Chapter 8) in its function. However, it is different in the way that it works. Samba is a more complex system and must be run as a separate process from the kernel. NFS is simpler and is built into kernel.

If you want to share file systems from one Linux or UNIX computer to another, then NFS provides many useful features. Red Hat Linux comes preconfigured to act as an NFS client. Please consult the documentation and `man` pages on NFS for more information.

Network Information Service

The Network Information Service (NIS) provides a mechanism for sharing information across a network. You configure one or more Linux or UNIX computers to act as NIS servers, but that's beyond the scope of this book. Other machines can then use one common database of user names and passwords from any machine that uses NIS.

NIS, when combined with automounter, can also be used to provide automatic mounting file system services. NIS/automounter can be used to mount your home directory, for instance, on any NIS machine that you log on to. You can program any file system to follow you around as you log onto various machines. Red Hat Linux provides this service. Please look on the CD-ROM for the ypbind, ypserv and yp-tools RPMs and the accompanying documentation for more information.

Introducing Network Usage and Security Policy

Every company and organization needs to address the issue of proper network usage in a formal way. Your organization needs to prioritize what your network is to be used for, and if you use only the single telephone connection to the Internet described in Chapter 11, you should probably limit the amount of web browsing that your employees can do. You may want to devise a formal document that every system user must sign.

Without a formal use document, you ultimately will have very little formal control over what your network is used for. Written guidelines can make it much less difficult to enforce your policies. For instance, if you decide to keep the firewall rules described in Chapter 11, which allow Web browsing, then you will implicitly allow web browsing. However, if you also state formallythat viewing pornography on company time with company equipment is prohibited, then you'll be able to take action against anyone who violates the policy.

- ◆ In addition to the formal use policies, you can also control what your users are capable of doing by modifying your company's server and workstation configurations. For instance, if you eliminate NFS from your Linux server, no one will be able to use it (one way that you can do that is by removing the NFS RPMs and then stopping any running NFS daemons with `killall -9 nfsd`). If you do not intend to use NFS, then eliminating it also enhances your computer and network's security by running one less service that might be used to break into your system.

Disaster Recovery

The subject of disaster recovery is an amorphous one. That is because defining what and how long it takes to recover from a disaster can mean totally different things to different businesses.

The definition of disaster can vary. For this discussion, *disaster* means anything that prevents your operation from functioning, even in a minimal way. That definition includes anything from a fire, earthquake, or flood to a burglary or a security breach. Rather than focus on what can cause a disaster, it is better to concentrate on how to recover from one.

Once again, the process of recovery depends on who you are and what you do. An author can recover from disaster by borrowing a friend's computer or running down to the local computer store with credit card in hand (as long as the manuscripts are backed up). A medical supply company, on the other hand, must have a completely documented recovery plan and all the parts in place.

Here are some suggestions for those who must be able to recover in a systematic way:

- Decide on the scale of disaster that you want to be ready for. Do you want to be able to recover from a local or regional disaster such as an earthquake or flood? Or do you want to limit your scope to disasters that just affect you and your operation, such as fire or vandalism?

- Decide on the level of recovery that is right for you. This is an economic decision that should match the type of work that you do. Once again, at the low end of the scale, the technical writer might only require a word processor to start. That word processor can be rebuilt with cheap used equipment for instance, and Applixware and Linux can be run on an old 486 computer as well. Such equipment is easily available from many sources and can quickly be purchased. However, the small retail store with point of purchase hardware can not go to the local used computer shop to regain its vital equipment. Spare equipment or service contracts with guaranteed replacement agreements are required for the latter.

- Determine the recovery time frame that matches your company. The catalog or financial services company has a different recovery time requirement than, say an architectural firm. The latter probably can depend on spending a weekend, unless in the middle of a deadline, while the catalog company must think in terms of minutes or hours to recover.

- Documentation and training are essential. There is a great deal of room for confusion when more than one or two people are involved in a recovery. It is essential to write down the steps to take, who is needed during the crisis, and how they can be contacted. It's also essential that everybody involved is aware of the location of the documents.

- The only way to be sure, or reasonably sure, is to practice. Otherwise, you can be sure that your recovery will not go as hoped. Training can be as simple as asking people to go get you the recovery plan, or as difficult as walking, driving, or flying to wherever your recovery site is and loading your backup tapes.

- Keep offsite backup clones and make direct copies of your backup tapes. At the very least, clone your most essential data. Keep the copies in a different location than where they are made. The offsite location can be another office, your home, a safety deposit box, or anywhere else, as long as it is not connected with your everyday system. Match the distance from your primary site by the scope of your disaster plan. If you are planning for a fire, then any separate building is adequate. If you are planning for an earthquake, then consider another city or state.

- Finally, expect the unexpected. Disaster recovery is an inexact science. Be ready to think on your feet.

Troubleshooting

Your network consists of numerous parts. The computers and printers that are connected to wires and network equipment all must speak the same language (protocol) in order to communicate. It's a complex animal.

When things don't work right, there are several actions that you should take, which are discussed in the following sections.

Make Simple Checks First

Check for the simple problems first. Make sure that the power is turned on to all the devices. Check that the wiring is okay; remember, Thinnet must be terminated at both ends and not have any breaks in between and Thinnet connectors (BNC) are prone to problems if they are poorly made or if they get stepped on. Make sure that your cables and connectors are in good working order. You can wiggle the cable at the connector to attempt to fix it. If that doesn't work, then you can try replacing the cable segment with another one.

Check Your Linux Computer

Once you have checked the obvious, you can check the computers and printers. On a Linux computer you should check the following.

USING THE PING COMMAND

Ping yourself. The `ping` command sends a simple ICMP packet to the logical loopback device — `lo` — and waits for a response.

On your Linux server, login as root and enter the following command:

```
ping 127.0.0.1
```

You should get the following response.

```
PING 127.0.0.1 (127.0.0.1): 56 data bytes
64 bytes from 127.0.0.1: icmp_seq=0 ttl=64 time=0.4 ms
64 bytes from 127.0.0.1: icmp_seq=1 ttl=64 time=0.2 ms
```

The response is continuous, so stop it by pressing Ctrl-C. This indicates that your basic networking is working.

Next try pinging your Ethernet interface by entering the following command:

```
ping 192.168.1.254
```

You should get a response similar to the previous example. In this case, `ping` is sending an ICMP packet to your Ethernet NIC. This is the device that you must have working in order to communicate with the rest of your LAN.

If you do not get any response to this or the previous ping, then there are several possible causes to look at.

CHECKING THE NETWORK INTERFACES AND ROUTES

First, check the status of your network interfaces. In the case of a failed loopback device ping, enter the command:

```
ifconfig lo
```

This should give you the following response:

```
lo        Link encap:Local Loopback
          inet addr:127.0.0.1  Bcast:127.255.255.255  Mask:255.0.0.0
          UP BROADCAST LOOPBACK RUNNING   MTU:3584  Metric:1
          RX packets:55 errors:0 dropped:0 overruns:0 frame:0
TX packets:55 errors:0 dropped:0 overruns:0 carrier:0  collisions:0
```

The important parts of the response is the `inet` address on the second line and the UP flag on the third line. The address (addr) shown here (127.0.0.1) is the correct one for a loopback device. The UP flag indicates that the interface is running.

You can also use the ifconfig command by itself. It will show all of your network interfaces. Any interface that it shows automatically means that the interface is working. Conversely, any interface that you do not see means that it is down.

In this case your loopback interface is correct. The next place to look is at your routing table. Enter the command:

`netstat -r -n`

The results, in this case, show that the routes for both the loopback and Ethernet interfaces are correct. You know that because your network address 192.168.1.0 is that of your local network (as defined by the example network `paunchy.net` in this book); class C networks are defined by the first three numbers - 192.168.1 - and the zero is just a place holder. The local (logical or internal) network is always 127.0.0.0.

```
Destination    Gateway    Genmask        Flags  MSS Window  irtt Iface
192.168.1.0    *          255.255.255.0  U      1500 0      0 eth0
127.0.0.0      *          255.0.0.0      U      3584 0      0 lo
```

If you do not see the loopback interface route then you need to add it. Enter the command:

`route add -net 127.0.0.1 dev lo`

Then try to ping your loopback interface. If it works, then great. Otherwise, several things could be wrong that are beyond the scope of this book. Your best option, at this point, is to go back to the `netcfg` or LinuxConf GUIs and reinstall the network from scratch.

PING THE ETHERNET INTERFACE

If you do not get a response from pinging your Ethernet interface, then run the command.

`ifconfig eth0`

This should give you the following response:

```
eth0 Link encap:Ethernet   HWaddr 00:20:AF:38:6A:AA
     inetaddr:192.168.1.254 Bcast:192.168.1.255 Mask:255.255.255.0
     UP BROADCAST RUNNING MULTICAST   MTU:1500  Metric:1
     RX packets:10725 errors:0 dropped:0 overruns:0 frame:0
     TX packets:8110 errors:0 dropped:0 overruns:0 carrier:0 collisions:6
     Interrupt:11 Base address:0x310
```

As before, the important parts of the response is the `inet` address on the second line and the `UP` flag on the third line. The `inet` address should match up with the one that you set for a Ethernet device. The `UP` flag indicates that the interface is running. The RX and TX lines show the receive and transmit statistics. The final line shows the interrupt and IO address that the NIC is known as to the PC. The computer uses them to communicate with the card, and this communication will vary from Ethernet card to Ethernet card.

The output of the `ifconfig` command, in this case, shows a correct configuration. If your NIC displays similar results, then it probably is not the culprit. The next place to look is at your routing table. Enter the command:

`netstat -r -n`

The results, in this case, show that the routes for both the loopback and Ethernet interfaces are correct.

```
Destination    Gateway    Genmask         Flags  MSS   Window  irtt  Iface
192.168.1.0    *          255.255.255.0   U      1500  0       0     eth0
127.0.0.0      *          255.0.0.0       U      3584  0       0     lo
```

If you do not see the 192.168.1.0 interface route, then you need to add it (the last zero in the address indicates your entire class C network). Enter the command:

`route add -net 192.168.1.0 dev eth0`

Then try to ping your Ethernet interface. If it works, then great. Otherwise, several things could be wrong. It might be that the Linux kernel does not recognize your Ethernet NIC. Run the following command.

`lsmod`

The results will look something like this:

```
Module          Pages   Used by
3c509           2       1 (autoclean)
```

This command lists the modules that the kernel currently is using to interact with the computer. In this example, an 3Com 3C509 ISA Ethernet NIC is being used. If you do not see a module that corresponds to your NIC, then you need to load one. Please refer to the `modprobe` and `insmod` man pages for information on the use of those programs. You can also refer to the Hardware-HOWTO and Ethernet-HOWTO in the `/usr/doc/HOTWO` directory for more information

Some network cards and drivers, of poor quality, can intermittently hang (stop working). Network cards can also hang if they are configured to use the wrong interface. You can try to diagnose such problems by unloading and then reloading the Linux module (driver). The following commands first show the modules that are loaded. Look for the module (lsmod) that corresponds to your network card and then remove it (rmmod). Reload the module and then test to see if it works again.

```
lsmod
rmmod driver
modprobe driver
```

If you can not get your Ethernet interface to work, then your best option, at this point, is to go back to the netcfg or LinuxConf GUIs and reinstall the networking from scratch.

Linux often has problems working with Plug-and-Play (PnP) devices. PnP devices are designed to work with Windows operating systems. Their interface parameters (such as interrupt values) are changed dynamically in conjunction with Windows. The idea is to make the addition and subtraction of peripherals transparent to the user. If you have problems configuring your Ethernet NIC, then PnP might be the cause. You should turn off the PnP option of your device by using the configuration software that comes with your device. This type of software generally runs under MS-DOS so you might have to use a DOS boot floppy to run it.

Ping your Network

If your network media is good and your Linux network interface and routes are working correctly, then you need to check the response of other computers on your network. Check the response of your Windows computer by using ping as follows:

```
ping 192.168.1.2
```

You should get a response similar to the local pings described earlier, except the IP address should correspond to the computer being pinged.

If you do not get a response, then it is likely that the computer is not configured correctly or is not working. Before you attempt to fix that computer, try pinging another one on your network (if another one exists). The second computer responds to the ping, the first computer you pinged has a problem, and you should check it out. If the second computer also fails to respond, the problem is with the first computer. The overall idea is to narrow down the possible cause of a problem.

Check your Windows Computer

If you suspect that your Windows computer is misbehaving, then you should check the Ethernet NIC and routes in the same manner as with your Linux machine. You can work from an MS-DOS window. Recall from Chapter 1 that the DOS commands that are equivalent to the Linux `ping`, `ifconfig`, `route` and `netstat` are PING, IPCONFIG, ROUTE and NETSTAT.

Windows also provides an interactive troubleshooting system called the Network Troubleshooter. From the Windows desktop click on Start→Help. Search for the Network Troubleshooter. It asks you questions and narrows down the possible causes depending on your answer. It can not solve every possible problem but is surprisingly good in fixing windows networking problems.

If you still have problems

This section is by no means an exhaustive description of troubleshooting your network. It covers the simplest and some of the most frequent problems and solutions. If you continue to have problems please look at the HOWTOs and FAQs. Recall that they are installed in your `/usr/doc` directory or can be by installing the `howto-5.2-2.noarch.rpm` on the companion CD-ROM.

You can also use the Internet to look for answers. Connecting your computer and network to the Internet is discussed in Chapters 11 and 12. Skipping ahead and connecting to the net can be problematic if you are having trouble getting your LAN going, so in that case try to find a computer with an existing connection that you can use.

Once on the Internet, you can ask for help by using one of the many newsgroups or by going to Red Hat directly. Follow their rules and requirements as necessary.

Summary

This chapter focused on the process of network administration. If you can start by focusing on the high-level aspects of managing a network, then the low-level jobs become more manageable. Your network will run more smoothly and efficiently if you take a holistic approach.

- ◆ Network administration is discussed in general terms. The policies that you make or inherit determine what you do and how you do it. The more that you do to shape policy, the better you can control your network.

- ◆ Network security is an ongoing job. The subject is a complex and ever-evolving one. No one solution or technique exists, and the process is the most important aspect of the subject. You must use good judgment and experience to manage the ever-changing dangers.

- If you are managing a network used by others, then your job as the network administrator is to serve them.

- You must plan ahead for disasters. The level and depth of your plans will vary depending on your business and your customers. You should make judgements about how fast you need to recover, where the recovery is to take place, and who should be involved. All considerations must be weighed against the cost of the course taken.

- The internet protocols were introduced. The protocols provide the common language that makes the Internet possible. Your Linux computer runs the same protocols as other computers across the world. The same protocols are used to network the computers in your office.

- A simple LAN is described. The paunchy.net network example consists of a few Linux and Windows boxes and is used in all the remaining examples in the book.

- The parameters necessary to connect a Linux computer to the network are described. These parameter types are generally the same for any Linux computer but vary in the specific addresses and such.

- The parameters necessary to connect a Windows computer to the network are described. These parameter types are generally the same for any Windows machine, but vary in the specific addresses and such.

- The NFS and NIS systems are introduced. If you work with multiple Linux and UNIX computers than these systems provide a great deal of flexibility.

- Some specific troubleshooting techniques are described. Several systems have to be in place for a computer to communicate over a network. The systems can be checked out and reconfigured if necessary. If the problem can not be found then the online documentation and Internet resources can be used to possibly find the solution.

Chapter 8

Sharing Files and Printers with Samba

IN THIS CHAPTER

- Understanding Samba fundamentals
- Exploring the Samba Configuration File
- Understanding Samba permissions
- Using the Samba utilities
- Learning Samba by example

SAMBA IS A SOFTWARE suite that speaks the same language as Windows NT. Samba enables you to access files and printers on a Linux server directly from Windows computers. It reduces or eliminates the need for an NT server and no third party software is required by the Windows clients.

Samba is not installed by default during the Red Hat installation process. You can select it for installation during that process, but otherwise you must install it manually. Log in as root, mount the CD-ROM, and enter the following command:

rpm -ivh /mnt/cdrom/RedHat/RPMS/samba*

Understanding Samba

Samba consists of several programs that use and understand the Microsoft *Session Message Block* (SMB) protocol; SMB is also referred to as *NetBios* or *LAN Manager*. That protocol is used by Windows 95, 98, and NT to share and access files and printers across a network. Andrew Tridgell reverse engineered the protocol for UNIX and Linux systems. Samba is now supported by Tridgell and the Samba Team. You can find more information about Samba at http://www.samba.org.

The heart of the Samba software suite consists of two daemons—smbd, which processes file and print sharing across the network, and nmbd, which provides share browsing. A single configuration file, smb.conf, controls the behavior of the system. Several utilities—`smbstatus`, `testparm`, `testprns`, and `smbclient`—provide troubleshooting and other services.

The `smbmount` system provides access to Samba or NT services from a Linux computer. The `smbmount` program comes as part of the `smbfs` RPM package. It was developed and is supported separately from the Samba project. It enables a Linux machine to mount a Samba share.

Understanding the Samba Daemons

A Linux-Samba server needs to respond to file and print share requests from network clients automatically. The monitoring function requires that some process needs to be waiting for requests for monitoring services. This job is handled by the Samba daemons `smbd` and `nmbd`.

Samba Shares

A *share,* or *service,* refers to the files, directories, or printers that are physically located on the Samba server that can be mounted by a client computer. When a share is mounted by a remote client, the files, directories and printers can be used as if they were connected directly to that machine.

smbd and nmbd

The `smbd` and `nmbd` daemons are the heart of the Samba system. Recall that daemons are processes that run constantly in the background—they don't need to interact with you directly. The `smbd` and `nmbd` monitor the network ports that are defined in the `/etc/services` files. If you look at that file, you'll see the Samba configuration information:

```
netbios-ns      137/tcp         nbns
netbios-ns      137/udp         nbns
netbios-dgm     138/tcp         nbdgm
netbios-dgm     138/udp         nbdgm
netbios-ssn     139/tcp         nbssn
```

The Internet protocols—referred to in general as TCP/IP—set up a system where a *port* is combined with IP address (for instance, 192.168.1.254 is an IP address) to handle networked-based communication between processes. That convention is used in order to allow multiple functions to be processed on one computer or one IP address.

TCP and *UDP* refer to the Transmission Control Protocol and User Datagram Protocol respectively. TCP makes sure that each packet reaches its destination, while UDP passes that responsibility to the application program. Applications like Netscape Navigator, Telnet, and FTP use TCP. Systems like name lookup and NFS use UDP.

For instance, when you browse the Internet with your Web browser and click `http://www.idgbooks.com`, your Web browser sends IP packets to the IDG Books World Wide Web server. The IP packets encapsulate TCP packets, which in turn contain the HTTP packets, which correspond to port 80. If you look at the `/etc/services` file again you'll see the line that corresponds to the HTTP service.

```
http            80/tcp              # www is used by some broken
```

The Web server listens to TCP port 80, so when it sees your IP packets, it acts on them as is appropriate. If that same server is also acting as a Samba server, it is also listening to ports 138 and 139 for SMB requests. With this networking model, a computer can differentiate and between different types of requests and act on them accordingly.

The `netbios-ns` lines refer to the name service port and is used by `nmbd` to provide share browsing to the network. The `netbios-dgm` line refers to the SMB datagram port and is used by `smbd` to provide the actual files and directories of the Samba shares.

The `smbd` and `nmbd` daemons can handle both TCP- and UDP-based packets. The TCP packets provide a virtual connection while there is no guarantee when the UDP packets are processed. These packet types are discussed more completely in Chapter 7.

Starting and Stopping the Daemons

The start-up links for `smbd` and `nmbd` are installed in the `/etc/rc.d` directories when the Samba RPM package is installed. If you look at the run-level directories (see Chapter 6) such as `/etc/rc.d/rc3.d` and `/etc/rc.d/rc5.d`, you should see the `S91smb -> ../init.d/smb` soft link file (recall that a soft link file contains the name of another file or directory and acts like a pointer). That link points to the `/etc/init.d/smb` script, which is responsible for starting and stopping the `smbd` and `nmbd` daemons. Depending on the run level declared in the `/etc/inittab` file, the system executes each script pointed to by the soft links in the run-level directory (for instance, `/etc/rc.d/rc5.d`) during the system boot. Thus, `S91smb` is executed, which executes the `/etc/init.d/smb` script that starts the Samba daemons.

You can use the `/etc/init.d/smb` script to manually start and stop the Samba daemons. Log in as root and run the following command to stop the Samba daemons:

```
/etc/init.d/smb stop
```

You can start the daemons again by entering:

```
/etc/init.d/smb start
```

You can restart the Samba daemons as follows:

/etc/init.d/smb restart

Exploring the Samba Configuration File

The smb.conf file provides the configuration information to the smbd and nmbd daemons. It is stored in the /etc directory on Red Hat based systems. Every time that you request a Samba share, a new smbd daemon is started, which reads the /etc/smb.conf configuration file in order to determine what it should do. The tasks of each smbd daemon are determined by three types of Samba configurations: the *global, homes,* and *printers* sections of the smb.conf file.

Understanding Global Settings

The [global] setting section is described at the beginning of the /etc/smb.conf file. A sample of the global settings are shown below. Note that both the pound sign (#) and the semicolon (;) specify a comment.

```
[global]
# workgroup = NT-Domain-Name or Workgroup-Name
workgroup = MYGROUP
# server string is the equivalent of the NT Description field
   server string = Samba Server
# This option is important for security. It allows you to restrict
# connections to machines which are on your local network. The
# following example restricts access to two C class networks and
# the "loopback" interface. For more examples of the syntax see
# the smb.conf man page
;   hosts allow = 192.168.1. 192.168.2. 127.
# if you want to automatically load your printer list rather
# than setting them up individually then you'll need this
   printcap name = /etc/printcap
   load printers = yes
# It should not be necessary to spell out the print system type
# unless yours is non-standard. Currently supported print systems
# include: bsd, sysv, plp, lprng, aix, hpux, qnx
;   printing = bsd

   {... some lines deleted for brevity ... }
```

```
# Security mode. Most people will want user level security. See
# security_level.txt for details.
   security = user
```

The `workgroup` setting describes name of the *browse* group that the Samba server shows up as when you use the Network Neighborhood or Windows Explorer on a Windows machine. This group doesn't have anything to do with Web browsing. You can also limit the subnets that can access the Samba services with the `hosts allow` parameter. The printer-related parameters describes how Samba treats printer shares. Finally, the security = user specifies that all shares will be authenticated by the Samba server itself (please see the section "Understanding the [homes] Section" for more information).

There are numerous other global parameters to consider. The ones that are important within the context of this book are discussed in later sections. For information about the other parameters, you can consult the `man` pages for `smb.conf`, `smbd` and `nmbd`. You can also consult the Samba documentation in the `/usr/doc/samba-2.0.3` directory.

Understanding the [homes] Section

The `[homes]` section controls how users' home directories are shared. The section is shown here:

```
[homes]
   comment = Home Directories
   browseable = no
   writable = yes
```

The `browseable` option controls whether the home shares are displayed in the list of available shares from Windows machines (or any computer capable of browsing the network). Normally, you don't want to do this, and the default is no. The `writable` option means that Samba gives permission to write to the share; this option can be dangerous if you do not properly authenticate your shares.

When using the *user security* mode each Linux user account home directory becomes the default share for that user. For instance, if you are working from a Windows machine as user X with password Y, if there is a user account X with the password Y on the Linux-Samba server, you automatically can access that share. User security mode is the Red Hat Samba default, and is discussed in the "Understanding Authentication" section.

Understanding [printers] Shares

These shares by default define the Samba spool directory and the access rights to your printers. Any printers that are defined in your `/etc/printcap` file (see

Chapter 9, in the "Introducing the LPD Daemon" section) are accessible via this section.

Understanding Authentication

The version of Samba that comes with the Red Hat distribution on the CD-ROM accompanying this book understands both plain-text and encrypted passwords. However, you must configure Samba to accept encrypted passwords. The later versions of Windows 95, most versions of Windows NT 4.0 with Service Pack 3 (SP3) or higher, and all versions of Windows 98 use encrypted passwords.

If you want to use plain-text passwords, you can turn off password encryption by modifying the Windows Registry. Use Regedit (or a similar registry editing utility) and go to the HKEY_LOCAL_MACHINE\System\CurrentControlSet\Services\VxD\VNETSETUP key. Change the DWORD named EnablePlainTextPassword the value of 1. Your Windows computer should now use a plain-text password.

Modifying the Windows Registry is a potentially dangerous operation. If you misconfigure it, you can render your computer unusable.

You can set up Samba to use encrypted passwords by either pointing it to a Windows NT domain controller or else by using its own encrypted password database. The following sections describe how to configure Samba to use both methods.

Configuring Samba to Use Encrypted Passwords

To make Samba understand encrypted passwords, you must modify the `smb.conf` file and create an `smbpasswd` file. First, edit the `/etc/smb.conf` file, and make sure that the security setting reads `security = user`. Next, uncomment the following two lines:

```
encrypt passwords = yes
smb passwd file = /etc/smbpasswd
```

Next, create the `smbpasswd` file from your `/etc/passwd` file by running the following command:

```
cat /etc/passwd | mksmbpasswd.sh > /etc/smbpasswd
```

The first few lines of the `smbpasswd` file look like the following (some of the X's have been deleted so that the entries fit onto the page):

```
#
# SMB password file.
#
root:0:XXXXXXXXXXXXXXXXXXXX:XXXXXXXXXXXXXXXXX:root:/root:/bin/bash
bin:1:XXXXXXXXXXXXXXXXXXXXX:XXXXXXXXXXXXXXXXXXXXXXXXX:bin:/bin:
daemon:2:XXXXXXXXXXXXXXXXXXXXX:XXXXXXXXXXXXXXXXXXXXXX:daemon:/sbin:
adm:3:XXXXXXXXXXXXXXXXXXXXXX:XXXXXXXXXXXXXXXXXXXXXXX:adm:/var/adm:
lp:4:XXXXXXXXXXXXXXXXX:XXXXXXXXXXXXXXXXXX:lp:/var/spool/lpd:
```

Delete any lines that don't start with the username of a user on your system. Leaving the entries for the system users (root, daemon, bin) can create a security hole.

Next, you need to create a Samba password for each user that you want to provide with Samba access. Run the `smbpasswd` command as follows, where *iamauser* is the name of the user whose password you want to set:

smbpasswd *iamauser*

The `smbpasswd` program prompts you to enter the password twice. The `iamauser` entry in the `/etc/smbpasswd` should now look something like the following:

```
iamauser:500:834A03B3B453DD1:8XE3ED80EBE5326::/home/iamauser:/bin/bash
```

The X's have been replaced with the encrypted password. Next, you need to repeat this process for each user.

Restart the Samba daemons:

/etc/rc.d/init.d/smb restart

Log on to your Windows machine and enter a username and password that correspond to a user you have entered in the Samba password file. You should see that user's home directory in the Windows Network Neighborhood folder.

If you configure Samba to accept encrypted passwords, it still accepts plain text ones as well. When using encryption, Samba first tries to authenticate a share request against the encrypted version of the associated password. If that fails, Samba attempts to authenticate against the plain text password.

For further information on configuring Samba for encrypted passwords, read the `ENCRYPTION.txt`, `Passwords.txt`, `Win95.txt`, and `WinNT.txt` files in the `/usr/doc/samba-1.9.18p10/docs` directory.

Configuring Samba to Authenticate from an NT Server

Samba can also use an NT domain controller to authenticate requested shares. (The discussion of NT domain controllers are beyond the scope of this book.) In this case, you need to modify the `/etc/smb.conf` file to point to the NT controller. Change the security parameter to specify the use of an NT domain controller as follows:

```
security = server
```

Next, uncomment the following line:

```
;   password server = <NT-Server-Name>
```

Next, edit this line to include the name of the NT server, which in this case is called *my_pdc*:

```
password server = my_pdc
```

The name of your domain controller should convert into the IP address of your NT primary domain controller via DNS. Please take note that you could specify the IP address if you desire. For instance, if your controller address is 192.168.1.100, then you could enter the following line:

```
password server = 192.168.1.100
```

You must, of course, have an account on the primary domain controller.

Understanding Samba Permissions

Samba provides control over how much access is given to each share. Access such as read and write is controlled by the configuration in the `/etc/smb.conf` file. However, the Linux file system permissions take precedence over that of Samba.

Linux controls access by the permissions that are set on a file or directory. Recall from the section "Managing Files, Permissions, and Ownership" in Chapter 2, that every file and directory has settings that allow or disallow reading, writing, and execution of the file or directory. The owner, the group membership, and everyone else each have these settings.

For example, if Samba allows a file to be written to, but Linux does not, then that file can not be written to. The same is true for directories. Linux permissions take precedence over Samba permissions.

Using the Samba Utilities

There are several utilities that provide access to Samba shares and also debugging and testing capabilities: smbstatus; smbclient; nmblookup, testparm, and testprns; and smbmount.

smbstatus

The smbstatus utility shows the status of the Samba smbd daemon. It also shows any shares that are currently being used. Log in as root and run the smbstatus program. You should see this response:

```
Couldn't open status file /var/lock/samba/STATUS..LCK
```

That response indicates that the Samba lock file has not been created. That file is not created when Samba is installed via RPM. Create it by entering the command:

touch /var/lock/samba/STATUS..LCK

Run the smbstatus command again and you should get the following response:

```
Samba version 1.9.18p10
Service      uid      gid      pid      machine

No locked files
Share mode memory usage (bytes):
   102232(99%) free + 112(0%) used + 56(0%) overhead = 102400(100%) total
```

That response shows that Samba is running but no shares are being accessed. It also shows information on memory usage.

smbclient

The smbclient program provides a way to access Samba shares directly from your Linux server. Any Linux computer can use it to access the Samba shares from across a network too. Log in as root and enter the command:

smbclient //chivas/root /mnt -c chivas -U root

This connects you to the root user share. Recall that each Linux user is given a share by default. (The root user is used for this example because it is guaranteed to exist on the Linux server.) When `smbclient` connects to a share, it gives you a prompt like this:

```
smbclient>
```

You can get a list of the `smbclient` commands by entering h at the command line. You can do things like list the files in the share, move around the directories—if any—in a share, and transfer files. It is similar to an FTP system.

Now, try running the `smbstatus` program again and you get a response that shows your open root share.

```
Samba version 2.0.3
Service  uid   gid  pid     machine
root     root root 11571    chivas (192.168.1.254) Mon Apr  5 13:56:48 1999

No locked files
Share mode memory usage (bytes):
   102232(99%) free + 112(0%) used + 56(0%) overhead = 102400(100%) total
```

nmblookup, testparm, and testprns

The `nmblookup, testparm, and testprns` are useful programs for test and debugging Samba shares. They are introduced in the "Troubleshooting" section in this chapter.

smbmount

You can mount a Samba share from a Linux machine by using `smbmount`. From any Linux computer, enter the following:

```
smbmount //chivas/root /mnt/tmp -c chivas
```

You are prompted for the root user's password. Enter it and then run the `df` command and you should see that root's home directory has been mounted on the `/mnt/tmp` directory.

```
Filesystem        1024-blocks    Used Available Capacity Mounted on
/dev/hda8             254169    34214    206828     14%   /
/dev/hda1              15856      803     14223      5%   /boot
/dev/hda6            1738711     8895   1639955      1%   /home
/dev/hda5            1738711   760285    888565     46%   /usr
/dev/hda7             254169     9526    231516      4%   /var
```

/dev/hdc	560606	560606	0	100%	/mnt/cdrom
//chivas/root	254168	47340	206828	19%	/mnt/tmp

The `smbmount` program can be used across a network.

The `smbmount` program is not part of the Samba project. It is distributed with the Samba software because it is a useful program. If you have any problems with it, your complaints should not be directed to the Samba project.

Learning Samba by Example

The following examples give a flavor of what Samba is capable of. They are straightforward, but also quite useful. Much, if not most, of Samba's power is found in the simple sharing of files and directories.

These examples make use of a backup copy of the `/etc/smb.conf` stored as `/etc/smb.conf.bak`. This is done to make the examples work from exactly the same configuration. Please make a copy with the following command:

```
cp /etc/smb.conf /etc/smb.conf.bak
```

Sharing your CD-ROM is the first Samba example. You can use this example to share the contents of a CD-ROM to all of your users.

Sharing your CD-ROM

Log in to your Linux server as root and mount the CD-ROM drive. Edit the `/etc/smb.conf` file, and find the section that refers to the public share as shown below. (You can use any existing share definition as your template or create a new one. The `public` share is used here because it is a reasonable fit for the example.)

```
;[public]
;   comment = Public Stuff
;   path = /home/samba
;   public = yes
;   writable = yes
;   printable = no
;   write list = @staff
```

Uncomment the first six lines by deleting the semicolon. Leave the last line (the `write list` line) alone. Change the `/home/samba` line to `/mnt/cdrom`. The `writable = yes` parameter is technically wrong but the CD-ROM is not writable so it is superfluous in this case. However, it is good practice to change it to "no". The file should now read:

```
[public]
   comment = CD-ROM contents
   path = /mnt/cdrom
   public = yes
   writable = no
   printable = no
```

Restart the Samba daemons:

```
/etc/rc.d/init.d/smb restart
```

From a Windows computer, double-click Network Neighborhood, and then double-click the Linux server icon (chivas). The shares available on the Linux server are shown. Now, double-click the public icon. You should see the contents of the companion CD-ROM displayed in the window as shown in Figure 8-1.

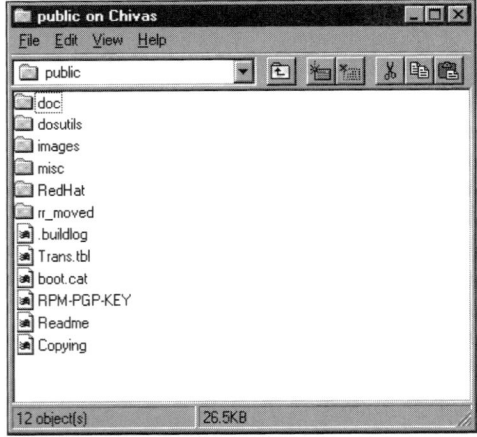

Figure 8-1: The CD-ROM contents displayed

On the Linux server, run the `smbstatus` command. The open Samba shares are displayed as shown here:

```
Samba version 2.0.3
Service   uid    gid    pid machine
-----------------------------------
public    nobody nobody 1243 toluca (192.168.1.3) Mon Mar 29 14:45:15 1999
```

In this case Samba is providing the public service. It sees the user and group id as the user nobody; that is because the public share maps to the user id 99, or nobody, unless the guest account parameter is set to some other value. The pid is the process id of the `smbd` daemon that is managing this service. (One `smbd` process is spawned by the original `smbd` process for each share that is in use.) The machine name and IP address that has mounted the share is displayed along with the date and time of its access.

Sharing Your /var/tmp Directory

Sharing a writable file system is a good variation of the CD-ROM example to experiment with. By publicly sharing a temporary directory you create a convenient place to store and transfer files. For instance, if you frequently need to transfer files to many different computers all the time, you can set up a common transfer point, instead of using a system like FTP. That simplifies life for everyone.

Log in to your Linux server as root. Restore the original copy of the `smb.conf` file (`cp /etc/smb.conf.bak /etc/smb.conf`). Edit the `/etc/smb.conf` file and find the section that refers to the public share, as in the previous example.

Again, uncomment the first six lines, but leave the last one alone. Change the `/home/samba` line to `/var/tmp`. This time, it's important to change the writable parameter to `writable = yes`. The file should now look like this:

```
[public]
   comment = Temporary storage space
   path = /var/tmp
   public = yes
   writable = yes
   printable = no
```

Restart the Samba daemons:

```
/etc/rc.d/init.d/smb restart
```

From a Windows computer, double-click Network Neighborhood, and then double-click the Linux server icon (`chivas`). The shares on the Linux server are shown. Now double-click the public icon. You should see the contents of the `/var/tmp` directory (if there are any) displayed in the window, as shown in Figure 8-2.

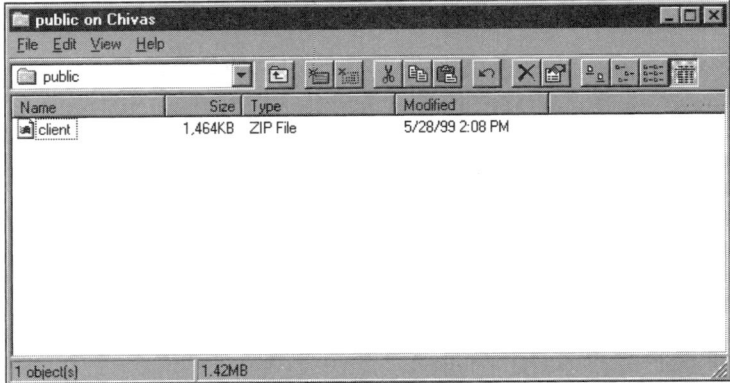

Figure 8-2: The /var/tmp contents displayed

On the Linux server, run the `smbstatus` command and the open Samba shares are displayed as shown below.

```
Samba version 2.0.3

Service    uid      gid    pid    machine
-----------------------------------------------

public     nobody   nobody 12479  toluca (192.168.1.3) Mon Mar 29 14:45:15 1999
```

In this case Samba, is providing the public service that points to the `/var/tmp` directory. It is similar to the CD-ROM example, except that it is a writable directory. If, from the Linux server, you look at the directory with the `ls /var/tmp` command, you will see the same files as shown in the Samba share.

 This is a useful example. The [tmp] share is used in Chapter 10 to install the Arkeia client software to a Windows machine.

Accessing Your Home Share

By default, the Red Hat distribution of Samba defines the home directory of all Linux users as a share. If you Look in the Share Definitions section of the `smb.conf` file and you see the standard [homes] share defined:

```
[homes]
    comment = Home Directories
```

```
browseable = no
writable = yes
```

To make use of the home directory shares, your Windows usernames and passwords must match up with their counterparts on the Linux server. For instance, to use the root user share, you must have a root user with the same password on your Windows computer. (If you create a usernamed root on your Windows computer, it will have no special privileges.)

This example requires that the you to add user `emerckx` to both the Windows client and the Linux server. Add the user `emerckx` onto both machines. Use the `useradd` or `LinuxConf` to add the user onto the Linux machine. On the Windows computer, use the New users icon in the Control Panel.

Open the Window's computer Network Neighborhood and double-click the chivas icon. If your username and password is the same on both machines, then you should see your home directory displayed in the in the `emerckx on Chivas` window. Double-click the emerckx icon, and you will see the contents of the `home` directory displayed, as seen in Figure 8-3.

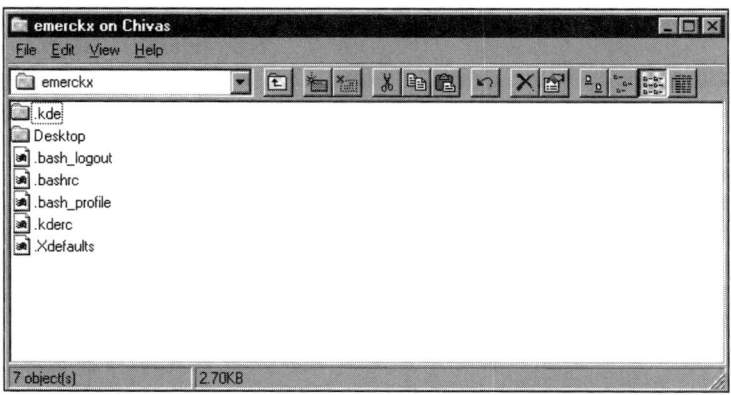

Figure 8-3: The contents of emerckx's home directory displayed

When you check the active shares with `smbstatus`, you see the results somewhat different than in the previous two examples.

```
Samba version 2.0.3
Service    uid    gid    pid    machine

emerckx emerckx emerckx 1280 toluca (192.168.1.3) Mon May 28,1999
No locked files
```

In this case the share name is the same as the user and group name — emerckx. That is because Samba automatically assigns the user home directory to a share defined in the [home] service. The user and group names match the share name.

Using Macros

Samba has a macro facility that dynamically allocates various resources based on which machine, user, and so forth is asking for a share. This facility allows you to custom tailor your services in a precise manner. A macro comes in the form of two characters, the first of which is a percent (%) sign. Table 8-1 lists the macros.

TABLE 8-1 SAMBA MACROS

Macro	Description
%S	Current service or share (if any exist)
%P	Root directory of the current service or share (if any exist)
%u	Username of the current service or share (if any exist)
%g	Primary group name of %u
%U	Session username the client requested, but not necessarily the one received
%H	The home directory of the user given by %u
%v	Samba version number
%h	Host name of the Samba server
%m	NetBIOS name of the client computer
%L	NetBIOS name of the Samba server
%M	Internet name of the client computer
%d	Process ID of the current server process
%a	Architecture of the remote server
%I	IP address of the client
%T	Current date and time

Login to your Linux server as root. Restore the original copy of the smb.conf file:

cp /etc/smb.conf.bak /etc/smb.conf

Edit the /etc/smb.conf file and find the section that refers to the [pchome] as shown below.

```
;[pchome]
;   comment = PC Directories
;   path = /usr/pc/%m
;   public = no
;   writable = yes
```

Uncomment the first five lines. Change the path line to /home/%u.

```
[pchome]
   comment = User emerkx working directory
   path = /home/%u
   public = yes
   writable = yes
   printable = no
```

The %u macro expands to the username on the Windows machine; /home/%u becomes /home/emerckx. Restart the Samba daemons:

/etc/rc.d/init.d/smb restart

From a Windows computer, open Network Neighborhood and, then double-click the Linux server icon (chivas). Next, click the emerkx share. You should see the contents of emerckx's home directory displayed again, as in Figure 8-3.

When you check the active shares with smbstatus, you see that the user and group name is emerckx, accessing the pchome share. This is the same directory that was accessed in the previous example.

```
Samba version 2.0.3
Service  uid    gid    pid machine
----------------------------------
pchome emerckx emerckx 13063 toluca (192.168.1.3) Mon May 29 1999
```

This share provides the same service by using the macro facility as the previous example using the [home] service.

Introducing SWAT

The Samba team has introduced the *Samba Web Administration Tool* (SWAT) in the Samba 2.0 distribution. SWAT is a Web-based tool that enables you to use your Web browser to configure Samba. This tool was introduced during the writing of this book. It appears to be a good tool and should only get better with time.

SWAT uses a specialized version of the `httpd` daemon to act as the interface to your Web browser. When you open SWAT with your browser, the `inetd` daemon kicks off the `swat` daemon.

The `inetd` daemon is used for kicking off other daemons on a per-use basis. The `inetd.conf` configuration file controls the action of `inetd`.

Start up your Web browser and enter the `http://localhost:901/` URL in the Location window. You are prompted to enter a username and password. Enter root as the username and enter the root password. You are then presented with the SWAT interface window shown in Figure 8-4.

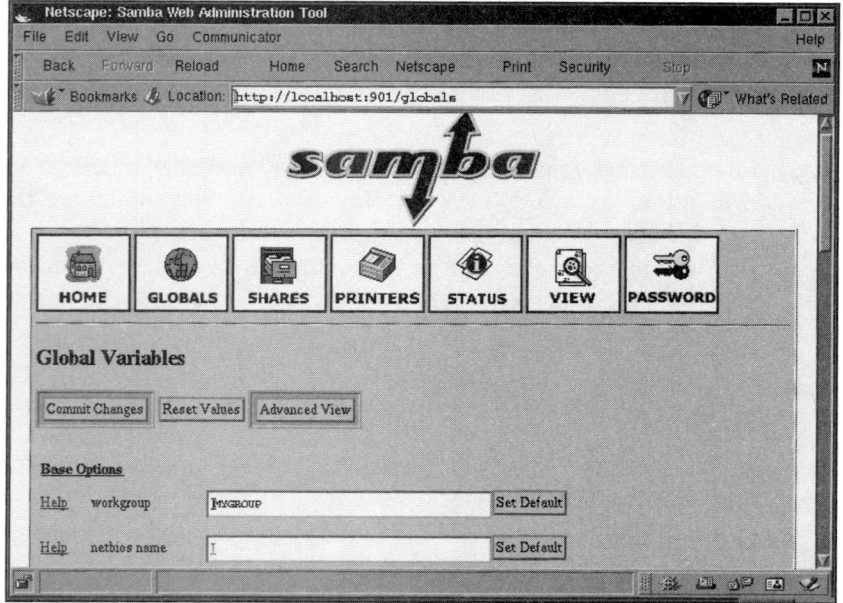

Figure 8-4: The Samba SWAT window is displayed

SWAT is in an early phase of development. It currently enables you to do all the things that you can do by manually modifying the `smb.conf` file. It allows you to modify the global parameters; add, modify, and create shares (printer shares too); and view the status of open shares. For instance, to modify the Samba workgroup, click GLOBALS, change the name from WORKGROUP to MYGROUP, and then click the Commit Changes button.

Next, look at the `/etc/smb.conf` file and you see that SWAT not only has changed the workgroup parameter, but it has completely rewritten the file.

```
# from localhost (127.0.0.1)
# Date: 1999/03/30 12:15:12

# Global parameters
        workgroup = MYGROUP
        server string = Samba Server
        log file = /var/log/samba/log.%m
        max log size = 50
        socket options = TCP_NODELAY
        dns proxy = No

[homes]
        comment = Home Directories
        read only = No
        browseable = No

[printers]
        comment = All Printers
        path = /var/spool/samba
        print ok = Yes
        browseable = No
```

SWAT replaces the original `smb.conf` file with one that does not include all the comments. Any changes that you make with SWAT are written into this new file.

One of SWAT's best features is that you can return any parameter back to its default value by clicking the Set Default button to the right of the field. It also prevents you from specifying incompatible parameters. You can display help on a subject by clicking the Help button to the left of the field.

Troubleshooting

If you have problems using Samba, then there are several troubleshooting processes that you can try. They are divided between checking your network connectivity and your Samba configuration.

Checking Your Network

You should first verify that your Windows machine is speaking to your Linux server across the network. Try pinging the Linux machine by opening a MS-DOS window and executing the following command:

```
ping 192.168.1.254
```

The numeric IP address is used to avoid any problems that might exist in the DNS server. You should see the pings returned from the Linux machine:

```
PING chivas.sandia.gov (192.168.1.254): 56 data bytes
64 bytes from 192.168.1.254: icmp_seq=0 ttl=64 time=0.4 ms
64 bytes from 192.168.1.254: icmp_seq=1 ttl=64 time=0.2 ms
64 bytes from 192.168.1.254: icmp_seq=2 ttl=64 time=0.2 ms
```

If you do not get that response (the "time" parameter in this listing refers to the response time of the pinged computer, and can vary), at least part of your problem lies with your network or your computers. Refer to the network troubleshooting techniques discussed in Chapter 7.

Checking the Samba Daemons

The `smbd` and `nmbd` daemons must be running for your clients to access the Samba server. Check that they are running with the following command:

```
ps x | grep mbd
```

At least one `smbd` and one `nmbd` daemon should be displayed.

```
301  ?  S    0:00 smbd -D
310  ?  S    0:01 nmbd -D
```

There can be more than one `smbd` running, because one daemon is allocated for each Samba share that is accessed. Both `smbd` and `nmbd` should be running. If they are not, then restart them by using the `smb` script (or by manually starting them):

```
/etc/rc.d/init.d/smb restart
```

Try accessing Samba again. If it still does not work, proceed to the next section.

Check the Lock Files

Samba requires a lock file to be in place in order to work correctly. There should be a STATUS..LCK in the /var/lock/samba directory. If it does not exist, create it as follows:

touch /var/lock/samba/STATUS..LCK

Case is important in this command. Restart the Samba daemons:

/etc/rc.d/init.d/smb restart

If Samba still fails, proceed to the next section.

Checking the Samba Log Files

The default Samba configuration contains the parameter log file = /var/log/samba/log.%m in the /etc/smb.conf file. This tells Samba to copy all log messages to a files with suffixes based on the NetBIOS name of each computer that tries to access the server (the %m macro expands to the NetBIOS name of the calling computer). The amount of information recorded is based on the debuglevel parameter, which can be defined in the /etc/smb.conf file. The log files are stored by default in the /var/log/samba directory.

The information contain in those files can be used to debug Samba. For instance, the log file for the Windows 95 computer toluca might contain the following message:

[1999/03/31 14:56:26, 1] smbd/password.c:pass_check_smb(500)
    Couldn't find user 'iamauser' in smb_passwd file.

This means that the /etc/smb_passwd file has not been configured correctly, if at all, for the user iamauser. That user's home share is not accessible from the Windows computer, and the solution is to edit the Samba password file and then use the smbpasswd iamauser command to set the password.

There are too many possible problems like this to discuss within the context of this book. However, many (if not most) messages are decipherable to the average reader. Consult the Samba documentation to find further information.

The next section follows the outline of the troubleshooting process found in /usr/doc/samba-2.0.3/docs/textdocs/DIAGNOSIS.txt for Samba 2.0.3. Consult those files for more detailed troubleshooting information.

Checking the Samba Configuration

There are several tools that come with the Samba distribution that are useful in checking its configuration.

USING TESTPARM

The `testparm` utility checks the `smb.conf` file for misconfigured parameters. It produces several pages of text, so you should pipe its output to the `more` filter.

```
testparm | more
```

The first page should look as follows for the default `smb.conf`:

```
Load smb config files from /etc/smb.conf
Processing section "[homes]"
Processing section "[printers]"
Loaded services file OK.
If a parameter is misconfigured, then testparm should point it out:
Load smb config files from /etc/smb.conf
ERROR: Badly formed boolean in configuration file: "Yees".
Processing section "[homes]"
Processing section "[printers]"
Processing section "[test]"
Loaded services file OK.
```

In this case, what should have been the string *Yes* was misspelled.

If you continue to have problems, then the next step is to check out Samba from the Linux server.

USING SMBCLIENT

`Smbclient` provides an interactive, command line interface to Samba. Log in as root and run the utility so that it tries to connect with the Samba server.

```
smbclient -L
```

If you are asked to enter a password, you have achieved at least partial success. Enter a blank password. If you are not granted access, there are several possible causes. The following lists some possible solutions:

- In the case where `smbclient -L` fails completely, consult the `DIAGNOSIS.txt` file for possible solutions.

- If you see the message `Bad Password`, check your `smb.conf` file for incorrect `Hosts allow`, `Hosts deny`, or `Valid users` entries. Run

Chapter 8: Sharing Files and Printers with Samba

`testparm` again and look specifically for incorrect entries for those parameters.

◆ If you see the message `connection refused`, the `smbd` daemon probably is not running. Restart it if necessary.

◆ If you see the message `session request failed`, and if it says `your server software is being unfriendly`, then you may have one or more invalid entries in `smb.conf`, or `smbd` may not be running, or another service may be running on port 139, which is reserved for NetBIOS. In the first two cases, you can check to see that the `smbd` daemon is running and that the `smb.conf` file is configured correctly. For the latter case, you can check the port by running the `netstat - | grep 139` command. Nothing else should be running on port 139.

◆ If all this fails, read the `DIAGNOSIS.txt` file for more hints.

Once the blank password is entered, you should be presented with the available Samba shares.

```
Added interface ip=192.168.1.254 bcast=192.168.1.255
nmask=255.255.255.0
Server time is Tue Mar 30 17:15:10 1999
Timezone is UTC-7.0
Password:
Domain=[MYGROUP] OS=[Unix] Server=[Samba 2.0.3]
security=user
Server=[CHIVAS] User=[root] Workgroup=[MYGROUP] Domain=[MYGROUP]
        Sharename      Type         Comment
        ---------      ----         -------
        IPC$           IPC          IPC Service (Samba Server)
        root           Disk         Home Directories
This machine has a browse list:
        Server                  Comment
        ------                  -------
        Chivas                  Samba Server
This machine has a workgroup list:
        Workgroup               Master
        ---------               ------
        MYGROUP
```

You should be able to connect with a share by using `smbclient`. Run the command:

`smbclient //chivas/root`

You should be prompted for the root password. Enter it correctly and you get the `smbclient` prompt.

```
Domain=[MYGROUP] OS=[Unix] Server=[Samba 2.0.3]
security=user
smb: \>
```

You can access the help screen by entering `help` at the prompt.

The `smbclient` utility enable you to `get` and `put` files to the Samba share, as well as many other functions. It is useful for transferring files between Linux machines as well as for troubleshooting.

USING NMBD

Samba uses the `nmbd` daemon to process browsing requests. You can use the `nmblookup` utility to test it and also do text-based browsing across a network:

```
nmblookup -d 2 "*"
```

This command returns the IP address of every Samba (SMB) server on your network. Thus, you should see your Linux server displayed if `nmbd` is working correctly.

```
Added interface ip=192.168.1.254 bcast=134.253.156.255 nmask=255.255.255.0
Got a positive name query response from 192.168.1.254 ( 192.168.1.254
)192.168.1.254 *<00>
```

If you don't get this type of response, check to see if the `nmbd` daemon is running, as explained earlier.

You can check the services running on the Samba server more precisely as follows:

```
nmblookup -B chivas __SAMBA__
```

This command should return the following:

```
Sending queries to 192.168.1.254
192.168.1.254 __SAMBA__<00>
```

CHECKING SAMBA FROM YOUR WINDOWS PC

The next step is to check Samba from your PC. You should be able to browse your Linux server from the Network Neighborhood window of your PC. If it doesn't show up there, then try using the following command from an MS-DOS window:

```
net view \\chivas
```

If successful, this command should show the available shares on chivas. If that doesn't work, then try connecting directly to a share:

`net use e: \\chivas\root`

This should mount the root user's share (/root) as drive E.

If both of these Windows based tests fail, then check the `DIAGNOSIS.txt` file again. Next, you can consult the Samba FAQ that is found in the `/usr/docs/samba-2.0.3/docs/textdocs` directory. Finally, you should also consider posting your query to the appropriate newsgroup (see Chapter 3).

Summary

This chapter provides you with a basic understanding of how Samba works and how to use it. Samba is the system that enbles a Linux server to provide the same file and print services as a Windows NT computer. It mimics the NT server by using the same SMB protocol that NT uses. Other Windows computers can access those shares without any additional software; Linux and UNIX computers can use those shares too.

- The Samba system is introduced. The ability to mimic an NT server makes a Linux computer into an powerful, inexpensive server. By using Samba you can power your business with inexpensive, reliable Linux PCs.

- The heart of Samba is the `smbd` and `nmbd` daemons. `Smbd` transfers the data to the SMB clients and `nmbd` provides the browsing service. They are both controlled by the `smb.conf` configuration file.

- The Samba configuration file, `smb.conf`, is described. It tells `smbd` and `nmbd` how to behave. You can customize it by hand or use its default configuration to access your Linux home directories.

- Password authentication is described. Windows 98 and newer versions of Windows NT and Windows 95 use encrypted passwords by default. You must modify Samba to accept encrypted passwords. If you use encrypted passwords, Samba still understands plain text passwords.

- Samba provides control over who can read and write to individual shares. However, the file permissions on the Linux server always override the Samba permissions.

- There are several utilities that come with the Samba RPM package. They are useful for both debugging problems as well as using Samba from other Linux computers.

- Several examples are described. A couple of simple ones such as sharing a CD-ROM drive and a temporary directory are useful examples. Samba also provides macros that dynamically define shares.

- The Samba Web Administration Tool (SWAT) was introduced with Samba version 2.0. SWAT provides a Web-based configuration tool that is easy to use and simplifies the configuration process.

- Troubleshooting techniques are described. There are several processes that you can use to systematically track down and fix bugs or misconfigurations. If they fail, you can access the on-line documentation or use newsgroups for interactive help.

Chapter 9

Sharing Printers

IN THIS CHAPTER

- Configure a Linux printer
- Configure a Samba print share
- Print from a Windows computer
- Print from a Linux client

LINUX IS A GOOD platform for providing print services. The Red Hat installation process allows you to configure a printer, (and that printer configuration can be used to provide print services to other computers). It is also simple to configure additional printers.

Your Linux print server can control locally attached (parallel printer port, or serial port or other type of directly attached) printers, as well as network printers. Printers attached to other Linux and Windows computers can be accessed too.

Introducing the LPD Daemon

Red Hat Linux comes configured with the `lpd` daemon. By default, `lpd` periodically checks the print spool directory which is `/var/spool/lpd/lp` for print jobs. Print jobs are created by the `lpr` program (applications such as Applixware and Netscape also call on `lpr` when you use them to print).

The Printcap Configuration File

When `lpd` is started it reads the `/etc/printcap` file for information about what printers it can access and how they are configured. The `printcap` file can be edited by hand (a difficult process) or configured via the Control-Panel or Linuxconf utilities. The following sections use those tools for the examples.

Print Filters

The `lpd` daemon is capable of sending simple text data to a printer. When you want to print more complex graphics or use PostScript then more processing has to be done. The data has to be converted into PostScript unless the printer understands PostScript. For instance, HP LaserJets use PCL.

The conversion can take place by using a print filter. There are a number of print filters available for Linux, and you can write simple ones yourself. Print filters come with Red Hat Linux and you can configure your printer to use them as described in the next section Configuring a Local Printer.

Configuring a Local Printer

Configuring a printer is a straight-forward process. Attach a printer to your Linux computer's parallel (printer) port. Login in as root and start the Control-Panel by clicking Start → Programs → Administration → Control Panel. Next, click on the Printer icon, which is the third from the top, and you'll see the window shown in Figure 9-1.

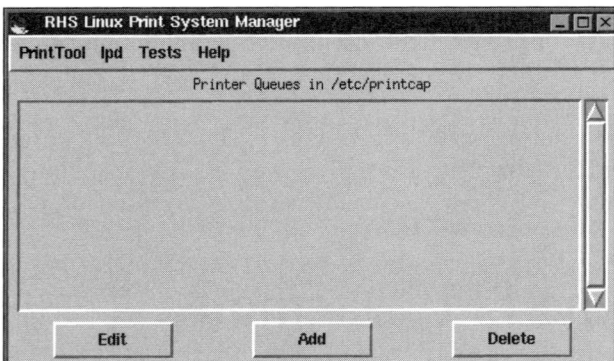

Figure 9-1: The RHS Linux Printer System Manager window

If you have not already configured a printer, then you'll get a blank screen. To add a printer, click on the Add button and you'll get the Add a Printer Entry window show in Figure 9-2.

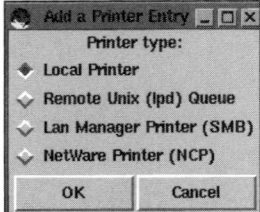

Figure 9-2: The Add a Printer Entry window

The Local Printer radio button should already be set. Choose OK and the printer port(s) that is detected is shown. Click OK and you are given the Edit Local Printer Entry window shown in Figure 9-3.

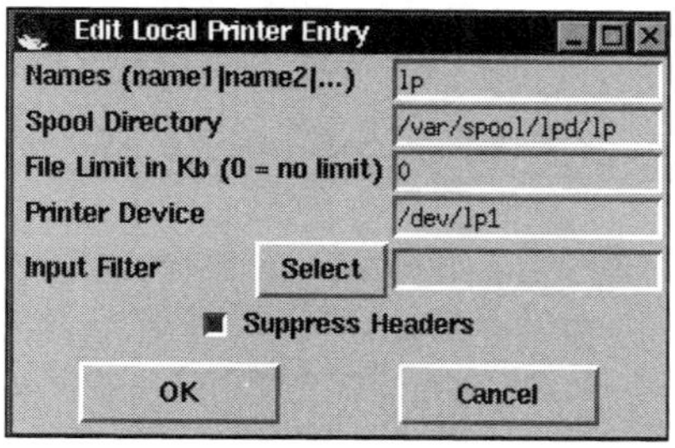

Figure 9-3: The Edit Local Printer Entry window

The default values for the printer name, spool directory and file limit fields should all be acceptable. (You can choose any name for the printer that you want but by convention the default name is lp. You can assign multiple names to a single printer.) If your printer port is detected, it should show up in the Printer Device field; if it doesn't, then choose the port yourself. Click the Input Filter Select button and you'll get the window shown in Figure 9-4.

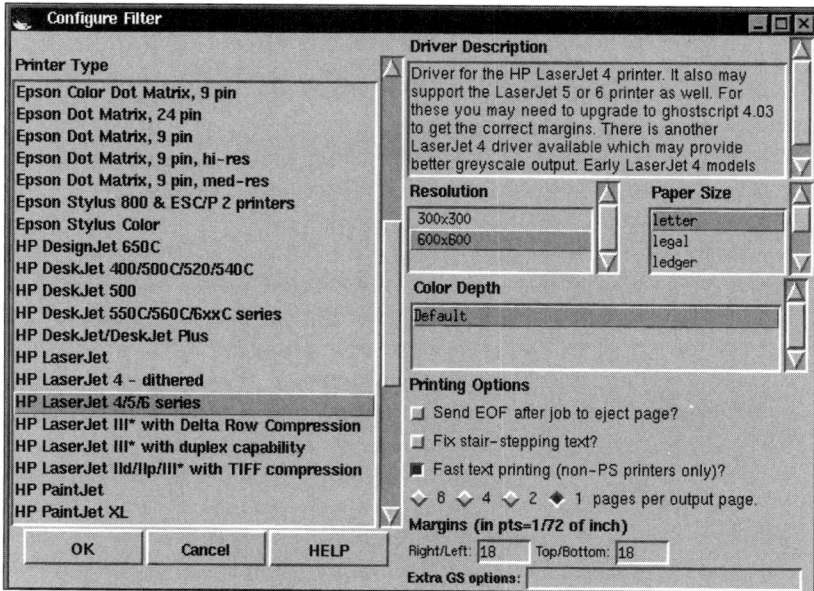

Figure 9-4: The Configure filter window

Highlight and select the printer type that you are using and click OK, and control will be sent back to the Edit Local Printer Entry window. Click OK and you are sent back to the RHS Linux Printer System Manager window and your new printer is displayed.

Test your new printer by first restarting the print daemon and then use the Tests → Print Postscript test page. Enter the command:

```
lpr /etc/printcap
```

Then, from the Red Hat Print System Manager window, click on the Tests → Print Postscript test page (you can also choose to print a plain text file). The PostScript, or text file should be printed. You can try a more complex job by using an application like Netscape (included on the companion CD-ROM).

Configuring a Remote Printer

You can access to a printer that is attached or controlled by another Linux or UNIX server; you can also print directly to a printer connected to your LAN. The entry in the `printcap` file that specifies the local port that the printer is attached to is replaced by an entry that points to the remote server or the printer itself.

The RHS Linux Printer System Manager is used to configure such a printer. Login as root and start the Control-panel by clicking on the Start → Programs → Administration → Control Panel. Click the Add button, select the Remote Unix (lpd) radio button and click on the OK button.

You need to enter the network name—or IP address—and the queue name in the Remote Host and Remote Queue sections. Figure 9-5 shows the entries for the LJ5_myoffice from the model network described in Chapter 6.

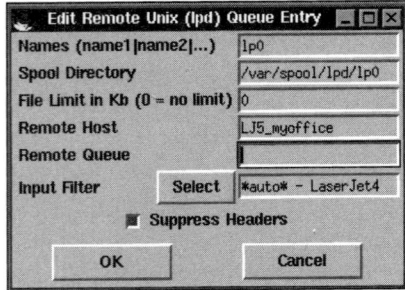

Figure 9-5: The Edit Local Printer Entry window for the printer LJ5_ myoffice

Test your new printer by first restarting the print daemon (`killall -1 lpd`) and printing out the text and Postscript files from the Test menu in the RHS Linux Print System Manager window. Alternatively, you can use the `lpr` program to manually print from the command line.

```
lpr /etc/printcap
```

The text file should be printed. You can try a more complex job by using an application like Netscape Navigator (included on the companion CD-ROM).

Configuring a Samba Printer

You can create a Samba share for a printer. The Samba share uses an existing entry in the `printcap` file.

The RHS Linux Printer System Manager can be used to configure Samba-based printers. (You can also hand edit the `/etc/smb.conf` if you wish.) Login in as root and start the Control-panel by clicking the Start → Programs → Administration → Control Panel. Open the printer manager by clicking the Printer Configuration button, which is the third from the top. Next, click the Add button, select the Lan Manager Printer (SMB) button and click on the OK button.

A warning message is displayed. This informs you that when entering a username and password for the printer share, the password file is stored in plain text. Because of this, your file can be read by anyone and your password can be easily exposed.

The default Samba configuration does not require that a username and password be supplied to use a local or remote Linux printer. However, if you wish to limit access to the Samba printer share that you are creating, then you should peg a Linux user account to it. In that case, it is advisable to create a specific Linux user account (such as printuser) to isolate your regular passwords. In another window use the `useradd printuser` to add the new user. Enter a password for the printuser with the `passwd printuser` command. Once you have added the new user, click the OK button.

You need to enter the network name of the Samba server in the Hostname of Printer Server box; you can optionally enter the IP address too. The Printer Name is the Samba share name that you want the printer to be known as. Enter the printuser and password in the User and Password boxes respectively. Next, use the Select menu to choose the printer type. Figure 9-6 shows the entries for the printer LJ5_myoffice (this is a printer on the model network described in Chapter 6).

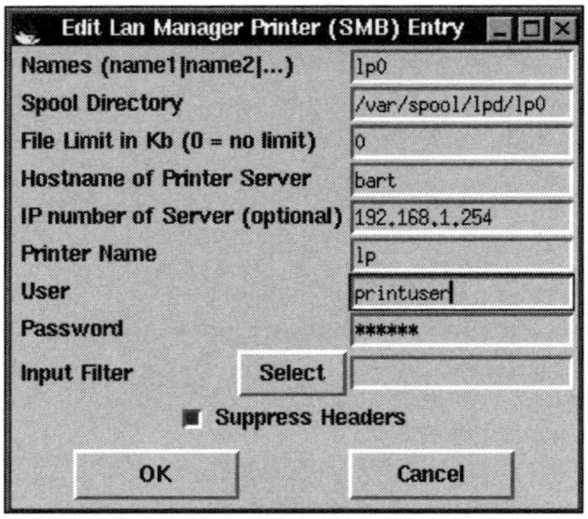

Figure 9-6: The Samba printer LJ5_myoffice

Test your new printer by printing out the text and Postscript files from the Test menu in the RHS Linux Print System Manager window. Alternatively, you can use the lpr program to manually print from the command line.

lpr /etc/printcap

The text file should now be printed. You can try a more complex job by using an application like Netscape (included on the companion CD-ROM).

Printing From a Windows Machine

You can access a local, remote, or Samba printers from your Windows computer. From the Windows desktop, open the Network Neighborhood. Next, double click the chivas icon. You should see the printer share lp (and the LJ5_myoffice share if you created it) in the window as shown in Figure 9-7.

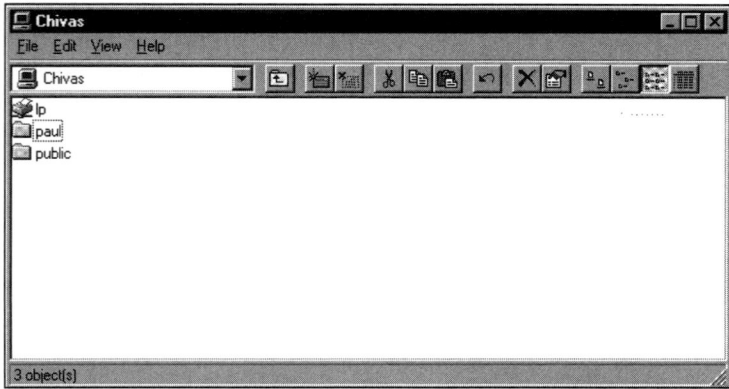

Figure 9-7: The lp printer share

Double click the lp icon. If your Windows machine does not already have a driver for the printer installed, then it prompts you to enter the driver and, if necessary, supply the software. Otherwise you should see the Windows print queue window for the remote Linux printer as shown in Figure 9-8. If you click the File menu, then you have the choice of making the printer your default printer.

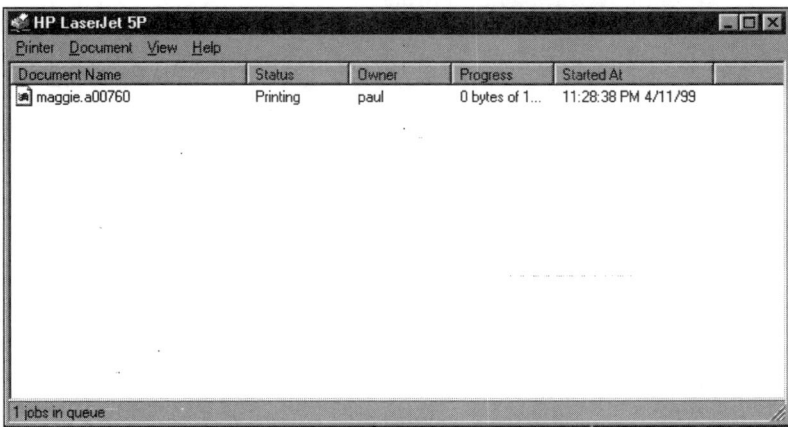

Figure 9-8: The Windows lp printer share

Any print jobs that you send to this queue are displayed in the window until they are sent to the Linux server. You can connect your Windows computer to as many printers as you set up on the Linux server or servers.

Troubleshooting

If you are having problems printing to a local printer, then first check that the printer cable is in good condition and attached properly. If your printer appears to be the problem, then first check that the power cable is connected and that the power is on. Next check that there is paper available and that the printer is not jammed.

Check that the lpd daemon is running and use the lpc program to check the status of the printer queue. Form the lpc> prompt enter the stat command and you see the status of all the queues (you can also use the lpq command from the command line to see the queue status). You can enter the restart all command to possibly get a stuck queue going again. Consult the lpd and lpc man pages.

If you are having problems using a remote printer, then use the troubleshooting techniques described in Chapter 6 to make sure that your network is working. Next, use the tips described in the previous chapters if another Linux machine is acting as the remote printer server. If you have a network printer, then check it for problems;

many printers now have fairly complete network configuration controls on their front panels.

If you are having trouble getting a Samba printer share to work, then first use the `testprns` command. It tells you if there are any problems with the printer shares in the `/etc/smb.conf` file.

The Samba troubleshooting techniques discussed in Chapter 8 apply for Samba printer shares too. If you have problems getting it to work, then consult Chapter 8 to make sure that the underlying Samba system is working.

Summary

This chapter describes how to set up your Linux server as a print server. It shows how to configure both local and remote printers. It also extended the discussion of Samba to printers.

- ◆ An introduction to the Linux printer daemon `lpd` is given. It's responsible for knowing when a print job has been submitted. It also must communicate with the printer being accessed and transmit the information to be printed. The `/etc/printcap` configuration file controls how `lpd` interacts with the printer(s) that it controls.

- ◆ A description of using a local printer is given. A local printer is attached—usually through the parallel printer port—directly to the Linux server. It can be configured via the RHS Linux Print System Manager or by manually editing the `/etc/printcap` file.

- ◆ A description of using a remote printer is given. A remote printer can be attached to another Linux server or directly connected to a network. It can be configured via the RHS Linux Print System Manager or by manually editing the `/etc/printcap` file.

- ◆ A description for using a Samba printer is given. A Samba print share can be configure by using the RHS Linux Print System Manager or by manually editing the `/etc/smb.conf` file. A Samba print share can access either a local or remote printer.

- ◆ A description of using Windows computers to access Linux printers via Samba is given. You use the Printer Manager to browse and then connect to the Linux printers. You can make a Samba printer your default printer if desired.

- ◆ An introduction to troubleshooting techniques is given. Troubleshooting Samba print shares is no different than troubleshooting Samba shares as discussed in Chapter 8. Troubleshooting locally and remote printers is a matter of checking the connecting cables or the network.

Chapter 10

Automating Network-wide Backups

IN THIS CHAPTER

- Introducing the advantages of automated, networked based backups
- Introducing the Arkeia backup software
- Installing the Arkeia software
- Configuring Arkeia backups
- Monitoring your backups
- Troubleshooting backup problems

THE PROCESS OF MAKING local backups is introduced in Chapter 6. Making local backups is a complex process because although the mechanics are important, the human factors are even more so. Managing the whole process at the minimum requires a disproportionate amount of your time as a reluctant system administrator.

The solution to your time management problem is an automated, network-based, client-server backup system. Until recently such software was either very expensive or unavailable on Linux. However, there are now numerous companies vying for your business. One such company, Knox Software produces a network backup product called Arkeia 4.0. Their system works on platforms such as Linux and Windows and is included on the CD-ROM.

 Another backup system is called BRU2000. It's made by Enhanced Software Technologies and more information about it can be found at: http://www.estinc.com. The `taper` program also provides another backup system, and comes as part of the Red Hat distribution.

Introducing Arkeia

Arkeia 4.0 is based on the client-server model. The Arkeia server controls the backup media and the backup schedule. The media can be anything from simple floppy disk(s), disk file(s), a single tape device or a tape library. The schedule can be daily, weekly or monthly; and a backup can be the total file system(s) or only files that have changed since the last backup. A client is any machine that you want to have backed upand the the server can be a client to itself.

Tape libraries, also known as autoloaders or jukeboxes, combine one or more tape drives, multiple tape slots, and a robotic arm mechanism to transfer the tapes from the slots to a drive. The whole system is generally contained within a simple box with a door on the front. (The biggest libraries have an slot for inserting and removing individual tapes without opening the front door.) Tape libraries are generally connected to their server but can also be connected by other methods.

The Arkeia backup server maintains indexes (databases) of what client backups have been done and where they exist. The indexes allow you to interactively browse the existing backups. Additionally, the indexes keep track of which tapes were used for each backup. This relieves you of the burden of keeping manual logs of the data located on each tape. You can use the browser to retrieve any backups via a GUI.

Both the backup server and client agents run daemons. The server daemons are responsible for starting the scheduled backups, informing the client daemons to start their backups, and maintaining the backup indices.

The server maintains a schedule of what to back up and when. When the server determines that a client has reached its scheduled backup time, the server daemon communicates with the client daemon to initiate the backup. The two sides manage the transfer of the data corresponding to the file systems being backed up across the network. The data is received by the server and written to the storage media.

Knox Software allows their software to be downloaded from their Web site to help you facilitate upgrades and patches and you can also download a time-limited demo or a home-use shareware version.

Knox Software Corp has provided a demo version of Arkeia (with a limited use license). They provide three RPM packages that run under Linux, including a client, server, and X Window interface. They also provide a Windows client that is packaged in a Zip format. All of the Arkeia software is included on the companion CD-ROM in the /mnt/cdrom/IDG/Arkeia directory.

Knox Software maintains a web site at www.knox-software.com, which provides general information about the company. More information on their Arkeia product can be found at www.arkeia.com.

Installing Arkeia on the Linux Server

The installation process is simplified by the use of the RPM format. You need at least 50MB of free space on the file system that you install it on.

In order to install Arkeia on your Linux machine, login as root, mount the companion CD-ROM, and run the following commands:

```
rpm -ivh /mnt/cdrom/arkiea-client*
rpm -ivh /mnt/cdrom/arkiea-server*
rpm -ivh /mnt/cdrom/arkiea-gui*
```

Most of the files are stored into the /usr/knox directory. The Arkeia manuals are stored into the /usr/doc/arekeia-server/html directory and can be viewed with your browser.

TIP The FSSTND suggests that all third party software be installed in the /usr/local directory. However, to keep it simple, I will let the software installed in its default location. If you want to follow the FSSTND guidelines, I suggest first creating the /usr/local/knox directory and then creating a soft link to ln -s /usr/local/knox /usr/knox and finally installing the RPM packages.

Configuring the Arkeia Server

To understand Arkeia you need to understand its underlying philosophy. The philosophy is to break down the backup process into component parts, which are then used as building blocks to 'build' your backup. By decomposing the backup process into parts, system flexibility and scalability are achieved. The parts are called the *Drive(s)*, *Drivepack*, *Tape Pools*, *Tapes*, *Savepacks*, and *Libraries*, respectively, and they are configured by the Server Administration GUI.

Server Administration

The *server administration screen* is the central control system for Arkeia, and the place where all other components are reached. This screen, broken down into four major areas, includes system menus, server/job status, message area, and the icon bar. The *system menu* area allows you to access all features and function, while the *icon bar* provides shortcuts to the most frequently used functions. The *server/job status* area, (center of the screen), shows the backup server you are attached to, user id/user class, and the current date and time. Additionally, it shows all active backup or restoration jobs, and when nothing is running, it indicates that. The *message area* shows general system status messages.

Drives management

The *Drive Management* component is used to logically define the read/write device(s), (typically the tape drive), to Arkeia. The Drive Management screen allows you to define one or more tape drives according to its specific characteristics, as well as providing the connection between Arkeia and the tape drive(s). By using logical drive definitions, Arkeia refers to the tape drive by its own internal logical name without needing to know how it is defined by the operating system. This allows you to change the drive definition, if required, without changing any other Arkeia settings.

Drivepack

The Drivepack is used to group one or more tape drives into a single processing group, which allows Arkeia to determine how many drives to use during a backup. On a system with one tape drive, this isn't important since the drive can only be used for one task at a time. However, on a backup server with multiple tapes drives, or with libraries that have multiple tape drives, this feature lets you easily perform independent operations (like simultaneous backups and restores) very easily. For example, on a backup server with a library that contains 4 tape drives, a drivepack can be defined with just two of the four drives leaving the other two drives available for other backups. When the backups run, only the two drives in the drivepack will be used, which leaves the other two drives available for performing restore operations. Because of its multi-processing design, Arkeia can simultaneously backup data from one client while restoring data to a different client.

Savepack

The Savepack concept specifies which client machines, file system(s), or individual files are to be backed up.

When you configure a Savepack, you might tell the Arkeia server that you want to backup XYZ files on client C. The savepack concept is meant to provide the necessary flexibility to backup a diverse network of computers, which allows you to back up several client-related computers as a single unit. Your grouping could be anything from all machines in the company, to just those in a certain department or floor.

Pools Management

The Pools Management screen is used to define a general purpose storage pool. A pool is the set of one or more tapes, and so by using separate tape pools, you can control where your data is saved. For example, you might perform a total backup once a week and an incremental backup each other night during the week. By using different pools, you can assign different retention periods to the backup. This allows you to retain, and keep valid, your total backup for say 12 months while letting the incremental backups expire after just one month. Tape pools can be used to separate data in whatever fashion makes sense for your company. A default 'scratch' pool is provided and can be used to hold tapes in reserve in case you run out logical definitions in your regular pools.

Dividing your tape volumes between pools can also separate the types of data by the person who generates the data. This generally makes sense in several ways. One way is computers used for different tasks generally generate different amounts of data. For instance, if you use your Linux machine as a file server to your Windows machines, then your Linux server probably will need to store much more data than the client Windows machines. By creating different pools, you can assign more volumes to the server pools than your client pools. When you advance to the point of using tape libraries, this capability becomes advantageous. Because a library has a fixed number of slots you can put more tape in the more heavily used pools than the lesser used ones. Thus, the tape library doesn't run out of tapes as frequently as if it had only one pool of tapes.

Tapes Management

The Tapes Management screen is where you create the logical definitions of the tapes that will be used during backup and restore operations. Again, Arkeia uses logical definitions of the tapes so that the backup and restore processes don't have to consider the underlying attributes of the media.

Libraries Management

Libraries combine volumes into either actual tape libraries or virtual ones. A tape library is a device that, under control of the backup software, automatically mounts one tape from a selection of many tapes into a tape drive. A virtual library mimics the action of a tape library. but creates volumes on a disk drive, instead of on tapes. Using virtual libraries is a good way to experiment and learn about making backups. Arkeia can select volumes from both real and virtual libraries.

The System

When the Savepacks, the Drivepacks and Pools are combined by Arkeia, you are able to automatically backup almost any size network. The packs and pools can be used to build both interactive and scheduled backups. Once the component parts are built, the detailed administration is taken care of by the Arkeia and your function becomes the much more high level one of monitoring the process. You need to make sure that previous night's backups ran successfully and if not then either re run them or troubleshoot the cause. You also need to maintain the system by supplying new and recycled tapes but the worry of keeping track of the individual files on the individual tapes is removed.

Creating a Null Backup

The Arkeia configuration documentation recommends configuring a null device to begin with. This is a good idea because it eliminates the need to deal with actual devices and their messy details, thereby letting you focus on overall system installation and configuration. It's also an excellent way to learn the system. A null device in this case means the Linux device /dev/null. This is a standard mechanism that UNIX systems send output to when the output is not to be saved or otherwise acted upon. The binary stream copied to the /dev/null file is simply discarded.

You can obtain help information at any time by clicking the information icon in the extreme upper left of the Arkeia GUI. It provides help related to the window that you are currently viewing.

To start, login as root and start X Window if it's not already running. Run the following command to start the Arkeia GUI:

/usr/knox/bin/arkx

When you install the arkeia-gui RPM it installs the shell script /usr/bin/ARKEIA. You can start the GUI by entering ARKEIA from the command line.

Next you'll see the introduction window as shown in Figure 10-1. Please note that in the Arkeia interface, the green checkmark button serves the same purpose as Windows' "OK" button—it indicates that you want to accept what you've entered in the window and move on. The red "X" button is the same as a Windows "Cancel" button—it indicates that you want to close the window and discard your changes.

Chapter 10: Automating Network-wide Backups

Figure 10-1: The Welcome to Arkeia window

The first time that you start the arkx GUI there is no Arkeia based password for the root set yet. Leave the password field blank this time and click on the checkmark button. The next window is the server administration window shown in Figure 10-2.

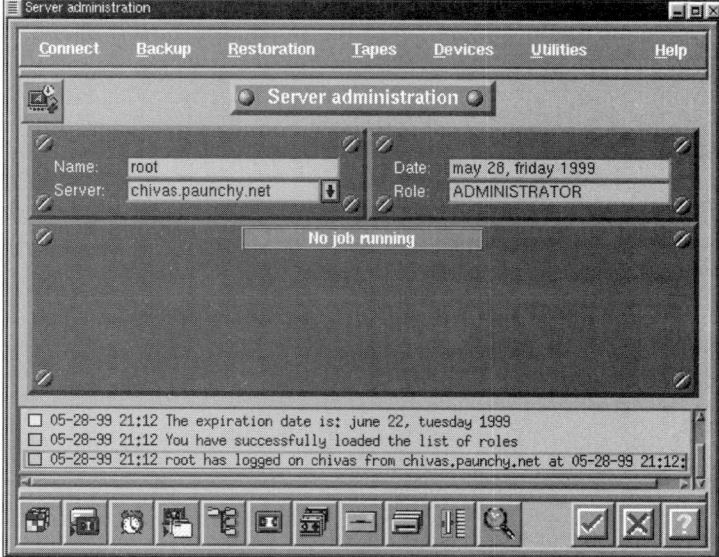

Figure 10-2: The Server administration window

Now is a good time to set a password for the Arkeia root user, which is different from the Linux root user. You should make the Arkeia root user's password different from the Linux root user; this permits other users to manage the Arkeia system without knowing the Linux root password. Click on Utilities → Users Management and you should see the user root displayed in the right half of the window. Click it and control is passed to the Users management window. Click the root user with the right mouse key and select the change password option (click with the left key on that item to select it). Leave the old password blank; enter the new password in the in the new password field, and enter the same password in the Confirm password field. Click the checkmark and your password becomes active. Exit from the Users management window and control returns to the Server administration window.

CREATE A NULL DRIVEPACK

Back in the Server administration window click on the Devices → Drives management. The Drives management window shown in Figure 10-3 is displayed.

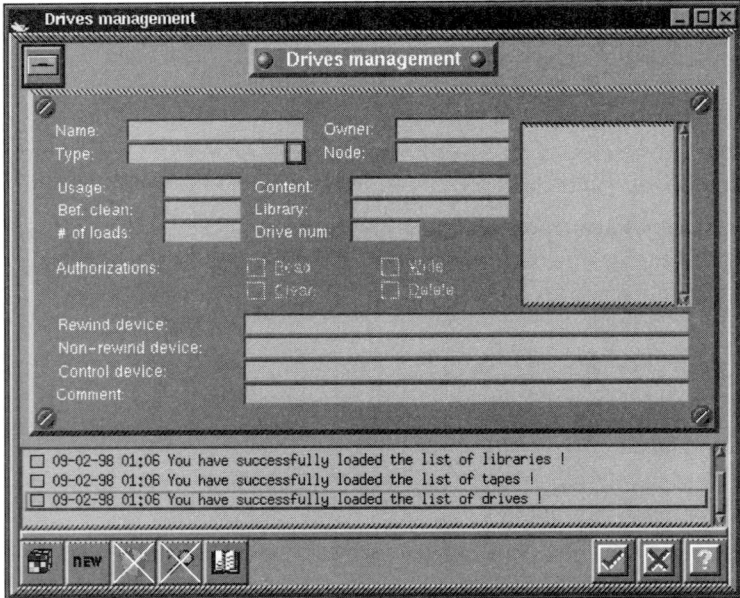

Figure 10-3: The Drives Management window

Click on the New button near the lower left hand of the window. A window similar to the Drives Management window is displayed. Fill in the entry field items: use the name NullDrive for the drive name, NULL for the drive type, and /dev/null for the devices, as shown in Figure 10-4.

Chapter 10: Automating Network-wide Backups

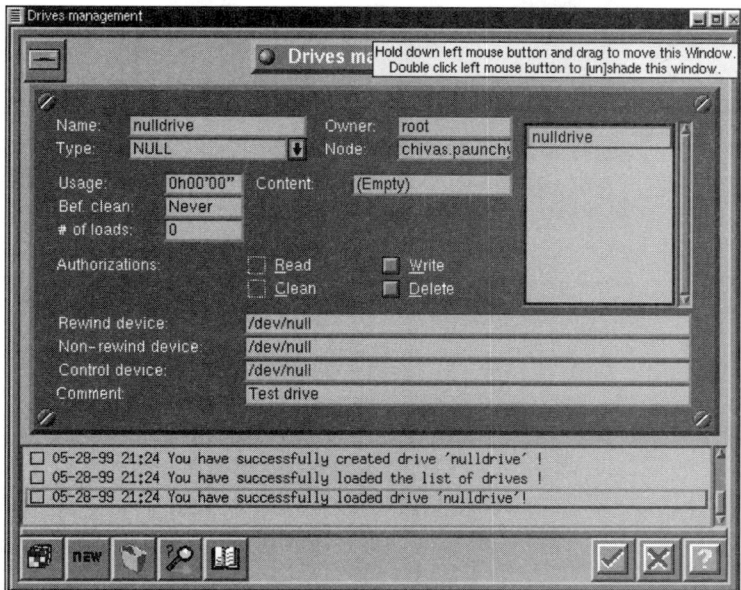

Figure 10-4: The completed Drives Management window

The information entered in this window is:

- **Name:** The name that you want to call the device.

- **Type:** The device type of the drive that you are using. In this case it is a NULL device, which is not an actual device.

- **Rewind, Non-rewind,** and **Control** devices: The device files are found in the /dev directory. When using a tape drive or a tape library, the rewind device specifies that the tape gets rewound after every access to it. The non-rewind device, of course, does not rewind it. The control device specifies the communication channel (usually a SCSI device) to the tape library robotic device.

- The **Authorizations** section enables you to configure the drive as a read, write, clean and delete capable device. Again, this is really unnecessary because nothing is being saved to the device, but it is indicative of what options you have to set for a real backup device.

Click the checkmark twice and you return to the Server administration window. Click Devices → Drivepacks. The Drivepacks window is opened as shown in Figure 10-5.

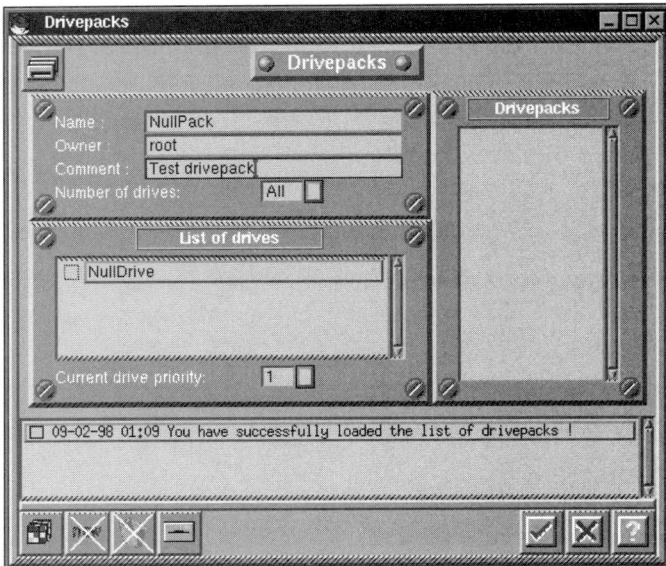

Figure 10-5: The Drivepacks window

Click the New button. Enter the drivepack name NullPack and click on the NullDrive drive as shown in Figure 10-6. (Clicking on the NullDrive drive button associates that drive with the new Drivepack.)

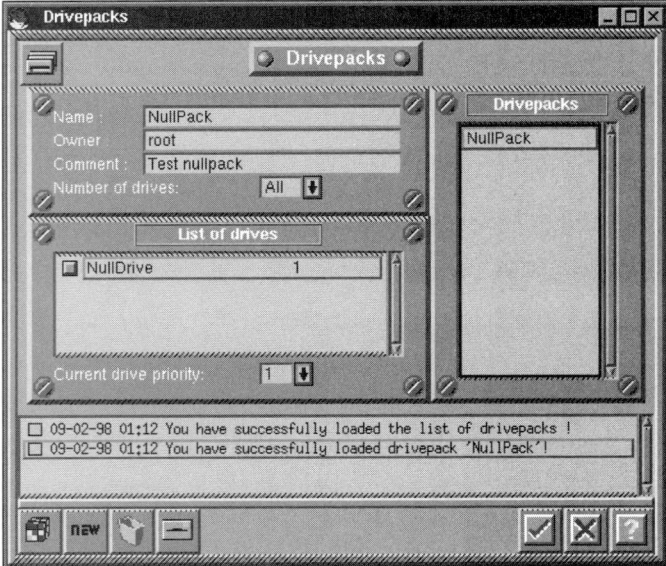

Figure 10-6: The completed Drivepacks window

Click on the checkmark again and the NullPack Drivepack shows up in the Drivepacks window at the right of the screen. Click on the checkmark once more and control is returned to the Server administration window.

CREATE A NULL POOL

The next step is to configure a tape pool. Click on Tapes → Pools management. The window shown in Figure 10-7 is displayed.

Figure 10–7: The Pools Management window

Click on the New button and the Pool creation window is activated.

Enter a name, optional comments as shown in Figure 10-8. The name NullPool is used for this example.

Figure 10–8: The completed Pool creation window

Click the checkbox in the Pool creation window and you go back to the Pool management window. Next, click on the checkbox in the Pools management window and control returns to the Server administration window.

You need to create a null tape for the null pool. Click on the Tapes → Tapes management menus. You'll get the Tapes management window shown in Figure 10-9.

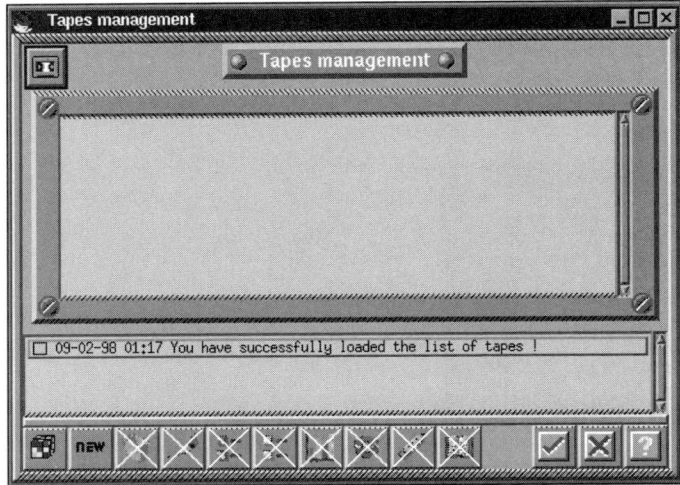

Figure 10-9: The Tapes management window

Click the New button to get the Create tapes window.

Because multiple tapes are used, the tape name that you specify becomes the prefix for all the tapes that you use for your backups. That is, if you use a tape name of XYZ, then tapes 1 through 3 are labeled as XYZ1, XYZ2, and XYZ3. In this case, the name (prefix) of NullTape is used and the five virtual tapes used in this example are labeled as NullTape1 through NullTape5.

Leave the Bar Code field empty. For this example, enter 1 and 5 respectively for the First number and Last number fields. Specify the NULL tape type by pulling down the submenu in the Type field.

You must also associate tapes with a pool. To do so, click the down arrow next to the Current pool field, and select the NullPool. The Create tapes window is shown in Figure 10-10 with the information entered as described.

Chapter 10: Automating Network-wide Backups 219

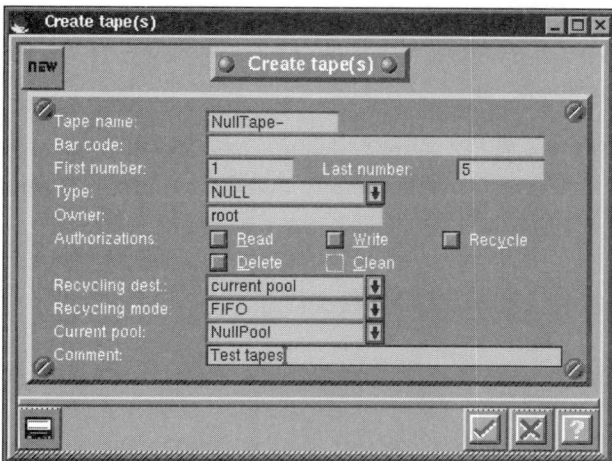

Figure 10-10: The completed Create tape(s) window

Click on the checkbox to save the settings. The Tapes management window is returned as shown in Figure 10-11. It now contains the 5 tapes, from NullTape-1 through NullTape-5, that you just created. Click checkmark to return to Server administration window.

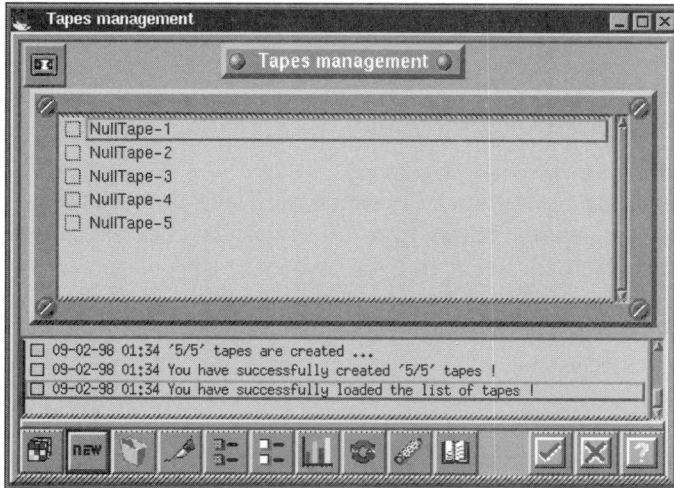

Figure 10-11: The Tapes management window

CREATE A SAVEPACK

Back in the Server management window, select Backup → Savepacks. The Savepacks management window is displayed.

Create a new Savepack by clicking on the New button. A window appears asking for the name of the Savepack. Enter Testsp as the name for this Savepack and click on the checkmark. The Savepack management window shows your new Savepack as shown in Figure 10-12.

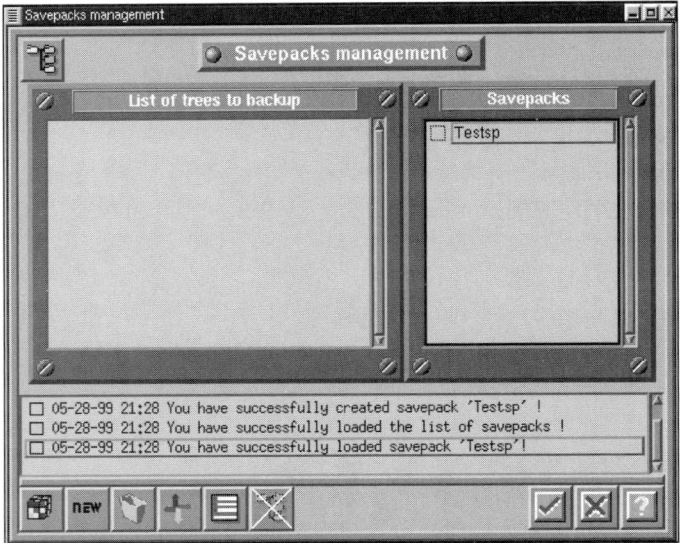

Figure 10-12: The Savepacks management window

The next step is to associate Testsp with a file system(s) to backup. Click the button to the left of the Testsp menu (the button turns orange). Next, click the navigator button, fourth button from the left (with the arrows) at the bottom of the Savepack management window.

The Select via navigator window is displayed as shown in Figure 10-13. This is a graphical display of your file system.

Chapter 10: Automating Network-wide Backups 221

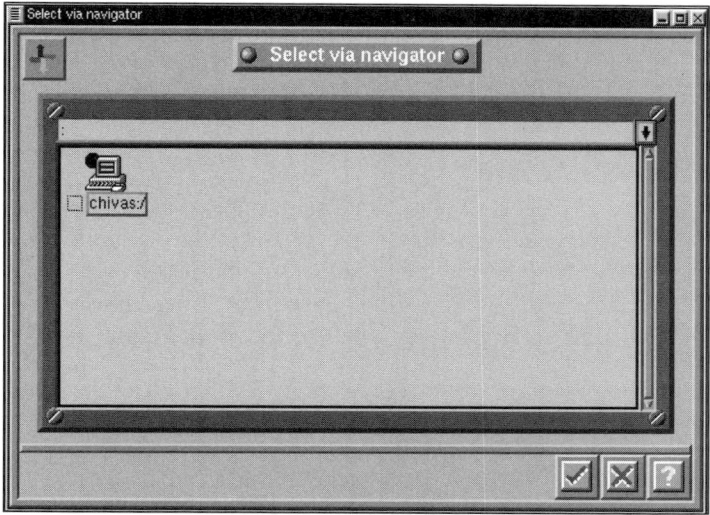

Figure 10-13: The Select via navigator window

If you click on the button to the left of the machine name chivas, then the entire machine is selected to be backed up. Otherwise, if you double click on the machine icon then you see a display of your root level directories. For this example, the /etc directory is chosen to be backed up by clicking on the selection box to the left of the /etc directory icon as shown in Figure 10-14.

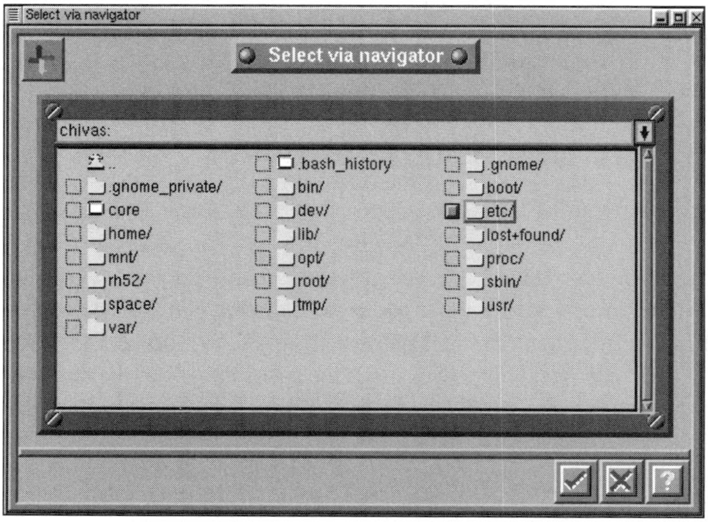

Figure 10-14: Choosing the files to backup

Click the checkmark and control is returned to the Savepack management window. This window now contains the files to be backed up in the List of trees to backup subwindow. Click the checkmark and you go back to the Server administration window.

MAKE AN INTERACTIVE BACKUP

Now that you have set up a Drivepack, a Pool, and a Savepack you can test your system by running an interactive backup. Remember that nothing is going to be backed up because the null device discards the backup data that it is fed.

From the Server administration window click Backup → Interactive backup menus. Then you'll enter the Interactive backup window shown in Figure 10-15.

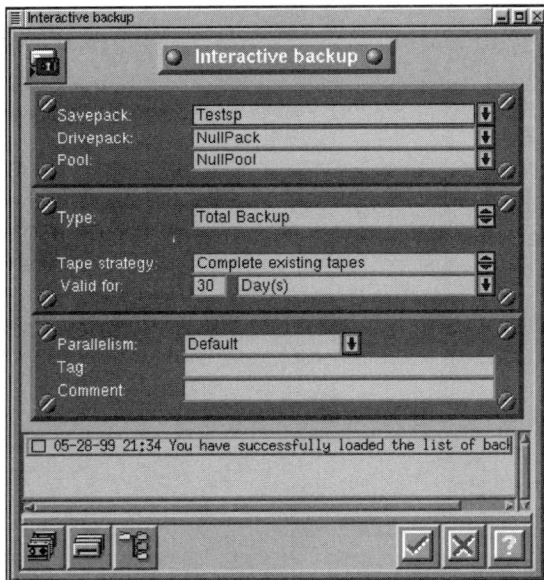

Figure 10–15: The Interactive backup window

Now you'll see the names of the Savepack, Drivepack, and Pool that you just configured. Other information such as the backup type is displayed too. Later, when you have other backups defined you can select them from this window.

To test the system click the checkbox. If everything is set up properly, then you see the status window shown in Figure 10-16.

Chapter 10: Automating Network-wide Backups

Figure 10-16: Arkeia status window

The speed in megabytes per second is displayed prominently, along with other progress indicators. You have the option of stopping the backup by clicking the Stop backup button in the lower left hand of the screen.

 One informative aspect of running a null backup is that it gives you a good indication of the maximum throughput of your machine. Since the data is not being written to any mechanical device, the speed that you see is most likely the maximum that your computer is capable of. Everything happening on the storage side (data is, of course, being read from a mechanical disk) is electronic with no slow mechanical tape or disk drives slowing up the process.

SCHEDULE AN AUTOMATIC BACKUP

Next, try scheduling a backup. From the Server management window click Backup → Periodic backup. The Periodic backup window is displayed, as shown in Figure 10-17.

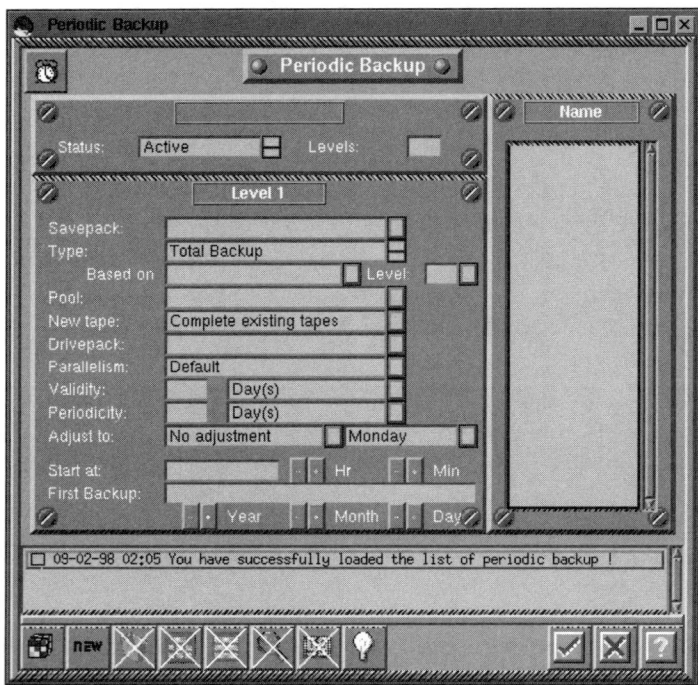

Figure 10-17: The Periodic backup window

To create a periodic backup click on the new button. Enter the name NullBackup for the new backup.

 **TIP** Arkeia provides a periodic backup assistant to help you create an automatic backup. From the : Server administration window, click on Help → Assistants → Periodic backup. The assistant walks you through the process of setting up a schedule by giving some predefined examples.

Click the checkbox and control returns to the Periodic backup window.

You need to specify the Savepack, Pool, and Drivepack to use. You also can change the default start time to any time that you want. Click on the plus (+) and minus (-) buttons on the Start and First backup menus to change the start time.

In this example the Savepack, Pool, and Drivepack values are Testsp, NullPool and NullPack respectively. Fill in the subwindow in the Periodic backup window as shown in Figure 10-18.

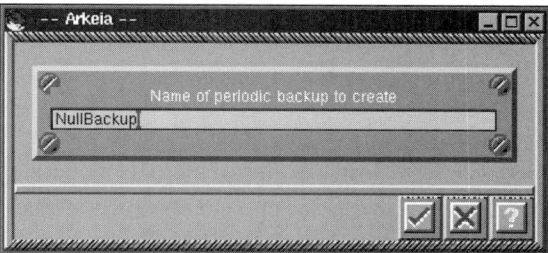

Figure 10-18: Creating a periodic backup

 You can optionally change from a total backup to an incremental one (a total backup copies every file, while the incremental backup copies files created or changed since the last full backup - or variations on that theme). Consult the Arkeia documentation for information on these and other optional periodic backup topics.

Using Real Backup Media

Running a backup to a null device is an excellent method for learning the Arkeia basics and testing the software. The configuration process requires some attention and patience; but, if you set up a null backup two or three times, you'll begin to understand how things fit together. The knowledge that you've gained can now be used to create a real backup.

Arkeia provides the ability to use a disk drive as the backup media. The disk can be a floppy or Zip disk as well as a hard disk (it is possible to use other types of disks as well). When a disk is used it is referred to as a file. Under Arkeia, a file is an abstraction for a physical storage medium. (Most backups today make use of tapes. So the file concept is added to provide a generic method for accessing a disk.)

Configuring a Zip Drive Backup

The following example makes use of a Zip disk (sometimes referred to as a Zip diskette). Zips do not store much data compared to DAT or DLT tapes, but can be useful for small operations and are certainly well suited for learning the Arkeia system. They are fairly common and thus provide another learning tool that almost everyone will have access to.

You can also use a hard drive to store data. A hard drive is generally not a good place to save long term data, but it does provide another good mechanism to learn how to set up your backups.

In some cases, a hard drive is a good backup alternative. For instance, a medium size retail chain in New Mexico, with 70 stores, uses a UNIX server for each store, with an extra hard drive installed in each machine for backups. The backups are made daily and are recycled on a monthly basis. In this case, hard disks work better than tapes because they are cheaper and do not require as much maintenance. The backups are made with a simple tar command that is executed from cron. Arkeia would make sense for this retail chain's circumstances because it has more functionality than tar and is inexpensive.

The previous example showed almost every graphical menu that you'll encounter while running Arkeia. The method is used to make the example easier to follow the first time. The following example, however, is given in list form without any illustrations.

MOUNT A ZIP DISK

Arkeia requires that a mounted file system be used in conjunction with the File media type. For this example you must mount a blank Zip disk.

Login as root. Insert a Zip disk into the drive and enter the following command:

```
mount /dev/hdb /mnt/zip
```

The /dev/hdb is used in this example. An IDE Zip drive device can be /dev/hda, /dev/hdb, /dev/hdc or /dev/hdd

If you want to use a DOS formatted Zip disk, then use the following command.
```
mount -t msdos /dev/hdb4 /mnt/zip
```
To use a floppy disk the command should be:

```
mount /dev/fd0 /mnt/floppy
```

CREATE A FILE DRIVE

Open the Drives management window, then from the Server administration window, click Devices → Drives management. Create the new drive called File Drive. From the Drives management window, click New, enter the name File Drive, and the type FILE. Click the checkbox and the new drive name appears in the menu on the right. Click the checkbox again to return to the Server administration window.

CREATE A DRIVEPACK

Open the Drives management window, then from the Server administration window click Devices → Drivepacks. Create the new drive pack called File Drive. From the Drivepacks window, click New, enter the name FilePack, and click the FileDrive in the List of drives menu. Click the checkbox and the new drivepack name appears in the menu on the right. Click the checkbox again to return to the Server administration window.

CREATE A NEW POOL

Open the Pools management window, then from the Server administration window click tapes → pools management. Create the new file pool called File Pool. From the Pools management window, click New, enter the name File Pool, and click on the checkbox. Click the checkbox in the Pools Management window to return to the Server administration window.

ADD TAPES TO POOL

Open the Tapes management window. Then, from the Server administration window, click Tapes → Tapes management.

Open the Create Tape(s) window. From the Tapes Management window, click the New button and enter the following values in the Create tape(s) window:

- Tape name: FileTape-
- Bar code: /mnt/floppy (/mnt/zip for a Zip drive)
- First number: 1
- Last number: 5 (Five simulated tapes for a Zip drive)
- Type: FILE 20MB (100MB for a Zip drive)
- Current pool: FilePool

Click the checkbox button. If you are using a tape drive or library that allows bar codes, then you would specify it here. Bar code labels can be placed on tapes so that they can be identified and inventoried automatically. In this example, however, the bar code field is used to specify the device being used as the back up media. No bar code is used in this case. You should see five tapes in your pool corresponding to 20MB of space on your Zip disk.

 If you list the contents of your floppy disk (ls /mnt/floppy), then you should see directories corresponding to those new files (/mnt/floppy/FileTape-1, through /mnt/floppy/FileTape-5).

CREATE A FILE LIBRARY

A file library is not used for a null drivepack. However, any backup that uses the file drive/file tape abstractions, requires that a library be defined. The file library is used as a virtual library to facilitate the file tape/file drive concept. When you use a disk drive (floppy, Zip, hard disk) as your storage media, the directories appear as a library containing individual tapes. (Backups done using a standalone tape drive, do not need a library to be defined. If you have a tape library for your tape drive, then you will need to define and configure the library prior to doing any backups.)

Open the Libraries management window. From the Server administration window, click Devices → Libraries management.

Create the new library called FileLib. From the Libraries management window click new button, enter the name FileLib and click on FILE in the Type menu. Click the checkbox and the new library name appears in the menu on the right.

Click the Drive Options button, which is the sixth button from the left on the bottom. The Drive of library: FileLib window should now appear.

Click the Attach Drive button which is in the lower, left corner of the window and the Attach drive in library: FileLib window activates.

Click the checkbox and Arkeia attaches, or associates, the Zip disk drive (FileDrive) with the library.

Click the checkbox button and control returns to the Libraries management window.

Click the Slot usage button which is the seventh button from the left (to the right of the Attach drive button) and the Slots in library: the FileLib window should appear. There should be 100 slots listed each with the No Tape indicator set in the Tape field. Click the button in the Slot field for each of the first five slots. (If your X Window color mapping is correct, then the buttons should turn orange when set.)

Click the Set tape button which is at the lower, left hand corner of the window. The Tapes management window should activate with the tapes (FileTape-1 through FileTape-5).

Select tapes 1 through 5 by clicking the button to the left of each tape name; you can also use the Select All button which is the fifth button from the left at the bottom of your window. If your X Window color mapping is correct, then the buttons should turn orange when set.

Click the checkbox button.

You now return to the Slots in library: FileLib window and should see FileTape-1 through FileTape-5 in the Slots in library: FileLib window (they should also be listed as `/mnt/zip/FileTape-1`, `/mnt/zip/FileTape-2` in the Voltag subwindow).

Click the checkbox to return to the Library management window and again to return to the Server administration window.

CREATE A SAVEPACK

Open the Savepack management window. From the Server administration window click Backup → Savepacks.

Create the new Savepack called FileSave, and then from the Savepacks management window click on New, enter the name FileSave and click the checkbox.

Attach a file system(s) to the savepack. From the savepacks management window click the box next to the FileSave item in the savepacks submenu (the box should become orange). Click the Navigator button which is the fourth button from the left on the bottom of the screen.

Remember that before you selected to back up your server's entire file system by clicking the button to the left of your server icon (chivas in this case). However, since in this example we're using a floppy, it's not possible. Instead, double click on the chivas icon and you'll see all the top-level directories displayed. Click on the `/etc` directory and then on the checkbox and control returns to the savepacks management window.

Click the checkbox and the Server administration window returns.

MAKE A TEST BACKUP

Open the Interactive backup window. From the Server administration window, click Backup → Interactive.

The Interactive backup window appears. The original Testsp hould appear in the Savepack submenu. Click on that menu and select the FileSave Savepack.

Click the checkbox and the Arkeia window. It displays the information on your backup as before. The backup should run quickly with information on the results appearing at the bottom of the window.

Please take note that when configuring the interactive backup you have the choice of associating different savepacks with different drivepacks and also different pools. This provides you with a flexible way of using your resources.

Using a SCSI Tape Drive or Tape Library

To make better use of this backup system, you are most likely going to need a device(s) capable of storing gigabytes of information. The most common media is a DAT tape drive. They are briefly discussed in Chapter 6.

This book does not describe the process of using a DAT drive, or a real tape library, in any detail. The following paragraphs provide some information on how to find information on a DAT drive if you have one. It also points out what parts of the previous example you should change in order to accommodate such drives.

Short of purchasing a tape library, you can use a 4mm or 8mm DAT drive. They are generally SCSI devices. It is best to purchase a good SCSI controller to work with a DAT. (Technically, tapes used for data storage are referred to as DDS but are commonly referred to as DAT.)

If you want to use a SCSI DAT drive, then consult the `/usr/doc/HOWTO/HARDWAREHOWTO` for details on installing it. Linux comes with numerous SCSI drivers. Once installed and configured the DAT device shows up similar to `/dev/st0` or `/dev/st1`.

Arkeia provides installation and configuration information in its on-line documentation. Use your browser to look at the `file:/usr/doc/arkeiaserver-4.0.9/html/install/setup.htm` and `file:/usr/doc/arkeiaserver4.0.9/html/install/setup.htm` for detailed information on configuring Arkeia for DAT tapes, tape libraries and other devices.

Configuring a Windows Client

Arkeia has provided a Windows 95 client. It is stored in the `windows.zip` file in the `/mnt/cdrom/IDG/Arkeia` directory on the companion CD-ROM. To install the Windows client, log in as root, install the unzip program (gunzip does not work on .zip files) and unzip with the following commands:

```
rpm -ivh /mnt/cdrom/RedHat/RPMS/unzip*
mkdir /var/tmp/arkeia
cd /var/tmp/arkeia
unzip /mnt/cdrom/IDG/Arkeia/client
```

You could copy the unzipped files to your Windows machine and then run the installation program. However, a more elegant method is to leave a single set of files on the Linux server, mount that directory on your Windows computer, and then run the installation program. This method is efficient because you do not make multiple copies of the file. If you install this, or any program, on more than one machine, then you do not end up with copies on multiple machines.

Edit the `/etc/smb.conf` file by hand or with SWAT and add a share for the `/var/tmp` directory.

```
[Arkeia]
        path = /var/tmp/arkeia
        public = yes
```

From your Windows computer, mount the Arkeia share by opening your Network Neighborhood, double click on the Chivas icon and then double click the Arkeia share. You should see the `Setup.exe` program. Double click on that icon and the software installs itself. (You need to have the Microsoft Virtual Machine, available at `http://www.microsoft.com/java/vm/dlvm32.htm`, installed for the Java based Arkeia GUI to work under Windows 95 or Windows 98.) The MS Java VM must be installed before installing the Arkeia Windows client and GUI software.

Next, locate the Knox software submenu in the Start → Programs menu. Click on the Arkeia ... selection. The Arkeia server GUI, shown in Figure 10-19, is functionally the same as the Linux Server Administration window.

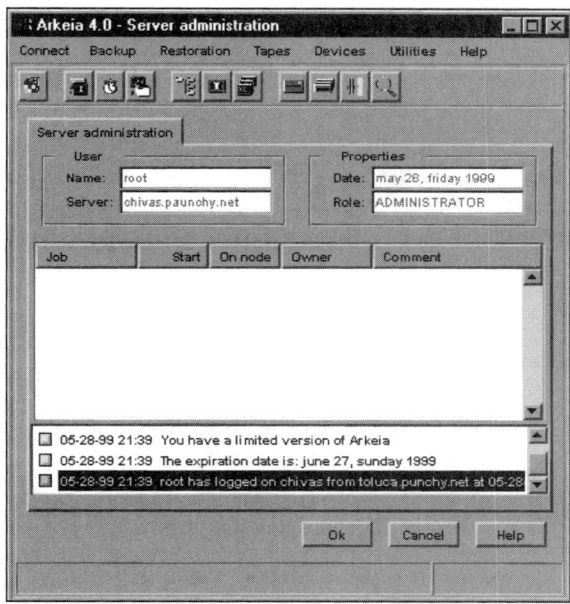

Figure 10-19: The Arkeia Windows Server administration window

Create a savepack for you Windows client. Use the same process as for creating a Linux savepack. Finally, go to the Interactive Backup and select the new savepack and one of the existing drivepacks. Click the OK button and the backup should start.

Restoring Data

You can restore data to a computer by using the Restoration → Restoration menu in the Server administration window. Double click the client that you want to restore.

The files and directories that have been backed up are displayed. Click on any or all of the icons that you want to restore. Click the checkbox and the Restoration window activates.

This window displays all the files and directories that are scheduled to be restored. It is often advisable to restore files and directories to a different location than they were originally stored on. This is because you often want manually sort through restored files to choose want you want to use; it is also good to restore to a temporary locations while you are learning the new system. Enter the new directory by entering the path name in the Redirection box towards the lower half of the window. You can also search for files by clicking on the Search button which is the 8th button from the left.

Click the checkbox and the restoration begins.

Troubleshooting

Arkeia is a sophisticated system. A full troubleshooting manual is beyond the scope of this book. However, this section provides an overview of the Arkeia system plus a few specific hints. By understanding the system as a whole, then it is easier to overcome problems when they occur.

Keep in mind that Knox Software maintains considerable documentation on their Web site in addition to the text provided on the companion CD-ROM. The Arkeia GUI also contains context sensitive help screens. You can obtain 30 days of free support by filling out their registration form on the http://www.arkeia.com/download.html page.

The Arkeia client-server backup system consists of three parts: the client, the server, and the interface GUI. The client daemon and server daemon can operate on the same machine as in the case of the backup server. The client can also operate on computers that are on the same network as the server.

When the Arkeia client is on a different machine than the server then you need to make sure that all the normal connectivity works. That is, if a client workstation can not communicate with the server (ping, telnet, etc.) then the backup will not work. If you are having problems making a backup work then make sure the network is okay before you look to the backup software as the problem.

The Arkeia server has five components that all need to work for backups to succeed. Arkeia uses the concept of Pools, Tapes, Drives, Drivepacks, and Savepacks. These components separate the hardware from the software. The computer(s) backups do not need to know anything about the underlying hardware that the data is to be stored to.

The Pool concept logically combines one or more backup media—such as DAT tapes—into a single object. Arkeia controls the object that maintains all the bookkeeping details on which volume(s) belong to it, which files and directories from which clients are contained on each volume and where that volumes can be found. A volume is an abstraction for physical media; a volume can be a tape, a disk file, a floppy file, a Zip file or any number of other devices.

When creating tapes of the File type care must be taken when creating tape in the Tape management window. The device, such as Zip drive, must be mounted and have a Linux ext2 file system. The value that you enter in the Bar code field in the Create tape(s) window must include the mount directory and the name of the simulated tape (for instance, `/mnt/zip/FileTape-`). Otherwise, the simulated tapes are created in the same directory as the mount directory. If you use the Bar code value of `/mnt/zip`, then the simulated tapes are created in the root directory file system as `/mnt/zip/FileTape-1`, `/mnt/zip/FileTape-2`, etc. In that case, your data is written to your hard disk and not the Zip disk.

Drivepacks link together one or more backup devices. It is another logical device. You must define at least one drive before you can create a drivepack.

Libraries define where a volume or volumes can be accessed. If you have a tape library, the library management system controls it. (A tape library is a device that combines multiple tapes, one or more tape drives and a robotic arm to load and unload the tapes, into a single case.) Otherwise, the library management system logically divides a volume such as a Zip disk into directories that mimic individual volumes in separate slots.

Savepacks combine the client's file systems to be backed up with a drivepack. A savepack makes it easy to make a client backup. For instance, to backup your server Chivas you simply specify that, for instance, the directory XYZ on Chivas uses drivepack W. You can then execute the Savepack manually or schedule it to run at some specific time.

The log files contain a good source of information that can be useful for debugging purposes. Click Utilities → Log management from the Server administration window and you are given a choice of five logs. The logs cover the backups finished, general information and the drives, tapes and restorations that you have done. Log information is displayed in all the windows that you access from the Server administration interface.

Once you have configured the four Arkeia systems, then it becomes a simple process to backup any computer with the software. You are divorced from having to execute, verify and maintain manual systems as you would with `tar`. Arkeia runs the show and you are left to monitor it and keep it fed with volumes.

If you have problems configuring the system or making backup, then there are several places that you can look for help. As mentioned there are numerous documents available to you - both locally (for instance, `file://usr/doc/arkeia-server-4.0.9/html/install/solving.htm`) and at the Arkeia web site. There is also the information that is displayed on the Server administration GUI. Arkeia also maintains several log files that can be accessed from the Server administration window by clicking on the Utilities → Log management menus.

Summary

This chapter provides you with the information to get a simple Arkeia client-server backup system working, with two examples highlighted. The first is trivial, but excellent for learning the basics of the system and how to get it working. The second is a real world example everyone should be able to get working. The more complex process of using a SCSI DAT tape drive system and even a robotic tape library is discussed in general terms. Other general topics such as scheduling are described.

- An introduction to the Arkeia client-server backup system is given. Arkeia is an automated system (it can also be run manually) that allows you to step back from the details of making backups.

- A description of its installation is given. Arkeia is contained on the companion CD-ROM and is in RPM format.

- A description of the configuration and operation of a null backup is given. This backup makes use of the Linux `/dev/null` device which exists solely in the mind of the operating system. The null backup writes to the null device which simply discards the data. This is the simplest method for verifying and learning the backup system.

- A description of the configuration and operation of a file backup is given. The file can be any kind of Linux disk drive. A floppy is used in this case because it's the only device that nearly every reader is guaranteed to have—the floppy can readily be Zip, hard disk, or other device. This example allows you to create actual backups and is a good way to practice. In some cases, it might be all that you need to use (I used a Zip drive for the daily backup of this manuscript).

- Most operations of any size require at least a single DAT tape drive. The details of doing so are not discussed in this book but the best places to research this are discussed. You should be able to configure a DAT, and even a tape library, if you use the examples and change the details to reflect the new equipment.

- A discussion of installing and configuring a Windows client is given. With this client you can backup you Windows machine to your Linux server.

- A discussion of the recover of data is given. Arkeia makes it a simple process to restore files and directories.

- A brief discussion of scheduling backups is given. Total backups are performed less frequently than the incremental ones. Incremental backups include files and directories that have changed since the total backup (incrementals can also be referenced to other incrementals). Total backups can be scheduled on various schedules. There are other scheduling operations that you are encouraged to investigate on your own.

◆ A general discussion of troubleshooting is given. Arkeia is a complex system to configure at times. Since it is beyond the scope of this book to discuss the many things that are interrelated, the general, overall logic is described. Arkeia also provides free help for 30 days if you register with them. They also provide considerable help systems both online and at their Web site.

There are many more functions that Arkeia can perform. You are encouraged to get the simple examples described in this chapter and then experiment with the more advanced features.

Part III

Connecting Your Network to the Internet

CHAPTER 11
Connecting to the Internet

CHAPTER 12
Creating a Simple Firewall

CHAPTER 13
Configuring a Linux E-mail Server

Chapter 11

Connecting to the Internet

IN THIS CHAPTER

◆ Learn how to connect to an Internet Service Provider

◆ Learn how to connect your entire network to the Internet

◆ Learn how to connect into your network via the phone system

◆ Configure a simple DNS server

◆ Learn how to troubleshoot your Internet connection

CONNECTING TO THE INTERNET from a single computer is the extent of the online experience for many people. That's the type of connection you use when you dial into an Internet Service Provider (ISP) from your home computer. The networks used by most large companies, institutions, and educational establishments are directly connected to the Internet via high speed, permanent connections. The term *direct* is used somewhat loosely for simplicity's sake. To get a more detailed and precise description of how networks are connected to the Internet please refer to a book that specializes in that subject. But for this discussion, think of the Internet as a single entity represented by your ISP.

Introducing Dial-Up Networking

Linux provides all the tools to connect your network to the Internet. The tools are Linux's general networking software, the *Point-to-Point Protocol* (PPP), the automated dial-up system (`diald`) and IP masquerading (`ipchains`). Add them all together and your network becomes part of the Internet—a full-fledged part with all the capabilities found in traditional, large institutions.

PPP is a protocol that piggybacks the IP protocol; PPP encapsulates IP and allows it to be sent over a serial line. When you use a modem to connect with another modem you have a *serial line connection* that is made over a regular telephone connection. PPP converts that serial phone connection into a complete, but not fast, Internet connection.

The `diald` software monitors the network you created in Chapters 1 and 7 for IP packets that want to go to the Internet. For instance, if you fire up Netscape Navigator and click on Search, then Navigator requests a connection to an external

IP address (the network configuration described in this book means any IP address that is not 192.168.1.*X*). When the `diald` program starts, it automatically creates a default route. The Netscape packet is routed by Linux to the default route; and then `Diald` sees it, picks up the modem, dials the ISP and establishes a PPP connection. All external packets can then find their way out and then back in via that connection. Your network is connected.

The `ipchains` system allows your private network's public IP addresses to work on the Internet. When you connect your individual Linux or Windows computer to the Internet via PPP without `ipchains`, that computer uses the single IP address that the ISP assigns to it. No other computer on your private network can use that address. However, by using `ipchains` your entire private network can share a single PPP address. Thus, each of your computers appear to the Internet as a valid IP address. All Internet traffic from your network is routed through your Linux gateway, which does the IP masquerading (also known as IP Network Address Translation, or NAT).

 There's an exception if you have a registered domain with valid IP addresses. In that case, IP masquerading is not necessary and your Linux gateway can simply route the packets back and forth to the Internet. However, IP masquerading can still be useful in that case because it provides extra security by hiding your real IP behind a temporary one.

Combine all three systems together and you get to connect your network to the Internet. The following sections describe the process for configuring these tools. Keep in mind that the description assumes that you use an ISP that can provide you with the information to configure the systems. If your ISP uses Linux servers then you most likely will not have problems.

Choosing an ISP

Choosing a reliable and technically astute ISP is the essential prelude to connecting to the Internet. ISP's are still pretty new as a business and it is difficult to separate the good from the bad. The more information that you can gather on your potential ISPs, the better chance you have of finding a good one.

Your potential ISP's web page is a good place to start looking for information. Try to assess how professionally they conduct their business and obtain their price and service information. The customer service and technical help that a company can offer is more important than their price. You should evaluate your ISP's level of professionalism as you would any other vendor that provides a service your company is going to rely on.

Talking to an ISP's technical support people is another good way to judge competence. This can be something of a chicken and egg dilemma because making a technical judgement at this stage in your technical development can be problematic. However, it should be possible to gain some idea of how they conduct their business and treat their customers.

The technical assistance that an ISP can give you is far more important than the price of their connection. Connecting to the Internet is not rocket science, but it can be difficult. Consider that any time that you spend sorting through the initial confusion of getting your connection working is money lost. Alternatively, any time spent waiting for an ISP to handle network outage or a cracker attack is also wasted.

High Speed Connections

There are several ways to obtain high speed Internet connections. The phone system connections discussed in this book reach up to 56 Kilobits per second (Kbps) of throughput (the amount of data passing over the wire) and should support a small operation if used judiciously. However, it is possible to multiply that speed by 5, 10, 20, and even 60 times if you are willing to pay for it. The technologies available for this include Frame Relay, ISDN, DSL, satellite, and cable modems. Frame Relay is universal in the United States and is available through the Baby Bells and many smaller companies. Satellites (which provide one and two-way connections) can work almost anywhere. The other technologies are available in some areas but not others. Please consult the World Wide Web (WWW) or your local ISP for more information.

Obtaining Network Information

Once you have selected an ISP, do your homework before attempting to connect your network. To make a PPP connection, you need to find out if you are going to be supplied with a dynamic or static IP address (dynamic address is by far the most common method today), what the dial-up phone number(s) are and what your PPP account password is. You will need this information to configure your software.

In addition you need to know what the prompt strings the PPP server uses. The `diald` program described in this chapter requires some specific information about the PPP server's prompt. If your ISP can provide you with the information, then great. If not, the `diald` software can make some reasonable guesses. If that doesn't work, then you can always determine the information yourself by using the manual configuration method described in the section "Manually Connecting to the Internet" later in this chapter.

Deciding on the Connection Type

The following sections describe several methods for establishing a PPP connection.

The Red Hat LinuxConf and Control Panel administration tools provide connection systems. They are automatic in the sense that they negotiate the dial-up process, as well as the authentication and kick off of the `pppd` daemon. However, they both need to be started and shutdown by you, the Linux user.

The `dip` program is completely manual (unless you configure it to use the `chat` scripting program, but that process is not discussed in this book). You run `dip` from the command line and provide it with the information to connect, including the PPP account user name and password.

The `dial d` program is totally automatic once it is configured (you supply the information to it about how to connect to your ISP). `Diald` constantly monitors your network for traffic destined for the Internet. Once detected, `diald` dials the ISP, enters your PPP account name and password, and then fires off the `pppd` daemon. In starting `pppd`, `diald` also creates a default route through which all external traffic is shunted. (`Diald` is not limited to creating a default route but can create any route that you tell it to.) However, most simple networks—those that are not permanently connected to the Internet—generally need only a default route.

Connecting to the Internet via a Dial-Up Connection

The simple yet ubiquitous telephone is largely responsible for creating the modern Internet. Without this cheap and universal method for making connections, the Internet would still be the domain of the large company or institution. However, with a phone line and the right software, anyone can become a complete part of the net. Linux takes the process a step further, and permits the entire private network to become part of the Internet.

The following sections describe how to connect your Linux server and network to the Internet via your ISP. The first section uses the Red Hat Control Panel GUI to make the connection. Next, `dip` is used to show how to manually connect to the Internet, and is also used to show some of the details of the connection process in anticipation of configuring `diald`. Finally, a description of using `diald` and making use of the information gleaned by using `dip`.

Building a Dedicated Linux Gateway

The Linux computer that you use as a *gateway* to the Internet is an essential part of your private network's security. You can use your Linux file/print server, called chivas in this book, as your gateway, but it is best to use a separate machine. The fewer software packages that you have running on your Linux gateway, the less opportunity there is for mistakes and mischief. The idea is to build a minimalist Linux computer that can only perform as a gateway and a firewall, as explained in Chapter 12.

Chapter 11: Connecting to the Internet   243

There are several ways to make a dedicated Linux gateway. You can install the basic Red Hat installation on a PC and then remove all but the necessary packages, or you can create a specialized Red Hat installation via the Kickstart function. You can also use a Linux distribution, such as Trinux (www.trinux.org) that's designed for the purpose.

Since this is an introductory book, the first method is used. It is recommended that you install Red Hat Linux on another PC dedicated as a firewall. Don't worry if you're using a 486 PC; they do quite well in that function because bottlenecks generally occur at the network interfaces. Also, a 486 computer can generally readily keep up, even with a fast T1 interface.

After installing Red Hat again, reduce the packages by running the `make_firewall.sh` script found in the `/mnt/cdrom/firewall` directory on the companion CD-ROM. Log in as root and run the script:

```
/mnt/cdrom/firewall/make_firewall.sh
```

The script uses the `rpm -e` command to remove all the unnecessary RPM packages and you are left with a minimalist Linux computer suited for running a firewall. The Linux computer atlas, shown in Figure 11-1, is used as the Internet gateway and firewall in this book.

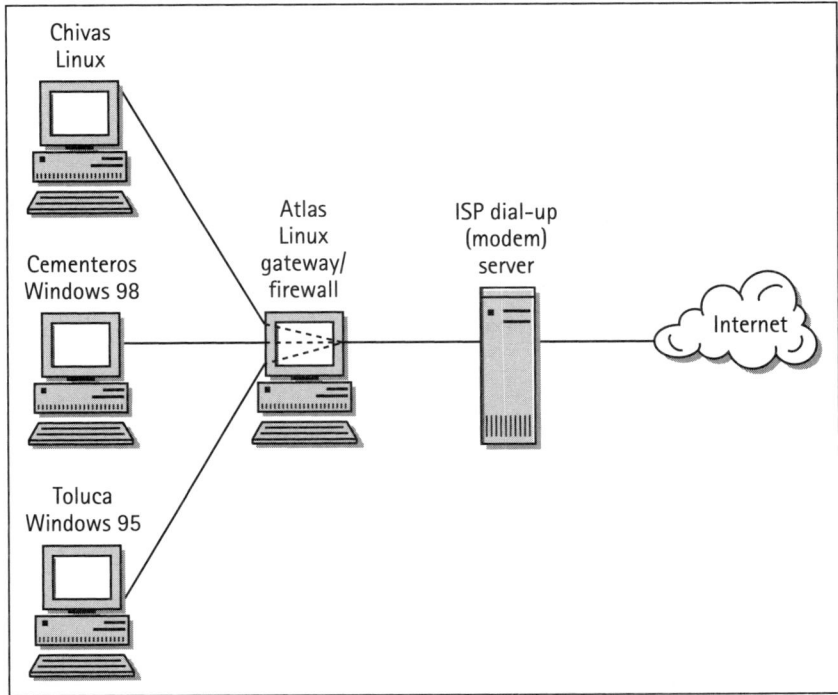

Figure 11-1: Network diagram for connecting to the Internet

Setting up Your Modem

You should first make sure that your modem is working correctly. Unfortunately, if you have a Winmodem, it will not work with Linux. Winmodems are internal modems that are designed to work only with Windows. Second, if you have a modem with Plug and Play capabilities, you should turn them off if you can.

It is easiest to work with external modems. You can turn them on and off at will; something that's useful when your modem gets stuck for whatever reason. You can also see the transmit and receive lights as well as the connection indicators. External modems need to connect to one of the two serial ports that are standard on PCs and please consult your modem manual for more information about making connections.

Internal modems are more difficult to install and configure. The difficulty lies in the necessity of opening up your computer case and plugging in the modem. Internal modems also require their IRQ and IO ports to be set correctly. Some modems can be changed from their DOS-based configuration software while on others, you need to physically change switches or dip connectors. Please consult your modem manual for more information about configuring it.

PCMCIA modems require loadable modules that match the modem type and manufacturer. PCMCIA modems are generally used in laptops and are beyond the scope of this book.

Once you have connected and configured your modem, it's useful to set a soft link to point to the device file that controls it. Table 11-1 shows which devices correspond to which IO addresses (the DOS equivalent is also shown).

TABLE 11-1 SERIAL IO AND INTERRUPT ADDRESSES

Device	IO Address	IRQ	DOS Equivalent
/dev/ttyS0	0x03f8	4	COM1:
/dev/ttyS1	0x02f8	3	COM2:
/dev/ttyS2	0x03e8	4	COM3:
/dev/ttyS3	0x02e8	3	COM4:

 Notice in Table 11-1 that the four potential ports share only two interrupts. If you try to use two devices sharing the same interrupt, your system will hang. One way around this is to use one or more internal modems and specify different interrupts for each (consult your modem manual for the settings).

If, for instance, you have a modem attached to device `/dev/ttyS1`, then enter the following command to create the link.

`ln -s /dev/ttyS1 /dev/modem`

You can see the link by listing the directory as follows:

`ls -l /dev/modem`

You can see that the link is created.

`lrwxrwxrwx   1   root    root    4   Jan 18  21:14   /dev/modem@@>/dev/ttyS1`

Instead of using the `/dev/ttyS1` when configuring your PPP dial up connections, you can use `/dev/modem` instead. The latter file is much easier to remember than former.

You can also use the Modem Configuration GUI in Control Panel to perform the same job.

Please see the `/usr/doc/HOWTO/Hardware-HOWTO`, `/usr/doc/HOWTO/Modem-HOWTO` and `./usr/doc/HOWTO/Serial-HOWTO` files for more information.

Using the Network Configurator to Connect to the Internet

Log in as root. Click the Gnome start (the little gnome footprint in the lower left corner of your screen). Click the System menus → Control Panel buttons. Now the Control Panel is activated and you should click the Network Configuration button, which is second from the top. The Network Configuration (`netcfg` from the command line) window, with the Names tab active, is displayed.

Click the Interfaces tab and the Network Configuration screen with the Interfaces information, as shown in Figure 11-2, is displayed.

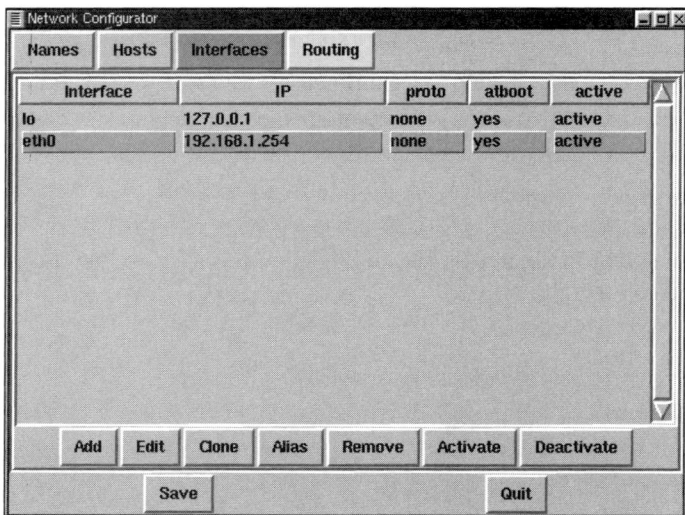

Figure 11-2: The Network Configuration - Interfaces window

You need to add the PPP interface now. Click the Add button and the Choose Interface Type window is activated as shown in Figure 11-3.

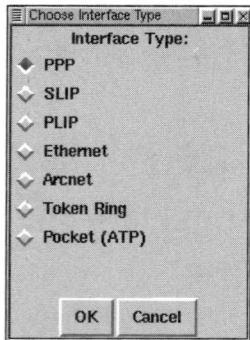

Figure 11-3: The Choose Interface Type window

The PPP button is active by default. Click OK and the Create PPP Interface window is started as shown in Figure 11-5.

You can have multiple PPP interfaces and therefore the first one created is ppp0. Enter your ISP's phone number, your PPP login name and PPP password. If your ISP supports encrypted PPP passwords, then you can click the PAP button. Fill in the window as shown in Figure 11-4. Note that the password is displayed in clear text in this situation. Please be careful not to let anyone see it as you type it in.

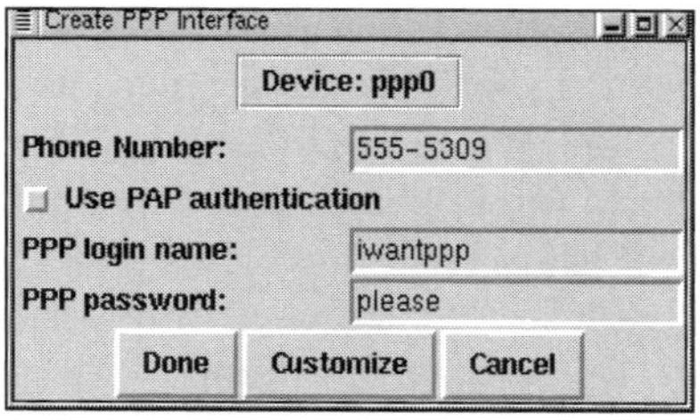

Figure 11-14: The completed Create PPP Interface window

Click Done and you are prompted to Save or Cancel your selections. Click on Save and control is returned to the Network Configuration window.

To make the connection, click the Activate button. The Network Configuration GUI then attempts to connect you to your ISP. If all goes well, you hear your modem pick up, dial and make the connection.

Once you are connected to the Internet, you need to configure your system to use the *domain name server* (DNS) provided by your ISP. DNS converts Internet names (for instance, www.idgbooks.com) to their numeric IP addresses (206.175.162.15). From the Network Configurator window, click the Names tab. Click anywhere in the Nameservers sub window and enter the numeric IP address of your ISP's DNS server. Your entry should look something like that shown in Figure 11-5.

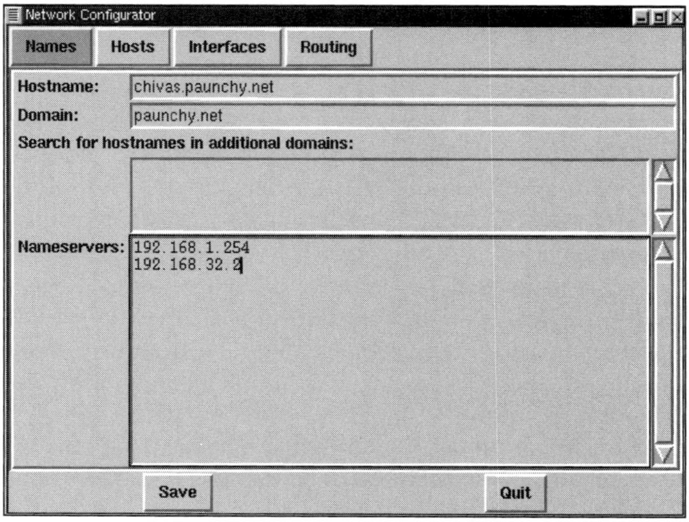

Figure 11-5: The DNS server address entered in the Network Interface window

The primary DNS server address (192.168.1.254) points to the Linux server chivas (the DNS function is kept on chivas instead of atlas in order to keep the gateway/firewall as simple as possible) and was configured as part of the Red Hat installation process described in Chapter 1. Instructions for configuring Chivas as a DNS are given later in this chapter in the section "Configuring a DNS Server". The local DNS server will give addresses for local machines. If you do not intend to configure a local DNS, then you can set the primary DNS server address to your ISP.

The secondary nameserver address is your ISP's DNS server (reached only when you have an active PPP connection) allows you to find any valid Internet address. For instance, if you enter the command nslookup www.idgbooks.com, then the IP address of 206.175.162.15 is returned.

The Network Configurator saves your information in the /etc/resolv.conf file. It should look something like the following:

```
search paunchy.net
nameserver 192.168.1.254
nameserver 192.168.32.2
```

You can manually edit the /etc/resolv.conf file if you wish. Use your favorite editor and add or change the values in that file as is appropriate.

When you want to disconnect your PPP connection, click the Interfaces tab again and then the Deactivate button. If you do not use your connection for some time, then it is likely that your modem or ISP will disconnect from you. However, your pppd might still be active and you should still use the Deactivate button to stop it.

Configuring a DNS server

It is convenient, but not necessary, to configure a local DNS server. If you set one up, then every machine on your private network can find the IP address of any other machine on the private network without having to include every host name/IP address in every Linux /etc/hosts file or every Windows lmhost fil. By configuring one local DNS server, you save having to duplicate the same address information on every computer on your private network.

Configuring a DNS server from scratch can be very difficult at first. DNS is a complex system and requires several configuration files to work together. Rather than go through the instructions for setting up the simple system needed by the paunchy.net, the configuration files for paunchy.net are included on the companion CD-ROM.

The Linux server chivas is used as the DNS server in this example. That function is kept off of atlas in order to keep that machine as simple as possible. There is no technical reason why the DNS server can not be put on any Linux computer as long as all the machines on your network point to it.

Chapter 11: Connecting to the Internet

Log in as root and install the caching-nameserver and bind RPM packages:

```
rpm -ivh /mnt/cdrom/RedHat/RPMS/bind-8*
rpm -ivh /mnt/cdrom/RedHat/RPMS/caching-nameserver*
```

Install the configuration files as follows:

```
cp -f /mnt/cdrom/dns/named.conf /etc
cp -f /mnt/cdrom/dns/named.ca /var/named
cp -f /mnt/cdrom/dns/named.local /var/named
cp -f /mnt/cdrom/dns/named.paunchy /var/named
cp -f /mnt/cdrom/dns/named.reverse /var/named
```

The `/etc/named.conf` file looks as follows.

```
// Boot file for paunchy.net name server
options {
        directory "/var/named";
};
zone "." {
        type hints;
        file "root.hints";
};
zone "0.0.127.in-addr.arpa" {
        type master;
        file "named.local";
};
zone "1.168.192.in-addr.arpa" {
        type master;
        file "named.reverse";
};
zone "paunchy.net." {
        type master;
        file "named.paunchy";
};
```

The first section tells `named` to use the `/var/named` directory as its home directory. The section defining the `named.local` file is used to set up name resolution for the `localhost` network. The `paunchy.net` section deals with converting IP names to numeric addresses for the paunchy.net-based devices. The 1.168.192 zone (`named.reverse`) provides reverse lookups — numeric IP addresses to names — for the `paunchy.net`.

Start the `named` daemon by using the start up script.

```
/etc/rc.d/init.d/named start
```

Modify your /etc/resolv.conf file to look as follows:

```
domain paunchy.net
nameserver 192.168.1.254
nameserver 192.168.32.2
```

Where the last nameserver entry is a fake one and should be replaced the IP address of your ISP's nameserver.

Test its operation by starting the nslookup program. At the nslookup prompt, enter a network name like atlas.

```
nslookup>atlas
```

The nslookup utility should return the numeric IP address of atlas:

```
Name:      chivas.paunchy.net
Address:   192.168.1.250
Aliases:   atlas
```

If you enter an address that is not found within the named files in the /var/named directory, then your ISP nameserver is accessed. In the case where you enter a name of a network device on your own network, then the name lookup fails. You should enter the device name and address information in your local named configuration files.

Using DIP to Connect to the Internet

The dip package is part of the default Red Hat installation. To use it log in as root and enter the command dip -t from the command line. You get the DIP> prompt as shown.

```
DIP: Dialup IP Protocol Driver 3.3.7o-uri (8 Feb 96)
Written by Fred N. van Kemp, MicroWalt Corporation.
DIP>
```

Dip is in *command* mode. Every valid word that you enter is interpreted as a command. (Enter help for a list of commands.) You need to tell dip where to find the modem so enter the following command at the DIP> prompt.

```
DIP>port modem
```

The modem parameter was set in Setting up Your Modem earlier in the chapter. Next, change into terminal emulation mode as follows:

```
DIP>term
```

Dip goes into *terminal emulation* mode.

```
[Entering TERMINAL mode.   Use CTRL-] to get back.]
```

Everything that you type in now is sent to the modem. If you type Ctrl], then dip returns to control mode.

Tell the modem to dial your ISP as follows:

```
atdt 5555309
```

The at characters tells the modem to pay attention. The d character tells it to dial and the t to use *t*one dialing. Substitute your ISP's phone number for the one used here. Once you press the return key, your modem dials up your ISP.

A Linux or UNIX-based ISP typically gives you the following prompt.

```
myisp login:
```

Enter your PPP account name (not your normal Linux user name) and then the PPP account password. If you ISP is configured to set up a PPP connection then you should see a line or two of garbled looking text. That is the ISP PPP daemon trying to *handshake*, or connect, with your PPP client.

Next, return to your dip command mode by entering the CTRL-] key sequence (press **Ctrl-]**). You should see the DIP> prompt again. You need to tell dip to get the dynamic IP address assigned to your Linux gateway by entering the following command.

```
DIP>get $local 0.0.0.0
```

Dip queries the remote PPP server about its new IP address and assigns it to the internal DIP variable local. The default route is designated by the numeric IP address 0.0.0.0.

 You are not limited to assigning your PPP connection to the default route. If you are connecting to another network with, say, the 192.168.16.0 network (which is fake, in this case), then you would use the instruction DIP>get $local 192.168.16.0.

To complete the PPP connection, enter the command:

```
DIP>mode PPP
```

Dip hesitates for a second or two and then exits, returning you to your `bash` shell. If all went well, then you can use the `netstat -i` command to see your new `default` route to the Internet as show below (the `ppp0` is the route to the Internet).

```
Kernel Interface table
Iface   MTU Met   RX-OK RX-ERR RX-DRP RX-OVR   TX-OK TX-ERR TX-DRP TX-OVR Flg
eth0    1500  0       0      0      0      0      59      0      0      0 BRU
lo      3924  0    2869      0      0      0    2869      0      0      0 LRU
ppp0    1500  0       5      0      0      0       5      0      0      0 OPRU
sl0     1500  0       0      0      0      0     187      0      0      0 OPRU
```

The `ppp0` is the default route to the Internet via your ISP.

If your ISP assigns you a static IP address, then it is necessary to slightly change the DIP connection process. Substitute the `get $local 0.0.0.0` command with the following two: `get $locip 192.168.1.250` and `$rmtip 192.168.64.2` where you substitute the numeric IP that your ISP assigns to you for the dummy value 192.168.64.2 (but keep your local IP 192.168.1.250).

Please keep in mind that the information about what kind of PPP log in prompts are used by your ISP can be useful in setting up the `dial d` system described in the "Connecting Automatically to the Internet with Diald" section.

Try out your connection by pinging your ISP (`ping www.myisp.com`) or using Netscape Navigator. To shut down your connection enter the command:

`dip -k`

If you have problems, consult the Troubleshooting section at the end of this chapter.

Connecting Automatically to the Internet with Diald

`Diald` uses two configuration files: `/etc/diald.conf` and `/etc/ppp/connect`. The `diald.conf` holds the `diald` configuration parameters (you can enter the same parameters manually on the command line). The `connect` file contains the phone number, PPP user login name, password, the expected prompt strings, and other information. When `diald` starts as a daemon, it reads those files to obtain its configuration.

When `diald` detects an outgoing IP packet, it fires up the `chat` program which is designed to negotiate such things as mode dial-ups and PPP authentication. `Diald` sends the information contained in `/etc/ppp/connect` to chat. You can view the process by using the `ps x` command as root.

The `diald` system is included in an RPM format on the companion CD-ROM in the `/mnt/cdrom/ppp` directory. To install it, log in as root and install the two packages (`diald16` and `diald16-config`).

```
rpm -ivh /mnt/cdrom/ppp/diald16*
```

Sample `diald.conf` and `connect` scripts are stored in the `/etc/diald` directory. The `connect` script should stay in the `/etc/diald` directory but the `diald.conf` should reside in `/etc`. Copy it to the appropriate directories as follows.

```
cp /etc/diald/diald.conf /etc
```

Create the start up links so that `diald` is started automatically at boot time as follows:

```
ln -s /etc/rc.d/init.d/diald /etc/rc.d/rc3.d/S99diald
ln -s /etc/rc.d/init.d/diald /etc/rc.d/rc5.d/S99diald
```

You can also use LinuxConf or Control panel to create the links.

You next need to modify the `diald.conf` and `connect` scripts to match your and your ISP's installation. The default `diald.conf` script (`diald16-conf` RPM) is modified below to reflect the ISP used in creating this book.

```
# stuff to set up the diald connection
device /dev/modem
speed 115200
lock
mode ppp
# We may get another terminal server, thus use
# 'dynamic' and do not tell PPP the IP number of the other end
# For use with gated, comment out the 'dynamic' option, and
# set remote to be the same as local
dynamic
local 127.0.0.2
remote 127.0.0.3
pppd-options name anappp :
# Delay sending packets for 5 seconds after PPP device opens -
# this allows routes to be established back to the appropriate
```

```
# dialup server.
up-delay 5
defaultroute
modem
crtscts
connect /etc/diald/connect
redial-timeout 10
fifo /etc/diald/diald.ctl
```

Some of the important lines are as follows:

- The `connect /etc/diald/connect` parameter tells `diald` to get the modem dialing information from the connect script in the `/etc/diald` directory.

- The `device` parameter points to your modem device file. If you have not set the modem soft link, then please refer to the instructions in the section "Setting up Your Modem".

- The `local` and `remote` IP address create the proxy routes. Proxy routes do not use any physical devices but are logical ones. The proxy routes receive IP packets destined for the Internet in this case. Once a packet shows up on one, `diald` sees it and starts the connection. Once the connection is established, `diald` creates a default route that uses the PPP connection.

- The `dynamic` option tells `diald` that your ISP assigns you a dynamic IP address for your connection. In the case that you use static IP address, then you omit the `dynamic` option.

- The `defaultroute` parameter tells `diald` to use the PPP connection that it creates as the default route. You can use `diald` to create non-default routes too. In that case, you do not use the `defaultroute` parameter.

Next, set up your `/etc/ppp/connect` script shown below. This sample script is included on the companion CD-ROM at `/mnt/cdrom/IDG/ppp/connect`.

```
#!/bin/sh
# Copyright (c) 1996, Eric Schenk.
#
# This script is intended to give an example of a connection script that
# uses the "message" facility of diald to communicate progress through
```

```
# the dialing process to a diald monitoring program such as dctrl or
# diald-top.
# It also reports progress to the system logs. This can be useful if you
# are seeing failed attempts to connect and you want to know when and why
# they are failing.
#
# This script requires the use of chat-1.9 or greater for full
# functionality. It should work with older versions of chat,
# but it will not be able to report the reason for a connection failure.
# Configuration parameters
# The initialization string for your modem
MODEM_INIT="ATZ&C1&D2%C0"
# The phone number to dial
PHONE_NUMBER="555-5309"

# The chat sequence to recognize that the remote system
# is asking for your user name.
USER_CHAT_SEQ="ogin:"
# The string to send in response to the request for your user name.
# Set this to empty if you are using PAP or CHAP.
USER_NAME="Piwantppp"
# The chat sequence to recognize that the remote system
# is asking for your password.
PASSWD_CHAT_SEQ="ssword:"
# The string to send in response to the request for your password
PASSWORD="franksearlyyears"
# The prompt the remote system will give once you are logged in
# If you do not define this then the script will assume that
# there is no command to be issued to start up the remote protocol.
PROMPT="PPP session"
# The command to issue to start up the remote protocol
PROTOCOL_START="ppp"
{...snip...}
# Dial the remote system.
>/var/log/diald.connect
{...the rest of the script is not shown because it should not
require modification...}
```

This `bash` shell script is used by `chat` to both dial the modem and negotiate the authentication during the log in process; some of the documentation lines have been removed to help accentuate the important parameters. The important lines are as follows:

- The phone number is that of your ISP's dial-up phone line.

- USER_CHAT_SEQ="ogin:" The string `ogin:` defines the prompt that diald/chat expects to see at the start of the PPP authentication process. The remote PPP server of your ISP responds to your modem connection (one that is assigned to handle PPP connections) with a login prompt. This is similar to the login prompt that you are given when logging into your Linux computer. The `chat` program uses the string `ogin:` as the indication that it should send your PPP login name. Note that the first character, which is a capital L (Login) is left out in order not to get confused by a system that happens to use a lower case l. USER_CHAT_SEQ is the variable that `diald/chat` uses to store the string.

- USER_NAME="Iwantppp" The `Iwantppp` string is the name of your PPP account. The capital P in front of the user name is a widely used convention to designate a PPP account from a normal user account. USER_NAME is the `diald/chat` variable used to store the string.

- PASSWD_CHAT_SEQ="word:" The string word: defines the prompt that diald/chat expects to see before entering the password. The partial word is used again because it has a higher probability of being constant across PPP servers. PASSWD_CHAT_SEQ is the variable that `chat` uses to store the string.

- PASSWORD="franksearlyyears" The string `franksearlyyears` is the password for your PPP account. It is also analogous to the password supplied for a normal user account. PASSWORD is the `diald/chat` variable used to store the string.

- PROMPT="PPP session" The `PPP session` is the string that `diald/chat` expects to see once the PPP server has authenticated you and started a PPP connection. PROMPT is the variable that `diald/chat` uses to store the string. Of all the parameters mentioned, this string is most likely to vary from one PPP server to another.

- PROTOCOL_START="ppp" The command that `diald/chat` sends to the ISP to start the session. If the PROMPT="" is left blank, then `diald/chat` does not send any connect command.

- >/var/log/diald.connect This is the `syslog` file used to store information about all dial ups and PPP connections.

Once you have completed modifying /etc/diald.conf and /etc/ppp/connect to match your set up, start the diald daemon as follows:

```
diald
```

You should be able to view the daemon by using the ps x | grep diald command. You can also verify that the proxy routes are configured as follows:

```
netstat -i
```

This results in the following display:

```
Kernel Interface table
Iface  MTU  Met  RX-OK RX-ERR RX-DRP RX-OVR TX-OK TX-ERR TX-DRP TX-OVR Flg
eth0   1500  0      0     0      0      0     67     0      0      0  BRU
lo     3924  0   2972     0      0      0   2972     0      0      0  LRU
sl0    1500  0      0     0      0      0      0     0      0      0  OPRU
```

Next, fire up your connection. You can use a program like Netscape Navigator or Telnet to access an external site. For instance, start Navigator and enter www.idgbooks.com in the Location field, and diald should pick up the modem, dial the ISP, and make a PPP connection. After a short delay, the Web page should load.

The connection dies after all of the open connections time out. Web connections typically take two minutes to time out, while interactive sessions such as Telnet and FTP take ten minutes. The following section describes a GUI based diald control system.

Using DCTRL

The dctrl script is a nice GUI-based interface to diald. It is part of the diald RPM and can be found in the /usr/bin directory. To run it, log in as root and set up your X Window System as follows:

```
xhost +
export DISPLAY=:0.0
```

These commands allow you to display dctrl to your own window.

```
dctrl -dstatus -tload -gload -pqueue -dlog
```

That command starts up dctrl and activates all of its display functions. You should see the interface shown in Figure 11-6.

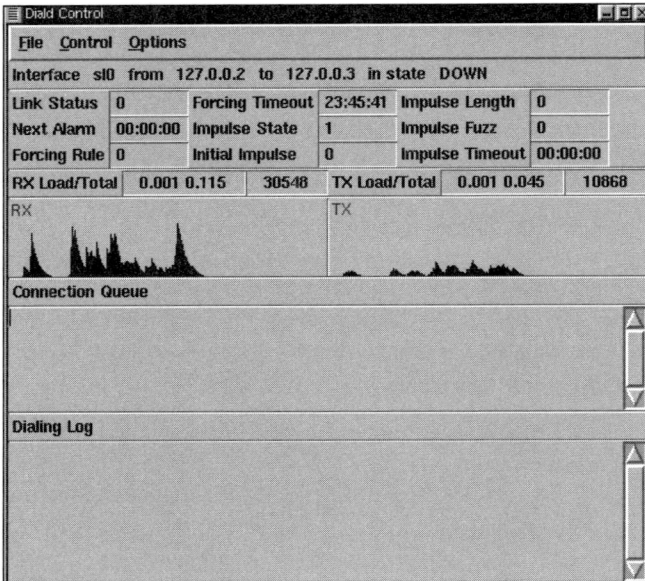

Figure 11-6: The dctrl window

If you click Control → Forced up, dialed connects to your ISP and remains connected until you click on Control → Forced up again. At that time, if there are no more open connections, then dialed takes down the connection. The open connections are displayed in the Connection Queue sub window.

If you click Control → Up, then dialed also starts up a connection. It, however, remains up only while there is an open connection is present.

By clicking Control → Down, any open connections are removed from the connection queue and if the Forced Up item is not active, then your connection is broken.

Selecting the Control → Block connection choice kills any open connections and prevents any new ones from being started.

Controlling diald Manually

You can also control the diald connection manually. Diald monitors the /etc/diald/diald.ctl file, which is a First In First Out (FIFO) queue. You can send signals to that file and diald acts as appropriate.

The signals are block, unblock, force, unforce, up, and down. They are similar to the menu selections and are mostly self explanatory; see the man page dialdcontrol for more information.

For instance, to start up a PPP connection enter the command:

```
echo "up" > /etc/diald/diald.ctl
```

To stop it do the following:

```
echo "down" > /etc/diald/diald.ctl
```

Troubleshooting

This troubleshooting section is divided up according to the sections of this chapter.

Modem trouble

If you have trouble getting your modem to connect, then there are several things you should check.

If you have an external modem, then make sure that it's connected properly. Can you see the Light Emitting Diodes (LED) flicker when you interact with it? For instance, if you use `dip -t`, then you should be able to see the LEDs flicker when you enter keystrokes.

If you have an internal modem, check that it is seated properly on the system board. Can you manually communicate with it via a program like `dip`? If not, then it might have an IRQ or IO port setting that is conflicting with another device. You can check its current settings against the other installed devices by looking at the `/proc/ioports` and `/proc/interrupts` files (for instance, `cat /dev/ioports`). You also can check the device file that it is supposed to be using. If, for instance, you have a soft link pointing to `/dev/ttyS0`, then check to see if that is correct. You might have to change the link to `/dev/ttyS1` for instance. Try using the `dip` command to communicate directly with another device (`DIP>port ttyS1` for instance). Keep in mind that if you have a PnP modem, then you might have to turn that feature off to make it work with Linux. A WinModem will not work with Linux.

Using the Control Panel to Connect to the Internet

If you have set up your modem correctly, then most problems that you encounter using the Network GUI in Control panel probably result from the misconfiguration of your ISP settings. If you have problems getting a connection going, then check that your ISP PPP login name and password are set correctly. You might also need to check that your ISP is not using unusual settings; go through the options in the Network Interfaces window and make sure that each one is correct.

Using DIP to Connect to the Internet

The good aspect of `dip` is that you can see everything that is going on. Any problems that occur are immediately visible. If you are having problems connecting via dip, turn on its debug mode. You can do that by using the verbose mode - `dip -t -v`:

```
DIP: Dialup IP Protocol Driver version 3.3.7o-uri (8 Feb 96)
Written by Fred N. van Kempen, MicroWalt Corporation.
DIP: name=root home=/tmp
     host=atlas.paunchy.net IP=192.168.1.250
     prot=SLIP MTU=296
Modem set to "HAYES".
DIP [0   ]>
```

The output shows information about what computer you are working on. Set the port to the modem and you see information about the modem - `DIP [0   ]>port modem`.

```
PORT: terminal port set to "modem".
DIP: tty_open: /dev/modem (3) DIP: tty_open: IBUF=1024 OBUF=1020
DIP: tty: set_speed: 38400
DIP: tty: set_databits: 8
DIP: tty: set_stopbits: 1
DIP: tty: set_parity: N
DIP [0   ]>
```

You'll enter into terminal mode as usual. Try dialing your ISP and then authenticating your PPP as usual too. Escape back to your `DIP>` prompt and proceed as described before. If there is a problem with any of your settings, then you receive more information about the problem.

If you continue to have problems getting your PPP connection to work, then make sure that you don't already have a default route set up. If you have `diald` running, then that can also create problems. You can also check the `/var/log/messages` file for any messages about `dip`.

Connecting Automatically to the Internet with Diald

`Diald` is the most complex of all connection methods described in this chapter. It uses two systems, both `diald` and `chat`, to make connections. It also works non-interactively and problems are not as obvious.

If you are having problems getting it to work, then it is best to start from the beginning. Make sure that you can connect to your ISP by using either Network or `dip` methods to verify your connection. Next, make sure that the information in the critical `/etc/ppp/connect` and `/etc/diald.conf` files are correct. Pay particular attention to the prompt string fragments like `USER_CHAT_SEQ="ogin:"`, `PASSWD_CHAT_SEQ="word:"` and `PROMPT="PPP session"`. It is essential that each one match up with the strings that your ISP sends you. For instance, if `diald/chat` is expecting the PPP session prompt (as defined in `/etc/ppp/connect`) but your ISP sends the string `XYZ session`, then `diald/chat` never finishes up the connection process and you don't get your PPP connection.

You should also check the `/var/messages` log file for dialog from the `diald` startup process. It shows the progress of each `diald` session and might includ insights into your problem. For example, if you have set up `diald` and everything looks okay but no connection is occurring, then take a look at the end of the messages file.

```
tail -20 /var/log/messages
```

It might show something like the following:

```
Apr 18 atlas diald[1312]: Specified device '/dev/modem' not a
character device.
```

There's something wrong with the soft link file `/dev/modem`. In this case, the link is pointing to the `/dev/ttyS0` device file. Use the following command to find out what serial ports are in use.

```
cat /proc/tty/driver/serial
```

It returns the following information:

```
serinfo:1.0 driver:4.27
0: uart:16550A port:3F8 irq:4 tx:0 rx:0
1: uart:16550A port:2F8 irq:3 baud:1200 tx:8 rx:59382 brk:5 RTS|DTR
2: uart:16550A port:3E8 irq:4 baud:115200 tx:359592 rx:8684037
RTS|CTS|DTR|DSR|CD
3: uart:unknown port:2E8 irq:3
```

The first port (0) looks like it is unused. The second port, (1) is probably a serial mouse because 1200 baud modems have not been in use for years. The third one, however, has a 115,200 baud, which is a high bandwidth connection (for a serial port device). Modems don't run at that speed but they do communicate with the computer at that rate. It's a good bet, so change the soft link to refer to the new device.

```
ln -s /dev/ttyS2 /dev/modem
```

In this case, that was the problem. Restart the `diald` daemon (`/etc/rc.d/init.d/diald restart`) and it now works.

If you have trouble with `dctrl`, then make sure that you have read/write privilege with the `/etc/diald/diald.ctl` file. You also need to be able to display to the X Window so make sure that you have run `xhost +atlas` and `export DISPLAY=:0.0`.

Configuring Linux for Dialing In

If you are having problems with dialing in to your network, then start by making sure that you can dial in to your incoming modem. If you can get the incoming modem to answer, then that means your `mgetty` is working at least partially. Next check that the `mgetty` configuration files, `login.config` and `mgetty.conf` are configured correctly.

You can also back off and try a simple login—non PPP—to your Linux server by changing the `login.config` file. Comment out the `/AutoPPP/` line and try a simple login. Check the `/usr/doc/mgetty-1.1.14/FAQ`, the `mgetty` man page for more information. Lastly, the default debug level is four (see the `mgetty.conf` file) and can be bumped up to as high as nine.

Summary

This chapter shows you how to connect your Linux network to the Internet. Several connection methods are described. Once connected, your network is part of the Internet. A dial-in PPP connection handles incoming network traffic, and this approach is taken to allow a simple one-way IP filtering firewall to be used (described in Chapter 12).

- A introduction to the dial-up network is discussed. The PPP protocol is the basis for this system.

- A discussion of how to choose an ISP is covered. Not all ISPs are built the same and the local ISP with good technical capability is worth a few extra dollars per month. The less time that you spend correcting problem the more money you save.

- Preparing for your connection is worth some effort. The connection systems described in this chapter require that you know parameters such as the dial up numbers and such.

- Configuring your modem is an important place to start your connection configuration.

- Red Hat provides a ISP connection GUI. You can access it via the Control panel. You need to enter a handful of parameters and the GUI will make the connection and start up PPP for you.

- A discussion of the manual connection method is discussed. The utility is the `dip` program that you interact with yourself. Much useful information is gained by manually connecting because you see the responses from your ISP. (If you have problems with the Control Panel or the `diald` systems, then this information can be used to get things right).

- The `diald` program detects outgoing network traffic and automatically dials and connects to your ISP. `Diald` uses your simple modem to effectively make your network look as though it is continuously connected to the Internet (although there are delays while the connection process is in progress.)

- The `dctrl` GUI is used to manually control `diald`. Sometimes you want to manually start and stop your network connection. The combination of `diald` and `dctrl` gives you the best of both worlds — automatic and manual connections. `Dctrl` also shows the network connections in progress.

- A description of building a simple DNS server is covered. DNS is used to convert Internet domain names into numeric IP addresses. By running your own internal DNS system, you can avoid having to enter all the host names on your private network into every machine. Scripts are provided to allow you to set up a simple DNS server. The scripts are oriented around the `paunchy.net` network used in all examples in this book.

- Configuring your modem for dial in is a matter of configuring the `mgetty` and `inittab` systems is discussed. `Mgetty` detects the incoming phone call and answers it. At that point it kicks off the `pppd` daemon which handles the authentication process. Once authenticated your incoming phone line acts as a PPP server and your remote computer becomes part of your local network. (That is much the same as when your local network becomes part of the Internet when you connect to your ISP's PPP server.)

- A discussion of troubleshooting techniques is covered.

Chapter 12

Creating a Simple Firewall

IN THIS CHAPTER

- Introducing firewalls
- Connecting your LAN to the Internet via masquerading
- Protecting your Internet connection with a hybrid firewall
- Monitoring your firewall
- Monitoring your server for break-ins
- Keeping track of the bad guys
- Testing your firewall with `nmap`
- Verifying your Server with `Tripwire`
- Learning more about firewalls and security
- Troubleshooting your firewall

Introducing Firewalls

A *firewall* is a computer, router, or a dedicated device that is configured to prevent unauthorized access to one network from another network. For the purposes of this book, a firewall is a Linux computer set up to protect your simple business network from troublemakers on the Internet.

This book uses terminology that is somewhat different than what you'll find in the technical literature. Your small business network is referred to as the *private network*; the private network is often referred to as the *protected network* in other places. The Linux computer that functions as a firewall is called the *firewall server* (in other circles that machine is often referred to as a *Screening Router*). Hopefully, the terms used here are descriptive and clear.

Firewalls come in two primary flavors: *filtering* and *proxy*. Filtering firewalls look at each IP packet and decide whether to pass or reject the packets based on a set of rules that you set; they work at the OSI Network layer (see the section "The OSI Network Layer Model" in Chapter 7 for more information). Proxy firewalls act as an intermediary between a program client and its server by replicating the communication. They work at the OSI application layer.

There are several strategic locations to place a firewall within a network. Two common configurations put a firewall either directly on the private network or on a separate network dedicated to security. The former allows a simple firewall to be easily constructed and depending on what services it provides, can be reasonably safe. The latter is more difficult to configure but provides a higher degree of safety; this book refers to the latter as a *Firewall Network* but the general term is the *DMZ* or *Demilitarized Zone*.

IP Filtering Firewalls

Filtering firewalls look at each packet coming into and going out of them, and compare the source IP and port as well as the destination IP and port to a set of rules. The packet is either permitted to pass or not depending on these rules, which you, the network administrator, choose.

Red Hat Linux comes with the `ipchains` package, which provides filtering capabilities. This package allows the filter rules to be configured dynamically and also can perform numerous levels of logging. The `diald` program described in Chapter 11 can automatically set up the `ipchains` rules. This allows you to completely automate both your Internet PPP connection and firewall.

Filtering firewalls are relatively easy to configure. They are also efficient; an Intel 486 firewall server can easily handle a medium sized network (dozens of computers) connected to the Internet through a T1 Frame Relay connection (1.45 Mbps). They also are safe as firewalls when providing one-way communication to the Internet.

The problem with IP filters is that once you start allow incoming connections from the Internet you are poking holes in your firewall. For instance, if you want to interactively connect into your private network from your home computer (assuming that they are not one in the same), then you need to set a rule(s) that allows incoming Telnet connections. There are tools (for instance nmap, which is discussed in the section Using NMAP to Test Your System) that can potentially find those holes and use them against you.

Proxying Firewalls

Proxying firewalls allow you to add application-level authentication to permit incoming connections. For instance, if you want to connect to your private network from your home computer, a proxying firewall forces you to provide a password before allowing you through. Using one-time passwords makes it very difficult to gain unauthorized access to your system.

The problem with proxying firewalls is that they are relatively difficult to set up, are somewhat inefficient, and are vulnerable to software bugs and new attack methods.

The difficulty of configuration is because each application that you want to proxy requires its own configuration. (The SOCKS system, however, only has one configuration.) It is inefficient because the communication processing is doubled for every application because every packet has to be rewritten as it passes through the proxy.

It's somewhat vulnerable to new attacks because any attack that finds an opening can only be fixed by the programming of the proxy itself. For instance, when Denial of Service attacks first appeared, any proxy that fell victim to it had to be reprogrammed. Unfortunately, this isn't something that a pressed administrator can do easily, if they can do it at all. (Filtering firewalls, while not immune to new attacks, can readily be reprogrammed to simply deny the IP packets that carry the new attack.) The fact that a proxying firewall is often sitting out on the Internet means that potentially everyone on the Internet can pound away at your firewall. The more attempts made on your firewall the higher the probability that a weak spot can be found.

Don't assume that proxying firewalls are inadequate for the job; the potential hazards are pointed out for completeness. Proxying firewalls are not used in this book because a better alternative (for the needs of the network being built in this book) exists in the hybrid system described in the next section "Hybrid Firewalls."

 One of the most widely used proxy firewall systems is the TIS Firewall. It is freely available for US citizens by way of the Internet. Please check the www.tis.com web page for license and download instructions.

Please refer to the Firewall-HOWTO in the /usr/doc/HOWTO directory for more information on proxying firewalls.

ipchains

The ipchains RPM package provides IP packet filtering for your Linux gateway. You can configure it to accept or deny each IP packet going into and out of your Linux gateway. Install the ipchains packages as follows:

```
rpm -ivh /mnt/cdrom/RedHat/RPMS/ipchains*
```

You can get a short informational listing by entering the command rpm -qi ipchains.

The `ipchains` has replaced the `ipfwadm` system with the introduction of the Linux 2.2 kernel 2.2. `Ipchains` is similar to `ipfwadm` but has several improvements (please refer to the ipchains HOWTO document for a full account). If you have an older Red Hat, or other Linux distribution, then you should download `ipfwadm` from a Red Hat mirror site.

Creating a Filtering Firewall

If you have built the Linux server described in Chapter 1 and connected it to the Internet as described in Chapter 11, then you'll need to protect it with a firewall. The following section describes how to set up simple filtering rules. You should keep in mind that until you construct the full firewall described in this chapter, you are potentially vulnerable to attack while connected to the Internet. This is probably a small risk right now, because you are connected via a dial-up phone connection, which is invulnerable when not connected. Also, the system constructed in this book has no valuable information on it other than the passwords (unless you have put information and data on it yourself). You can judge the potential danger for yourself.

In order to test and build the chains described in this chapter you need to be connected to the Internet (a *chain* is simply a series of filtering rules). If you are experienced with IP filtering, then you can translate the rules to apply to an internal connection; a good idea if you don't want to risk being unprotected.

Building a Simple Filter

You can make a simple filter as follows. The Linux computer atlas is used as the firewall in this example. To enhance security it is best to use a separate computer for your firewall. By using a dedicated machine you can reduce the services and software that it provides in order to minimize potential vulnerabilities.

Log on to your Linux server atlas as root and connect to your ISP:

```
echo "force" /etc/diald/diald.ctl
```

The following instructions should be carried out from your Linux server's console. The rules are oriented towards shutting off all but a few Internet connections, but if you make a mistake, then you can accidentally shut off your private network communication. If that happens and your remote session freezes, then you can run the `/mnt/cdrom/firewall/ipchains.reset` script to turn off the filters.

Chapter 12: Creating a Simple Firewall

You should see the following results if you have not configured any filtering rules yet:

```
Chain input (policy ACCEPT):
Chain forward (policy ACCEPT):
Chain output (policy ACCEPT):
```

The results shows that there are no output, input and forwarding rules set and that the default policy is to accept any IP packet to come into or out of your network. Your system is completely open.

SETUP DEFAULT POLICY

From atlas add the following rules.

```
ipchains -P input   DENY
ipchains -P output  DENY
ipchains -P forward DENY
```

Those rules set your output, input and forwarding rules on atlas to deny any IP packets in any direction; the following list shows the `ipchains` filter commands. You now have a very safe firewall. However, it does not allow you to access the Internet either.

- `-A`   Append one or more rules to a chain
- `-D`   Delete one or more rules from a chain
- `-R`   Replace a rule from a chain
- `-I`   Insert a rule into a chain
- `-L`   List the rules in a chain
- `-F`   Flush a chain — all rules are lost
- `-N`   Create a new chain
- `-P`   Set a policy for a chain
- `-M`   Masquerading rules to follow

Please consult the `ipchains man` page for more information (`ipchains -help` will display the same information too).

FLUSH ALL EXISTING RULES

Enter the next command to flush out any existing rules.

```
ipchains -F
```

The following lists the some of the more oft-used `ipchains` parameters.

- `-p` Set the protocol (for instance, tcp, udp, icmp) for the rule or packet to check. The rules in a chain only apply to packets that match the protocols. The available protocols can be found in the `/etc/protocols` file.

- `-s` Source address to check packets against. Every IP packet has a source and destination address; they also have a corresponding source and destination port. Any packet with a source address that matches an `ipchains` rule is then checked against the rule to determine whether it passes through the firewall or not.

- `-d` Destination address to check packets against. Every IP packet has a source and destination address, as well as a corresponding source and destination port. Any packet with destination address that matches an `ipchains` rule is then checked against the rule to determine whether it passes through the firewall or not.

- `-i` Interface name to peg a chain against. You can optionally specify an interface to configure rules on.

- `-h` Display a help screen.

SETUP INPUT AND OUTPUT TCP RULES

The following rules set your firewall to allow you to browse the World Wide Web.

```
ipchains -A output -p TCP -j ACCEPT -i ppp0      -d 0.0.0.0/0 www
ipchains -A input  -p TCP -j ACCEPT -i ppp0 ! -y -s 0.0.0.0/0 www
```

- The destination and source addresses — 0.0.0.0/0 — indicates the entire Internet addresses space

- The first command sets up a filter that only allows TCP packets originating at the PPP connection (within the Linux gateway atlas) to go out to any location.

- The second command allows only the return packets from connections that originate from within the private network by using the ! -y parameter. For instance, if you Telnet to an external computer, every outgoing Telnet packet that you send a response packet to comes back to you. That response packet has its SYN (for synchronize) flag set. Thus, with this filter rule set only the return packets can get back through the firewall. It is highly unlikely that any bad guy can take advantage of this arrangement.

Chapter 12: Creating a Simple Firewall

Note that these rules apply to your first PPP (-i ppp0) network interfaces and will act on network traffic to and from your Linux server via the Internet. You can apply ipchains rules to any network interface by using the -i parameter. For instance, to apply rules to the first Ethernet interface you should use the option -i eth0. If you omit the -i parameter, then the rules will apply to all network interfaces.

SETUP INPUT AND OUTPUT UDP RULES

The following rules configure the firewall to allow DNS queries to go out to the Internet and the response to come back in. DNS uses UDP and is identified as the *domain* service.

```
ipchains -A output -p UDP -j ACCEPT -i ppp0 -d 0.0.0.0/0 domain
ipchains -A input  -p UDP -j ACCEPT -i ppp0 -s 0.0.0.0/0 domain
```

UDP is a simpler protocol than TCP so there is less configuration required. Outgoing UDP packets

- The first filter rule specifies that UDP packets of the type domain can leave the firewall and go anywhere. This rule allows you to access external DNS services.

- The second rule allows the return UDP domain packets from anywhere to come back in with the DNS information.

The following lists some of the more widely used ipchains options.

- -b Forces a rule to work in both directions. For example, the previous examples two rules for the UDP protocol could be replaced by one rule. This does not work if you wish to limit incoming packets with the SYN (! -y) parameter.

- -v Verbose. By using this option with the -L list command, more information about each chain is displayed.

- -n Numeric output. Display IP numbers instead of names.

- ! -y Only allow packets with their SYN bit set through. Typically used for limiting network traffic to only the return packets of existing, outgoing connections.

These rules create a simple, but quite effective firewall. The more advanced filtering rules described in the next section, Building a Working IP Filter, give you a more complete firewall.

It is often quite useful to turn off all your IP filters and set them to accept mode. The script /mnt/cdrom/firewall/ipchains.reset is shown here, and does just that.

```
/sbin/ipchains -F
/sbin/ipchains -P input    ACCEPT
/sbin/ipchains -P output   ACCEPT
/sbin/ipchains -P forward  ACCEPT
```

Once the connection is established, enter the following command to see the status of your IP filters.

```
/sbin/ipchains -L
```

Building a Working Filter

There are two approaches that you can take in designing filters: deny everything and add rules to allow specific access, or allow everything and write rules to deny specific access. The latter can make sense if you desire to provide public service access to your system. However, the former mode is used in this book in order to provide the maximum security.

The filter script used for this firewall can be found in /mnt/cdrom/firewall/ipchains.rules on the companion CD-ROM. Most of its rules are listed here, but the some of the comments and the *Type of Service* (TOS) rules, which are used for optimizing the modem connection, have been omitted for brevity's sake.

```
#!/bin/bash
# i------ Define variables ------
# High (non well-known ports)
HI="1024:65535"

# Define the default network address
ALL="0.0.0.0/0"
# Define the private network's address
PRIV_NET="192.168.1.0/24"
# Define localhost address
LOCAL_HOME="127.0.0.1"
# Get dynamic PPP IP address (your ISP assigns this to you at connection time
```

Chapter 12: Creating a Simple Firewall

```
PPP_IP=`/sbin/ifconfig ppp0 |grep 'inet addr'| awk '{print $2}'| \
   sed -e "s/addr\://"`
echo $PPP_IP
# ------ General Rules ------
# Flush out all existing rules
/sbin/ipchains -F
# Flush out any existing chains
/sbin/ipchains -X

# Set default filters to deny everything
/sbin/ipchains -P input   DENY
/sbin/ipchains -P output  DENY
/sbin/ipchains -P forward DENY

# Allow all internal network traffic
#/sbin/ipchains -A input  -i lo -j ACCEPT
#/sbin/ipchains -A output -i lo -j ACCEPT

# Allow all internal network traffic
#/sbin/ipchains -A input  -i eth0 -j ACCEPT
#/sbin/ipchains -A output -i eth0 -j ACCEPT

# Deny spoofed packets
/sbin/ipchains -A input  -j DENY -i ppp0 -s $PPP_IP -d $ALL
/sbin/ipchains -A output -j DENY -i ppp0 -s $PRIV_NET    -d $ALL
# --- TCP ---
/sbin/ipchains -A output -p tcp  -j ACCEPT -i ppp0      -s $PPP_IP -d $ALL
/sbin/ipchains -A input  -p tcp  -j ACCEPT -i ppp0 ! -y -s $ALL    -d $PPP_IP
# --- UDP ---
/sbin/ipchains -A output -p udp -j ACCEPT -i ppp0 -s $PPP_IP   -d 0.0.0.0/0
/sbin/ipchains -A input  -p udp -j ACCEPT -i ppp0 -s 0.0.0.0/0 -d $PPP_IP
# --- Masqurade (Network Address Translation) ---
# Masquerade your private network
# (see the section "Configure Linux Networking for Masquerading"
# in this chapter for more information.)
# (all local IPs appear on the Internet as your PPP IP address)
###/sbin/ipchains -A forward -j MASQ -s 192.168.1.0/24 -d 0.0.0.0/0
```

Understanding IP masquerading

Using *IP masquerading* is an elegant method for attaching your network to the Internet. IP masquerading (also call Network Address Translation, or NAT) converts an IP source address into another address. In this example, the source addresses of packets originating from within the private network get converted into the source address of the PPP connection on the Linux gateway/firewall. Once on the Internet they all appear to be coming from a single machine. No matter what computer on the private network you are using, all packets appear to come from a single computer.

If you use IP masquerading, then you do not need any official registration to allow your network to access the Internet. Without masquerading you would have to register with he InterNIC (the organization that distributes IP addresses) to obtains IP addresses for your network. It also conserves the quickly diminishing pool of IP addresses.

IP masquerading also provides the advantage of hiding your network behind a single address. Anyone trying to probe or attack your private network has to go through your single (and typically dynamic) address. Since IP masquerading is in effect a one-way street, most (if not all) attacks on your networked computers will die on the vine. That is because packets originating from the outside will not get translated into the address of a private network machine and, thus, never find their way to any computer.

The only way for a probe or attack to get a foothold is to hijack an existing connection. However, even if that's possible, the packets will have to be part of an existing connection originating from the private network. The packets will be treated as return packets and should never be able to start a new connection. IP masquerading has the affect of making your firewall safer than without it.

The last line in the `ipchains.rules` script, in section "Building a Working Filter," describes the masquerading rule for the `paunchy.net` network. IP masquerading converts one IP address into another IP address. That translation permits one or more computers to masquerade as single IP address. If that IP address is your dynamic, dial-up IP address, then your entire network can access the Internet.

What the rule says is that any local IP address 192.168.1.0 (the /24 specifies a subnet mask of 255.255.255.0) that shows up at the Linux gateway that is destined for the default route 0.0.0.0 are masqueraded. The default route is pegged to the PPP connection—`ppp0`—which has a dynamic IP address given by your ISP. The source address of the packets destined for the Internet is changed to the dynamic IP address. For instance, if your PPP connection has an address of 192.168.32.15 and the packets from the Windows machine toluca have a source address of 192.168.1.2, then the packets that get sent to the Internet get the source address of 192.168.32.15. The computer toluca appears to the rest of the world as 192.168.32.15.

A little more happens during masquerading than just the source address translation. The source port also gets converted to another port. Recall that the TCP/IP protocols make use of both IP addresses and ports. Ports are used to separate network communication between different applications. For instance, the standard Hypertext Transport Protocol (HTTP) uses port 80 by default. If you look at the `/etc/services` file, then you see all the standard applications and protocols along with their ports; the ports below 1024 are referred to as *Well Known ports*. During masquerading, the port gets changed to a number above 1024. This process allows the ipchains software to demasquerade the returning, masqueraded packets back to their original locations.

When a response occurs to a masqueraded packet, the reverse translation is performed. The returning packets have their destination IP address converted back to the originating IP address. The destination port is also converted back to the original port number.

Configure Linux Networking for Masquerading

Modify the following `FORWARD_IPV4` line in the `/etc/sysconfig/network` script on your Linux gateway atlas. IP masquerading requires forwarding to work.

```
NETWORKING=yes
FORWARD_IPV4=no
HOSTNAME=atlas.paunchy.net
DOMAINNAME=paunchy.net
GATEWAY=0.0.0.0
GATEWAYDEV=eth0
```

Your new `network` file should look as follows:

```
NETWORKING=yes
FORWARD_IPV4=yes
HOSTNAME=atlas.paunchy.net
DOMAINNAME=paunchy.com
GATEWAY=0.0.0.0
GATEWAYDEV=eth0
```

Uncomment the masquerading rule (the last line) in your `ipchains.rules` script.

```
ipchains -A forward -j MASQ -s 192.168.1.0/24 -d 0.0.0.0/0
```

Any IP packet that shows up on atlas's Ethernet NIC and is destined for an external location (any non 192.168.1.*x* address) gets masqueraded as the dynamic PPP interface address; any packets originating within atlas do not get masqueraded because they inherit the PPP address.

Restart your network to put the change into effect.

```
/etc/rc.d/init.d/network restart
```

Give it a try from any computer on your private network. If, for instance, you open a Web browser on a Windows machine and click on www.swcp.com/~pgsery/LNTK, your Linux gateway should dial up and connect to your ISP and then—after a few tens of seconds—you should see the Web page.

Automatically Starting Your Firewall

Whenever you connect to the Internet you should start your firewall as well. One simple and effective way of doing that is to have `diald` run the `ipchains.rules` once the PPP connection has been established. This can be done by adding the following commands to the end of the `/etc/diald.conf` file.

```
ip-up /usr/local/etc/ipchains.rules
ip-down /usr/local/etc/ipchains.reset
```

The `ip-up` parameter forces diald to run the script that configures the `ipchains` rules. The `ip-down` runs the script that flushes all the `ipchains` rules and sets the default policies to `accept`.

Configuring Your Network for External Access

The firewall described in this chapter works best when configured for one-way connections to the Internet. IP filtering can present a formidable wall with this configuration. However, when you start allowing connections from the outside, then your internal services can become exposed to attack. You can replace your services with proxies (for instance, the TIS firewall or www.tis.com/) to protect yourself, but that makes designing your firewall a more complex and difficult process. For small networks, my advice is to pay an ISP to provide general services, such as Web pages, and take the risks.

If you do want two-way communication, then a reasonable method is to keep the one-way IP filtering firewall and create a dial-in PPP server of your own. You then connect to your own network from outside by using the same methods as for connecting to the Internet. If you add a one-time password system such as SecureID (www.securid.com), then your private network will be reasonably protected. However, since SecureID is a physical device that must be purchased, its use is beyond the scope of this book.

Another alternative is to use Secure shell for incoming connections on your Linux gateway/firewall. Secure shell can be configured to provide both host and user authentication, and can determine whether an incoming connection is from a trusted computer. It can also authenticate the incoming user (separate from the normal Linux user login process). Secure shell is essentially an application-based firewall.

By modifying the IP filtering firewall to allow only incoming Secure shell (port 22) you maintain the most of the firewall's integrity. There's only one possible port of entry and, if Secure shell is configured correctly, there is very little that an cracker can attack. Using Secure shell is discussed in Appendix A.

Managing the Firewall

Maintaining a firewall is a lot of work, and there is no way around that fact. The following maintenance and observation tips are oriented towards pointing you in the right direction and should not be considered to be definitive. Firewall management, like every other aspect of computer security, is a moving target.

There are several areas that are important enough that you should pay attention to them on a regular basis (some of these items can readily be categorized as general purpose security tools but are placed here, rather in Chapter 10, because they are also effective firewall tools as well).

- The people and organizations who attempt to gain unauthorized access to your firewall and private computers are diverse in both scope and ability.
- Your log files provide a good mechanism to observe what is happening to your firewall.
- You can effectively test your firewall with the `nmap` program.
- The Tripwire program can tell you which files and directories have changed or been modified.
- You can check your user passwords regularly with the `crack` system.

Know your Enemies

There is a great deal of media hype about computer and network break-ins. The problem that you face, now that you are concerned with such issues, is making intelligent decisions about who and what the threats are.

Probably the best place to start is in a neutral position. Don't view the threat as overwhelming or as trivial. Many of the crackers out there do not have an intimate understanding of computers and the internet protocols. They are referred to as *scriptkiddies* because they make use of readily available scripts and cracking tools. This appears to be true because a considerable amount of the suspicious Internet traffic can be deduced to come from such tools.

On the other hand, there are enough smart crackers out there to worry about. There are both individuals and organized groups that make their living that way.

The professionals have varying degrees of ability, of course, but they all should be treated as significant threats in both terms of intelligence and ability.

Whatever direction you are being attacked from, you can do a lot to protect yourself. The firewall described in this chapter is the essential corner stone. Once in place, you need to actively monitor and manage it to assure that you present your best defense.

Know Their Tools and Methods

There are numerous tools available to the unscrupulous cracker. One of them—nmap—is described in the section "Using NMAP to Test Your System" in this chapter. Other tools can be investigated by searching the net.

There are also numerous methods for attacking systems. For instance, if one can gather information about a system or network, then you can go search the manufacturer's bug and vulnerability lists. By comparing the two lists you might be able to walk through an open door or slither through a crack. Another way is the well publicized *denial of service* attack. By sending incorrect and incomplete packets into a computer it is often possible to overload the internal network buffers of that computer and shut the service or entire computer down. No break in occurs but the operators and users of the computer or network suffer a temporary breakdown.

Again, this book is not intended to be an reference for security matters. It deliberately avoids the detail on subjects such as this in order to concentrate on specific solutions. Please refer to the URLs listed in the section "Education is Your Firewall Too" to study this issue further.

Monitoring your Log Files

Your log files are often your best way of knowing what is happening, and has happened to your system. They record system information about users and system processes. You can keep track of user logins and failures; modem/PPP connections to the Internet and many other functions.

There are numerous flags that you should keep an eye out for. Some of the most important are failed logins, logins at odd hours (that don't fit your users' general profiles), logins from unrecognized machines, etc. Also keep a close look at super user (root) log ins. Limit the distribution of the root account password to yourself and one or two other people. Don't write down the password either. In that way, it is possible to know when an unauthorized root login has occurred. The `last` command lists user logins. The `lastlog` shows the time of the last login for each of the users.

Keep an eye out for unusual `/var/log/messages` system information. The system logs much of its information to that file.

Other logs of interest are `secure`, `xfer.log` and the `samba` logs. The `secure` log records incoming connections to the Linux services (Telnet, imap, etc.). The `xfer.log` keeps track of data transfers from the Linux computer. The `samba` logs keeps track of external Samba connections.

Using NMAP to Test Your System

The `nmap` program is a powerful security tool. It can be used for good purposes or not. It can be used against you so, since it can be obtained off the Internet, you should use it to protect your network.

You should not, under any circumstances, use `nmap` to scan machines that you do not have or have permission to do so. Using `nmap` in an unauthorized manner is similar to walking up to a house and rattling the door. It is okay to test your own door, but not someone else's.

`Nmap` does three things: simple and flexible pings, port scans, and computer fingerprinting. The functions are as follows:

- **Pings.** You can use `nmap` to see what machines are up on a network. The ping program sends out simple ICMP packets and displays their response. It is a workhorse for system administrators who want to see if a network device is alive.

- **Port scan.** This is the process where `nmap` sends `tcp`, `udp` and `icmp` packets with various settings are sent to a host or entire network and the response monitored. `Nmap` can determine what ports are available (listening) depending on what the response is.

- **Fingerprinting.** A variation of the port scan sends out packets of varying type and setting. The responses can be correlated to determine what operating system is running on the target.

When you put all three (especially the latter two) functions together, you can gather a great deal of intelligence about individual machines and entire network. The more that one knows about a network, the more possibilities there are for attack. You should know at least as much about your network as an intruder, and `nmap` can help you do that.

`Nmap` is a difficult system to master, because it takes a good understanding of the underlying TCP/IP protocols to make complete sense of the information that it can give you. The following examples are meant to give you a sense of what `nmap` can do and how to utitilize the results (the ping function is useful but is skipped over in this discussion for the sake of brevity).

 Most of the interesting scans must be performed as root.

PORT SCAN YOUR OWN LINUX SERVER

Login as root on your Linux Internet gateway—atlas—and install the nmap package.

```
rpm -ivh /mnt/cdrom/firewall/nmap*
```

Run the following nmap scan against yourself.

```
nmap -sS 192.168.1.254
```

This is SYN scan. It sends the first part of a tcp handshake used for opening a tcp connection such as a Telnet session. When a response is sent, nmap sends another packet that immediately clears the connection. The result is that you can get a response from all active ports and the target system probably doesn't log any of the partial connections. That means you get the information but probably don't leave any trace.

The results from the default Red Hat installation without any firewall is as follows.

```
Starting nmap V. 2.07 by Fyodor (fyodor@dhp.com,
www.insecure.org/nmap/)
Interesting ports on atlas.paunchy.net (192.168.1.250):
Port    State       Protocol    Service
21      open        tcp         ftp
23      open        tcp         telnet
25      open        tcp         smtp
37      open        tcp         time
53      open        tcp         domain
70      open        tcp         gopher
79      open        tcp         finger
98      open        tcp         tacnews
109     open        tcp         pop-2
110     open        tcp         pop-3
111     open        tcp         sunrpc
113     open        tcp         auth
139     open        tcp         netbios-ssn
143     open        tcp         imap2
```

```
513       open        tcp         login
514       open        tcp         shell
515       open        tcp         printer
963       open        tcp         unknown
984       open        tcp         unknown
989       open        tcp         unknown
994       open        tcp         unknown
1024      open        tcp         unknown
1080      open        tcp         socks
6000      open        tcp         xterm
7100      open        tcp         font-service

Nmap run completed — 1 IP address (1 host up) scanned in 1 second
```

That list corresponds to the /etc/services file. Those are the ports that are potential targets for all sorts of mischief. One way to tighten up your system is to eliminate all the services that you don't use. Services such as finger, gopher, and such can be removed or commented out of your /etc/services file.

PORT SCAN ANOTHER LINUX MACHINE
Run a Stealth FIN port scan against another Linux machine on your network. Enter the command.

```
nmap -sF 192.168.1.100
```

This scan attempts to uses a combination of tcp packet flags to hide from detection programs. The results from an unprotected Linux computer are similar to the previous listing, and is not shown here for brevity's sake. But the end result is the same—more information about a system without necessarily revealing yourself.

PORT SCAN A WINDOWS COMPUTER
Run a port scan against a Windows machine.

```
nmap -sS 192.168.1.1
```

Returns the following:

```
Starting nmap V. 2.07 by Fyodor (fyodor@dhp.com,
www.insecure.org/nmap/)
Interesting ports on toluca.paunchy.net (192.168.1.1):
Port      State       Protocol    Service
139       open        tcp         netbios-ssn
617       open        tcp         unknown
Nmap run completed — 1 IP address (1 host up) scanned in 1 second
```

There is an unknown and a netbios port. You could potentially use this information to attack the Windows machine. For instance, a denial of service attack might be mounted against the netbios.

FINGERPRINT YOUR NETWORK

Now try detecting the operating systems that are running on your network. Enter the command.

```
nmap -sS -O 192.168.1.0/24
```

You should see all the unprotected network devices as follows:

```
Starting nmap V. 2.07 by Fyodor (fyodor@dhp.com,
www.insecure.org/nmap/)
Interesting ports on toluca.paunchy.net (192.168.1.100):
Port     State       Protocol    Service
139      open        tcp         netbios-ssn

TCP Sequence Prediction: Class=trivial time dependency
                        Difficulty=0 (Trivial joke)
Remote operating system guess: Windows NT4 / Win95 / Win98

TCP Sequence Prediction: Class=truly random
{... the Linux ports edited out to reduce the length of this
listing...}
                        Difficulty=9999999 (Good luck!)
Remote operating system guess: Linux 2.0.35-36
Nmap run completed — 256 IP addresses (2 host up) scanned in 56
seconds
```

This shows that the paunchy.net network has two machines running without firewalls (and where Fydor's preferences are!). Both operating systems are accurately detected; in fact almost the exact Linux version is found.

STOP SCANNING BY TURNING ON YOUR FIREWALL

This example uses the Linux machine atlas. Log in to it and install the ipchains package, if necessary. The simple filter shown below turns off all network connections, so you need to be at the console to enter the rules. (You can make your own filter script that allows, say, a Telnet connection if you want.) Enter the rules.

```
ipchains -P output DENY
ipchains -P input DENY
ipchains -P forward DENY
```

Run any of the scans from the previous examples; or try new ones. Enter the following:

```
nmap -sX atlas
```

After about a minute nmap returns the following:

```
Starting nmap V. 2.07 by Fyodor (fyodor@dhp.com,
www.insecure.org/nmap/)
Nmap run completed — 0 IP addresses (0 hosts up) scanned in 80
seconds
```

Nmap was not able to detect any open ports because the filter either prevented the packets from ever getting to the Linux machine's network layer or else the filter prevented any return packets from getting back to the nmap server.

Read the Web page maintained by the nmap creator at www.insecure.org for much more in depth—and interesting—discussion of nmap.

Using Tripwire to Monitor Your System

Tripwire is a tool for computing and storing the digital signature of files. There is always the danger of your system being broken into by a subtle intruder. Once inside the cracker doesn't do any thing obvious and does not attract any attention. Then, sometime later, the break-in is discovered but it is not know when it first occurred.

You are left unsure about which files are valid and which might be hidden disasters. The technology and skill of some crackers is such that they can modify or substitute a file and leave the obvious check sums the same as the original. For example, your /bin/ls command might be replaced with another program that provides the features of a normal ls but also does some other nasty process.

Tripwire creates its own database of digital signatures that can, and should, be stored on some read-only media. You can periodically check the state of your important systems files. In the case of a break-in, you can check your system against the Tripwire database.

Tripwire is included on the companion CD-ROM. Log in as root and install it.

```
rpm -ivh /mnt/cdrom/firewall/tripwire*
```

Tripwire is controlled by the /etc/tw.config file. If you look at the file, then you see the lines like /dev @@DEVM. These tell Tripwire what and how to check the files. The macros, such as @@DEVM are defined earlier in the file and expand to $+pnugsci12 for instance. Without going into the detail of what each character means, that particular example tells Tripwire to check every possible change that can occur in a file.

This example leaves the default Tripwire configuration as is. To run Tripwire you need to have initialize its signature data base. Enter the command and be prepared to wait a while for it to finish.

```
/usr/sbin/tripwire -init
```

Tripwire chugs away. If it finishes without problems, it then stores its signature database in the /root/databases directory.

Make a trivial change to a file as follows:

```
touch /bin/ls
```

Next, run Tripwire in interactive mode:

```
tripwire -interactive
```

When it finishes, you see that it reports /bin/ls as having been changed.

It is best to store a Tripwire database in a read-only media. If you can burn it into a CD-ROM, then that is probably the best solution. Then nobody with access to your physical plant can easily alter your database. (Paranoid? Maybe, but it *is* a possibility.)

You can run Tripwire on a daily, or other frequent, basis from the cron daemon. Then it is a matter of checking the results and using your judgement about what changed files make sense and which ones do not. Use your judgement as to how often that you review the logs. In some cases, you might want to only run Tripwire so that you have an audit trail should you ever get broken into.

Using crack to Test Your Passwords

Passwords are your first and last line of defense. Now that you are connected to the Internet, it is necessary to test your passwords regularly just in case your firewall is compromised.

The crack RPM is included on the companion CD-ROM and is used to guess passwords. Linux passwords are stored in encrypted form in either the /etc/passwd or /etc/shadow files. Crack goes through international dictionaries and encrypts each and every word or phrase. It then compares the two encrypted entities and if a match occurs, then it knows your password.

Log in as root and install the crack RPM.

```
rpm -ivh /mnt/cdrom/firewall/crack*
```

The cracklibs and cracklib-dicts RPM packages, needed by crack, should already have been installed during the Red Hat installation process.

Chapter 12: Creating a Simple Firewall

Next, run `crack` against your `/etc/passwd`. Make a copy of the password file in, for instance, `/root/passwd.crack`. Then run the `crack` command.

`/root/crack-4.1f/Crack /etc/passwd`

If you have installed shadow passwords, then you need to unconvert the `/etc/shadow` file before running crack. Run `pwunconv` to restore the passwords. Copy the newly restored `/etc/passwd` file to some other temporary location like `/root/passwd.crack`. Make it readable only by `root`: `chmod 400 /root/passwd`. Finally, restore the shadow password file; `pwconv`.

`Crack` displays the results of each password that it works on. In the case where a user account is not a login account it displays a result like follows:

```
join: Apr 10 02:41:18 User uucp (in /etc/shadow) has a locked password; - *
```

If you have set good passwords, then it is likely that `crack` will not discover it. But just to be sure, try using a trivial password in one of the accounts (don't forget to change it back to a good one!) and see what happens. When `Crack` finds the password it gives the system administrator a good jolt.

Don't forget to delete the `/root/passwd.crack` file once you have finished checking it.

There is another way to discover passwords. You can use a packet sniffer to look at and store every packet that travels across your network. Red Hat Linux comes with the package `tcpdump` that includes a sniffer. If you record every packet on a private network, then you can filter through the information and possibly pick out plain text passwords. You have to have physical access to a network but if that can be obtained, then the rest is easier. The only real solution is to use encryption. Use encrypted Samba passwords for file sharing and Secure shell for interactive communications. The Secure shell ssh tools can be found at `ftp://ftp.cs.hut.fi/pub/ssh`.

Education is Your Firewall Too

It should be emphasized that the security methods discussed here are effective but not complete. They are a reasonable place to start. However, firewall security and security in general is a big topic. It is wise to treat all of this as a process. If you continue to educate yourself on the subject, then you stand a much better chance of keeping ahead of the wolves.

There are several places to look at on the Internet:

- The Computer Emergency Response Team (CERT) web page at www.cert.org
- http://www.cis.ohio-state.edu/text/faq/usenet/computer-security/top.html
- http://olympus.cs.ucdavis.edu/
- http://www.cs.pdx.edu/~mchugh/cs510sc.html
- http://www.cs.umsl.edu/~sanjiv/security.html
- http://www2.pitt.edu/HOME/Security.old/
- http://www.insecure.org (one of my favorites and also one of the best!)

The following are newsgroups:

- comp.linux.security
- comp.firewalls

If you can find a college course on Internet or computer security, then that is certainly worthwhile. There are conferences that are very good at disseminating a great deal of information in a short time. Look up the schedules at www.sans.org and www.usenix.org for instance.

Troubleshooting

The two most difficult systems to install and maintain are the ipchains filtering firewall and the DNS server. Some basic troubleshooting hints and techniques are described in this section. The other systems discussed in this chapter deal with the monitoring and maintenance of the above services and are not difficult to set up or use.

IP Chains

Setting up IP chains can be a confusing task at first. It's difficult to understand which packets are going where and through which interface. It is also hard to keep track of how the source and destination addresses – and port numbers – interact with the filtering rules.

When designing new rules or modifying existing ones, it is best to write out the rules on a piece of paper in order to get a better understanding of them. Make separate diagrams and lists for each direction: outgoing packets, incoming, and forwarding. (If you continue to use a simple network with a single Linux gateway, then the only forwarding rule that you'll probably ever need is the masquerading one.)

Once you have put into place the new rules, or are trying to better understand existing ones, then you can use the `dctrl` and `tcpdump` utilities.

The `dctrl diald` connection GUI provides a display of open tcp and udp network connections. The source, destination and port information is shown. You can see new connections open up and old ones end. It is quite useful for seeing what is going on at your PPP connection.

The `tcpdump` is a packet sniffer. It comes as part of the Red Hat distribution and can be installed by logging in as root and entering the command `rpm -ivh /mnt/cdrom/RedHat/RPMS/tcpdump*`. This is a powerful tool because you can see every network packet that goes through your PPP connection. (You can also see every packet that goes by any network connection on your machine. This is one of the commonly used tools for sniffing information off a network. With enough experience and patience, you can discover passwords and other vital information. Beware.) If you are having problems getting a filter to work, then you can watch what packets are showing up at your PPP interface. With some work it is possible to then relate those packets back to your rule set and hopefully find the errant filtering rule.

Finally, you can try backing off on your filtering rules. Define a rule set that sets up default deny policies – as done in this book's `ipchains` scripts – but then set up input and output rules in each direction that allow all packets. For instance, try the following rules.

```
ipchains -F
ipchains -P output DENY
ipchains -P input DENY
ipchains -P forward DENY
ipchains -A output -j ACCEPT -s 0.0.0.0/0 -d 0.0.0.0/0
ipchains -A input -j ACCEPT -s 0.0.0.0/0 -d 0.0.0.0/0
```

These rules first flush out any existing rules (it is essential to start from scratch when debugging filtering rules) and then setting up a uniform denial policy. At that point your firewall is shut down tight. The final two rules open up the firewall to tcp, udp, and icmp packets, coming from any location and going to any location from any port. Your firewall is now completely open.

Test your system and whatever Internet access you are after should work. The next step is to discover what IP protocol is getting stuck. Change the rules to include separate ones for both the TCP and UDP protocols as follows:

```
ipchains -F
ipchains -P output DENY
ipchains -P input DENY
ipchains -P forward DENY
ipchains -A output -p tcp -j ACCEPT -s 0.0.0.0/0 -d 0.0.0.0/0
ipchains -A input  -p tcp -j ACCEPT -s 0.0.0.0/0 -d 0.0.0.0/0
ipchains -A output -p udp -j ACCEPT -s 0.0.0.0/0 -d 0.0.0.0/0
ipchains -A input  -p udp -j ACCEPT -s 0.0.0.0/0 -d 0.0.0.0/0
```

You have now separated out the tcp and udp protocols; the icmp protocol is ignored in this example for simplicity and because it doesn't play a factor in nearly as many transactions as the other two do. Try modifying the source and destination addresses to their correct values (for instance, for outgoing udp packets set the source address to your PPP IP address.) You should consult the `ipchains.rules` script for the details of the process.

Test your system again. Once you have narrowed the problem down to a protocol, then you need to find out the port.

Next, try setting up rules for the individual interfaces. You should pay particular attention to your internal interfaces such as `eth0` and `lo`. It is very easy to set up rules for those interfaces that interfer or deny communication on your private network. Once again, please refer to the `ipchains.rules` script for more details.

Without going into more detail you get the idea. Like in all other troubleshooting, you want to successively narrow down the problem until you arrive at the solution.

Masquerading

If you are having problems getting masquerading to work, then first check that you have enabled IP forwarding in your Linux gateway. Check the file `/etc/sysconfig/network` and make sure that the `IPFORWARD_IPV4` line is set to `yes`.

```
IPFORWARD_IPV4=yes
```

You need to restart your Linux networking to make the new rule take effect.

```
/etc/rc.d/init.d/network restart
```

Next, check that the masquerading rule has atcually been set up with the `ipchains -L` command. You should see the following.

```
Chain forward (policy DENY):
target     prot opt    source            destination        ports
MASQ       all  ----   192.168.1.0/24    anywhere           n/a
```

If you still can not find the problem, then refer to Chapter 7 to make sure that your network connections are working correctly. Next, check the HOWTO documents and man pages.

DNS

If you have problems with the DNS server, then you should first look in the `/var/log/name.run` log file. It show basic information about what is going on with the system both during the startup process and general operation. Make sure that all the files defined in the `/etc/named.conf` file exist and are in their correct directories.

Keep in mind that the local DNS server is optional. From the Linux server's perspective, it can easily keep track and find the other machines on the network as long as the `/etc/hosts` file is accurate and up to date. All of your machines can find their way around on the Internet by using your ISP's DNS server. Make sure that your `/etc/resolv.conf` file has the correct ISP DNS server in it. You have to suffer the delay while your Linux gateway connects to the Internet before getting domain names resolved but it you will get your IP numbers.

Summary

This chapter describes how to set up a firewall to protect your private network from the worst of the Internet. The `ipchains` system is used as the heart of the firewall. It provides IP filtering that provides excellent protection when used in conjunction with the hybrid firewall described in Chapter 11. When combined with monitoring and testing tools, the firewall can be maintained in order to continuously provide maximum protection.

- ◆ An introduction to firewalls is duscussed and the three basic types are described. The advantages of each are briefly discussed and the reasoning for the use of a hybrid firewall in this book is given.

- ◆ An introduction to the `ipchains` system is given. Its basic functions are explained. A simple example is given.

- Configuring a simple filtering firewall is described. A basic set of `ipchains` rules are described so that you can interactively experiment with them. By getting a feel for how the system works you can better install and manage the full rule set.

- A description of a full filtering rule set is described. It is displayed in the text but also is stored on the companion CD-ROM. The rule set provides a template that allows the major protocols (such as www and FTP) to work through your firewall. You can modify the script to allow other protocols through your firewall as desired.

- The process of checking your log files is discussed. Log files provide you with the history of your system. By studying them, you can discover problems and possible break-ins before they progress to far.

- The `nmap` system is described. `Nmap` is a powerful tool that can be used to `port scan` networks. Port scanning can mine information about your computers and network. The information can be used against you. By proactively scanning your own network and computers (and nobody else's), you can take a big step towards short-circuiting the bad guys.

- The Tripwire utility is introduced. It creates signatures for any file or file system that you want. The signatures (or fingerprints) can be stored on read-only media to provide a means of checking your files for unauthorized access or modification.

- The `crack` program is introduced. It checks your encrypted passwords against any word or phrase that can be contained in a dictionary (you must have the dictionary of course). By regularly checking your passwords you can proactively find and eliminate ones that do not meet your specifications.

- If you educate yourself on the ever changing Internet hazards, then you have a chance of staying ahead of the threats. Managing and using firewalls is a process that includes education as well as tools. There are many resources available on the Internet as well as traditional sources such as schools and seminars.

Chapter 13

Configuring a Linux E-mail Server

IN THIS CHAPTER

- Connecting your e-mail client to your ISP
- Configuring Sendmail for local e-mail
- Using Fetchmail to retrieve e-mail from your ISP
- Troubleshooting e-mail problems

CONFIGURING E-MAIL SYSTEMS IS one of the more complex tasks that you can do. There are numerous e-mail servers and clients, and getting them all to interact is definitely not a trivial task.

In order to simplify your e-mail configuration, this chapter uses two types of e-mail systems. One is simple and easy to configure but is not very flexible, and the other is not so easy to set up but is somewhat more flexible. You can choose the best solution for your operation.

Using the Netscape E-mail Client

Once you have subscribed to an ISP and connected to the Internet, you can use the ISP as your e-mail server. This is quite simple in concept and execution because your ISP gives you a login account and that login account comes with an e-mail address. Your ISP also provides *Post Office Protocol* (POP) and *IMAP* protocol capabilities, which means that you can download and/or view your e-mail from your Private Network.

The POP and IMAP protocols are designed to allow access to e-mail via an external network or connection. Traditionally, one would have to log into an account and access e-mail directly from that machine, but the introduction of the POP and IMAP protocols makes that unnecessary.

Netscape provides an e-mail client that is capable of using either POP or IMAP. You can configure the Netscape e-mail client to access your remote ISP account to send and retrieve e-mail. You pay your ISP to manage your e-mail, and don't have to worry about anything other than configuring the Netscape client. Figure 13-1 shows an e-mail system based around an ISP server. Connections are made through the Linux gateway Atlas, and local workstations send and receive mail through the ISP.

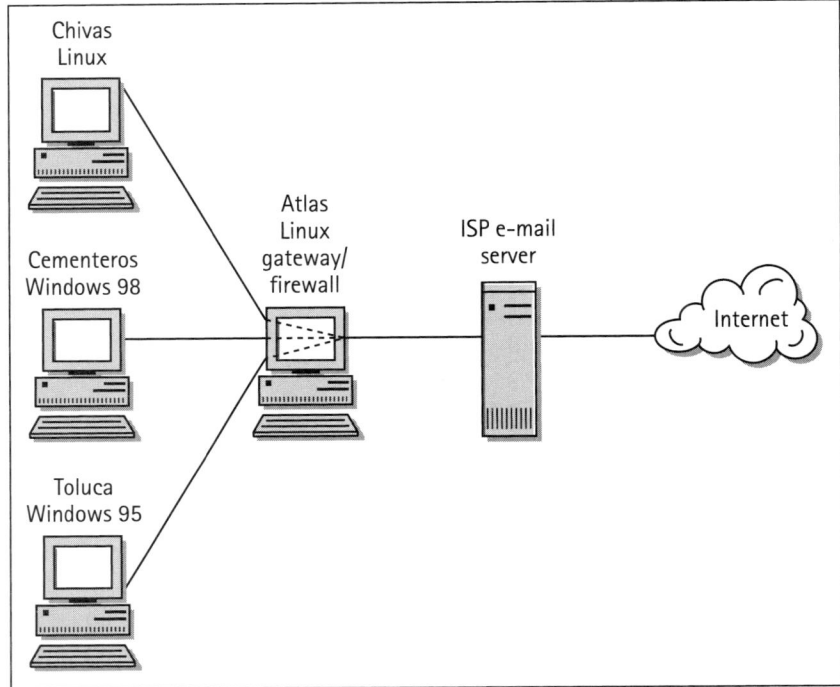

Figure 13-1: An ISP based e-mail system

 You are not limited to Netscape as your e-mail client. There are other clients available that work with POP and IMAP. For instance, the simple, text based PINE client can be used. The Netscape client is used as the example in this chapter because it is included in the Red Hat distribution included on the companion CD-ROM, and it is also easy to use and powerful.

Netscape is installed as part of the Red Hat installation process. Log in as any user and click on the Netscape (N) button on the Main menu panel. When the Netscape window opens up, click Edit → Preferences. The Preferences screen is displayed.

Chapter 13: Configuring a Linux E-mail Server

Click Mail and Groups, then click Mail Server. Enter the information about your user name (as it exists on your ISP's mail server) and the names of your outgoing and incoming server.

Click either the POP3 or IMAP4 radio buttons depending on what protocol your ISP provides you.

- POP3 is a one-way protocol. It is used to retrieve, but not send, e-mail. If you do not want to run a sendmail daemon on your local computer (for security, or other reasons), then use IMAP.

- IMAP4 is a two-way protocol. You can use it to both send and receive e-mail. It is the newer of the two protocols and has reached a state of maturity where you should not have any problems with it.

Your entries should look something like the window shown in Figure 13-2.

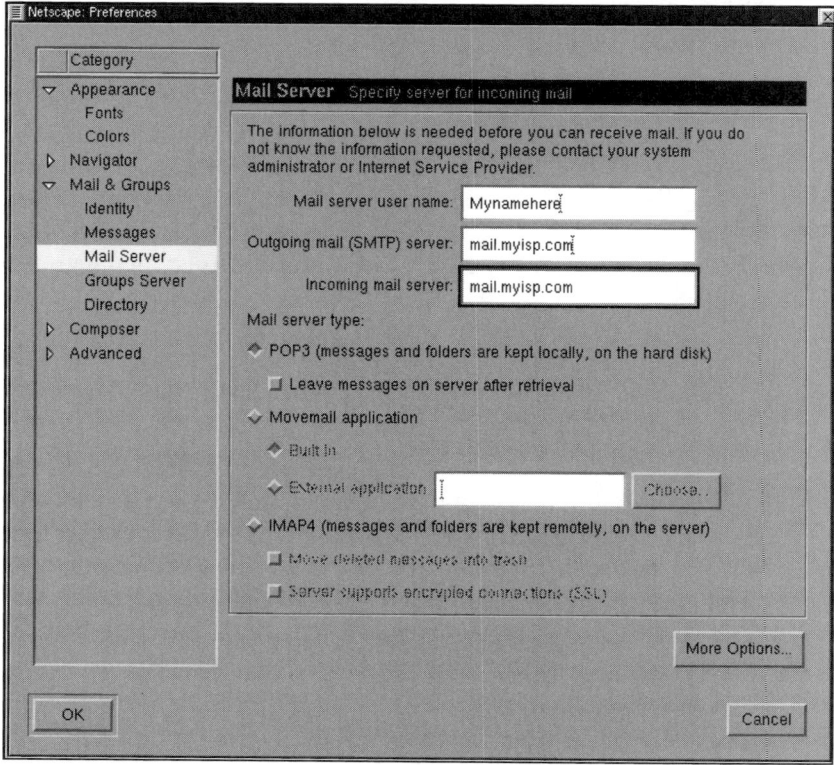

Figure 13-2: The Netscape Mail Server window

Next, click the Identity item and enter your full e-mail address, and optionally your real name, organization, and signature file.

Click OK and try to send yourself some e-mail. You should be able to click the Get messages button and receive your e-mail.

The caveat to this method is that each user on your network will need an e-mail address provided by your ISP. That typically costs some money, but not much, and is quite reasonable for even the smallest business. Also, since all of your e-mail is queued through your ISP, you have to have a PPP connection activated in order to access it. So if users on your Private Network want to communicate with each other, then they have to all go out to the ISP to do so. This is probably not a problem until your operation grows beyond a dozen people or so.

Another advantage to this method is that you can retrieve e-mail from any location. As long as you have a way to connect to your ISP, then you can retrieve your e-mail. For instance, if you have a lap top with a modem, then you can configure it to retrieve your e-mail and all you have to do is dial in to your ISP and get it.

Even if you have a lot of e-mail traffic this method still might make sense as long as you have a fast connection to your ISP. For instance, if you have a T1 (1.45 Mbps), then you very likely will not have any problems. However, if you little modem has to manage megabytes of e-mail traffic every day, then you need either a bigger Internet pipe or you need to reduce the load by keeping local traffic within your network. The next section, "Configuring a Local E-mail Server," describes that process.

Configuring a Local E-mail Server

If you have a significant amount of e-mail traffic (especially local traffic) then using your ISP as your e-mail server might not be practical. This section describes a hybrid system where your Linux Internet gateway, or atlas, acts as the local e-mail server using the *sendmail, fetchmail,* and *imap* software. E-mail destined for locations outside of your network is forwarded to your ISP. Incoming e-mail traffic is retrieved from your ISP via fetchmail. Fetchmail feeds the retrieved e-mails to sendmail, which distributes it to the rest of the network. Figure 13-3 shows the configuration of the local e-mail system. The Linux IMAP server cementero downloads all e-mail from the ISP's mail server. The local workstations send and receive e-mail via atlas.

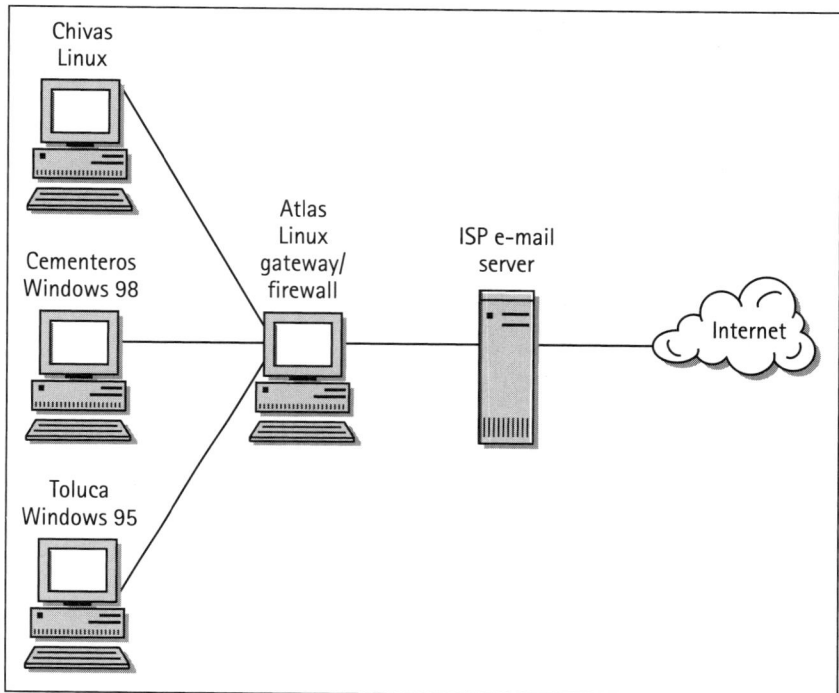

Figure 13-3: A locally based e-mail system

There are four parts that need to be configured together to make this system work: the e-mail client, local delivery, external delivery, and external retrieval. They are described in that order.

The fictitious user rodbush is used in the examples for this configuration. Log in as root and create the user by running the commands:

adduser rodbush
passwd rodbush

Configuring the Netscape E-mail Client

This e-mail system depends one the use of the Netscape mail client on each computer on paunchy.net. Netscape should be configured to use IMAP4. You can use the instructions previously given in the section "Using the Netscape E-mail Client."

However, instead of entering the name of your ISP as the incoming and outgoing server, you should enter atlas.paunchy.net instead. The Linux e-mail server atlas directs all local e-mail traffic and forwards or retrieves e-mail destined for or coming from the Internet via the ISP server.

Please see the section "Configuring your Netscape E-mail Client" in Chapter 14 for more information on configuring Netscape for your local system.

Configuring Sendmail for Local E-mail

The default sendmail configuration requires all the names that your e-mail server is known as to be listed in /etc/sendmail.cw. Modify the file as follows.

```
# sendmail.cw - include all aliases for your machine here.
chiva
paunchy.net
```

Your ISP must know what name you are known as too. That process is discussed in the section Registering your Domain Name later in this chapter.

The /etc/sendmail.cf file must be modified too. Modify the parameter #Dj$w.Foo.COM as shown below.

```
Dj$w.paunchy.net
```

This line tells sendmail what the local domain name is.

Configuring Sendmail for External Delivery

To send mail from your network to the outside world through your ISP, you need to make a another modification to the /etc/sendmail.cf file. Log in as root and edit the sendmail.cf file. Find the section that looks as follows:

```
# "Smart" relay host (may be null)
DS
```

Modify the DS parameter to DSmyisp.com which tells sendmail to deliver external mail to your ISP.

The modified configuration file should look like the following.

```
# "Smart" relay host (may be null)
DSmail.myisp.com
```

Next, comment out the following line to allow your messages to be relayed to your ISP. This line can be found at, or around, line 1033 in the /etc/sendmail.cf file.

```
# anything else is bogus
###R$*                    $#error $@ 5.7.1 $: "550 Relaying denied"
```

Restart the Sendmail Daemon to Activate the Changes

You need to restart the sendmail daemon in order to put the changes into effect. Use the sendmail startup script to restart the daemon.

`/etc/rc.d/init.d/sendmail restart`

You should be able to test your system. While logged on as root, enter the command

`mail rodbush@myisp.com`

This is a simple e-mail client. Type whatever you want on the subject line, and then everything that you type in is part of the message that you are composing. Finish the message by entering a period (.) as the first character on a line and then press the Enter key. Press the Enter key once more at the CC: prompt.

If you have a PPP connection to your ISP, then your message should be delivered immediately. Otherwise, your `diald` program will make the connection and your message is delivered. Log on to your ISP account and check for your message. It's great if it works, but if it doesn't, check the Troubleshooting section in this chapter.

Restart the sendmail daemon to make it reread its configuration files.

`/etc/rc.d/init.d/sendmail restart`

Installing imap

The imap RPM package needs to be installed in order for the Netscape clients to access the e-mail distributed by sendmail. Log in as root and add it as follows:

`rpm -ivh /mnt/cdrom/RedHat/RPMS/imap*`

The `imapd` daemon is kicked off by the `inetd` daemon. If you look in the `/etc/inetd.conf` file, then you see that there is an entry for `imapd`. Whenever Netscape, or any other `imap` based e-mail client, queries atlas (the e-mail server) the `imapd` daemon is started and negotiates the delivery of the e-mail.

You could use the Post Office Protocol (POP) for this function. However, POP does not deliver outgoing mail, and that would require you to setup sendmail on each client workstation. That is not terribly difficult but it enhances security if you remove sendmail completely from every Linux workstation except atlas. Also, Windows machines do not run sendmail and so the only site wide solution is to use imap.

Configuring Fetchmail for External Retrieval

Fetchmail can be used to retrieve e-mail queued up for an individual user on a remote account. When used for a single user it works in much the same way as you can use your Netscape e-mail client; it uses POP or IMAP to download your e-mail to your local e-mail client.

Fetchmail can be used on an individual basis to download each user's e-mail. This is reasonable if your network has only a few people. Please see the section "Configuring Fetchmail for a Single User" for instructions.

Fetchmail can also download e-mail for multiple local users from a single remote account. This is called *Multidrop mode* and is the method used here. See the section "Configuring Fetchmail for Multiple Users" for instructions.

In order to make use of multidrop mode you must have a registered domain name. The domain name must be registered so that more than one individual can receive e-mail. For example, if you have just a single ISP login account, then only that user name can receive e-mail. However, if you have registered domain name such as `paunchy.net`, then any user that you give an account on your own network (`paunchy.net`) can receive e-mail from the Internet.

The following section Registering your Domain Name describes the process of registering your domain name.

REGISTERING YOUR DOMAIN NAME

The local e-mail server as described in this chapter relies on funneling all e-mail through a single e-mail account at your ISP. This means that you need to register an domain name with the InterNIC. This is a simple process if you pay your ISP to process the paperwork for you. It costs $70 (as of spring, 1999) for two years of registration. You can have your ISP create an alias in their own e-mail system to map your registered domain name to your single e-mail address.

The alternative to registering a domain name and routing all of your user's e-mail through a single account is to pay your ISP to create an e-mail account for every user on your system. You need to create a separate fetchmail process to retrieve each of your users e-mail.

Once that you have registered your domain and had your ISP configure their system for you, then any mail addressed to that domain should show up at your ISP login account. For instance if your login account name is `widget_inc`, at isp.com and someone sends e-mail to `rod_bush@paunchy.net`, then that message shows up in the mail queue for `widget_inc`.

The trick is to download that mail queue to your local server and then distribute it to the appropriate individual mail queues. The following sections describe how to do that.

CONFIGURING FETCHMAIL FOR A SINGLE USER

Fetchmail gets its configuration from the `.fetchmailrc` file in a user's home directory. The `fetchmailconf` program provides an interactive configuration GUI. However, a sample configuration file is provided here that can be used with the `paunchy.net` network. It is used in this example for the example user rod_bush.

To configure your own fetchmail, log in as root, mount the CD-ROM and install fetchmail.

```
rpm -ivh /mnt/cdrom/RedHat/RPMS/fetchmail*
```

Create the sample user Rod Bush.

```
useradd rbush
passwd iwantmail
```

Copy the configuration file from the companion CD-ROM.

```
cd /home/rbush
cp /mnt/cdrom/IDG/e-mail/fetchmailrc.sampleuser ./.fetchmailrc
chown rbush.rbush /home/rbush/.fetchmailrc
```

Change it to include your ISP login name and password.

```
# Configuration created Fri Apr  9 22:28:57 1999 by fetchmailconf
set postmaster "root"
poll mail.myisp.com with proto POP3
user "rbush" there with password "iwantmail" is rbush here
options fetchall
```

- ◆ The `set postmaster` parameter informs the sendmail program that any unrecognized or such messages should be forwarded to the root user.
- ◆ The `poll mail.myisp.com with proto POP3` tells fetchmail to go to your ISP's mail server and use the POP3 protocol (IMAP and other protocols can be used too).

- The `user` line tells fetchmail that your ISP user name and password are `rbush` and `iwantmail` and that any e-mail in that account should be sent to the local user Rod Bush.

- The fetchall option tells fetchmail to download all messages in the `widget_inc` e-mail queue.

Your .fetchmail file contains your ISP password, so change the permissions so that only the user can read and write to it by entering:

```
chmod 0600 .fetchmailrc
```

Once fetchmail is run and the e-mail for rod_bush is downloaded, then the Netscape e-mail client (or any e-mail program that speaks POP or IMAP) can be used to view the e-mail.

You can modify the `.fetchmailrc` file to get the e-mail for another user by changing the local user name. For instance, to use that script to get the e-mail for garagon just change the `user` line as follows (you should also create the account - adduser gabe_aragon).

```
user "rbush" there with password "iwantmail" is garagon here
```

The problem with this method is that every individual who wants to receive e-mail needs a separate e-mail account at the ISP. This can certainly be arranged and should not be prohibitively expensive. It works in much the same way as when you use Netscape to go directly to your ISP as described earlier in the section "Using the Netscape E-mail Client."

The advantage of using fetchmail, on an individual basis, is that it automatically downloads the e-mail for a particular user without configuring your local sendmail, fetchmail and procmail systems. When you receive e-mail from mailing lists, delivery can become a problem. Mailing lists typically do not have your explicit e-mail address. Using fetchmail on an individual basis solves that problem because every message is directly downloaded to each user's local account.

CONFIGURING FETCHMAIL FOR MULTIPLE USERS

Fetchmail can be run by root to retrieve an entire Private Network's e-mail. This is called *multidrop mode*. In multidrop mode, fetchmail is configured to read the e-mail's destination fields and convert it to a local domain's users. If the two fields do not match up completely (for instance, I receive e-mail from the list samba@samba.anu.edu.au which does not match up with my ISP user name), then the mail will not be delivered to your local account. Instead, it is sent to the postmaster which, in this example, is root.

To use this method, log in as root and create the following user.

```
adduser widget_inc
passwd widget_inc
```

Chapter 13: Configuring a Linux E-mail Server

Copy the sample multidrop `.fetchmailrc` file to the root home directory.

cp /mnt/cdrom/email/fetchmailrc.multidrop /root/.fetchmailrc

Your `.fetchmail` file contains your ISP password, so change the permissions so that only the user can read and write to it.

chmod 0600 .fetchmailrc

The fetchmail configuration file with multidrop is shown below.

```
# Configuration created Fri Apr  9 22:08:58 1999 by fetchmailconf
set postmaster "root"
poll mail.myisp.com with proto POP3
    localdomains paunchy.net
        user "widget_inc" there with password "iwantemail" is * here
options fetchall
```

- The `localdomains` line is added to tell fetchmail that the Private Network's domain name that it is servering is `paunchy.net`. This tells fetchmail to transfer e-mail from one domain to another. For instance, e-mail that shows up for `rod_bush@paunchy.net` at your ISP account widget_inc is transferred to the local e-mail account for rod_bush.

- The `user` line substitutes the asterix metacharacter (*) for an individual user name. That informs fetchmail that any e-mail that shows up with a `paunchy.net` domain name is to be downloaded and converted to the appropriate local e-mail account.

- The `fetchall` option tells fetchmail to download all messages in the `widget_inc` e-mail queue.

Now try and get your e-mail via your multidrop fetchmail. Log in to your ISP user account and send e-mail to two or more of your local users.

From your Linux e-mail server (atlas), log in as root and run fetchmail. Your `diald` should dial your ISP and make the PPP connection.

SCHEDULING FETCHMAIL FETCHES

You can configure fetchmail to automatically retrieve your company's e-mail in couple of ways.

One way is to run fetchmail in daemon mode and have it periodically download mail. It must be run as root and must be run in multidrop mode. For instance, if you run it as `fetchmail -d 300`, then fetchmail downloads your e-mail once every 5 minutes (or 300 seconds). If you run fetchmail in this mode, then you need to start it automatically every time that you boot your Linux machine. A good way to start up a system that does not have a startup script in the /etc/rc.d/init.d directory is to use the /etc/rc.local file. Log in as root and add the following lines to the rc.local file.

```
if [ -f /etc/fetchmail ]; then
   /usr/bin/fetchmail -d 300
fi
```

Another method is to have cron kick off a fetchmail process. Log in as root and run the crontab -e command. It starts up vi (or whatever you default text editor is) and edits the crontab file for the user root. Add the line like the following:

```
# Fetch mail from mail.myisp.com
0,20,40 * * * * /usr/bin/fetchmail -v
```

Cron starts the fetchmail process as the user root every 20 minutes. Please refer to the crontab man page for information about the scheduling details.

Finally, you might want to opt to download mail whenever you connect to your ISP. You can modify the /usr/local/etc/ipchains.rules to include the following line at the end of the file.

```
/usr/bin/fetchmail -d 60 -v
```

Once the PPP connection is made, diald/chat kicks off a fetchmail daemon that checks for e-mail once every 60 seconds (you can choose any interval that you want).

Add the following rule to the /usr/local/etc/ipchains.reset script to stop the fetchmail daemon when PPP is disconnected.

```
killall -9 fetchmail
```

You can use this method by itself or in conjunction with the previous two methods. There is no reason why you shouldn't download your e-mail every time you connect. It doesn't cost you anything other than the filling up your PPP connection with the e-mail coming across.

Troubleshooting

Designing and maintaining an e-mail server can be a very complex job. Fortunately, the default Red Hat installation provides a ready made sendmail system that works for a small network. By adding fetchmail to get remote e-mail, a complete e-mail system can readily be constructed. Please test your new e-mail system before using it as your primary e-mail system.

However, keep in mind that if you have problems configuring it, you can always configure e-mail clients like Netscape to send and receive e-mail directly from you ISP.

Using the Netscape E-mail Client

If your Netscape e-mail client refuses to read your mail queued up at your ISP, then first check that you have a PPP connection. Next check that your ipchains based firewall has rules set to allow POP or IMAP (depending on which protocol you use). A quick and potentially dangerous way to do this is to simply turn off the filtering rules. If you can then get your e-mail, then you know that a modification of your firewall is in order; consult Chapter 12 for a discussion of filtering rules.

If you still can't get your e-mail, then make sure that your Netscape preferences are set correctly. Look at the server name and protocols as well as check that your user name and e-mail address are correct. Consult the /var/log/messages and /var/log/maillog files for any hints to your problems. You might also consult with your ISP for their advice.

In If you are running your own e-mail server and your e-mail client can't access it, first check that your network connection is functioning correctly (Chapter 7 discusses network troubleshooting). If your network is okay, then check to see if the sendmail daemon is running correctly. That can be tested with a simple ps x |grep sendmail or /etc/rc.d/init.d/sendmail status commands as well as logging in to your server and running Netscape. Change the preferences to use Movmovemail and if you get your mail, then sendmail is fine. Change back to POP or IMAP and try again. If e-mail still fails, then check the /etc/services and /etc/inetd.conf files to make sure that they have POP and/or IMAP entries. Use RPM to check that POP or IMAP is installed (rpm -qa | grep -i pop). Also check your /var/log/messages and /var/log/maillog for any hints that you might glean. Finally, check out the Usenet news groups like comp.mail.sendmail for advice and information on your problem.

Fixing Problems with Local E-mail

The sendmail daemon is configured out of the box by Red Hat to serve a small Private Network. If you never need to go outside your own network and you are not getting e-mail, then check first that sendmail is running. Second, check the sendmail installation with the rpm -V sendmail command. If it still does not work, then consult your /var/log/messages and /var/log/maillog for insights. The last step is to consult the Usenet news groups like comp.mail.sendmail.

When a message fails to get sent, it is returned to the sender or the postmaster, or in the case where it can not be delivered to either, a message will be written to the /var/log/maillog file. The return message has information about why it failed. It is beyond the scope of this book to discuss the many possible reasons for this to happen. Please refer to the sendmail man page as well as the FAQ and other documents in the /usr/doc/sendmail directory for further information.

Fixing Problems with External Delivery

Configuring sendmail to forward e-mail destined for the outside world is a simple matter of modifying one parameter in the /etc/sendmail.cf file (see the section "Configuring Sendmail for External Delivery" in this chapter for details). If you cannot get your e-mail delivered, then the problem most likely lies in either your Internet connection or your sendmail installation. Use the troubleshooting techniques described in Chapters 11 and 12 to investigate the former. The latter can be checked by using the rpm -V sendmail command; don't hesitate to reinstall sendmail, because you only have three parameters in the sendmail.cf to change.

Fixing Problems with External Retrieval

Fetchmail is another system that depends on having your ISP PPP connection in place and your firewall filtering rules correct. If you are having problems getting it to work then use all the network and firewall troubleshooting hints given in Chapters 11 and 12 to verify your Internet connection. You can use the verbose flag to see how the connection and downloading process is going by using the fetchmail -v command. Pay attention the login and authentication process. When fetchmail has authenticated with the POP or IMAP server it should say that it's downloading the text or data of each message. Once that is done, then you should see sendmail related handshaking messages displayed. Any errors are displayed during this process. When all else fails, check with your ISP and the Usenet comp.mail.sendmail group.

Summary

E-mail is an essential part of any business or organization. You can configure your Linux network to use the very simple method of having each e-mail client directly access an individual e-mail account at your ISP. If that is not sufficient, then you can set up your Linux server to act as a local e-mail server and fetch and forward external e-mail via your ISP.

- ◆ Using your Netscape e-mail client to directly access e-mail queue at your ISP is covered. This is a simple and nearly bullet proof method. Your ISP takes delivery of e-mail addressed to you. Netscape is configured to pull your messages across your PPP connection via POP or IMAP. Each user on your network requires a separate account for this method to work.

- Using your Linux server to handle local e-mail delivery while forwarding or fetching external e-mail from your ISP is covered. This requires four separate functions to be performed: local deliver, external forwarding, external fetching and domain name registration.

- Obtaining a domain name is necessary so that your ISP can forward messages to individual users based on your domain name is covered. Your ISP can handle the registration process for a small fee.

- Configuring your Linux machine to act as a local e-mail server is covered. Messages destined for people on your network can be handled by the Red Hat default sendmail installation. No modification of the /etc/sendmail.cf configuration file.

- Modifying one parameter in your /etc/sendmail.cf file takes care of the e-mail forwarding process. That line simply points to your ISP's e-mail server.

- Using fetchmail to retrieve external messages queued at your ISP finishes your Linux e-mail server configuration. There are several ways to configure fetchmail; either on an individual retrieval basis or for your entire domain. The individual method is straightforward but the group (maildrop) method is not much more difficult.

- Troubleshooting e-mail problems is discussed. Much of the troubleshooting is based on basic network and PPP connection methods. Beyond that you can use the log information that sendmail, fetchmail, and procmail produces.

Part IV

Getting Work Done

CHAPTER 14
Using Office Productivity Tools

CHAPTER 15
Configuring an Intranet Web Server

Chapter 14

Using Office Productivity Tools

IN THIS CHAPTER

- Installing and using Applixware
- Using Applixware Words word processor
- Using Applixware Graphics and Presentation manager
- Introducing Applixware Spreadsheet
- Introducing Applixware E-mail client
- Using Applixware SQL Database Interface
- Configuring Netscape Navigator
- Troubleshooting application problems

THE EMPHASIS OF THIS book has been placed on properly building your Linux-based network. Linux-based networks are powerful and inexpensive, and you can use one to run your business network.

However, Linux is more than just a server. It can also be used as a general-purpose workstation. Products such as Applixware, StarOffice, WordPerfect, and many others, provide the personal productivity tools that turn an inexpensive Linux PC into your new personal workstation.

This chapter is intended to give you an introduction to some of the tools that are turning Linux into a complete productivity tool.

Introducing Applixware for Linux

Most of this book was written using the *Applixware Words* word processor. It is a full function *what-you-see-is-what-you-get* (WYSIWYG) word processor that has most of the functionality of Microsoft Word. It has most of the functions that one expects — formatting, cutting and pasting, graphics, spell checking and such. It also has the advantage of being able to run satisfactorily on less than top-of-the-line equipment; it runs under Linux and Linux just does not require as powerful a computer as other operating systems.

The only significant limitation that was found while writing this book is that Applixware Words can only track changes that occur within a line whereas Microsoft Word can detect changes down to the letter.

A lesser limitation is that the Microsoft Word template files that IDG Books uses could not be loaded directly. A simplework around was found by importing an existing Word document, with the template attached, into Words and stripping the old text old. This problem is more likely due to my inexperience with Words than any limitation of the product. On the other hand, the fact that I wrote the book using a word processor unfamiliar to me is a testimonial to the ease of use of Words.

Installing Applixware

Installing Applixware is a straightforward process. The demonstration software is found in the /mnt/cdrom/applixware directory on the CD-ROM that accompanies this book. Log in as root and change your working directory with the following command:

cd /usr/local/src

Mount the second CD-ROM and untar the single file as follows:

tar xvf /mnt/cdrom/applixware/applixdemo*

That process extracts several files to the /usr/local/src directory. The README.install file contains information about what type of systems Applixware can run on. The applix_demo.tgz contains the actual software and the install axdemo file is the script that installs the software.

Change your working directory to the applixdemo directory:

cd applixdemo*

Run the install axdemo script as follows:

./install-axdemo

The Applixware installation and setup system starts its job. An informational screen is shown. (Note that you'll need 142MB to install the demo system.) Press Enter to proceed.

Next, you are asked if you want to install Applixware into the /usr/local/applix directory. (If you have created a /opt directory, you are asked if you want to install there.) This book uses the /usr/local directory to install third-party application software, so press Enter to proceed.

The installation process then prompts you to create the /usr/local/applix directory if you have not already done so, during a previous installation. Press the Enter key again.

Applixware is then installed. You get the message:

Installing Applixware for Linux demo. . .

It takes a few minutes to install depending on your system's speed. Once complete you get the simple message:

```
Applixware for Linus has been installed. To run Applixware, type:
                /usr/local/applix/applix
For more information on purchasing your own copy of Applixware
for Linux, please visit our web site at
                http://linux.applixware.com/
```

Remove the temporary tar file:

```
rm -rf /usr/local/src/applixware*
```

Starting Applixware

You can start Applixware from the command line or from the Gnome desktop. To start it manually, log in (as any user or root) and enter the following:

```
/usr/local/applix/applix
```

You should see the Applixware main menu window as shown in Figure 14-1.

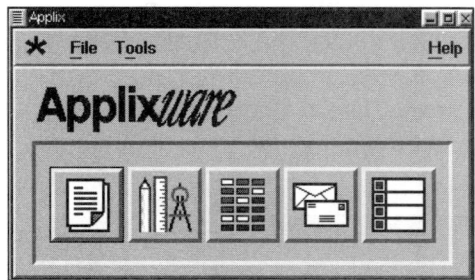

Figure 14-1: The Applixware Main Menu window

This is the launching point for all five main Applixware components, plus the *font installer*, the *license generator*, and the *help system*, which are accessed from the Tools and Help menus along the top of the window. The font installer is used for installing custom fonts, and the license generator is used to switch an existing temporary license to a permanent one. If you like this system, and purchase a full-blown license, then you can use this system to convert. The font installer and license generator are not discussed in this book.

Using the Applixware Help System

From the Applixware main menu window, click the Help menu. The Help window pops up and you need to slide the mouse up and down to select the help subsystem.

Highlight the On Context selection and a question mark replaces the mouse cursor. A help window is displayed for any item on the menu bars that you click.

Next, try selecting the On Words item and the screen shown in Figure 14-2 is displayed.

312   Part IV: Getting Work Done

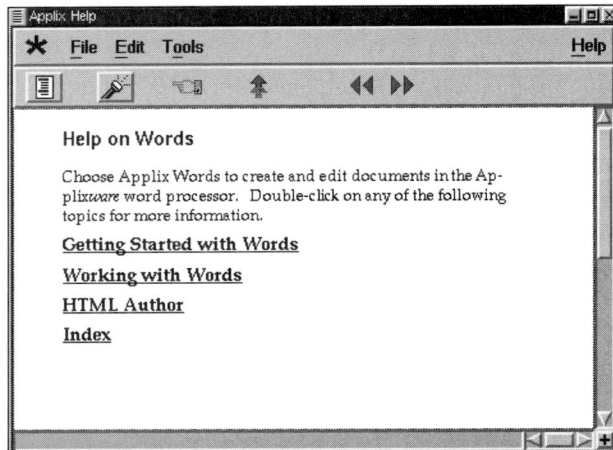

Figure 14-2: The Help on Words help window

Double click any of the menu items and additional selections are displayed. Double click any of the submenus to display a short explanation of the subject.

For more in-depth topic coverage, click Help → Words On-Line Books. If you installed the Words books during the installation process, the books selections are displayed.

Click Help → Tutorial to get instructions on various subjects, as shown in Figure 14-3. Lessons are avaliable on topics such as formatting and spell checking.

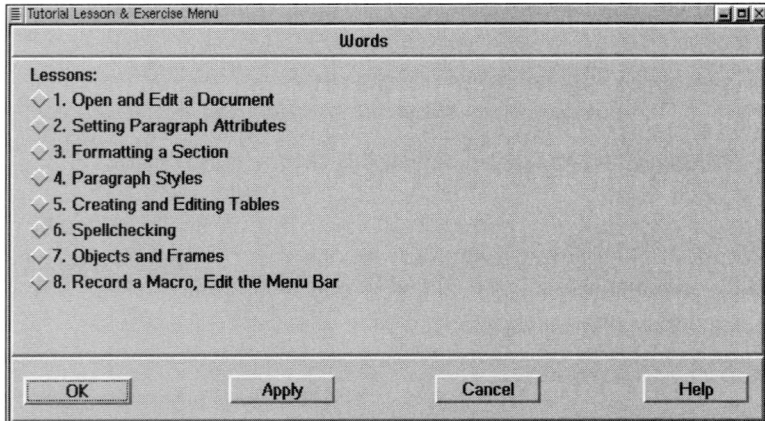

Figure 14-3: The Applixware Tutorial Lession & Exercise window

There are several other help topics covered, including the other Applixware functions.

Using Applixware Words

If you are familiar with the Microsoft Word word processor, then you should be able to find your way around Applixware Words. The look and feel is not quite the same, but the idea is universal. This discussion touches on a few of the widely used functions. Please experiment with your own test documents and consult the on-line help for more information.

The main menu items are shown at the top of the window. The next bar down contains short cuts to frequently used functions and is called the *ExpressLine*. The *Ruler* bar is third from the top and contains the ruler and font short cuts. The ExpressLine and Ruler bars can be hidden by clicking the View menu and toggling their radio buttons.

THE FILE MENU

Documents can be opened and saved from the File menu. Figure 14-4 shows the various functions.

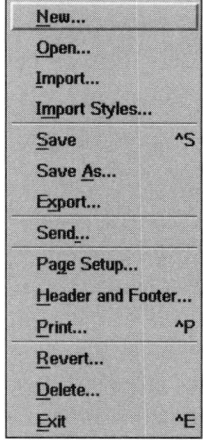

The Words file menu window

The New, Open, and Save functions work on Applixware Words files only; Words files have the aw suffix. Other file formats, such as Microsoft Word and HTML, must be imported and exported. The Import and Export selections are found within the File menu. To import a file, click on the Import item, and the Import window pops up. You can browse the Linux file system by double-clicking any of the directories (directories are distinguished by orange file folder icons). When you find a file to import, click it, and then select the file type from the submenu at the bottom of the window. Finally, click the Open button. Consult the help system for information on the other functions.

EDIT
The Edit menu provides all the functions that you are used to. The main functions are Cut, Copy, Paste, and Delete. You can also access the Find & Replace function from this menu. The Find & Replace menu provides a method for finding text strings and optionally replacing them with another string. You can search going forward or backward. You can replace one instance as well as all instances. Options include such things as activating case sensitivity (the default is no case sensitivity).

VIEW
The View menu displays or hides the various menu bars as described earlier. You can also have Words display its formatting characters and zoom the display in or out. The zoom function is quite nice for making smaller fonts more readable without changing a document.

INSERT
The Insert menu can be used to—you guessed it—insert many different special characters, objects, files, and macros. Special characters include various symbols that are not found in the normal character set. Objects include graphics, symbols, and figures. You can create your own figures with Applixware Graphics, described in this chapter. You can also insert macros and hyperlinks into your Words documents.

FORMAT
You can format Words documents at the character, paragraph, or document level. You can format a character's font, font size, color, and position. Provisions are also made for bold, italics, and strike-through formats.

TABLE
Tables can be inserted into a document. You have control over the number of rows and columns in a table. Words can automatically adjust the row height, or you can do it manually. The overall positioning can also be adjusted.

TOOLS
The main function that the Tools menu provides is access to the spelling checker, thesaurus, and change bar. The spell checker and thesaurus are self-explanatory. The *change bar* provides a change tracking mechanism that works at the line level. For example, if you change a single character or an entire line, then the change bars displays a marker pointing to the line that is changed. This is better than nothing, but obviously needs to be improved to mark changes, in color, at the character level.

HELP
The Help menu provides information that is described in the "Using the Applixware Help System" earlier in this chapter.

Introducing the Other Applications

Applixware is more than just a word processor; it's a full-featured office productivity suite. The other applications in the Applixware suite are briefly described here.

APPLIXWARE GRAPHICS

Applixware provides a graphical document editing and creation tool called Graphics. You can create slides and general-purpose graphics with this tool. Several of the figures in this book were created with Graphics. It works like one expects such a tool to behave, and no detailed explanation is given here. It is fairly intuitive if you is familiar with presentation and graphics tools. Give it a try.

APPLIXWARE SPREADSHEETS

Applixware Spreadsheets is a full featured spreadsheet program. Applix Spreadsheets is similar to other such tools. If you are familiar with spreadsheet software, then Spreadsheets should be straight forward to use.

APPLIXWARE MAIL

Applixware provides an e-mail client called Mail. However, because this book focuses on using the Netscape, e-mail client it will not be discussed.

APPLIXWARE DATA

If you run a SQL database, then you can use the Applixware Data interface. It provides a front end to your SQL database server back end. Click on the Star (*) button (or the data icon, on the far right in the Applixware main menu) to start the Data window.

This Linux distribution comes with the PostgreSQL database and client RPMs but not the data RPM. All three RPMs are included on the accompanying CD-ROM. You can install it by logging on as root and running the following command:

```
rpm -ivh /mnt/cdrom/db/postgresql*
```

MODIFY THE POSTGRES USER Installing the `postgresql` RPMs creates the postgres user in the `/etc/passwd` file. Modify the postgres user in that file and set its home directory and shell.

```
postgres:x:101:234:PostgreSQL Server:/home/postgres:/bin/bash
```

Set the postgres user password.

```
passwd postgres
```

Create the `postgres` home directory and populate it with the skeleton configuration files.

```
mkdir /home/postgres
cp /etc/skel/.* /home/postgres
chown -R postgres.postgres /home/postgres
```

Modify the `.bashrc` file to include the `postgres` environmental variables shown here.

```
export PGDATA=/var/lib/pgsql
export LD_LIBRARY_PATH=/usr/local/applixware/axdata/axshlib/lib
```

Log on as the postgres user.

```
su - postgres
```

START THE POSTMASTER Before you create the database, start the `postmaster` process, which handles communications between the database backup (engine) and any SQL queries.

```
nohup postmaster >/home/postgres/postmaster.log 2>&1 &
```

`nohup` is a command that starts a background process (a non-interactive process) that will not stop when the shell that initiates it is stopped. In this case, the postmaster process does not end when you exit from the bash shell that started it. The `postmaster.log` directs all logging and debugging messages to the specified file. The `2>&1` directs all standard error (`stderr`) messages to the controlling shell. Finally, the ampersand (&) directs the command to run in the background.

CREATE A SIMPLE DATABASE Create a simple database as follows.

```
createdb netdb
```

Start the `psql` SQL interface and create a table and enter a couple of records.

```
psql netdb
```

The `psql` start-up screen is shown below.

```
Welcome to the POSTGRESQL interactive sql monitor:
  Please read the file COPYRIGHT for copyright terms of POSTGRESQL

   type \? for help on slash commands
   type \q to quit
```

```
   type \g or terminate with semicolon to execute query
You are currently connected to the database: netdb
netdb=>
```

Enter the following commands to create a table with the names of hosts. This will be used as a simple private network machine database.

```
netdb=> create table hosts (
netdb@@> hostname varchar(80),
netdb@@> ip varchar(20),
netdb@@> alias varchar(20),
netdb@@> date date
netdb@@> );
```

The semicolon (;) specifies the end of the process. When you successfully finish defining the database, you should get the following message.

```
CREATE
```

Check your new database by using the \l command. You should see the information that you just entered in the following output.

```
netdb=> \l
datname   |datdba|encoding|datpath
----+----+----+----
template1|   124|       0|template1
netdb    |   124|       0|netdb
(2 rows)
netdb=>
```

INSERT DATA INTO THE DATABASE Next, add a couple of entries.

```
netdb=>insert into hosts
netdb=>values ('chivas.paunchy.net','192.168.1.254','chivas','04/23/99');
INSERT 18540 1
mydb=>insert into hosts
mydb=>values ('atlas.paunchy.net','192.168.1.250','atlas','04/23/99');
INSERT 18541 1
```

Check your table again.

```
select * from hosts;
```

You should see your new entries.

```
netdb=> select * from hosts;
hostname          |               ip|alias|     date
---------+---------+---+-----
chivas.paunchy.net |192.168.1.254|chivas |04-24-1999
atlas.paunchy.net|192.168.1.250|atlas|04-24-1999
(2 rows)
netdb=>
```

Quit by entering the \q command.

```
netdb=>\q
```

CREATE AN .ODBC.INI CONFIGURATION FILE   When you use Applixware Data to access an SQL database, it reads the .odbc.ini file in your home directory. Create the file and modify it to look like this:

```
# /home/postgres/.odbc.ini
[ODBC Data Sources]
rhbiz=PostgreSQL Database
[netdb]
Driver= /usr/lib/libpsqlodbc.so.0
Database=netdb
Username =postgres
Password = "mypasswd"
Servername=localhost
Port=5432
[ODBC]
Trace=1
TraceFile=/home/postgres/odbctrace.out
InstallDir=/usr/local/applixware/axdata/axshlib/lib
```

Log in again as root and modify the Applixware axnet.cnf **Configuration File** /usr/local/applixware/axdata/axnet.cnf. Modify the last two lines to look like this:

```
libFor elfodbc /usr/local/applixware/axdata/axshlib/lib
setenvFor elfodbc /usr/local/applixware/axdata/axshlib/lib
```

Chapter 14: Using Office Productivity Tools 319

When you query a database, Applixware uses `axnet` to access the database. The commands in the `axnet.cnf` file tell axnet where to find the ODBC libraries. Save the file and change back to the postgres user.

CONNECT TO YOUR DATABASE Fire up the Applixware main menu and click on the Data icon (the last button on the right). You should see the Applixware Data window shown in Figure 14-5.

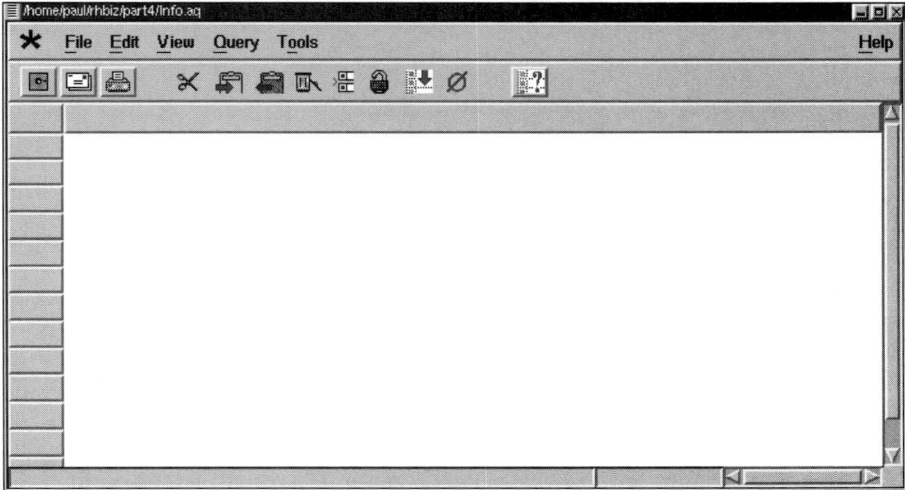

Figure 14-5: The Applixware Data window

Click on the Query → Server buttons to get to the Choose Server window.

If you are running one of the major database engines (Informix, Ingres, Oracle or Sybase), you can click on the appropriate tab. For *postgreSQL*, however, you need to use the ODBC tab. Click ODBC tab and then click the Browse button. You should see the `netdb` database that you just created. Click on the `netdb` line to highlight it and click OK again.

You should see your database—in this case `netdb`—listed in the window. Click the database name to highlight it and then click OK. Control returns to the Choose Server window and your database should show up in the List of Database Connections list, as shown in Figure 14-6. Click OK and you are prompted for your username and password. Enter the information and control goes back to the Applixware Data again.

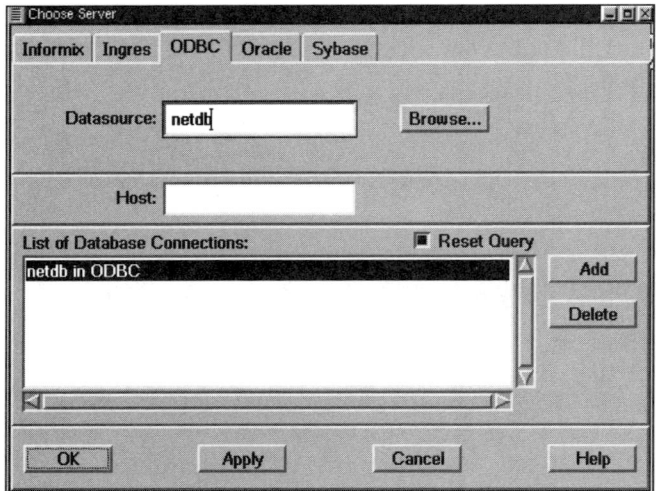

Figure 14-6: The Applixware netdb in the Choose Server window

The message "Starting elfodbc server" is shown in the lower left hand margin of the window. If it succeeds, then you are presented with the information stored in the netdb database. Otherwise, please consult the Troubleshooting section at the end of this window.

You can edit and otherwise modify your database now. With time I will modify this system to manage the sundry housekeeping chores of administering the paunchy.net network. Please check my Web page (www.swcp.com/~pgsery/RHBIZ) occasionally for information and scripts.

Introducing StarOffice

StarOffice is another desktop productivity suite. It is offered by Star Division, GinbH. It provides all the functions that one expects from such software. My early opinion is that it has more of the look and feel of Microsoft Office 97 than Applixware. On the other hand, it is quite a large distribution, weighing in at 70MB. You can find out more information on this tool at http://www.stardivision.com.

Please see the comparison review of both Applixware and StarOffice in issue 54 of the Linux Journal. The article is posted at http://www.linuxjournal.com/issue54/3080.html and was written by Fred Butzen, who is the co-author of *The Linux Network*, from MIS Press, 1998.

Using Netscape Communicator

Netscape Communicator hardly needs an introduction, but just in case, it is primarily a Web browser. A Web browser is used to view graphical information that can be stored on the Internet, your intranet, or on the computer that you are working from. Netscape can be installed as just a browser, Netscape Navigator, or as a multipurpose device in the Netscape Communicator suite, which is the Red Hat default.

When installed in Communicator form, Netscape provides an e-mail client, a newsgroup reader, some utilities and the browser. The browser and e-mail client are discussed in this section. The details on how browsers work can be found on the net or in many books. Netscape itself provides considerable information from its help menus.

Installing Netscape Communicator U.S. Version with 128-bit Encryption

The Netscape Communicator version that is installed by default during the Red Hat installation process is an international version with only 40-bit encryption. The U.S. version uses 128-bit encryption and is considerably more difficult to crack than 40-bit. You should consider downloading the U.S. version if you wish to use the Internet for commerce (send credit card information) and are a U.S. citizen. Please consult the download page at www.netscape.com for more information.

The current version of Netscape Communicator is 4.51 as of this writing. If you wish to download it for Linux and you accept the license agreement and meet the criteria, then download the tar package to /usr/local/src. Expand it to a temporary directory as follows:

```
tar xzf /usr/local/src/netscape* | (cd /var/tmp; tar xvf - )
```

Create a Netscape directory and Expand the .nif files:

```
mkdir /usr/local/netscape
cd /usr/local/netscape
tar xvf  /var/tmp/netscape.nif
tar xvf  /var/tmp/nethelp-v451.nif
tar xvf  /var/tmp/spelling.nif
```

Change the Gnome Netscape launcher on the main menu panel by clicking the icon with the right mouse button. Next, click the Properties menu and the Launcher properties window pops up. Change the file name in the Command submenu to /usr/local/netscape/netscape and click OK. The next time that you click the Netscape icon, the new version should start.

Using Netscape Navigator

Netscape Navigator is such a widely used tool that no general tutorial is given here. If you are unfamiliar with Web browsers, consult the Netscape help menu (click the Help menu in the upper right-hand corner of the window). Using Navigator for secure communications is important, however, and is discussed in the next section Setting Up Secure Netscape Communication.

Setting Up Secure Netscape Communication

You can use encrypted communication with Netscape Navigator. The level of encryption varies depending on the version. International versions use 40-bit encryption, while the U.S. version uses 128-bit encryption. 40-bit encryption can be theoretically broken in a matter of hours while 128-bit encryption would take much longer if it can be broken at all.

Speaking in general terms, 128-bit encryption is better than 40-bit encryption. Depending on what you are doing, 40-bit might be adequate. If you are simply browsing the net, then it might not matter that your packets can be broken because you are probably not sending information that will have any value in a couple of hours. However, if you are sending long-lived valuable information, such as credit card information, you should be concerned. Use your best judgement.

There are two basic security measures that need to be taken: using encrypted transactions, and verifying the validity of the web server that you are communicating with. The former is matter of setting up Netscape Navigator to use *Secure Socket Layer* (SSL) transactions and the latter requires the use of certificates.

USING ENCRYPTION

Use Navigator to connect to a Web site. Click Communicator → Tools → Security info menu in the Netscape window. The Netscape: Security Info window is displayed. Click on the Navigator menu and you see a window similar to that in Figure 14-7.

Chapter 14: Using Office Productivity Tools 323

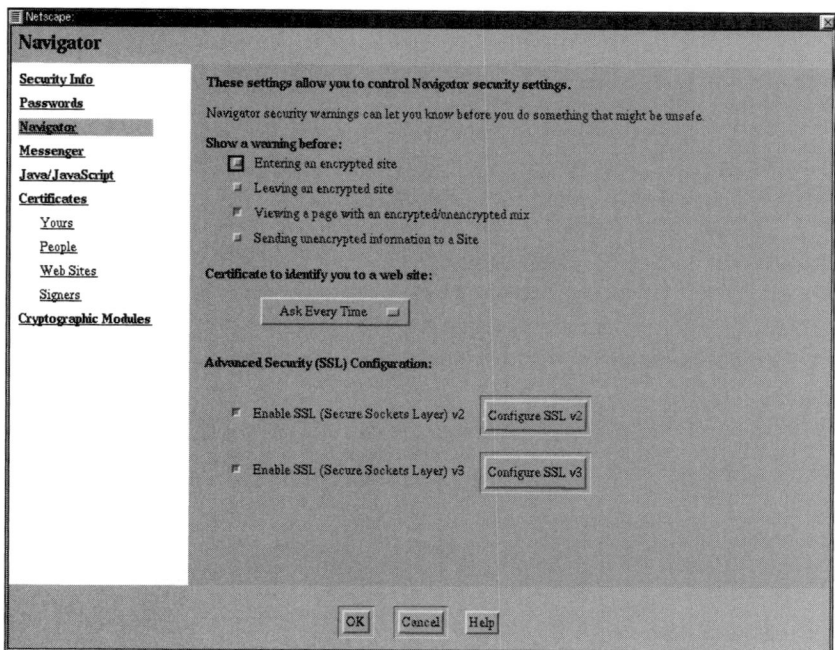

Figure 14-7: The Netscape Security Info window

You have the choice of setting Navigator to warn you of the status of Web sites that you are connecting to. For instance, if you click on the Sending unencrypted information to a Site selection, Navigator will warn you when you try to do that. If you select all of those choices, you might get too many warnings and end up ignoring them, to your own detriment. It's probably a good idea to start off by getting too much information and then back off as you gain experience with what warnings you want to pay attention to.

You should select both the Enable SSL (Secure Sockets Layer) v2 and Enable SSL (Secure Sockets Layer) v3options. If they are not, then activate both. That will automatically encrypt your transactions when you connect to a secure site. One way to verify that you have an encrypted connection to a Web site (a secure Web server is designated by a https URL prefix as opposed to an http prefix) is to look for the little padlock icon which is displayed in the extreme lower left corner of your Netscape window; you can also display the encryption status by clicking Communicator→Tools→Security Info. The closed padlock icon indicates an encrypted connection; otherwise, the open padlock indicates that your connection is not encrypted.

Most Web sites do not use SSL connections until you want to make a financial or other sensitive transaction. For instance, when you view books at www.amazon.com, your connections are not secured. However when you go to make an order, you connect to an SSL server and your communication is encrypted, if your browser has SSL enabled.

Secure servers use port 443 (see the /etc/services file). The HTTP protocol uses port 80 (sometimes ports like 8080 and 8001 are used too). If you can not connect to a secure server, you might have to modify your firewall to allow an unusual port. You can use the diald control panel (dctrl) to view the ports being used.

INTRODUCING CERTIFICATES

If your Netscape communication is perfectly encrypted, but you are connected to a fraudulent Web site, then the bad guys will get your perfectly encrypted information. This is called a *Man In The Middle attack*.

A secure Web server provides a server certificate to ensure that it is who it says it is. You can view the certificate by opening up the security info page (click on Communicator → Tools → Security Info menus) and click on the View Certificate button. If you don't see a certificate, then you should be very cautious about your interaction with the web site.

Configuring the Netscape E-mail Client

The Netscape Messenger Mailbox is the default e-mail client used in this book's paunchy.net network. Netscape provides all of the essential functions that are necessary to send and receive e-mail, plus some extras. From the Navigator window, click Communicator → Messenger to open the email system.

Netscape requires that you configure your e-mail address and server. Click Edit → Preferences and you get the Netscape: Preferences window. Click on Mail & Newsgroups, then click Identity, and the Identity window is shown. Enter your e-mail address. In the case of this book's example network, that should either be *myname*@paunchy.net or *myispusername*@myisp.com. The former corresponds to the case where your Linux server is acting as an email server as described in the section "Configuring a Local E-mail Server" in Chapter 13.

Next, click Mail & Newsgroups, then click Mail Server. Chapter 13 describes the two methods for accessing an e-mail server that this book uses. The following two sections outline how to configure Netscape to use the two methods.

CONFIGURING NAVIGATOR TO GET E-MAIL FROM YOUR ISP

If you wish to send and receive your e-mail directly from your ISP, then click the Add button and enter your ISP's e-mail server name in the Server Name sub window. Click the Server Type button and choose either the POP or IMAP protocols depending on what your ISP provides. Next enter your ISP username in the Username field. Click OK.

Back in the Preferences window, enter the IP address of your ISP's e-mail server name in the Outgoing mail (SMTP) server field. (The name of your outgoing and incoming ISP mail server might be the same or might be different. Consult your ISP for the proper names.) Finally, enter your username in the Outgoing mail server username field. Your configuration should look similar to Figure 14-8.

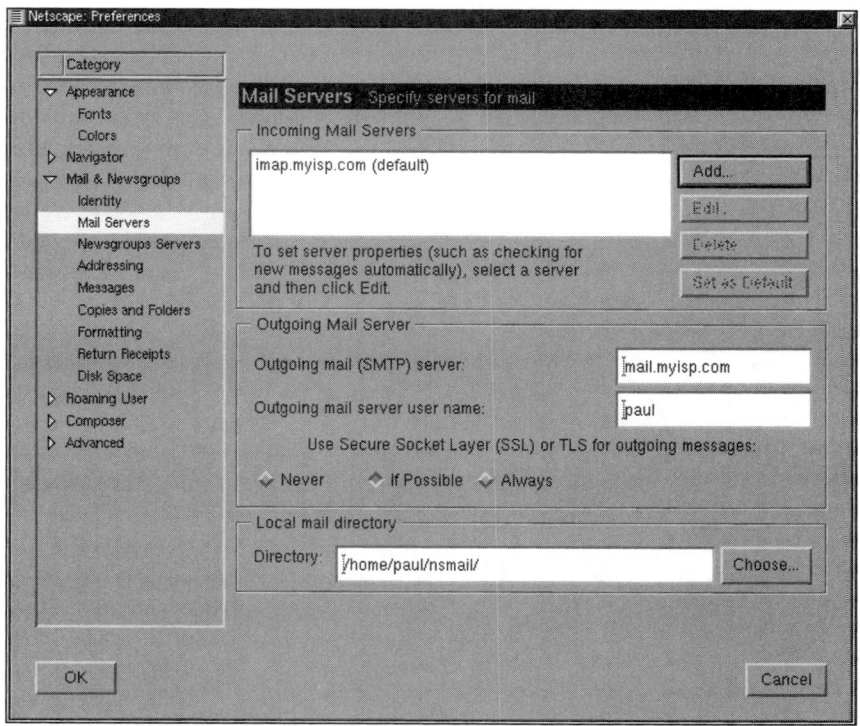

Figure 14-8: The Netscape Mail Server configuration window points to your ISP's e-mail server.

You will send and receive e-mail directly through your ISP. Every time you want access, your account `diald` has to make a connection (unless you have a permanent or semi-permanent connection). You also need a separate e-mail account (but not necessarily a login/PPP account) for each user who wants to receive e-mail this way.

CONFIGURING NAVIGATOR TO USE YOUR LOCAL LINUX SERVER

If you are using your own Linux server to provide local e-mail services, then proceed as follows. First, click Mail & Groups → Mail Server. Click the Add button and enter your local email server name in the Server Name field. Next, click the Server Type button and choose the IMAP protocol. Next, enter your username in the User name field. Click OK.

Back in the Preferences window, enter the IP address of your local e-mail server (atlas.paunchy.net in this example) in the Outgoing mail (SMTP) server field. (The name of your outgoing and incoming local mail server should be the same in this case.) Finally, enter your user-name in the Outgoing mail server username field. Your configuration should look similar to Figure 14-9.

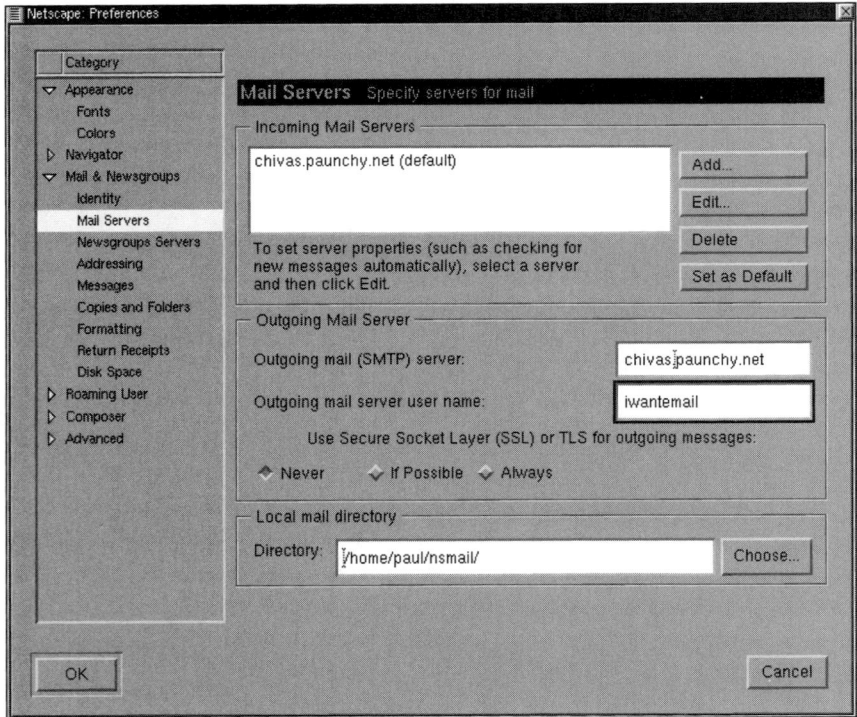

Figure 14-9: The Netscape Mail Server Preferences window points to your local Linux e-mail server.

The Local mail directory should default to your /home/username/nsmail directory. The IMAP server temporarily stores (spools) your email in the /var/spool/mail/username directory. For instance, if you send a message to the local user roger_retallack, the message gets stored in the /var/spool/mail/roger_ retallack file. You can read that file directly and see that user's messages; only root and the owner have privileges to read the information, however. Once Navigator gets your messages, either by you clicking the Get button, or by automatically polling every so many minutes, your email is transferred into the mbox file in your home directory. It stays there until you delete it or move it into your local imap folders. At that point, messages are transferred to files corresponding to your folders in the nsmail directory in your home directory.

Back in the Mail Server window, click the General tab, and you can also configure Netscape to save your e-mail password (your username password on the Linux e-mail server) by pressing the Remember my mail password button. You can also have Netscape check your IMAP email spool check every x minutes or not. Click OK to exit the Netscape: More Mail Server Preferences window. Click OK in the Netscape: Preferences window to save your changes.

You can now receive e-mail whenever your Linux e-mail (IMAP) server downloads messages from your ISP that are addressed directly to you. You can also receive locally delivered messages as well. All outgoing e-mail is directed to your Linux server and routed to your ISP if it is destined for the outside world, and to your local network otherwise.

More Linux Applications!

Please consult the Red Hat home page for information on other Linux applications. The address is: http://www.redhat.com/appindex/index.html.

Troubleshooting

The applications used in this chapter are relatively bulletproof. I have not experienced any problems except with using PostgreSQL and Applixware Data. The troubleshooting section for the SQL server connection is a bit more in-depth than the others. That is not to say that problems cannot occur. If problems occur that are not covered here, consult the appropriate documentation.

Applixware

If you able to install Applixware, there are not many problems that can occur. The most difficult system to use by far is Applixware Data. See the section "Postgres and Applixware Data" for more information on that subject. Otherwise, you should not have many problems using the systems. One thing to keep in mind is that Words can not read and write files that it does not have Linux permissions for.

Postgres and Applixware Data

Configuring PostgreSQL and Applixware Data is not an easy process. Both systems are quite complex and require a lot of work to learn in depth. The discussion here covers some of the more common hints and problems that one encounters.

- You need to have the `postgresql-data` RPM installed in order create a new database. You can create your own templates but it is much easier to do with the `postgresql-data` package.

- You should use the postgres Linux user and create, modify, and delete all databases from there.

- The postmaster process must be running in order to create a database with the `createdb` command. The postmaster should be started by the postgres or other non-root user.

- When creating tables and other SQL database objects, you need to pay close attention to the syntax of the commands that you use. Case is not important but characters like semicolons are.

- The same holds true for adding, modifying and deleting database records. Please pay close attention to syntax.

- The `.odbc.ini` and `axnet.cnf` files all need to be configured correctly in order for the Applix Data interface to work with a SQL database. Pay special attention to the library path names.

When trying to connect Applixware Data to your database, the following common messages can be remedied as shown (this information is derived from section Common Problems in Chapter 55 of the PostgreSQL tutorial and was contributed by Steve Campbell):

- `Cannot launch gateway on server.` The `eldodbc` driver can not find the `libodbc.so` library. Your `axnet.cnf` file is probably misconfigured.

- `Error From ODBC Gateway: IM003::[iODBC][DRIVER MANAGER]Specified driver could not be loaded.` In this case, the `libodbc.so` library cannot find the driver specified in the `.odbc.ini` file. Your `.odbc.ini` file probably needs to be reworked.

- `Server: Broken Pipe.` The driver process (`axodbc` in the case of Applixware Data) encountered some problem and stopped without completing its job.

Refer to the `usr/doc/postgresql-6.4.2/tutorial/tutorial.html` and other documents in that directory for more information on this process.

Netscape Communicator

Netscape Communicator is just about bulletproof in my experience. The only problems that tend to occur are due to misconfiguration, or are of the annoying but not deadly variety. If, for instance, you cannot browse the Internet, then make sure that your host computer's network configuration is correct; your Linux Internet gateway (`atlas`) must be specified; your network must be configured and IP masquerading enabled. Refer to Chapter 7 for more network configuration and troubleshooting information.

Summary

This chapter introduces a couple of the major applications available for Linux users. Linux is no longer limited to the server or specialized workstation arena. Software like Applixware, StarOffice, and Netscape Communicator provide desktop productivity tools that you can get your everyday work done with.

- The Applixware office productivity suite is introduced. Applixware provides the work-a-day functions like word processing, spreadsheets, and presentation graphics. A demo version is included on the CD-ROM accompanying this book so that you can experiment with its features.

- Applixware Words is described is some detail. Its basic functions, which should be familiar to any word-processor user, are introduced. This book was mostly written using Words.

- The other Applixware applications are introduced. Applixware has applications for creating slides and graphics, using spreadsheets, and sending e-mail.

- A simple example for creating a SQL database with postgreSQL is given. That data base is used to show how to use the Applixware Data application. Data is used as an interface to SQL databases.

- Netscape Navigator is introduced. The program is the most widely used Web browser in the world. It is included in the Red Hat distribution and used in examples throughout this book.

- Configuring and using Netscape Messenger is described. If you want to send and receive your e-mail directly through your ISP, then configuring Netscape is straightforward. However, if you want to use the Linux based e-mail server described in Chapter 13, then some further configuration is necessary. Both systems are described in this chapter.

Chapter 15

Configuring an Intranet Web Server

IN THIS CHAPTER

- Introducing the HTTP protocol
- Introducing the Apache Web server
- Installing Apache
- Creating a simple Intranet Web page
- Adding information to the simple Web page
- Accessing SWAT via your Web page
- Securing your Intranet Web page

Introducing the Apache Web Server

Apache stands for *a patchy server*. It was based on both existing software and a series of patch files (see the FAQ for the explanation) and thus got the name. It is part of the Red Hat distribution in RPM format. Most of the world's Web servers use Apache. The heart of Apache is the `HTTP` daemon, which runs in the background and listens on port 80 for `HTTP` packets.

The `HTTP` protocol defines how Web browsing works. When `httpd` receives a `HTTP` packet, it tries to interpret the packet. If successful, it looks by default to the `/home/httpd/html` directory. You can create *Hypertext Markup Language* (HTML) files and store them in the `/home/httpd/html` directory. `httpd` will then interact with those files, and display the information contained in them.

Installing and Configuring the Apache Web Server

The example in this chapter uses the Linux personal workstation veracruz, which has the IP address 192.168.1.1, as the Apache server.

Log in as root on veracruz and install the Apache RPM packages.

```
rpm -ivh /mnt/cdrom/RedHat/RPMS/apache*
```

Start the httpd daemon as follows:

```
/etc/rc.d/init.d/httpd start
```

Check to make sure that it is running:

```
ps x | grep http
```

You should see the daemon running:

```
2187     ?    S    0:00    httpd
```

Next, use your browser to see if you can access your new Web server. Enter the following URL in the location field (the localhost address refers to the internal 127.0.0.1 IP address of your Linux computer):

```
http://localhost
```

You should see the display shown in Figure 15-1 in your browser

Chapter 15: Configuring an Intranet Web Server

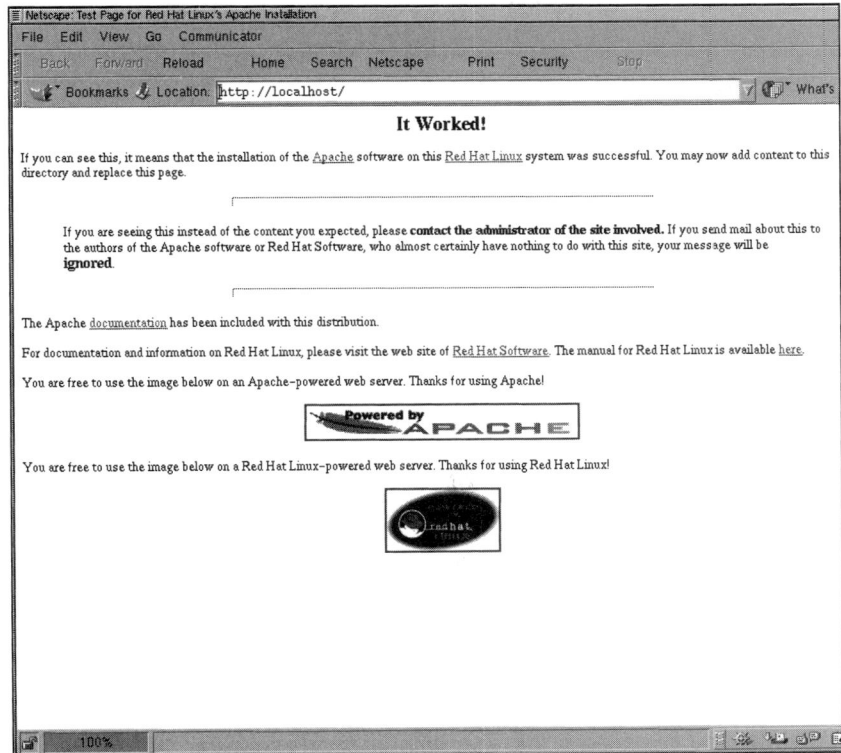

Figure 15-1: The Red Hat Apache test page window

That's it! Your Linux computer is now an intranet Web server.

Using Lynx to View Your Web Page

If you have not installed X, you can still view your new Web page with the text-based *lynx* program. Enter the following command.

```
lynx http://localhost
```

You should see the text part of the Web page displayed. Press the **H** key to display the help instructions. The up and down arrows move the cursor between the links within the page. The right and left arrows follow a link. Refer to the man page and help screen for more information.

Setting Up Simple Services

If you click the documentation link in the Red Hat Test Page, you see the page shown in Figure 15-2.

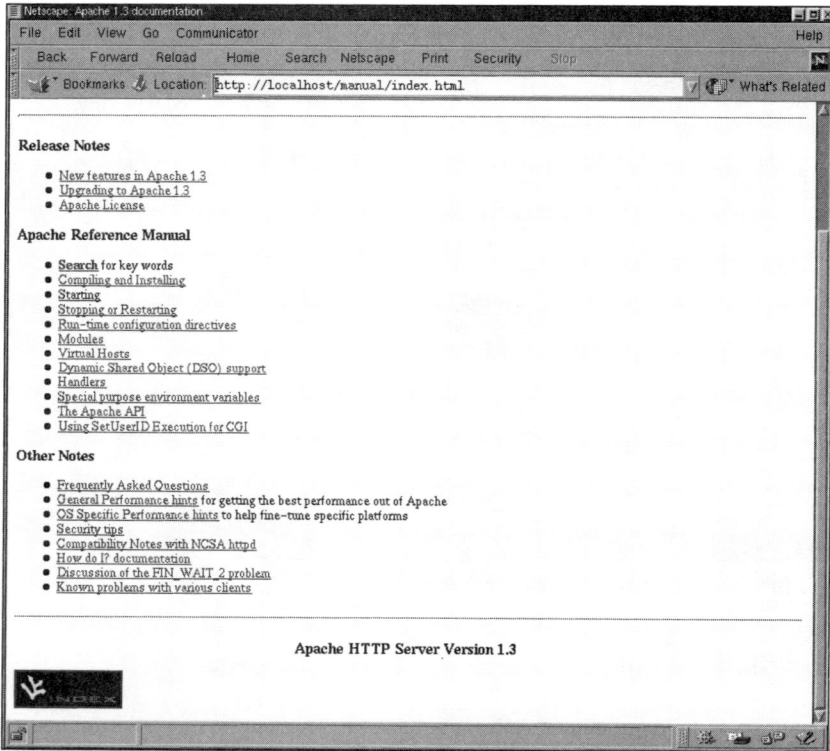

Figure 15-2: Apache 1.3 documentation

Not only does the page provide you with a wealth of information, it also illustrates where and how Apache stores and accesses information. The default Apache directory is `/home/httpd/html`. When you specify the localhost locations, `httpd` looks at the `index.html` file in the default directory. The documentation URL points to the file `index.html` file in the `/home/httpd/html/manual` directory. The information shown in Figure 15-2 is contained in that file.

Creating Your Own Intranet Web Page

The next step is to create your internal Web page. Open Applixware Words and enter some information that you would like to display to computer users within your company. Figure 15-3 shows information entered into Words about *Red Hat Linux in Small Business.*

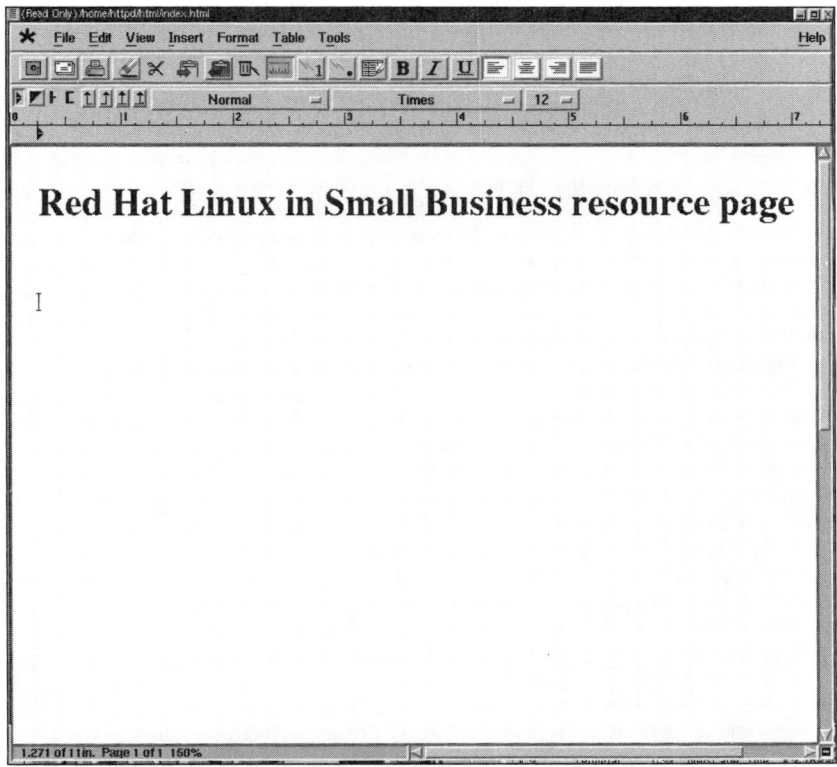

Figure 15-3: The Red Hat Linux in Small Business page being created in Words

This is admittedly a bland page, but it is simple enough to understand at a glance. Save the page in HTML format by using the export function, pick the /home/httpd/html/index.html file to save to, and select the HTML Export File Type. Click Export to save the new file.

Open up the http://localhost/index.html file in Netscape Navigator, and you should see your new Web page. Display the /home/httpd/html/index.html file and you can see the HTML code that comprises your new page.

```
<HTML>
<HEAD>
<TITLE>Title</TITLE>
<!-Created by Applixware HTML Author, Release 4.4 on Thu Apr 22 22:01:03 1999->
```

```
<!-Ax:WP:DocVar:HTMLOriginalPath@:"/tmp/ex01127d.aw"->
</HEAD>
<BODY>
<H1>Red Hat Linux in Small Business resource page</H1>
<P></P>
<P></P>
</BODY>
</HTML>
```

- The first line specifies that HTML is the language used.
- The next five lines are boilerplate created by Applixware Words.
- The `<BODY>` line indicates the start of the important HTML code.
- The `<P>` and `</P>` combinations create a paragraph break. In this example, that has the affect of creating a blank line.
- The `<P>` and `</P>` parameters also separate each line of text that were created.

You can read more information on understanding and using HTML with Words by clicking Help → Words and then double-clicking HTML Author.

Adding Some Useful Information

The page in Figure 15-3 shows only text. To add some content to the intranet Web page, mount the CD-ROM, click Insert → Hyperlink. Next, click File, enter `file:/mnt/cdrom/doc/HOWTO/INDEX.html` and click Open. In the Enter Text field, enter the text that you want to use for the link. This is what the user will see in the Web page, and where they will click to follow the link. Finally, click the OK button. The `INDEX.html` file points to the Linux HOWTO documents on the CD-ROM accompanying this book. Figure 15-4 shows the Insert Hperlink dialog box.

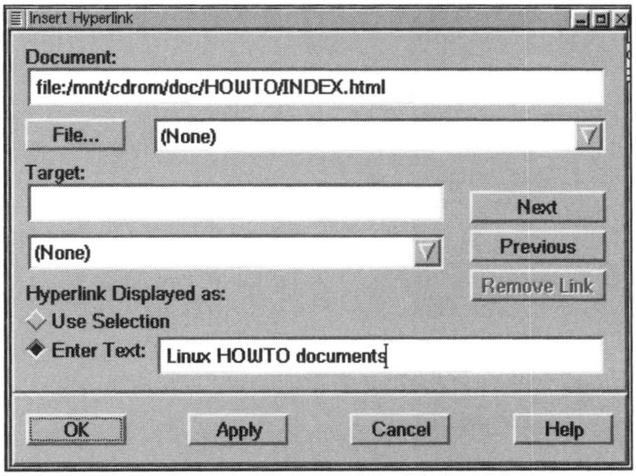

Figure 15-4: Add a hyperlink to the mini HOWTOs on the CD-ROM

Next, add a link to an external Web page. Open the Insert → Hyperlink menu again but add a link to `http://www.swcp.com/~paunchy/RHBIZ` in the Target field as shown in Figure 15-5.

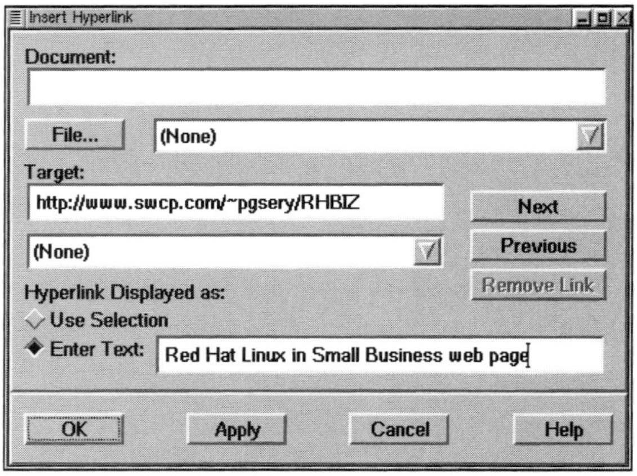

Figure 15-5: Add a hyperlink to my book page.

Finally, add a link to the SWAT interface (a configuration GUI for Samba, discussed in Chapter 8). Add the link `http://localhost:901` in the Target field as shown in Figure 15-6.

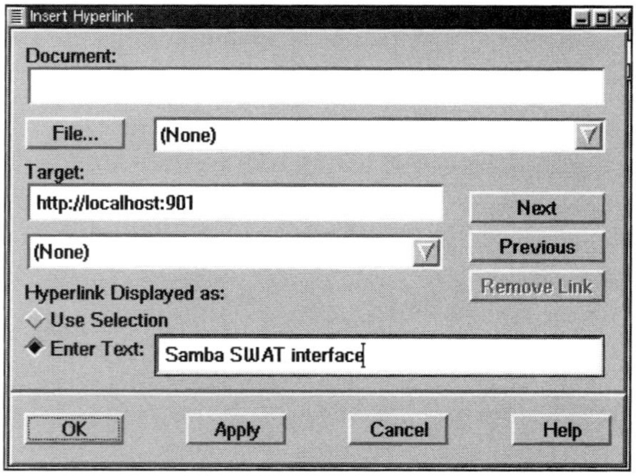

Figure 15-6: Add a link to the SWAT interface.

Export the new Web page to `/home/httpd/html/index.html` file. Open Netscape Navigator, enter the `http://localhost` address in the Location field, and press the Return key. The new page looks like that shown in Figure 15-7.

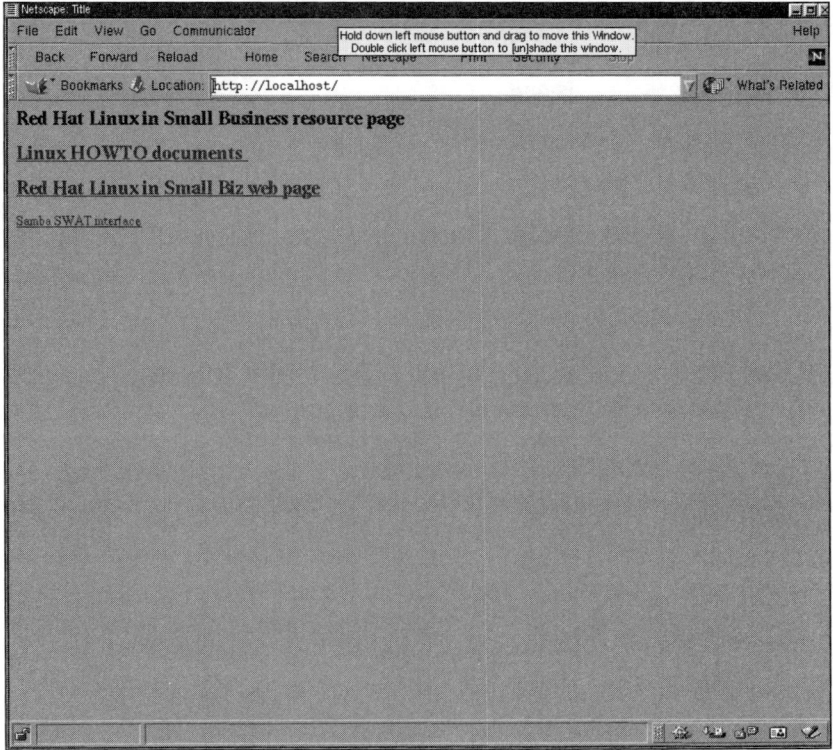

Figure 15-7: Open the new Web page

Okay, this is a boring page, but it does provide a hint of what you can accomplish with just a little more work. You can consult the numerous books available about both the technical and esthetic aspects of Web page design.

If you want to make the new Web page your home page (the first page you see when you start Navigator), open up Navigator. Click Edit → Preferences. Next, click Navigator. From within the Navigator preferences, click the Home page button and enter http://localhost in the Location field. Click OK and then click the Home button in the main browser. You should automatically see the new page that you've created.

There is another HTML file, /mnt/cdrom/rhlbiz.html, that has additional links about the book. Copy it to the /home/httpd/html/index.html file if you wish.

Introducing Advanced Intranet Web Pages

The Web page designed in this chapter is quite useful. I run a small Web page to provide extra information and help for my books. It is no more complicated than the type described here, and allows readers to download updated information and go to useful URLs. It demonstrates that you do not need to run a complex Web site to provide information to your target audience.

Of course, you can run more complex Web sites. A small company can save time and money by distributing basic (and advanced) information via a Web page. For instance, if you run a Simplified Employee Pension (SEP) plan, then you might want to put information about that up on your own intranet.

Not only can you give employees access to static information, such as the funds that your plan uses, but you can make it interactive. You might even make the forms related to the pension plan available via the Web page. That is a complicated process, and I won't go into it here. However, there are many books available on the subject, so I've mentioned it to spark your interest.

Securing Your Server

The firewall that you run is essential to securing your Intranet Web page from unauthorized access. Another essential element is the security of your Linux Web page server itself. All the security functions and topics discussed in this book are relevant to the subject. You should secure the files that contain the information with the appropriate file permissions. For instance, if you have information on your SEP program, you do not want to grant read privileges to the entire Internet.

You also have the distinct advantage of not giving access to the Web at large to your private Web page. I've assumed throughout this book that it is generally best for a small business or organization to pay an ISP to provide information to the Internet, which includes hosting your public Web pages for you. Unless you have a fast Internet connection like a T1, then running your Internet Web page on your own server will eat up your valuable bandwidth. The firewall described in this book can be altered to allow external access for Web traffic but that makes you more vulnerable to attack and misuse.

Troubleshooting

The Apache system is simple in concept and execution. There is not much that can go wrong with it. If you do have problems, it is generally best to make sure that your private network is working. Consult the configuration and setup instructions in Chapters 6 and 7. If your network looks okay, use the troubleshooting sections in those chapters first.

The next place to look is at your Linux Apache server. Make sure that your `httpd` daemon is running. Enter the command:

```
ps x | grep http
```

You should see the process running, like this:

```
467     ?     S     0:00     httpd
```

If you don't see it, start the process up again; enter:

```
/etc/rc.d/init.d/httpd start
```

If it doesn't start up, check that the Apache RPM is installed by using:

```
rpm -qi apache
```

This should show an information page about Apache. If it doesn't, reinstall Apache according to the instructions at the beginning of this chapter. If you still have problems, consult the HOWTOs and Usenet newsgroups for interactive help from experienced users.

Problems can occur in the formatting of the html files. For instance, hyperlinks act in a relative fashion when a URL is preceded by a pound (#) character, meaning that the server will look on the local network for the home page, and not on the Internet. If you have a URL `#http://www.swcp.com/~pgsery/RHBIZ`, the page will not load. Remove the pound sign, and it will work.

A file-based URL will not work if it has two slashes (//) instead of one (/). The `file:///mnt/cdrom/usr/HOWTO/INDEX.html` will not work properly but `file:/mnt/cdrom/usr/HOWTO/INDEX.html` does function properly.

Summary

This chapter describes how to set up your own intranet Web page. It is designed to serve your private network, which is also referred to as an intranet (not Internet). You can provide a surprising amount of information, and therefore value, to your own computer users. You can even provide interactive services.

- ◆ The installation of the Apache Web server is described. Apache is part of the Red Hat distribution in RPM format. Most of the world's Web servers use Apache.

- Apache provides a simple default Web page for you to use. It is installed in the /home/httpd/html/index.html directory. To access it, start Netscape Navigator (or lynx, or any browser) and enter /home/httpd/html/index.html as the location.

- You are shown how to build a simple Web page by using the Applixware Words HTML generator. Words can save files in HTML format.

- The simple Web page is expanded to include a link to the mini HOWTOs on the CD-ROM accompanying this book. There is a /mnt/cdrom/doc/mini/HOWTO/index.html file that points to the HOWTO files. The simple Web page provides a convenient method for accessing that information.

- The simple Web page is further expanded to include an Internet URL. The author's personal Web page is used in the example. It includes information about the book and other interesting URLs.

- The final example generates a link to the Samba SWAT program. Recall from Chapter 8 that SWAT is an interactive Samba configuration GUI.

- Basic Intranet Web security is introduced. The most important security measures that you can take are to create and run a good firewall and maintain good Linux server security. If you want further information about Intranet Web security, consult specialized books, HOWTOs, and Web pages.

- Basic troubleshooting is discussed. The Apache Web server examples shown in this chapter are fairly bulletproof. Most problems occur in the private network.

Appendix A

Using Secure Shell

The private network that is used in this book is potentially vulnerable to attack because all of the information traveling on it is in plain text. Anyone connected to the network can potentially look at the packets flying by. It is also possible for someone outside your private network to look at your information that travels out onto the Internet. This is called *packet sniffing*, and the `tcpdump` RPM that comes with Red Hat Linux can be used to display and log such packets. Those packets contain interesting information such as passwords and any information that is being passed on the network.

The firewall introduced in Chapter 12 is designed to allow network traffic originating from within the private network to go out to the Internet and allow return packets back in. No traffic originating from outside the private network—the Internet—is allowed back in. This creates an effective firewall but limits its use when you are not physically present at your network.

One solution to both problems is to use Secure shell. The newest version of secure shell (`ssh2`) encrypts the information contained in the network packets, which provides a high degree of privacy and safety for your valuable information. If you modify your firewall to allow Secure shell packets into your network you sacrifice a small amount of safety for the convenience of accessing your private network.

Introducing Secure Shell

Secure shell is a system that allows you to communicate between two computers via an encrypted connection. Secure shell also permits you to validate that the machine you are connecting to is the correct one.

Secure shell makes it very difficult for anyone to sniff your communication. Secure shell does not send your password or general communication in plain text. Communication programs like Telnet send everything in readable form; it is possible to intercept the packets and reconstruct them to reveal passwords and other information. Secure shell solves that problem.

Secure shell is based on a client-server model. You run a client program (`ssh2`) to connect to a server daemon—`ssh2d`—on a remote computer. Once connected, you can interact with the remote computer as if you were sitting at its console.

Encryption Methods

Secure shell uses several encryption methods: IDEA, three-key triple-DES, DES, or Blowfish. Discussion of these methods is beyond the scope of this book and you should look to the following URLs for more information:

http://www.employees.org/~satch/ssh/faq/ssh-faq-2.html#ss2.5.2
http://www.sunworld.com/sunworldonline/swol-02-1998/swol-02-security.html

The article at the second URL discusses the operation of the first version of secure shell. Please keep in mind that Secure shell 2 (used in this book) configures the keys differently than is discussed in the article but overall the concept is the same.

Public and Private Keys

Secure shell uses the concept of public and private keys to perform authentication. A *public key* is a sequence of randomly generated numbers that is available to everyone. A *private key* is a another random number that you do not share with anyone else. Information that is encrypted with a public key can only be decrypted by the private key and vice versa. The public and private keys are totally independent of each other and one can not be derived from the other. This method is called *RSA authentication.*

Host Authentication

Secure shell makes use of the public and private keys to verify that all parties are who they claim to be. When you attempt to connect to a remote computer both the client and server generate random strings. The strings are exchanged in such a way that the combination of public and private keys proves that both the client and server are valid. The details of the process is interesting but beyond the scope of this book. Please refer to the other documents and URLs mentioned in this chapter, and http://www.spotch.com/~robjen/sa/ssh/sshtalk-1/sld032.htm, especially slides 32 through 37.

 The first time that you connect to a Secure shell server, you do not have it's public key. You get the message "Accepting host chivas key without checking." This means that your client machine is recieving the public key of the server without being able to verify that the server is the correct server. The new key is stored in a file in the `.ssh/hostkeys` directory.

It is essential that both the client and server verify the true identity of those involved. Without verification, it is possible that a third party can pretend to be the client or server, a process called *spoofing*. For instance, you are computer A and want to connect to computer B. However, if computer C pretends to be B by using the same IP address as B, then you might connect to C and send your valuable information to C. This is called a *man-in-the-middle* attack.

However, if you encrypt a random string, and send it to C, but do not get the same string back, then you know that the computer you are talking to either has changed keys or is a fake. RSA authentication prevents DNS, IP, and routing spoofing.

User Authentication

When you are creating your user keys with `ssh-keygen2` (discussed later in this chapter) you are asked to enter a *pass phrase*. The phrase can be up to 20 characters long and include spaces. During the authentication process you are prompted for your pass phrase. Once it is correctly entered, you are logged onto the remote system. If the host authentication process fails, or you enter the wrong pass phrase, then secure shell reverts to the normal login process and you need to enter your regular login account password (You can turn off the normal login process in order to allow only pass phrase authentication. Please see the section Configuring General Parameters for more information).

Please see the URLs listed in the section "Encryption Methods" for more information on this subject.

Downloading Secure Shell

The Linux/UNIX version of secure shell is available via the Internet (`ftp://ftp.replay.com/pub/crypto/redhat/i386/`) for non-commercial users only. Secure shell must be purchased if it is to be used for commercial purposes. Please read the license agreement to determine whether you can legally use the publicly available version. The SSH Communication Security's home page at `http://www.ssh.fi` contains more product information.

Appendix A

TIP Data Fellows Ltd. at http://www.datafellows.com is a licensed reseller of Secure shell products. In addition to the commercial version of Secure shell, they also provide a free commercial trial version of it.

To download the RPM version of ssh2, log on to atlas as root and change to the /usr/local/src directory. Connect to http://www.shopthenet.net/publiclibrary/RPM/replay/crypto/redhat/test_rpms/ByName.html and download the ssh2, ssh2-client, ssh2-server, and ssh2-extras RPMs.

Installing and Configuring Secure Shell

Secure shell requires that the machine(server) that it's connected to runs the sshd2 daemon. You can connect to that machine from any other machine (the client) by using the ssh2 client program once you've configured both the client and server. The following sections describe how to configure both sides.

TIP Your secure shell server and client can be placed on the same machine. Simply translate the following instructions for installing and configuring your client machine to your server. This is a good method to test Secure shell if you do not have multiple Linux computers to work on.

Installing Secure Shell on the Server Computer

In this example, the Linux Internet gateway and firewall server atlas will function as the secure shell server. Any Linux computer on your network can provide this function. By placing one on the gateway, however, you can gain access to your private network from the Internet. (There is no limit on how many Secure shell servers you can have. If you want to make your internal network more secure, then every Linux computer that you interactively communicate with should be a Secure shell server.)

Log on to atlas as root and install the Secure shell packages as follows.

```
rpm -ivh /usr/local/src/ssh2*
```

This command installs the `ssh2`, `ssh2-clients`, `ssh2-extras`, and `ssh2-server` RPM packages. When the `ssh2` RPM (the base package) is installed, it generates the public key (`hostkey.pub`) and private key (`hostkey`) as shown:

```
Generating 1024 bit host key. This may take a while, go and have a
coffee ;)
Generating 1024-bit dsa key pair
1 oOo.oOo.oOOo
```

The process can take several minutes depending on the speed of your computer. The keys that it generates are stored in the `/etc/ssh2` directory.

When the ssh2-server RPM is installed it starts the `sshd2` daemon (and also installs the start up script `sshd2` in the `/etc/rc.d/init.d` directory). At that point, your Secure shell server is ready to accept connections from clients. However, you still need to configure your client.

Installing Secure Shell on the Client Computer

Only the Secure shell base (`ssh2`) and client package (`ssh2-clients`) need to be installed on a client computer. In this example, chivas, the Linux file and print server, is used as the client.

Log on to chivas as root and install the Secure shell base and client RPMs as follows.

```
rpm -ivh /usr/local/src/ssh2-2*
rpm -ivh /usr/local/src/ssh2-clients*
```

Creating a User's Public and Private Keys on the Client Computer

While the `ssh2` base package is installing it will generate the client's keys. However, you will need to generate your own user keys. In this example the user `gabearagon` is used. Create that user with the `useradd gabearagon` command and create a password. Change to that user with the `su - gabearagon` command and run the following command.

```
ssh-keygen2
```

The computer will spend more time generating the user's public and private keys. It will prompt you to enter a pass phrase, which is the Secure shell equivalent of a password. The phrase can be up to 20 characters long, and can include space characters. Use your good judgement in creating a good password.

Once you enter the pass phrase, `ssh-keygen2` places the public and private keys in the .ssh2 directory (that it creates). That directory is placed in the user's home directory which, in this case, is /home/gabearagon. The public file is called id_dsa_1024_a.pub and the private one is id_dsa_1024_a. Once again, the public file can be transported across the network, while private one should be kept secret.

Creating a User's Identification File on the Client Computer

Next, you need to create an identification file on the client. That file tells the ssh2 client where to go to find its private key - id_dsa_1024_a in this case. From the user's home directory, change to the .ssh2 directory.

```
cd ~/.ssh2
```

Enter the following command to create the identification file.

```
echo "IdKey id_dsa_1024_a" > identification
```

The contents of /home/gabearagon/.ssh2/identification file will be as follows.

```
IdKey id_dsa_1024_a
```

Secure shell looks to the `identification` file to find out the name of the user's private key. This arrangement means that you can have multiple private keys assigned to each user. However, this example does not make use of that capability.

Configuring the Server Computer

Now that you have created your personal public and private keys, you need to copy the public key to the server that you want access to. Log on to the secure shell server (atlas) as the user that you want to log on as - in this case gabearagon on atlas (Create the user with the `useradd gabearagon` command if necessary). From the user's home directory, /home/gabearagon, create the .ssh2 directory.

Go into the .ssh2 directory (cd ~/.ssh2) and copy the user gabearagon's public key - id_dsa_1024_a.pub - from the client computer. Use any method that you want—smbclient, FTP or even sftp—to make the transfer, but be aware that anyone who intercepts the key before you install it on the server conceivably will be able to perform a man-in-the-middle attack. This is probably a remote possibility for most people, but it is potential threat. Therefore, it is considered good practice to use a floppy or some other media to hand carry the public key from machine to machine in order not to transport the key over a possibly insecure network. Whether you want to such precautions is up to you and depends on the degree of security that you want to maintain.

Once you have copied the `id_dsa_1024_a.pub` file to the server, rename it. The `/usr/doc/ssh2*/SSH-QUICKSTART` document uses the convention of calling it `Local.pub`. However, I personally find it easier to reference the name of the key to the user who will use it to connect. In this example, the command is `mv id_dsa_1024_a.pub key_of_gabearagon.pub` to rename it.

Create the authorization file in the `.ssh2` directory on the server as follows.

```
echo "Key   key_of_gabearagon.pub" > authorization
```

The secure shell server daemon will look in the user's authorization file in the `.ssh2` directory for the file containing user's public key on the server.

Copying the Server's Public Key to the Client Computer

Both the server and client need to know the other's public keys for secure shell to work. The final configuration step requires you to copy the server's public key to your client. From atlas, copy the `/etc/ssh2/hostkey.pub` file to `key_22_atlas.pub` in the `/home/gabearagon/.ssh2/` directory. The new name contains the `sshd2` port number - 22 - and the name of the server - atlas.

Checking the Client and Server's Configuration Files

The user `gabearagon` should have the following configuration and key files on the client and server. Note that the file `random_seed` is not discussed here because it is used by the Secure shell programs and is not directly configured, or used, by the user and is not included in Table A-1.

TABLE A-1 SECURE SHELL 2 USER FILES

Computer	Directory	File	Purpose
chivas	/home/gabearagon/.ssh2/	id_dsa_1024_a	client private key
chivas	/home/gabearagon/.ssh2	id_dsa_1024_a.pub	client public key
chivas	/home/gabearagon/.ssh2	identification	public key file name
chivas	/home/gabearagon/.ssh2/hostkeys	key_22_atlas.pub	server public key
atlas	/home/gabearagon/.ssh2	key_from_chivas.pub	public_key
atlas	/home/gabearagon/.ssh2	authorization	pointer to public key
atlas	/etc/ssh	hostkey	private key of root
atlas	/etc/ssh	hostkey.pub	public key for root
atlas	/etc/ssh	ssh2_config	client configuration
atlas	/etc/ssh	ssh2d_config	server configuration

Connecting to Your Secure Shell Server

Try connecting to your Secure shell server. Log on to the client computer chivas as the regular user `gabearagon` and try connecting to your Linux computer (atlas) via secure shell.

```
ssh2 atlas
```

If you have configured both the client and server correctly, then you are prompted for the pass phrase that you entered while creating your client keys with `ssh-keygen2`.

```
Passphrase for key "/home/gabearagon/.ssh2/id_dsa_1024_a" with
comment "1024-bit dsa, created by gabearagon@chivas.paunchy.net Sat
May 29 19:27:40 1999":
```

Enter the correct pass phrase and you should be connected to the secure shell server via a secure, encrypted channel.

If your client machine does not have the server's public key the first time that you connect to it, then the `/etc/ssh2/hostkey.pub` file will be copied to the `.ssh2/hostkeys` directory in your home directory. Every subsequent time that you connect to atlas you will not see the "Accepting host chivas key without checking" line in the log in prompt. This is potentially a dangerous situation because full host authentication is not possible until each side has the other's public key.

If you have not configured the keys and other files correctly, then you can still connect to the remote secure shell server. You will be prompted for your regular password just as if you were connecting via Telnet.

```
gabearagon@atlas's password:
```

Enter your password and you will be connected. You are still connected over an encrypted channel, but secure shell is not able to correctly pass your public key back to your client machine. That means that you can not verify that the server you are connecting to is the correct one. You are potentially vulnerable to a man in the middle attack where someone spoofs the computer that you are trying to connect to. In that case you would be using a perfectly encrypted connection to a fake machine.

Once again, you should use your judgement to determine whether the danger of connecting to a false server is significant. If you are using Secure shell to connect within your private network, then the number of potential dangers should be clear or relatively so. If you are connecting from the Internet, then the potential danger might be much greater.

In this example, however, you are connecting to your own secure shell server from the server itself and thus have pretty good assurance that there is no fake server involved. Continue with your connection and Secure shell will create a known_host file in your home directory /home/encryptme/.ssh/known_hosts:

```
Host 'atlas' added to the list of known hosts.
Creating random seed file ~/.ssh/random_seed.  This may take a while.
myuser's password:
```

If you look in the newly created known_hosts in the .ssh directory in your home directory (/home/gabearagon in this case) then you see that Secure shell has created a key for your hosts.

Connecting to Different Computers

The previous example provides instructions for connecting from chivas to atlas only. If you want to go in the other direction, or want to connect to multiple computers, a little more configuration is necessary.

You do not want to copy your private keys from other machines. This would violate the secrecy of the private key concept.

You need to create new private keys on each new client machine. Follow the previous instructions on each client computer for creating public and private keys. On the client computer you will need to have the id_dsa_1024_a, id_dsa_1024_a.pub, and identification files in your .ssh2 directory; the public key such as key_22_server.pub should be put in the .ssh2/hostkeys directory. You also need to transfer the user's client public key to the user's .ssh2 directory on the server machine and create the authorization file that points to it.

 **TIP** If you have user accounts with different names on other computers, you can use the same keys to connect to them. The `ssh2 -l` option allows you to specify what account name to connect with. For instance, if your user account name is `gabe` on veracruz but you want to connect to chivas where your name is `gabearagon`, then you should use the command `ssh2 -l gabearagon chivas`. Otherwise, ssh2 will use your name gabe which will not match up with `gabearagon` on chivas.

Modifying your Firewall for Secure Shell

The firewall design from Chapter 12 is an effective and strong one. It gains much of its strength from the philosophy of not permitting any communication originating from the Internet into the private network; it allows only one-way communication. This model is quite useful but if you want to gain access to your network for outside — for instance, from your home — then it presents some problems.

A firewall based solely on IP filtering works very well in one direction. As soon as you allow IP packets from the Internet, you start opening potential holes in your firewall. For instance, I have used the network scanner `nmap` against this book's firewall defined by the `ipchains.rules` script found in the `/mnt/cdrom/IDG/firewall` directory. The firewall tests very well, as every `nmap` configuration that I can conjure fails to return any information about my network sitting behind the firewall. However, when I add a rule to allow Telnet sessions in from the Internet, `nmap` then is able to see that service. An attacker then knows that there is a computer and/or network at the IP address and can attempt to find a way in.

Allowing external access to network services like Telnet is not a direct danger in itself. However, it is a potential vulnerability for several reasons. First, if someone places a Trojan Horse on your network, then access to the network is possible. (Otherwise, with a one-way firewall, even if a Trojan Horse exists no one can gain access and use it.) Second, if there is a bug or back-door in a daemon like `telnetd`, then an intruder can take advantage of it if external access is available. Finally, if someone is sniffing your incoming network traffic, then it's quite possible that you passwords will be discovered and access to your internal network gained via a service like Telnet.

The solution is to run a secure shell server on your Internet gateway/firewall and provide external access only to the secure shell server. In this case, atlas is the secure shell server and an `ipchains` rule is added to allow external clients access to it. This arrangement is safer than others for several reasons.

- First, all communication is encrypted which makes all the information, such as passwords, very difficult to intercept, if not impossible.

- Second, if the authentication keys have been properly configured on both the client and the server, then you are assured that you are communicating with the correct machine. You cannot be spoofed by some third party on the Internet.

- Third, secure shell is in itself a type of firewall. It can be configured to require its own authentication before it will allow any access to itself (by turning off password-only authentication). Network packets coming in from the Internet and seeking access to the private network will be serviced by the secure shell daemon only. It essentially prevents unauthorized access to your private network just like an application-based firewall does.

- Finally, my `nmap` tests of my firewall with external access granted to secure shell do not show any response. That is, I scan the firewall and nmap does not see the Secure shell port which is listening for incoming connection. nmap does not see the network just as before. This is not an exhaustive test but a very good indicator that the firewall is not going to break easily. (`nmap` is one of the most widely used and respected scanners available. It is highly adaptive to new conditions and continually being improved.)

The following rule is used to provide external access to your private network from the Internet.

```
# allow secure shell connections originating from the outside
ipchains -A output -p TCP -j ACCEPT -i ppp0 -s $ALL ssh -t 0x01 0x10
ipchains -A output -p UDP -j ACCEPT -i ppp0 -s $ALL ssh -t 0x01 0x10
```

These rules can be found in the `/mnt/cdrom/IDG/firewall/ipchains.rules` file. The comments should be removed in order to activate them.

Using Secure FTP

Secure shell comes with a secure version of FTP called `sftp`. `sftp` can be used in place of FTP to transfer encrypted information. The `sftp` system is easy to use, you just enter the following command to connect to a computer (chivas in this case) running Secure shell.

```
sftp chivas
```

The secure shell daemon handles the entire process. Unlike FTP, there is only one communication channel for both commands and data.

Configuring General Parameters

By default, the `sshd2` configuration allows root logins. The better practice is to not allow direct root logins and force everyone to log in as a regular user. Those who have root privilege can use the `su` command to access root. That leaves an audit trail and also forces everyone to use two passwords instead of one to gain root access.

Edit the `/etc/ssh/sshd2_config` file and set the `PermitRootLogin` parameter from yes to no:

```
PermitRootLogin      no
```

Another useful change is to disallow password logins. The secure shell default operation is to revert to using the general Linux login password to authenticate the connection if the pass phrase fails. This could present an intruder with the possibility of gaining access if, for instance, the password file has been cracked or intercepted. Changing this option is not a panacea but does potentially provide extra protection. Change the parameter in the `/etc/ssh/sshd2_config` file to the following:

```
PasswordAuthentication    no
```

There are numerous other parameters that can be changed. Please consult the `sshd2` man page for more information.

Troubleshooting

For more information on secure shell, please consult the following `man` pages, documents and URLs.

- `man sshd2`
- `man ssh2`
- `man ssh-keygen2`

- `man sftp`
- `/usr/doc/ssh2*/SSH-QUICKSTART`
- `/usr/doc/ssh2*/README`
- `http://www.ssh.fi/sshprotocols2`
- `http://www.tac.nyc.ny.us/~kim/ssh`
- `http://www.sunworld.com/sunworldonline/swol-02-1998/swol-02-security.html`
- `http://www.sunworld.com/sunworldonline/swol-03-1998/swol-03-security.html`

You can also subscribe to the secure shell mailing list.

Send an email to: `majordomo@clinet.fi` with the string `subscribe ssh` in the body of the message.

Many common problems can be found in the mailing list archives:

```
http://www.egroups.com/list/ssh/info.html
http://www.progressive-comp.com/Lists/?l=secure-shell&r=1&w=2#secure-shell
```

The Usenet news group can be accessed for interactive information.

`comp.security.ssh`

Appendix B

What's on the CD-ROMs

CD-ROM #1 contains the Red Hat Linux distribution. CD-ROM #2 contains several demo applications, plus my own scripts. The applications include a demo version of the Applixware desktop suite (wordprocessor, spreadsheet, graphics, and database) and a demo of the Arkeia client-server network backup software.

CD-ROM #1

The official Red Hat distribution is included on CD-ROM #1. The major directories are:

- `doc`: Linux FAQs and HOWTOs
- `images`: The files that you create boot and ramdisk images out of (typically on a floppy).
- `RedHat`: Contains the Red Hat distribution RPM files, plus the installation image and a small file system archive.
- `dosutils`: Utilities used to assist in the installation of Red Hat. It includes MS-DOS programs for making Linux boot and ramdisk floppies.
- `misc`: Source files and installation trees.

The installation process for Red Hat is covered in detail in Chapter 1. Please refer to that chapter for instructions.

CD-ROM #2

CD-ROM #2 contains the Applixware office suite demo, Arkeia backup application demo, and scripts for firewalls, DNS, and e-mail servers:

Applixware

Applixware is a full-featured office productivity suite, including a word processor (Applixware Words), spreadsheet (Applixware Spreadsheets), SQL database (Applixware Data), e-mail client (Applixware Mail), and graphics and presentation editor (Applixware Graphics). The Applixware demo is found in the `/IDG/applixware` directory. Detailed instructions for installing and using the Applixware demo are included in Chapter 14.

Arkeia Backup Software

Arkeia is a backup system from Knox Software Corp. A demo version of Arkeia (with a limited use license) is included on CD-ROM #2 in the /IDG/Arkeia directory. Three RPM packages that run under Linux are provided — a client, server, and X Window interface. A Windows client that is packaged in a Zip format is also provided. Detailed instructions for installing and using Arkeia are included in Chapter 10.

Bonus Scripts

I've provided various scripts of my own for you to use in creating and configuring your Linux network. The following is a list of the scripts and where to find them:

- **PPP scripts:** These scripts provide a sample diald configuration. They are found in the ppp directory. These scripts are discussed in detail in Chapter 11.

- **DNS scripts:** These scripts will enable you to configure a DNS server on your local network. They are found in the dns directory. These scripts are discussed in detail in Chapter 11.

- **Firewall scripts:** These are scripts that will help you create a simple firewall. They are found in the firewall directory. These scripts are discussed in detail in Chapter 12.

- **E-mail scripts:** These scripts will help you configure a simple e-mail server. They are found in the e-mail directory. These scripts are discussed in detail in Chapter 13.

- **Bookmarks:** The URLs used in this book are contained in the bookmarks.html file.

Glossary

10base2 A version of Ethernet that transfers data at 10 megabits per second. It uses an RG58 coaxial cable. It's also referred to as Thinnet.

10baseT A version of Ethernet that transfers data at 10 megabits per second but uses twisted pair wires instead of coaxial cable. The twisted pair cable is similar to telephone cable in appearance. This is the most popular media for Ethernet networks.

100baseT A Version of Ethernet that transfers data at rates up to 100 megabits per second using special grades (category 5) of twisted-pair cables.

ATAPI CD-ROM Advanced Technology Attachment Packet Interface. This bus is used to connect a CD-ROM or tape device to a computer, using the standard IDE interface. ATAPI is an improvement over the first CD-ROMs that used proprietary interface adapters and drivers.

bash Bourne Again Shell. The standard Linux shell.

bit A binary cell of information. It can either be on (1) or off (0). A computer hard disk, floppy disk, Zip disk, or Jaz disk stores a bit magnetically on a small piece (the size depends on the density of the disk) of the disk. A CD-ROM or other optical disk stores a bit as a small distortion in the media that reflects a laser beam one way or another depending on the state (1 or 0) of the bit.

boot The process of powering on or resetting a computer.

bus The electrical interface between devices on a computer or a network. In a computer, it carries the data (in digital format), memory addresses and timing signals between the CPU, memory and its associated internal and external devices. On a network it carries information (in analog radio frequency format) that is converted into digital packet form at the network hosts; an example of a bus based network device is 10base2 (Thinnet) Ethernet. Every device on a bus − computer and network − receives all of the information being broadcast; each device uses or discards the information depending on whether it is addressed to the device or not.

byte A unit of 8 bits of binary information.

CD-ROM Compact Disk-Read Only Memory. Computer storage media that uses the same form as a music CD. It is a read only media although writable forms are available. It is the most commonly used form to distribute computer software and information.

Glossary

CPU Central Processing Unit. The chip that processes the instructions of the operating system and all other software.

directory A system for organizing individual files. Under Linux, a directory is a file itself that contains a list of files and directories that are assigned to it. A directory can be contained in another directory, in which case it is called a subdirectory.

Disk Druid The Red Hat utility used to create and edit disk partitions.

Distribution There are numerous companies and organizations that package Linux and its support software into a single entity. That combination is called a distribution. The Red Hat distribution is one example.

DNS Domain Name Server. Converts numeric IP addresses (for instance, 192.168.1.1) to names myserver.mydomain.net and vice versa.

Dual boot This describes the method of storing two or more operating systems on a single disk.

EIDE Enhanced IDE. An advanced version of the IDE bus. It is also referred to as ATA-2. ATAPI is part of this interface.

Ethernet A protocol that defines how network communication, in the form of packets, will take place on a single bus. That bus is physically shared by the one or more network devices that use the Ethernet protocol. The packets contain a header that describes the recipient.

FAQ Frequently Asked Questions. This type of document gives answers to typical questions about a given topic.

file A file is the collection of bytes that are stored on a device such as a hard disk or CD ROM.

file partition A partition is the way that Linux (and many other operating systems, including DOS and Windows) divides a disk device in order to create a file system on it.

file systems The file system is the way that the kernel logically organizes a physical device, such as a hard drive, to store information in the form of a file or directory. The kernel is connected to a file system when it is mounted.

firewall A system that protects one network from unauthorized access from another network. Typically a firewall protects an individual or organization's private network from the Internet.

GNU Gnu's Not UNIX. The GNU Project out of MIT (largely due to the efforts of Richard Stallman) produces and distributes a considerable amount of the software that Linux uses.

GPL GNU General Public License. The license that Linux and most of the software used in this book is published under.

GUI Graphical User Interface.

HOWTO A document that contains information about accomplishing certain tasks. Linux makes extensive use of such documents. This book's CD-ROM contains numerous HOWTO RPM packages in the /mnt/cdrom/usr/doc/HOWTO directory.

HTML Hypertext Markup Language. This language defines how World Wide Web pages are constructed.

IDE Integrated Device Electronics. This interface is used to connect disk drives, including CD-ROMs, to a computer's CPU via the motherboard. It is now the defacto standard used in PCs.

Internet The sum total of all the worlds computers and networks that are interconnected via the TCP/IP suite of protocols.

InterNIC The company (Network Solutions, Inc.) that is responsible for dispensing Internet domain names.

kernel The software that forms the center of the Linux operating system. It provides the interface between the computer's hardware and the higher level software that uses it.

LAN Local Area Network. Network devices (computers, printers, hubs, switches, etc.) that are connected together within a limited geography. Typically the geography consists of an single office or home.

Linux The term Linux refers to the Linux kernel, plus the cooperating daemons (processes running constantly in the background that providebasic services), plus all of the user commands, plus your computer's hard disk files.

man page Manual page. Linux/UNIX provides a simple mechanism for accessing information about commands and other system and application information.

metacharacters Characters that are expanded by a shell or program to another meaning. They are similar in concept to DOS wildcard characters.

mirror A mirror is a Internet connected computer that maintains a copy of the another site's files. For instance, since Red Hat's ftp.redhat.com download site is often too busy to allow new connection but numerous copies (mirrors) of that site are maintained to provide alternative download locations.

mounting The process where the Linux kernel is made aware of where it can access that particular file system. Under Windows/DOS the partition is intrinsically linked to the operating system.

multitasking An operating system such as Linux that allows more than one process (program) to run at the same time.

multiuser An operating system such as Linux that allows more than one person to be logged on at the same time.

NFS Network File System. A system used for sharing files and directories across a network.

NIC Network Interface Card. The physical device that connects the external network to a network device (for instance, a computer).

NIS Network Information Service. A mechanism that shares system services among machines on a network. For instance, a single password data base can be shared among computers on a network.

Operating system The software that creates an interface between a computer's hardware and the human operator/user.

permissions Under Linux/UNIX every file and directory has attributes that limit access. There are three sets of permission: owner, group, and other (everyone). The types of permissions are read, write, and execute.

pipe A system for transferring information from one process to another.

PPP Point-to-Point Protocol. Encapsulates IP packets for transport over a serial communication channel. This typically means a telephone connection and is the protocol that this book uses to connect a private network to the Internet.

public IP addresses Ranges of IP addresses that are set aside by the InterNIC for public use. These addresses are specified not to be routed by the Internet and are, thus safe to use on your own network.

RAM Random Access Memory. It is often referred to as memory. Used to store bytes of information electronically. It is much faster than hard disk storage but also more expensive.

Red Hat Linux The company that provides the Linux distribution included with this book.

RG58 The type of coaxial cable used by 10base2/Thinnet Ethernet.

RPM Red Hat Package Manager. Provides a self contained system for distributing software.

root The root user is the user on a Linux system that has nearly total control of it. It also refers to the root file system that is the center of any Linux file system.

router A device (dedicated, or a computer) used to direct (route) network packets from one network to another.

routing The method for directing network communications (in the form of IP, Ethernet or other packets) from one network to another. The IP protocol is used extensively for this purpose.

subdirectory See directory.

superuser Typically a synonym for the root user. See root.

SVGA Super Video Graphics

swap A disk partition that temporarily stores pages of RAM.

system administrator (sysadmin) The person who manages, engineers and otherwise keeps a network(s) and its components running and safe.

TCP Transmission Control Protocol. TCP is the basis for many interactive applications like www, Telnet, FTP, among others, because it guarantees the delivery of the packets. TCP uses the IP protocol to perform the routing (delivery) of the packets to the desired destination. TCP has more overhead than UDP.

TCP/IP Technically refers to the Transport Control Protocol and Internet Protocol. However, it really refers to the suite of networking protocols that allows both the Internet and small networks (LANs) to function.

Thinnet A synonym for 10base2.

UDP User Data Protocol. UDP is the basis for applications (typically non-interactive) like e-mail where the acknowledgement of delivery does not have to be guaranteed. The application program that uses UDP takes care of the acknowledgement. UDP doesn't have as much overhead as TCP/IP.

UNIX UNIX is a type of operating system that provides the interface between the computer's hardware and the human operator/user. UNIX and Linux are very similar in operation but Linux does not share the numerous copyrights that UNIX has.

user A person who logs onto a computer and uses it.

user account The login account that belongs to a user.

Virtual memory The system where pieces (pages) of memory are taken (swapped) out of RAM and placed onto disk storage (swap). This makes the memory "look" larger than it is.

X Window System Also X, X11, or X Window. A client-server graphical window system developed by the Massachusetts Institute of Technology (MIT). It is used extensively in the Linux/UNIX world.

World Wide Web (WWW) The sum total of all the computers connected to the Internet that serve information via the http protocol.

Index

Symbols

& (ampersand) 55
* (asterisk) 46, 140
` (back quotes) (back tics or grave accents) 137
\ (backslash) 47
<BODY> HTML tag 336
^ (caret) 66
: (colon) 47, 76
, (comma) 50
\l command 317
- (dash) 45, 49, 55
$ (dollar sign) 42
/etc/hosts table 153
/etc/ppp/connect script, setting up 254
/ (forward slash) 47, 96
> (greater-than sign) 56
/home/httpd/html (Apache default directory) 334
- (minus) button 224
- (minus sign) 50
/ (mount point) 22
(number sign) 140
<P></P> HTML tags 336
( ) (parentheses) 56, 138
% (percent sign) 188
| (pipe) 57, 138
+ (plus) button 224
+ (plus sign) 50
# (pound sign) 42, 176, 341
? (question mark) 96
; (semicolon) 56, 176, 183, 317
// (slashes) 341
~/ (tilde and forward slash) 56
/var/temp directory, sharing 185-186

A

Accept button 127
Activate button 161
Add a Printer Entry window 200
Add button 21
addresses
    IP 8, 254
    static ISP 252
Allen, Joseph H. 69
ampersand (&) 55
Apache Web server
    configuring 332-333
    /home/httpd/html (default directory) 334
    HTTP daemon 331
    installing 332-333
    services, setting up 334
    troubleshooting
    Web pages, viewing 333
application layer 150
applications, running 55
Applixware
    Applixware Data
        Data window 319
        data, inserting 317-318
        databases 316-320
        netdb in the Choose Server window 320
        .odbc.ini file, creating 318
        postgresql RPMs, installing 315-316
        postmaster process, starting 316
        troubleshooting 328
    Applixware Graphics 315
    Applixware Mail 315
    Applixware Spreadsheets 315
    Applixware Words 309-314
        help system 311-312
        installing 310
        Main Menu window 311
        Star Office, comparing to 320
        starting 311
        troubleshooting 327-328
        Tutorial Lesson & Exercise window 312
apropos command 63, 96
arguments commands 46

365

Index

Arkeia server
   asterisk (*) 46, 140
   automatic backups 224-225
   backup media 225
   BRU2000 207, 225-226
   configuring 209
   data, restoring 231-232
   Drive Management 210
   Drivepack 210
   GUI, starting 212
   hard drive backups 226
   help information 212
   indexes 208
   installing 209
   interactive backups 222-224
   Libraries Management 211
   null backup 212-214
   null drivepack 214-217
   null pool 217-219
   packs and pools 211
   passwords, setting 213
   Pools Management 211
   Savepack 210, 220-222
   SCSI tape drive or tape library 229
   server administration 209
   status window 223
   tape libraries 208
   Tapes Management 211
   troubleshooting 232-234
   Web site 233
   Windows client, configuring 230-231
   Windows Server administration window 231
   Zip drive backups, configuring 225-226
Atlas gateway 292-294
Attach Drive button 228
attacks
   crackers, tools and methods 277-278
   firewalls 267
   gaining footholds 274
   Man in the Middle 324
authentication
   configuration 30
   Samba 178-180
AUTOBOOT.BAT 13-15

autoloaders (tape libraries) 208
automated network backups. *See* Arkeia server
AutoProbe 83

B

back quotes (`) (back tics or grave accents) 137
backslash (\) 47
backups 116
   BRU 2000 125
   DAT drive 117-118
   data 131
   data retrieval 124-125
   file servers 111
   local 117
   records 123
   scheduling 122
   Systems Administration policy 111
   tar (Tape Archive) 117-118, 121-122
   verifying 123-124
   Zip drives 118-119
backups, automated network. *See* Arkeia server
bash shell (Bourne Again Shell) 42, 55, 256
Bash Shell commands 137
bind RPM packages, installing 249
boot floppy, making during installation 144
booting
   boot floppy disk 14-15
   daemons 28
   dual 9-10
   floppy 30
   protocol 25
   from Red Hat CD-ROM 14-15
Bootp services, DHCP (Dynamic Host Configuration Protocol) 8
bootstrap loader, LILO (Linux Loader) 12, 30
Bourne shell 42
Bourne, Stephen 42
BRU2000 Web site 207
buttons
   + (plus) 224
   - (minus) 224

Index

Accept 127
Activate 161
Add 21
Attach Drive 228
Commit Changes 191
Delete 22
Drive Options 228
Edit 22
Get messages 294
green checkmark 212
Help 191
Input Filter Select 201
Interface configuration protocol 160
Local Printer 201
Network Configuration 157
OK 22
Printer Configuration 203
Remote Unix (lpd) 202
Select All 228
Set tape 228
Slot usage 228
Star (*) 315
System Configuration 126
Butzen, Fred 320

C

C shell 42
cabling, coaxial or twisted-pair 153
caching-name server, installing 249
cards
    hang (stop working) 169
    video 31, 84
caret (^) 66
case sensitive text 45
cat command 36, 54
CD-ROMs
    HOWTO documents 8
    local drive 16
    sharing to learn Samba 183-185
CERT (Computer Emergency Response Team)
    Web page 286

certificates (Netscape Navigator) 324
checksum database 131
chgrp command 51
chivas 91, 204, 248
chmod command 50-51
Choose a Card menu 91
Choose Interface Type window 160, 246
chown command 51
classes
    custom 19
    IP addresses 160
    server 18
    Workstation 18-19
clients
    Windows, configuring 230-231
    X Client 89-92
    See also Netscape e-mail client
Clockchip, configuring 32
coaxial cabling 153
colon (:) 47, 76
comma (,) 50
command
    lines 54
    mode (vi) 73
commands 7
    apropos 63, 96
    arguments 46
    Bash Shell 137
    cat 36, 54
    chgrp 51
    chmod 50-51
    chown 51
    connecting processes 57
    cp 51
    Custom menu, Generic Monitor 84
    cw 76
    dip 251
    done 138
    echo 137
    env 55
    exit 55
    find 61
    fsck 142

continued

368 Index

commands *(continued)*
   grep 57, 138
   ifconfig 167-169
   installation troubleshooting 33-34
   ls 45
   kill 58-59
   less 54, 96
   Linux, help 95, 98
   locate 62
   makewhatis 96
   man 96-97
   metacharacters 46-47
   mkdir 53
   mode, inserting 73
   more 54
   mv 52
   output, redirecting 56-57
   parameters 45-46
   ping 166-167
   process 58
   ps 56, 58-59
   ps auxwww 59
   ps x 138
   put 76
   restart all 205
   rm 52
   rmdir 53
   rpm 133, 138, 143
   rpm -e 243
   running a series 56
   s 76
   smbpasswd 179
   smbstatus 181, 184, 186
   sort 57
   Start menu, Lock Screen 130
   strings 57
   su 55
   subshells 138
   testpms 206
   Tests menu, Print Postscript 202
   whatis 63
   whereis 61
   which 62
   x 75
xdm 87
xhost 90
\I 317
Commit Changes button 191
comparing commands and metacharacters 46
components 23-24
compressing data with tar 121
Computer Emergency Response Team (CERT)
       Web page 286
computers
   pinging 192
   preparing 8
   Windows 154-156, 171, 204-205
   Windows PC, checking Samba 196
concatenating files 54
configuration file (Samba)
   [global] setting section 176
   [homes] section 177
   [printers] shares 177
   subnets, limiting 177
   workgroup setting 177
   writable option 177
Configure filter window 202
configuring
   Apache Web server 332-333
   Applixware Data, troubleshooting 328
   Arkeia server 209-210
   authentication configuration 30
   Clockchip 32
   configuration files, general
       purpose 163
   Custom configuration 19
   DNS server 248-249
   e-mail servers 291, 294-295
   Fetchmail 298-303
   Linux
     installing 24-25
     dialing in toubleshooting 262
     network parameters 156-157
     networking for masquerading 275
   monitors 31
   mouse 25
   netcfg (Network Configurator) 157-158
   Netscape e-mail client 295

Netscape Messenger Mailbox 324-327
networks 25-27, 276-277
PostgreSQL, troubleshooting 328
printers 29
   local 200-201
   remote 202
   Samba 203-204
proxy routes, verifying 257
screens 31
SCSI (Small Computer System Interface) 19
sendmail 296
TCP/IP 26
time zones 28
Windows
   client 230-231
   computers 154-156
Xconfigurator 32
zip drive backups 225-226
connect /etc/diald/connect
       parameter 254
connect scripts 253
connecting to networks 153-154
consoles, virtual 43
control keys for pico (Pine Composer) 66
Control Panel 114-115, 242
   activating 245
   troubleshooting 142, 259
   utility 39
   window 116
conventions, Linux versus DOS 47-48
copying files 51
cp command 51
crack RPM, testing passwords 284-286
crackers 112, 277-279
Create tapes window 218-219
Ctr+Alt+FR keyboard combination 88
Ctrl-A keyboard combination 67
Ctrl-Alt-+ keyboard combination 86
Ctrl-Alt– (Control-Alt-Minus) keyboard
       combination 86
Ctrl-B keyboard combination 66
Ctrl-C keyboard combination 67, 83
Ctrl-D keyboard combination 67
Ctrl-E keyboard combination 67

Ctrl-G keyboard combination 68
Ctrl-J keyboard combination 67
Ctrl-K keyboard combination 67
Ctrl-Left-Alt-F2 keyboard combination 43
Ctrl-N keyboard combination 66
Ctrl-O keyboard combination 67
Ctrl-P keyboard combination 66
Ctrl-R keyboard combination 67
Ctrl-T keyboard combination 67
Ctrl-U keyboard combination 67
Ctrl-V keyboard combination 67
Ctrl-W keyboard combination 67
Ctrl-X keyboard combination 67
Ctrl-Y keyboard combination 67
Ctrl-^ (Ctrl-Shift-6) keyboard combination 67
Ctrl-_ keyboard combination 70
cursors, movement commands 74
custom
   class 19
   menu 85
Custom
   configuration 19
   menu commands, Generic Monitor 84
customer service 111-113
cw command 76

D

daemons 28, 58
   checking in Samba 192
   diald, starting 257
   HTTP (Hypertext Transfer
       Protocol 331
   httpd 190, 341
   imapd 297
   inetd 190, 297
   lpd 199
   nmbd 173-175, 196
   Samba 174-175
   sendmail, restarting 297
   smbd 173-175
dash (-) 45, 49, 55

Index

DAT (Digital Audio Tape) 117-118
data
    backing up 131
    restoring 231-232
    retrieving 124-125
Data window 315
databases
    Applixware Data 315-320
        troubleshooting 328
    indexes, Arkeia server 208
    tripwire checksum 131
dctrl
    script 257-259
    window 258
Debian distribution 132
dedicated Linux gateways 243
Default Gateway 26
default route 157
Delete button 22
deleting
    directories 53
    files 52
    text 75
Demilitarized Zone (DMZ) 266
device parameter 254
devices, cleaning 35
DHCP (Dynamic Host Configuration Protocol) 8
dial-up networking 239-240
    connecting to Internet 242
    Control Panel 242
    dip program 242
    gateways, dedicated 242-243
    LinuxConf 242
    modems, setting up 244-245
    Network diagram for connecting to the Internet 243
diald (dial-up system) 239-241
    bash shell script 256
    connect scripts 253
    connecting to Internet 252-256
    controlling manually 258
    daemon, starting 257
    diald.conf script 253
    /etc/ppp.connect script, setting up 254

    proxy routes, verifying configuration 257
    start up links, creating 253
    troubleshooting 260-261
dialog boxes
    Insert Hyperlink 336
    ScanDisk 10
Dialup IP Protocol. *See* DIP
Digital Audio Tape (DAT) 117-118
DIP (Dialup IP Protocol)
    connecting to Internet 250-253
    DIP> prompt 250
    troubleshooting 259-260
dip
    command 251
    program 242
directories 29
    changing 48
    creating 53
    deleting 53
    home 56
    /home/httpd/html (Apache default directory) 334
    listing 44-47
    man pages 97
    spool 29
disaster recovery for networks 149, 165
Disk Defragmenter utility 10
Disk Druid 20-22
disks 6
    Disk Druid 20-22
    floppy disk booting 30
    formatting partitions 23
    loading Linux 12
    partitioning 6, 9, 19-20
    swap space 22
    tar for backing up 117-118
    Zip 119, 226
DMZ (Demilitarized Zone) 266
DNS (Domain Name Server) 8, 247
    blind RPM packages, installing 249
    caching-name server, installing 249
    chivas 248
    configuring 248-249
DNS (Domain Name Service) 151

Index

troubleshooting 289
UDP, input and output rules setup 271
documents
   FAQ 24
   HOWTO 8, 24, 153
dollar sign ($) 42
Domain Name Server. *See* DNS
Domain Name Service. *See* DNS
domain names, registering 298
done command 138
DOS
   root directory 47
   shells 42
   versus Linux conventions 47-48
Drive Management 210
Drive Options button 228
Drivepacks 210, 227, 232-233
   window 216
drivers, hang (stop working) 169
drives 232
   DAT (Digital Audio Tape) 117-118
   File Drive 226
   Zip, backing up 118-119
Drives Management window 214-215
dual booting 9-10
Dynamic Host Configuration Protocol (DHCP) 8

E

e-mail
   Applixware Mail 315
   Atlas gateway 292- 294
   external delivery or retrieval,
      troubleshooting 304
   Fetchmail 294-295
      configuring 298-303
      cron star 302
      domain names, registering 298
      fetches, scheduling 301-302
      ISP passwords 300
      multidrop mode 298-300
      imap RPM package, installing 297

   local, troubleshooting 303
   Netscape e-mail client 291-294
      installing 292-293
   Netscape Messenger Mailbox, configuring
      324-327
   POP (Post Office Protocol) 291, 298
   receiving 294
   sendmail 296-297
   servers, configuring
      IMAP protocol 291, 293
      ISPs (Internet Service Providers) 291
      POP (Post Office Protocol) 291, 298
      POP3 protocol 293
      troubleshooting 303
echo command 137
Edit /etc/hosts 159
Edit button 22
Edit Ethernet/Bus Interface window 160
Edit Local Printer Entry window 201-202
Edit menu (Applixware Words) 314
Edit/etc/hosts window 159
editing
   control keys 66
   editors (text) 65-66
   Emacs editor 78
   joe (Joe's Own Editor)
      features and options 71
      files, multiple 70
      starting 69
   pico (Pine Composer), starting 66
   spell checking 78
   text
      deleting 75
      editing 67, 70-71
      inserting and moving 66
      searching for 77
   vi
      changes, undoing 75
      command mode 73
      deleting text 75
      editing text 76-77
      help 78
      insert mode 73

continued

Index

editing *(continued)*
    saving and exiting 77-78
    starting 72
    switching modes 73
    text insertions 72-73
    text searches 77
education for security methods 286-287
Emacs editor 78
encrypted communication (Netscape Navigator) 322-324
    Man in the Middle attacks 324
encrypted passwords 178-179
enemies (crackers), tools and methods 277-278
Enhanced Software Technologies Web site 207
Enlightenment
    GNOME (GNU Network Object Model Environment) 88
    Gnome footprints 88
    Gnome/Enlightenment window manager 87
    Start menu 88-89
    X clients on X servers, viewing 89-92
env command 55
Ethernet
    hubs 154
    interface, pinging 168-170
    NIC 37-38, 163
exit command 55
Expert Mode 15
exporting Web pages 338
external security 128

F

FAQs (Frequently Asked Questions) 8
    documents 24
    Web site 99
FAT file systems 11
fdisk program 9
Fetchmail 294-295
    configuring 298-303

    cron star 302
    domain names, registering 298
    fetches, scheduling 301-302
    ISP passwords 300
    multidrop mode 298-300
File Drive 226
file libraries 228
File menu (Applixware Words) 313
File Pool 227
file servers, backing up 111
file systems
    dual booting 9-10
    FAT 11
    inodes 6
    partitioning disks 6
    proc 36-37
files 7, 44-47
    backing up 116
        backup records 123
        BRU 2000 125
        DAT drive 117-118
        data retrieval 124-125
        incremental tar archives 122
        scheduling 122
        tar (Tape Archive) 117-118
        verifying 123-124
    concatenating 54
    configuration, general purpose 163
    configuration (Samba), 176-177
    copying 51-52
    data retrieval 124-125
    deleting 52
    File Drive 226
    file libraries, creating 228
    File Pool 227
    FileSave 229
    group 125
    groups, changing 51
    information listed 48
    listing 44-47
    lock, checking in Samba 193
    log 233
        checking in Samba 193
        monitoring 278-279

Index

messages 140
moving 52
multiple, working with 70
network 162
NFS (Network File System) 163
.odbc.ini, creating 318
ownership, changing 51
pages, displaying 54
password 125
permissions 49-51
printcap 199, 202
proc file system 143
rescue.img 14
searching 61-64
shadow password 125
smb.conf, modifying 178
   Share Definitions section 186
smbpasswd, creating 178
state of installation, checking 134
system logs, monitoring 139-141
transferring 138
viewing 54
writable option 177
See also editing; security
FileSave 229
filtering firewalls 266
   creating 268-269
   default policies, setting up 269
   filters, building 268
   flushing existing rules 269
   IP filters, adjusting settings 272
   ipchains options 271
   TCP rules, input and output setup 270
   UDP rules, input and output setup 271
filtering strings 57
filters
   building 268
   grep 137
   IP 266
   print 199
   TOS (Type of Service) 272
   working filters, building 272-273
Find & Replace menu (Applixware Words) 314
find command 61

finding man (manual) pages 96
fingerprinting (nmap program) 279
   networks 282
FIPS (First nondestructive Interactive Partition Splitting) 10-12
Firewall Network 266
firewalls
   attacks 267, 274
   CERT (Computer Emergency Response Team) Web page 286
   configuring Linux networking for masquerading 275
   crack RPM, testing passwords 284-286
   DNS servers, troubleshooting 289
   education for security methods 286-287
   enemies (crackers), tools and methods 278-279
   filtering 265, 268
      default policies, setting up 269
      flushing existing rules 269
      IP (Internet Protocol) filters, adjusting settings 272
      ipchains options 271
      TCP rules, input and output setup 270
      UDP rules, input and output setup 271
   Firewall Network 266
   Intel 486 266
   IP (Internet Protocol)
      chains, troubleshooting 287-288
      filters 266, 272
      masquerading 273-274
      packets 265
   ipchains RPM package 267
   Linux servers, port scan 280
   log files, monitoring 278-279
   managing 277
   masquerading, troubleshooting 288
   networks, configuring for external access 276-277
   nmap program to test system 279-280
   OSI Network layer 265

continued

firewalls *(continued)*
    packets 266
    placing within networks 266
    proxy 265, 276
    proxying 266-267
    scanning, stopping 282
    Secure Shell 276-277
    starting automatically 276
    TIS Firewall 267
    TOS (Type of Service) 272
    Tripwire, monitoring systems 283
    troubleshooting 286-289
    working filters, building 272-273
    See also security
First nondestructive Interactive Partition Splitting (FIPS) 10-12
floppy disk booting 30
footprints, Gnome 88
Format menu (Applixware Words) 314
formatting disk partitions 23
forward slash (/) 47, 96
Frame Relay 241
Frequently Asked Questions. *See* FAQs
fsck command 142
FSSTND (File System Standard) 7
    guidelines 209
FTP (File Transfer Protocol) 17
functions
    LinuxConf 114-116
    nmap program 279-280
    query 133
    virtual console 33

G

gateways, dedicated 242-243
Generic Monitor command (Custom menu) 84
Generic Multisync monitor 86
Get messages button 294
[global] setting section 176
Gnome
    footprints 88

Gnome/Enlightenment window manager 87
    Start menu 88-89
    X clients on X servers, viewing 89-92
GNOME (GNU Network Object Model Environment) 88
GNU (Gnu's Not UNIX) 43-45
GNU General Public License (GPL) 44
GNU Network Object Model Environment (GNOME), 88
GPL (GNU General Public License) 44
Graphical User Interface. *See* GUI
graphics, Applixware Graphics 315
greater-than sign (>) 56
green checkmark button 212
grep
    command 57, 138
    filter 137
group file 125
groups
    creating 126
    of files, changing 51
GUI (Graphical User Interface) 81
    guidelines, FSSTND 209
    starting in Arkeia server 212
Guides 100
gzip program 121

H

hackers, tools and methods 277-278
hang (stop working) 169
hard drive 16, 226
hardware, video cards, selecting 84
help
    Applixware 311-313
    Arkeia server 212
    connecting to networks 153
    disaster recovery 165
    FAQs (Frequently Asked Questions) Web site 99
    Guides 100
    HOWTOs 100

Index   375

Internet 101
joe (Joe's Own Editor) 71
LDP (Linux Documentation Project) 98
Linux
   commands 96
      Linux publications 104
   LUGs (Linux user groups) 104-105
   mailing lists 103-104
   man pages 95-96
   Netscape Communicator 322
   newsgroups 102-103
   pico (Pine Composer) 68
   user groups 104-105
   vi 78
   WWW (World Wide Web) 101-102
   X Window System 91-92
   Xconfigurator 91-92
   See also troubleshooting
Help
   button 191
   menu (Applixware Words) 314
Help on Words help window 312
high speed Internet connections 241
home
   directories 56
   pages, making 339
   share, accessing 186-187
[homes] section 177
HOWTO documents 8, 24, 153
HOWTOs 100
HTML (Hypertext Markup Language) tags
   <BODY> 336
   <P></P> 336
HTTP (Hypertext Transport Protocol) 274
   daemon 331
httpd daemon 190, 341
hubs 36
   Ethernet 154
hyperlinks 341
   adding to SWAT interface 338
   adding to Web pages 337
Hypertext Markup Language. *See* HTML
Hypertext Transport Protocol. *See* HTTP

I

icons
   chivas 204
   lp 205
   Printer 200
ICMP (Internet Control Message Protocol) 151
IDE devices 120-121
IDG Books Web site 175
ifconfig command 167-169
IMAP
   protocol 291
   servers 294
imap RPM package, installing 297
IMAP4 protocol 293
imapd daemon 297
indexes, Arkeia server 208
inetd daemon 190, 297
InfoWorld's Best Technical Support award 95
init process 5
inodes 6
Input Filter Select button 201
Insert Hyperlink dialog box 336
Insert menu (Applixware Words) 314
insert mode, navigating screens 73-74
Install Status window 24
installing 3, 13-14
   Apache Web server
   Applixware 310
   Arkeia server 209
   blind RPM packages 249
   boot floppy, making 144
   caching-name server 249
   classes 17-19
   components 23-24
   hard drives 16
   keyboard types 15
   Linux, 24, 33-39
   methods 15
   Netscape Communicator 321
   Netscape e-mail client 292-293
   paths 17
   postgresql RPMs 315-316

continued

376 Index

installing *(continued)*
   process, starting 15
   RPM (Red Hat Package Manager) 133
   Samba 173
   sources 17
Intel 486 firewall server 266
Interactive backup window 222
interactive
   backups 222-224
   mode 83
Interface configuration protocol button 160
interfaces
   checking 167-168
   Ethernet, pinging 168-170
   networks 159
internal security 128-129
International Standards Organization (ISO) 150
Internet 8
   chivas 248
   dctrl scripts 257-259
   dial-up networking 239-240
      connecting to Internet 242
      gateways, dedicated 242-243
   diald (dial-up system) 239-241
      connecting to Internet 252-256
      controlling manually 258
      start up links, creating 253
   DIP (Dialup Internet Protocol) 250-253
   DNS (domain name server) 247-249
   help 101
   IP (Internet Protocol)
      addresses 8, 25, 27
      masquerading 240protocol 239, 254
   ipchains system 240
   ISPs (Internet Service Providers) 239
      choosing 240-242
      dynamic option 254
      high speed Internet connections 241
      static addresses 252
   modems, setting up 244-245
      LED (Light Emitting Diodes) 259
   Network Configurator
      connecting to the Internet 245
      PPP interface, adding 246
   Network diagram for connecting to the
      Internet 243
   network information 241
   PPP (Point-to-Point) protocol 239-240
      connections, establishing 241
      disconnecting 248
      route parameter 254
   troubleshooting
      configuring Linux for dialing in 262
      Control Panel, connecting to Internet 259
      diald, connecting to Internet 260-261
      DIP, connecting to Internet 259-260
      modems 259
Internet Control Message Protocol (ICMP) 151
Internet Service Providers. *See* ISPs
InterNIC 8
intranets
   Web pages, creating 334-335
      advances 340
      content, adding 336
      exporting 338
      home pages, making 339
      hyperlinks, adding 337
      servers, security 340-341
      SWAT interface, adding hyperlinks 338
   Web servers, Apache 332-334
IP (Internet Protocol)
   addresses 8
      classes 160
      frequently used 27
      static 25
   chains, troubleshooting 287-288
   filters, adjusting settings 272
   masquerading 240, 273-274
   packets 265
   protocol 239, 254
ipchains
   RPM package 266-267, 271
   system 240
ipfwadm system. *See* ipchains, RPM package
ISO (International Standards Organization) 150
ispell 78
ISPs (Internet Service Providers) 239, 325
   choosing 240-242

DNS (domain name server) 247
dynamic option 254
e-mail servers 291
high speed Internet connections 241
Netscape Navigator, configuring for
    e-mail 326-327
Network Configuration GUI 247
passwords 300
static addresses 252

J

jobs, automating execution 139
joe (Joe's Own Editor)
    default editor, making as 71
    features and options 71
    files, multiple 70
    keyboard combinations 70
    starting 69
jukeboxes (tape libraries) 208

K

kernel 5
    parameter options 15
    proc files and directories 37
key combinations, virtual console functions 33
keyboard combinations 43, 70
    Ctrl+Alt+Fn 88
    Ctrl-A 67
    Ctrl-Alt- (Control-Alt-Minus) 86
    Ctrl-Alt-+ 86
    Ctrl-B 66
    Ctrl-C 67, 83
    Ctrl-D 67
    Ctrl-E 67
    Ctrl-F 66
    Ctrl-G 68
    Ctrl-J 67
    Ctrl-K 67

Ctrl-Left-Alt-F2 43
Ctrl-N 66
Ctrl-O 67
Ctrl-P 66
Ctrl-R 67
Ctrl-T 67
Ctrl-U 67
Ctrl-V 67
Ctrl-W 67
Ctrl-X 67
Ctrl-Y 67
Ctrl-^ (Ctrl-Shift-6) 67
Ctrl-_ 70
keyboards 15
keys, control for pico 66
keywords, man (manual) pages 63-64
Kickstart Mode 15, 83
kill command 58, 59
Knox Software Web site 209, 232
Korn shell 42
Korn, David 42

L

LAN (local area network) 4, 147
LAN Manager, printer, 29
    SMB (Session Message Block) 173
languages, choosing for Red Hat Linux 15
layering security 128
LDP (Linux Documentation Project) 98
    FAQs (Frequently Asked Questions) 99
    Guides 100
    HOWTOS 100
    Internet help 101
    Linux publications 104
    LUGs (Linux user groups) 104-105
    mailing lists 103-104
    newsgroups 102-103
    Web site 99
    WWW (World Wide Web) help
        101-102
LED (Light Emitting Diodes) 259

less command 54, 96
libraries 233
    file libraries, creating 228
Libraries Management 211
Libraries management window 228
Light Emitting Diodes (LED) 259
LILO (Linux Loader) 12, 30
lines, uncommenting 183
links, start up (diald), creating 253
    See also hyperlinks
Linux.See Red Hat Linux
Linux Documentation Project. See LDP
Linux File System Standard (FSSTND) 7
Linux Journal Web site 104, 320
LinuxConf 242
    functions 114-116
    troubleshooting 142
    user accounts, creating and modifying 126-127
    utility 39
LInuxLoader (LILO) 12, 30
listings, directories or files 44-47
loadable modules 25-26
loading Linux onto disk 12
local and remote IP address 254
local area network (LAN) 4, 147
local backups 117
local e-mail
    servers, configuring 294-295
    troubleshooting 303
Local Printer button 201
local printers 29
    configuring 200-201
    troubleshooting 205
locate command 62
lock files, checking 193
Lock Screen command (Start menu) 130
locked up processes, circumventing 60
locks on screens 130
log files 233
    checking 19
    monitoring 278-279
log off security 130
logging in as user root 53

logs, system, monitoring 139-141
lp icon 205
lpd daemon, print filters or printcap file 199
ls command 45
LUGs (Linux user groups) 104
    Web site 105

M

macros (Samba) 188-189
mailing lists,help 103-104
makewhatis command 96
man command 96, 97
Man In The Middle attacks 324
man (manual) pages 95
    directories 97
    finding 96
    keywords, looking for 63-64
    navigating 96
    organization of 97
    sections 96-97
masks, subnet 38
masquerading
    IP (Internet Protocol) 273-274
    Linux networking, configuring 275
    troubleshooting 288
MBR (master boot record) 140
media, backups 225
memory, videos 32
menus
    Choose a Card 91
    custom 85
    Edit (Applixware Words) 314
    File (Applixware Words) 313
    Find & Replace (Applixware Words) 314
    Format (Applixware Words) 314
    Help (Applixware Words) 314
    Insert (Applixware Words) 314
    Monitor Setup 91
    Pick a Server 91
    Table (Applixware Words) 314

Index 379

Tools (Applixware Words) 314
User accounts 127
View (Applixware Words) 314
messages file 140
metacharacters 46-47
mice, Mouseconfig 82
minus (-) button 224
minus sign (-) 50
mkdir command 53
modems
   LED (Light Emitting Diodes) 259
   modem parameter 250
   PCM CIA 244
   serial IP and interrupt addresses 244
   setting up 244-245
   troubleshooting 259
modes
   command 72-73
   insert 73
   interactive 83
   Kickstart 83
   permission, changing 49-51
   switching 73
modules
   loadable 25-26
   networking 36-37
   options 26
Monitor Setup
   menu 91
   screen (Xconfigurator) 85
monitors
   configuring 31
   custom menu 85
   damaging 85
   generic 86
   Generic Multisync Monitor 86
   selecting 84
more command 54
mount point (/) 22
mouse, configuring 25
Mouseconfig 82
moving files 52
msks profram 9

multidrop mode (Fetchmail) 298, 300
Multisync Monitor (Generic) 86
multitasking 58
mv command 52

N

names
   domains, registering 298
   machines, specifying 155
Namesever entry 26
NAT (Network Address Translation), IP masquerading 240, 273-274
navigating screens 73-74
NetBios, SMB (Session Message Block) 173
netcfg (Network Configurator), 157-158
Netscape Communicator
   certificates 324
   encrypted communication 322-324
   help 322
   installing 321
   Linux servers, e-mail services 326-327
   Man in the Middle attacks 324
   Messenger Mailbox, configuring 324-327
   SSL (Secure Sockets Layer) 323
   troubleshooting 329
Netscape e-mail client 291, 294
   configuring 295
   installing 292-293
   troubleshooting e-mail server 303
Netscape Mail Server
   configuration window 325
   Preferences window 326
   window 293
Netscape Security Info window 323
NetWare print server 29
Network Address Translation (NAT), IP masquerading 240, 273-274

Index

Network Configuration
  button 157
  GUI 247
  Interfaces window 246
  window 247
Network Configurator
  connecting to the Internet 245
  GUI 161
  Hosts window 158
  Interfaces window 159
  PPP interface, adding 246
  Network Configurator Names window 157
  Routing window 161
Network diagram for connecting to the Internet 243
Network File System (NFS) 16, 163
Network Information System (NIS) 30
network interface cards (NICs) 26
  Ethernet interface 37-38
network ports, monitoring 174
Network Troubleshooter 171
networking, configuring Linux for 275
  See also dial-up networking
networks 25
  administering 148
  application layer 150
  automated backups. *See* Arkeia server
  CERT (Computer Emergency Response Team) Web page 286
  checking in Samba 192
  Choose Interface Type window 159
  coaxial cabling 153
  configuration files, general purpose 163
  configuring 25-27, 276-277
  connecting to 153-154
  connections, checking 35-36
  default route 157
  disaster recovery 149, 165
  DNS (Domain Name Service) 151
  Edit /etc/hosts window 158
  Edit Ethernet/Bus Interface window 160
  education for security methods 286-287
  /etc/hosts table 153

Ethernet
  hubs 154
  interfaces, pinging 168-170
  NIC, configuring 163
fingerprinting 282
firewalls
  attacks 267, 274
  CERT (Computer Emergency Response Team) Web page 286
  configuring Linux 275-277
  crack RPM, testing passwords 284-286
  default policies, setting up 269
  DNS servers, troubleshooting 289
  education for security methods 286-287
  enemies (crackers), tools and methods 277-278
  filtering 266, 268-269
  fingerprinting networks 282
  Firewall Network 266
  flushing existing rules 270
  Intel 486 266
  IP chains, troubleshooting 287-288
  IP filters 266, 272
  IP masquerading 273-274
  ipchains options 271
  ipchains RPM package 267
  log files, monitoring 278-279
  managing 277
  masquerading, troubleshooting 288
  nmap program to test system 279-280
  packets 266
  passwords, testing 284-286
  placing within 266
  private 266
  proxies 276
  proxying 266-267
  scanning, stopping 282
  Secure Shell 276-277
  starting automatically 276
  TCP rules, input and output setup 270
  TIS Firewall 267
  TOS (Type of Service) 272
  Tripwire, monitoring systems 283

Index   381

UDP rules, input and output setup 271
working filters, building 272-273
hang (stop working) 169
hubs 36, 154
ICMO (Internet Control Message Protocol) 151
ifconfig command 167-169
interfaces 159
  checking 167-168
IP (Internet Protocol) addresses, classes 160
ISO (International Standards Organization) 150
LAN (local area network) 147
Linux
  network, parameters, configuring 156-157
  server, port scan 280
netcfg (Network Configurator) 157-158
Network Configurator
  GUI 161
  Hosts window 158
  Interfaces window 159
  Names window 158
  Routing window 161
network file 162
network layer 151
networking modules 36-37
Network Troubleshooter 171
NIS (Network Information Service) 164
OSI (Open Systems Interconnect) 150-151
parameters, configuring 156
passwords, testing 284-286
paunchy.net 151-153
physical/data link layer 151
ping command 166-167
pinging 170
PnP (Plug and Play) 170
policies 148
PPP connection 162
problems, sources for solving 171
restarting 162
routes, checking 167-168
routing 151

routing, checking 38-39
scripts 161-163
security 148-149, 164
stopping and starting 162
switches 154
TCP (Transport Control Layer) 151
Thinnet 35
transport layer 151
troubleshooting 166-171, 286-289
twisted-pair cabling 153
UDP (User Datagram Protocol) 151
usage policy 164
Windows computers, configuring 154-156
newsgroups, help 102-103
NFS (Network File System) 16, 163
NICs (network interface cards) 26
  Ethernet interface 37-38
NIS (Network Information Service) 164
NIS (Network Information System), authentication configuration 30
nmap program
  finger printing networks 282
  port scan 280-281
  scanning, stopping 282
  testing system, functions 279-280
nmbd daemon 173-175, 196-197
nmblookup utility 182
null
  backup 212-214, 223
  drivepack 214-217
  pool 217-219
NullPack Drivepack 217
number signs (#) 140

O

office productivity tools. *See* productivity tools
OK button 22
one-way protocols 293
Open Systems Interconnect (OSI) 150
  Network layer 265
operating system 5

382 Index

OSI (Open Systems Interconnect) 150
   Network layer 265
output of commands, redirecting 56-57
ownership of files, changing 51

P

packages, RPM (Red Hat Package Manager)
   blind, installing 249
   removing 135
   updating 135
   verifying 135
   versus tar files 136
packet sniffers 285
packets, ipchains 266
packs and pools for backups 211
pages of files, displaying 54
parameters 15, 250
   commands 45-46
   connect /ect/diald/connect 254
   device 254
   kerner options 15
   Linux network,configuring 156-157
   route 254
   security 180
   Windows network 156
parentheses ( ) 56, 138
partitions (disks) 6
   Disk Druid 20-22
   formatting 23
   partitions 9
   suggested partitions 19-21
   swap space 22
passwd files 125
passwords 29, 127
   Arkeia, setting in 213
   authentication 178-180
   encrypted 178-179
   packet sniffers 285
   plain-text 178
   root 29
   shadow 129, 285

   testing with crack RPM 284-286
paunchy.net 151-152, 248
   /etc/hosts table 153
PCMCIA modems 244
percent sign (%) 188
Periodic backup window 224
permissions
   of files, changing modes 49-51
   Samba 180
Pick a Server menu 91
pico (Pine Composer)
   control keys 66
   default editor, making as 67
   help 68
   text
      editing 67
      inserting and moving 66
PID (process ID) 59
Pine Composer. *See* pico
ping command 166-167
pinging
   Ethnernet interface 168-170
   Linux machine 192
   networks 170
pings (nmap program) 279
pipe (|) 57, 138
plain-text passwords 178
Plug-and-Play (PnP) 26, 170
plus (+) button 224
plus sign (+) 50
PnP (Plug and Play) 26, 170
Point-to-Point Protocol. *See* PPP
policies
   logging off 130
   networks 148, 164
   System Administration 110
      backups 111
      customer service 11-113
      security 111, 130-132
      troubleshooting 111-114
Pool creation window 217
Pools 232
Pools Management 211
   window 217

Index 383

POP (Post Office Protocol) 291, 298
POP3 protocol 293
port scan (nmap program) 279
    Linux
        machines 281
        servers 280
    Stealth FIN 281
    SYN scan 280
    Windows computers 281
ports, network, monitoring 174
Post Office Protocol (POP) 291, 298
postgresql RPMs, installing 315-316
PostgreSQL, troubleshooting 328
postmaster process (Applixware Data), starting 316
pound sign (#) 42, 176, 341
PPP (Point-to-Point Protocol) 239-240, 271
    connections, establishing 241
    disconnecting 248
    route parameter 254
Print Postscript command (Tests menu) 202
print working directory (pwd) 47
printcap files 199, 202
Printer Configuration button 203
Printer icon 200
Printer System Manager 202, 203
printers
    Add a Printer Entry window 201
    Configure filter window 201
    configuring 29
    Edit Local Printer Entry window 201-202
    filters 199
    Lan Manager 29
    local 29
        configuring 200-201
        troubleshooting 205
    lpd daemon 199-200
    NetWare 29
    printcap files 199, 202
    printer queues 29
    Printer System Manager 202-203
    printing from Windows computers 204-205
    queues, troubleshooting 205
    remote 29

    configuring 202
    troubleshooting 205
    restart all command 205
    RHS Linux Printer System Manager window 200
    Samba
        configuring 203-204
        troubleshooting 205
    spool directories 29
    testing 202-204
    testprns command 206
    troubleshooting 205
[printers] shared 177
private networks 266
probing monitors 86
proc file system 36-37, 143
process commands 58
process ID (PID) 59
Process Table 58-59
processes
    connecting 57
    locked up, circumventing 60
    signalling 59
productivity tools
    Applixware 309
        help system 311-312
        installing 310
        starting 311
    Applixware Data
        data, inserting 317-318
        databases 316-320
        .odbc.ini file, creating 318
        postgresql RPMs, installing 315-316
        postmaster process, installing 316
        troubleshooting 328
    Applixware Graphics 315
    Applixware Mail 315
    Applixware Spreadsheets 315
    Applixware Words 313-314
    Netscape Communicator
        certificates 324
        encrypted communication 322-324
        help 322
        installing 321

Linux servers, e-mail services 326-327
Man in the Middle attacks 324
Messenger Mailbox, configuring 324-327
SSL (Secure Sockets Layer) 323
troubleshooting 329
StarOffice 320
protocols
  boot 25
  DIP (Dialup Internet Protocol) 250-253
  FTP (File Transfer Protocol) 17
  HTTP (Hypertext Transfer Protocol) 274, 331
  ICMP (Internet Control Message Protocol) 151
  IMAP 291
  IMAP4 293
  IP (Internet Protocol) 239
  ISPs (Internet Service Providers), e-mail servers 291
  one-way protocols 293
  POP (Post Office Protocol) 291, 298
  POP3 293
  PPP (Point-to-Point Protocol) 239-240, 271
    connections, establishing 241
    disconnecting 248
    route parameter 254
  TCP (Transmission Control Protocol) 174
  TCP (Transport Control Layer) 151
  TCP/IP (Transmission Control Protocol/Internet Protocol) 26, 149, 174
  UDP (User Datagram Protocol) 151, 174
proxy
  firewalls 276
  routes, verifying configuration 257
proxying firewalls 266-267
ps auxwww command 59
ps command 56, 58, 59
ps x command 138
publications, *Linux Journal* 104
put command 76
pwd (print working directory) 47

Q

query function 133
question mark (?) 96
queues
  printers 29
  printing, troubleshooting 205

R

radio frequency (RF) 35
rebooting to troubleshoot 143
Red Hat Apache test page window 333
Red Hat Linux
  commands 95-98
  installing 3, 13-15
  machines, port scan 281
  root partition 47
  servers
    Arkeia, installing 209
    e-mail services 326-327
    port scan 280
  starting 140-141
  stopping 142
  system requirements 3-4
  Test Page 334
  user groups. *See* LUGs
  versus DOS conventions 47-48
  Web sites 101-102, 327
  See also RPM (Red Hat Package Manager)
Red Hat Linux in Small Business page 335
remote and local IP addresses 254
remote printers 29
  configuring 202
  troubleshooting 205
Remote Unix (lpd) button 202
removing. *See* deleting
Rescue Mode 15
rescue.img file 14
resources, CD-ROM 8
restart all command 205
restarting networks 162
Restoration window 231

Index

restoring data 231-232
RF (radio frequency) 35
RHS Linux Printer System Manager window 200
rm command 52
rmdir command 53
root
    partitions 47
    passwords 29
    user 44, 53
route parameter 254
routes, checking 167-168
routing 151
    default route 157
    networks 38-39
RPM (Red Hat Package Manager) 24
    blind packages, installing 249
    files, checking state of installation 134
    information, getting 133-134
    installing 133
    packages 135-136
    query function 133
rpm -e command 243
rpm command 133, 138, 143

S

s command 76
Samba
    authentication 178-180
    configuration file 176-177
    configuration, checking 194
    daemons 173-175
    home directory shares 187
    installing 173
    learning
        CD-ROM sharing 183-185
        home share, accessing 186-187
        /var/tmp directory, sharing 185-186
    log files, checking 193
    macros 188-189
    passwords 178-180
    permissions 180
    printers
        configuring 203-204
        testing 204
        troubleshoooting 206
    Samba SWAT window 190
    security, authentication 178-180
    shares 174, 184, 195
    SMB (Session Message Block) 173
    smb conf file, modifying 178
    smbmount system 174
    smbpasswd 178-179
    smbstatus command 186
    subnets, limiting 177
    SWAT (Samba Web Administration Tool) 190-191
    troubleshooting
        daemons, checking 192
        lock or log files, checking 193
        networks, checking 191-192
        nmbd daemon 196
        smbclient utility 194-195
        from Windows PC 196
    utilities 181-183
    Web site 173
Samba Web Administration Tool (SWAT) 190-191
Savepack 210, 220-222, 229, 232-233
    management window 220
ScanDisk utility dialog box 10
scanning packages to install 22
scans
    port scan
        Linux servers 280
        Windows computers 281
    scanning, stopping 282
    Stealth FIN port scan 281
    SYN 280
screens
    configuring 31
    Drive Management 210
    Drivepack 210

continued

386 Index

screens *(continued)*
   Libraries Management 211
   locks 130
   Monitor Setup (Xconfigurator) 85
   navigating 73-74
   Pools Management 211
   Savepack 210
   server administration 209
   Tapes Management 211
scripts 162
   bash shell 256
   connect 253
   dctrl 257-259
   diald.conf 253
   /etc/ppp/connect 254
   modifying manually 163
   Network Configurator GUI 161
   shell, creating and making executable 50
   writing 136
      Bash Shell commands 137
      done command 138
      echo command 137
      grep filter 137
      ps x command 138
      rpm command 138
      subshells 138
SCSI (small computer systems interface) 8
   configuring 19
   tape drive or tape library 229
searching files 61-64
Secure Shell 276-277
Secure Sockets Layer (SSL) 323
security
   Arkeia, setting in 213
   authentication 178-180
   CERT (Computer Emergency Response Team) Web page 286
   certificates 324
   checksum database 131
   crack RPM, testing passwords 284-286
   crackers 112
   data backups 131
   education for security methods 286-287

   encrypted communication (Netscape Navigator) 322-324
   enemies (crackers), tools and methods 277-278
   external 128
   fingerprinting networks 282
   internal 128-129
   layering 128
   log files, monitoring 278-279
   logging off 130
   login messages 131
   Man in the Middle attacks 324
   networks 148-149
      policies 164
   nmap program to test system 279-280
   parameter 180
   passwords 129
      authentication 178-180
      testing 284-286
   policy setting 130-132
   SSL (Secure Sockets Layer) 323
   Systems Administration 111-113
   tripwire program 131
   Tripwire, monitoring systems 283
   See also firewalls
Select All button 228
Select via navigator window 221
semicolon (;) 56, 176, 183, 317
sendmail
   configuring for external delivery 296
   daemon, restarting 297
Server administration
   screen 209
   window 213
server class 18
servers
   caching-name, installing 248
   DNS, troubleshooting 289
   e-mail, configuring 291
      IMAP 294
      local servers, configuring 294-295
   Linux, port scan 280
   securing 340-341
   X clients on X servers, viewing 89-92

Index   387

X Server 90
　See also Apache Web server; Arkeia server;
　　DNS (Domain Name Server); Linux,
　　servers
Session Message Block (SMB) 173
Set tape button 228
shadow passwords 125, 129, 285
Share Definitions section (smb.conf file) 186
shares 174, 195
　home directory 187
　[printers] 177
shell scripts 50
shells 6
　bash 42, 55
　Bourne 42
　C 42
　DOS 42
　Korn 42
　X Window System 41
slashes (//) 341
Slot usage button 228
Slots in library: FileLib window 228
Small Computer System Interface. *See* (SCSI)
SMB (Session Message Block) 173
SMB Image 17
smb.conf file, modifying 178
　Share Definitions section 186
smbclient utility 181-182, 194-195
smbd daemon 173-175
smbmount
　system 174
　utility 182-183
smbpasswd
　command 179
　file, creating 178
smbstatus
　command 181, 184, 186
　utility 181
software, FSSTND guidelines 209
sort command 57
spelling, checking 78
spool directories 29
spreadsheets, Applixware Spreadsheets 315
SSL (Secure Sockets Layer) 323

Star (*) button 315
StarOffice 320
Start menu 88-89
　commands, Lock Screen 130
starting
　Applixware 311
　firewalls automatically 276
　Linux 140-141
　X Window System 87
static IP (Internet Protocol) addresses 25
static ISP (Internet Service Provider) addresses
　252
Stealth FIN port scan 281
stopping Linux 142
strings, filtering or sorting 57
su command 55
subnet masks 38
subshells 138
SuperProbe 83
swap space (disk partitions) 22
SWAT (Samba Web Administration Tool) 190-
　191
Swat interface, adding hyperlinks 338
switches 154
SYN scan 280
syslogd 142
System Configuration button 126
system logs, monitoring 139-141
systems
　requirements 3-4
　smbmount 174
　testing with nmap program 279
　Tripwire, monitoring 283
Systems Administration
　backups 116-118
　BRU 2000 125
　Control Panel 114-115
　file servers, backing up 111
　IDE devices 120-121
　jobs, automating execution 139
　Linux, starting or stopping, 140-142
　LinuxConf functions 114-116
　MBR (master boot record) 140
　　　　　　　　　　　　　　continued

388 Index

Systems Administration *(continued)*
   passwords, shadow passwords 129
   policies 110-114
   RPM (Red Hat Package Manager) 132
   scripts, writing 136-138
   security 112-113, 128
   system logs, monitoring 139-141
   tar (Tape Archive) 117-118
   troubleshooting 142-144
   user accounts, managing 125-126
   Zip disks, formatting 119
   Zip drives 118

T

Table menu (Applixware Words) 314
tables, /etc/hosts 153
tags, HTML (Hypertext Markup Language)
   <BODY> 336
   <P></P> 336
Tape Archive. *See* tar
tape libraries 208
tapes 232
   Libraries Management 211
   Pools Management 211
   pools 217-219, 227
   SCSI tape drive or tape library 229
   Tapes Management 211
Tapes management window 218-219
tar (Tape Archive) 117
   backup records 123
   compressing data 121
   data retrieval 124-125
   incremental backups 122
   saving to Zip disk 121
   scheduling backups 122
   verifying 123-124
   versus RPM packages 136
   Zip drives, backing up 118-119
TCP (Transmission Control Protocol) 174
   rules, input and output setup 270
TCP (Transport Control Protocol) 151

TCP/IP (Transmission Control Protocol/Internet
   Protocol)
   26, 174
   application layer 150
   configuring 26
   DNS (Domain Name Service) 151
   ICMP (Internet Control Message Protocol)
   151
   ISO (International Standards Organization)
   150
   network layer 151
   OSI (Open Systems Interconnect) 150-151
   physical/data link layer 151
   routing 151
   TCP (Transport Control Protocol) 151
   transport layer 151
   UDP (User Datagram Protocol) 151
test backups 229
testing printers 202-204
testparm utility 182, 194
testpms
   command 206
   utility 182
Tests menu, Print Postscript command 202
text
   case sensitive 45
   inserting and moving around 66
   See also editing; joe; pico; vi
Thinnet 35
tilde and forward slash (~/) 56
time zones, configuring 28
TIS Firewall 267
tools. *See* productivity tools
Tools menu (Applixware Words) 314
TOS (Type of Service) 272
transferring files 138
Transmission Control Protocol (TCP) 174
   rules, input and output setup 270
Transport Control Protocol (TCP) 151
transport layer 151
Tridgell, Andrew 173
Trinux Web site 243
tripwirechecksum database or program 131
Tripwire, monitoring systems 283

troubleshooting 33-39
   Applixware 327-328
   Applixware Data 328
   Arkeia server 232-234
   boot floppy, making during
      installation 144
   configuring Linux for dialing in 262
   Control Panel 142, 259
   diald, connecting to Internet 260-261
   DIP, connecting to Internet 259-260
   DNS servers 289
   e-mail 304
   fsck command 142
   installation problems 33-39
   IP chains 287-288
   LinuxConf 142
   local e-mail 303
   masquerading 288
   modems 259
   Netscape Communicator 329
   Netscape e-mail client 303
   networks 166-171
   PostgreSQL 328
   printers 205
   proc file system 143
   rebooting 143
   Samba
     daemons, checking 192
     lock or log files, checking 193
     networks, checking 192
     nmbd daemon 196
     smbclient utility 194-195
     testparm utility 194
     from Windows PC 196
   syslogd 142
   Systems Administration 111-114, 142-144
   X Window System 91-92
   Xconfigurator 91-92
   See also help
twisted-pair cabling 153
Type of Service (TOS) 272

U

UDP (User Datagram Protocol) 151, 174
   rules, input and output setup 271
uncommenting lines 183
User account creation window 127
User accounts menu 127
user accounts, managing 125-126
   creating and modifying with LinuxConf
     126-127
   creating with useradd 126
   groups, creating 126
   passwords 127
User Datagram Protocol. *See* UDP
user groups, joining 104-105
user root, logging in 53
useradd, user accounts, creating 126
users, changing 55
utilities
   Control-Panel 39
   Disk Defragmenter 10
   LinuxConf 39
   local area network (LAN) 4, 147
   nmblookup 182
   Samba 181-183
   ScanDisk 10
   smbclient 181-182, 194-195
   smbmount 182-183
   smbstatus 181
   testparm 182, 194
   testprns 182

V

van Kemp, Fred N. 250
verifying
   printer configuration 29
   RPM packages 135
vi editor 67
   changes, undoing 75
   command mode 73
   editing 76-77

continued

Index

vi editor *(continued)*
  help 78
  insert mode 73
  saving and exiting 77-78
  starting 72
  switching modes 73
  text insertions 72-73
  text searches 77
video hardware
  cards, selecting 84
  finding with SuperProbe 83
videos
  cards 31
  memory 32
viewing
  files 54
  Web pages 333
virtual consoles 33-35, 43

W

waveguides 35
Web browsers. *See* Netscape Communicator
Web pages
  CERT (Computer Emergency Response Team) 286
  Intranet, creating 334-335
  advanced 340
  content, adding 336
  exporting 338
  home pages, making 339
  hyperlinks, adding 337
  servers, securing 340-341
  SWAT interface, adding hyperlinks 338
  viewing 333
Web servers, Apache
  configuring 332-333
  /home/httpd/html (default directory) 334
  HTTP daemon 331
  installing 332-333
  services, setting up 334
  Web pages, viewing 333

Web sites
  Arkeia 233
  BRU2000 207
  Enhanced Software Technologies 207
  FAQs (Frequently Asked Questions) 99
  IDG Books 175
  Knox Software 209, 232
  LDP (Linux Documentation Project) 99
  Linux 102
  Linux Journal 320
  LUGs (Linux user group) 105
  Red Hat 327
  Samba 173
  Trinux 243
Welcome to Arkeia window 213
what-you-see-is-what-you-get (WYSIWIG) 309
whatis command 63
whereis command 61
which command 62
wildcards 46
windows 24
  Add a Printer Entry 201
  Applixware Data 319
  Applixware Main Menu 311
  Applixware netcb in the Choose Server 320
  Applixware Tutorial Lesson & Exercise 312
  Arkeia status 223
  Arkeia Windows Server administration 231
  Choose Interface Type 160, 246
  Configure filter 202
  Control Panel 116
  Create PPP Interface 247
  Create tapes 218-219
  Data 315
  dctrl 258
  Drivepacks 216
  Drives Management 214-215
  Edit Ethernet/Bux Interface 160
  Edit Local Printer Entry 201-202
  Gnome/Enlightenment manager 87
  Help on Words 312
  Install Status 24

Interactive backup 222
Libraries management 228
Netscape Mail Server 293
Netscape Mail Server configuration 325
Netscape Mail Server Preferences 326
Netscape Security Info 323
Network Configuration 245-247
Network Configuration-Interfaces 246
Network Configurator Hosts 158
Network Configurator Interfaces 159
Network Configurator Names 158
Network Configurator Routing 161
Periodic backup 224
Pool creation 217
Pools Management 217
Red Hat Apache test page 333
Restoration 231
RSH Linux Printer System Manager 200
Samba SWAT 191
Savepacks management 220
Select via navigator 221
Server administration 213
Slots in library: FileLib 228
Tapes Management 218-219
User account 127
Welcome to Arkeia
Words File menu 313
XLock 130
Windows 95 client, configuring 230-231
Windows computers
   checking 171
   configuring 154-156
   machine name, specifying 155
   network parameters 156
   Network Troubleshooter 171
   port scan 281
   printing from 204-205
Windows PC, checking Samba 196
Windows Registry, modifying 178
Words file menu window 313
workgroup setting 177
working filters, building 272-273
Workstation class 18-19

WWW (World Wide Web)
   help, getting 101-102
   high speed Internet connections 241
WYSIWIG (what-you-see-is-what-you-get) 309

X

X Client 90
X clients on X servers 89-92
x command 75
X Server 90
X Window System 31, 41
   AutoProbe 83
   chivas 91
   custom menus 85
   Enlightenment 87-88
   Generic Multisync Monitor 86
   GNOME (GNU Network Object Model
      Environment) 88
   interactive mode 83
   Kickstart mode 83
   monitors, selecting 84
   Mouseconfig 82
   shells 41
   Start menu 88-89
   starting 87
   SuperProbe 83
   troubleshooting problems 91-92
   understanding 81-82
   video hardware
      cards, selecting 84
      finding with SuperProbe 83
   X clients on X servers 89-92
   Xconfigurator 82
Xconfigurator 31-32, 82
   AutoProbe 83
   interactive mode 83
   Kickstart mode 83
   Monitor Setup screen 85
   SuperProbe 83
   troubleshooting 91-92

Index

xdm command 87
xhost command 90
XLock window 130

Z

Zip
    backing up 119
    mounting 226
    using tar to save 121

Zip drive backups
    configuring 225-226
    Drivepack 227
    File Drive 226
    file libraries, creating 228
    File Pool 227
    Savepack 229
    tapes, adding to pools 227
    tar 118-121
    test backups 229

IDG Books Worldwide, Inc. End-User License Agreement

READ THIS. You should carefully read these terms and conditions before opening the software packet(s) included with this book ("Book"). This is a license agreement ("Agreement") between you and IDG Books Worldwide, Inc. ("IDGB"). By opening the accompanying software packet(s), you acknowledge that you have read and accept the following terms and conditions. If you do not agree and do not want to be bound by such terms and conditions, promptly return the Book and the unopened software packet(s) to the place you obtained them for a full refund.

1. **License Grant.** IDGB grants to you (either an individual or entity) a nonexclusive license to use one copy of the enclosed software program(s) (collectively, the "Software") solely for your own personal or business purposes on a single computer (whether a standard computer or a workstation component of a multiuser network). The Software is in use on a computer when it is loaded into temporary memory (RAM) or installed into permanent memory (hard disk, CD-ROM, or other storage device). IDGB reserves all rights not expressly granted herein.

2. **Ownership.** IDGB is the owner of all right, title, and interest, including copyright, in and to the compilation of the Software recorded on the disk(s) or CD-ROM ("Software Media"). Copyright to the individual programs recorded on the Software Media is owned by the author or other authorized copyright owner of each program. Ownership of the Software and all proprietary rights relating thereto remain with IDGB and its licensers.

3. **Restrictions On Use and Transfer.**

   (a) You may only (i) make one copy of the Software for backup or archival purposes, or (ii) transfer the Software to a single hard disk, provided that you keep the original for backup or archival purposes. You may not (i) rent or lease the Software, (ii) copy or reproduce the Software through a LAN or other network system or through any computer subscriber system or bulletin-board system, or (iii) modify, adapt, or create derivative works based on the Software.

   (b) You may not reverse engineer, decompile, or disassemble the Software. You may transfer the Software and user documentation on a permanent basis, provided that the transferee agrees to accept the terms and conditions of this Agreement and you retain no copies. If the Software is an update or has been updated, any transfer must include the most recent update and all prior versions.

4. **Restrictions on Use of Individual Programs.** You must follow the individual requirements and restrictions detailed for each individual program in Appendix B of this Book. These limitations are also contained in the individual license agreements recorded on the Software Media. These limitations may include a requirement that after using the program for a specified period of time, the user must pay a registration fee or discontinue use. By opening the Software packet(s), you will be agreeing to abide by the licenses and restrictions for these individual programs that are detailed in Appendix B and on the Software Media. None of the material on this Software Media or listed in this Book may ever be redistributed, in original or modified form, for commercial purposes.

5. **Limited Warranty.**

   (a) IDGB warrants that the Software and Software Media are free from defects in materials and workmanship under normal use for a period of sixty (60) days from the date of purchase of this Book. If IDGB receives notification within the warranty period of defects in materials or workmanship, IDGB will replace the defective Software Media.

   (b) IDGB AND THE AUTHORS OF THE BOOK DISCLAIM ALL OTHER WARRANTIES, EXPRESS OR IMPLIED, INCLUDING WITHOUT LIMITATION IMPLIED WARRANTIES OF MERCHANTABILITY AND FITNESS FOR A PARTICULAR PURPOSE, WITH RESPECT TO THE SOFTWARE, THE PROGRAMS, THE SOURCE CODE CONTAINED THEREIN, AND/OR THE TECHNIQUES DESCRIBED IN THIS BOOK. IDGB DOES NOT WARRANT THAT THE FUNCTIONS CONTAINED IN THE SOFTWARE WILL MEET YOUR REQUIREMENTS OR THAT THE OPERATION OF THE SOFTWARE WILL BE ERROR FREE.

   (c) This limited warranty gives you specific legal rights, and you may have other rights that vary from jurisdiction to jurisdiction.

6. **Remedies.**

   (a) IDGB's entire liability and your exclusive remedy for defects in materials and workmanship shall be limited to replacement of the Software Media, which may be returned to IDGB with a copy of your receipt at the following address: Software Media Fulfillment Department, Attn.: *Red Hat Linux 6 in Small Business*, IDG Books Worldwide, Inc., 7260 Shadeland Station, Ste. 100, Indianapolis, IN 46256, or call 1-800-762-2974. Please allow three to four weeks for delivery. This Limited Warranty is void if failure of the Software Media has resulted from accident, abuse, or misapplication. Any replacement Software Media will be warranted for the remainder of the original warranty period or thirty (30) days, whichever is longer.

(b) In no event shall IDGB or the authors be liable for any damages whatsoever (including without limitation damages for loss of business profits, business interruption, loss of business information, or any other pecuniary loss) arising from the use of or inability to use the Book or the Software, even if IDGB has been advised of the possibility of such damages.

(c) Because some jurisdictions do not allow the exclusion or limitation of liability for consequential or incidental damages, the above limitation or exclusion may not apply to you.

7. **U.S. Government Restricted Rights.** Use, duplication, or disclosure of the Software by the U.S. Government is subject to restrictions stated in paragraph (c)(1)(ii) of the Rights in Technical Data and Computer Software clause of DFARS 252.227-7013, and in subparagraphs (a) through (d) of the Commercial Computer – Restricted Rights clause at FAR 52.227-19, and in similar clauses in the NASA FAR supplement, when applicable.

8. **General.** This Agreement constitutes the entire understanding of the parties and revokes and supersedes all prior agreements, oral or written, between them and may not be modified or amended except in a writing signed by both parties hereto that specifically refers to this Agreement. This Agreement shall take precedence over any other documents that may be in conflict herewith. If any one or more provisions contained in this Agreement are held by any court or tribunal to be invalid, illegal, or otherwise unenforceable, each and every other provision shall remain in full force and effect.

GNU General Public License

Version 2, June 1991
Copyright (c) 1989, 1991 Free Software Foundation, Inc.
59 Temple Place - Suite 330, Boston, MA 02111-1307, USA
Everyone is permitted to copy and distribute verbatim copies of this license document, but changing it is not allowed.

Preamble

The licenses for most software are designed to take away your freedom to share and change it. By contrast, the GNU General Public License is intended to guarantee your freedom to share and change free software—to make sure the software is free for all its users. This General Public License applies to most of the Free Software Foundation's software and to any other program whose authors commit to using it. (Some other Free Software Foundation software is covered by the GNU Library General Public License instead.) You can apply it to your programs, too.

When we speak of free software, we are referring to freedom, not price. Our General Public Licenses are designed to make sure that you have the freedom to distribute copies of free software (and charge for this service if you wish), that you receive source code or can get it if you want it, that you can change the software or use pieces of it in new free programs; and that you know you can do these things.

To protect your rights, we need to make restrictions that forbid anyone to deny you these rights or to ask you to surrender the rights. These restrictions translate to certain responsibilities for you if you distribute copies of the software, or if you modify it.

For example, if you distribute copies of such a program, whether gratis or for a fee, you must give the recipients all the rights that you have. You must make sure that they, too, receive or can get the source code. And you must show them these terms so they know their rights.

We protect your rights with two steps: (1) copyright the software, and (2) offer you this license which gives you legal permission to copy, distribute and/or modify the software.

Also, for each author's protection and ours, we want to make certain that everyone understands that there is no warranty for this free software. If the software is modified by someone else and passed on, we want its recipients to know that what they have is not the original, so that any problems introduced by others will not reflect on the original authors' reputations.

Finally, any free program is threatened constantly by software patents. We wish to avoid the danger that redistributors of a free program will individually obtain patent licenses, in effect making the program proprietary. To prevent this, we have made it clear that any patent must be licensed for everyone's free use or not licensed at all.

The precise terms and conditions for copying, distribution and modification follow.

Terms and Conditions for Copying, Distribution, and Modification

0. This License applies to any program or other work which contains a notice placed by the copyright holder saying it may be distributed under the terms of this General Public License. The "Program", below, refers to any such program or work, and a "work based on the Program" means either the Program or any derivative work under copyright law: that is to say, a work containing the Program or a portion of it, either verbatim or with modifications and/or translated into another language. (Hereinafter, translation is included without limitation in the term "modification".) Each licensee is addressed as "you".

   Activities other than copying, distribution and modification are not covered by this License; they are outside its scope. The act of running the Program is not restricted, and the output from the Program is covered only if its contents constitute a work based on the Program (independent of having been made by running the Program). Whether that is true depends on what the Program does.

1. You may copy and distribute verbatim copies of the Program's source code as you receive it, in any medium, provided that you conspicuously and appropriately publish on each copy an appropriate copyright notice and disclaimer of warranty; keep intact all the notices that refer to this License and to the absence of any warranty; and give any other recipients of the Program a copy of this License along with the Program.

   You may charge a fee for the physical act of transferring a copy, and you may at your option offer warranty protection in exchange for a fee.

2. You may modify your copy or copies of the Program or any portion of it, thus forming a work based on the Program, and copy and distribute such modifications or work under the terms of Section 1 above, provided that you also meet all of these conditions:

a) You must cause the modified files to carry prominent notices stating that you changed the files and the date of any change.

b) You must cause any work that you distribute or publish, that in whole or in part contains or is derived from the Program or any part thereof, to be licensed as a whole at no charge to all third parties under the terms of this License.

c) If the modified program normally reads commands interactively when run, you must cause it, when started running for such interactive use in the most ordinary way, to print or display an announcement including an appropriate copyright notice and a notice that there is no warranty (or else, saying that you provide a warranty) and that users may redistribute the program under these conditions, and telling the user how to view a copy of this License. (Exception: if the Program itself is interactive but does not normally print such an announcement, your work based on the Program is not required to print an announcement.)

These requirements apply to the modified work as a whole. If identifiable sections of that work are not derived from the Program, and can be reasonably considered independent and separate works in themselves, then this License, and its terms, do not apply to those sections when you distribute them as separate works. But when you distribute the same sections as part of a whole which is a work based on the Program, the distribution of the whole must be on the terms of this License, whose permissions for other licensees extend to the entire whole, and thus to each and every part regardless of who wrote it.

Thus, it is not the intent of this section to claim rights or contest your rights to work written entirely by you; rather, the intent is to exercise the right to control the distribution of derivative or collective works based on the Program.

In addition, mere aggregation of another work not based on the Program with the Program (or with a work based on the Program) on a volume of a storage or distribution medium does not bring the other work under the scope of this License.

3. You may copy and distribute the Program (or a work based on it, under Section 2) in object code or executable form under the terms of Sections 1 and 2 above provided that you also do one of the following:

    a) Accompany it with the complete corresponding machine-readable source code, which must be distributed under the terms of Sections 1 and 2 above on a medium customarily used for software interchange; or,

b) Accompany it with a written offer, valid for at least three years, to give any third party, for a charge no more than your cost of physically performing source distribution, a complete machine-readable copy of the corresponding source code, to be distributed under the terms of Sections 1 and 2 above on a medium customarily used for software interchange; or,

c) Accompany it with the information you received as to the offer to distribute corresponding source code. (This alternative is allowed only for noncommercial distribution and only if you received the program in object code or executable form with such an offer, in accord with Subsection b above.)

The source code for a work means the preferred form of the work for making modifications to it. For an executable work, complete source code means all the source code for all modules it contains, plus any associated interface definition files, plus the scripts used to control compilation and installation of the executable. However, as a special exception, the source code distributed need not include anything that is normally distributed (in either source or binary form) with the major components (compiler, kernel, and so on) of the operating system on which the executable runs, unless that component itself accompanies the executable.

If distribution of executable or object code is made by offering access to copy from a designated place, then offering equivalent access to copy the source code from the same place counts as distribution of the source code, even though third parties are not compelled to copy the source along with the object code.

4. You may not copy, modify, sublicense, or distribute the Program except as expressly provided under this License. Any attempt otherwise to copy, modify, sublicense or distribute the Program is void, and will automatically terminate your rights under this License. However, parties who have received copies, or rights, from you under this License will not have their licenses terminated so long as such parties remain in full compliance.

5. You are not required to accept this License, since you have not signed it. However, nothing else grants you permission to modify or distribute the Program or its derivative works. These actions are prohibited by law if you do not accept this License. Therefore, by modifying or distributing the Program (or any work based on the Program), you indicate your acceptance of this License to do so, and all its terms and conditions for copying, distributing or modifying the Program or works based on it.

6. Each time you redistribute the Program (or any work based on the Program), the recipient automatically receives a license from the original

licensor to copy, distribute or modify the Program subject to these terms and conditions. You may not impose any further restrictions on the recipients' exercise of the rights granted herein. You are not responsible for enforcing compliance by third parties to this License.

7. If, as a consequence of a court judgment or allegation of patent infringement or for any other reason (not limited to patent issues), conditions are imposed on you (whether by court order, agreement or otherwise) that contradict the conditions of this License, they do not excuse you from the conditions of this License. If you cannot distribute so as to satisfy simultaneously your obligations under this License and any other pertinent obligations, then as a consequence you may not distribute the Program at all. For example, if a patent license would not permit royalty-free redistribution of the Program by all those who receive copies directly or indirectly through you, then the only way you could satisfy both it and this License would be to refrain entirely from distribution of the Program.

   If any portion of this section is held invalid or unenforceable under any particular circumstance, the balance of the section is intended to apply and the section as a whole is intended to apply in other circumstances.

   It is not the purpose of this section to induce you to infringe any patents or other property right claims or to contest validity of any such claims; this section has the sole purpose of protecting the integrity of the free software distribution system, which is implemented by public license practices. Many people have made generous contributions to the wide range of software distributed through that system in reliance on consistent application of that system; it is up to the author/donor to decide if he or she is willing to distribute software through any other system and a licensee cannot impose that choice.

   This section is intended to make thoroughly clear what is believed to be a consequence of the rest of this License.

8. If the distribution and/or use of the Program is restricted in certain countries either by patents or by copyrighted interfaces, the original copyright holder who places the Program under this License may add an explicit geographical distribution limitation excluding those countries, so that distribution is permitted only in or among countries not thus excluded. In such case, this License incorporates the limitation as if written in the body of this License.

9. The Free Software Foundation may publish revised and/or new versions of the General Public License from time to time. Such new versions will be similar in spirit to the present version, but may differ in detail to address new problems or concerns.

Each version is given a distinguishing version number. If the Program specifies a version number of this License which applies to it and "any later version", you have the option of following the terms and conditions either of that version or of any later version published by the Free Software Foundation. If the Program does not specify a version number of this License, you may choose any version ever published by the Free Software Foundation.

10. If you wish to incorporate parts of the Program into other free programs whose distribution conditions are different, write to the author to ask for permission. For software which is copyrighted by the Free Software Foundation, write to the Free Software Foundation; we sometimes make exceptions for this. Our decision will be guided by the two goals of preserving the free status of all derivatives of our free software and of promoting the sharing and reuse of software generally.

No Warranty

11. BECAUSE THE PROGRAM IS LICENSED FREE OF CHARGE, THERE IS NO WARRANTY FOR THE PROGRAM, TO THE EXTENT PERMITTED BY APPLICABLE LAW. EXCEPT WHEN OTHERWISE STATED IN WRITING THE COPYRIGHT HOLDERS AND/OR OTHER PARTIES PROVIDE THE PROGRAM "AS IS" WITHOUT WARRANTY OF ANY KIND, EITHER EXPRESSED OR IMPLIED, INCLUDING, BUT NOT LIMITED TO, THE IMPLIED WARRANTIES OF MERCHANTABILITY AND FITNESS FOR A PARTICULAR PURPOSE. THE ENTIRE RISK AS TO THE QUALITY AND PERFORMANCE OF THE PROGRAM IS WITH YOU. SHOULD THE PROGRAM PROVE DEFECTIVE, YOU ASSUME THE COST OF ALL NECESSARY SERVICING, REPAIR OR CORRECTION.

12. IN NO EVENT UNLESS REQUIRED BY APPLICABLE LAW OR AGREED TO IN WRITING WILL ANY COPYRIGHT HOLDER, OR ANY OTHER PARTY WHO MAY MODIFY AND/OR REDISTRIBUTE THE PROGRAM AS PERMITTED ABOVE, BE LIABLE TO YOU FOR DAMAGES, INCLUDING ANY GENERAL, SPECIAL, INCIDENTAL OR CONSEQUENTIAL DAMAGES ARISING OUT OF THE USE OR INABILITY TO USE THE PROGRAM (INCLUDING BUT NOT LIMITED TO LOSS OF DATA OR DATA BEING RENDERED INACCURATE OR LOSSES SUSTAINED BY YOU OR THIRD PARTIES OR A FAILURE OF THE PROGRAM TO OPERATE WITH ANY OTHER PROGRAMS), EVEN IF SUCH HOLDER OR OTHER PARTY HAS BEEN ADVISED OF THE POSSIBILITY OF SUCH DAMAGES.

End Of Terms And Conditions

Applixware Office for Linux

Applixware Office for Linux is a suite of full-featured productivity tools that takes true advantage of the multi-tasking and internetworking capabilities of the Linux operating system. Applixware is the leading Office Suite for Linux and offers:

- Words - WYSIWYG live-linking compound document editor
- Spreadsheets - Multi-plane, minimal recalculating spreadsheet
- Presents - Create and deliver presentations that incorporate other Applixware documents
- Graphics - Raster or vector drawing and pixel editing
- Mail - Organizes and filters email messages, enabled from every Applixware application
- Data - Browse and update data in RDBMS, incorporate into other Applixware applications
- Builder - Extend the capabilities of Applixware or create full scale applications using our object oriented, visual scripting tool
- HTML Author - Publish your Applixware documents on the web!

NEW Microsoft Office 2000 filters

SPECIAL OFFER!!
$10 off the regular price of $99

Offer limited to 1 copy per reader and expires 4/15/2000, shipping and handling charge of $8 to US residents, $25 to international locations. Orders only accepted on the form below.

Visit our Applixware for Linux site at http://linux.applixware.com

---

☐ Yes! send me a copy of Applixware for Linux incl. CD-ROM, the Make It Happen book and release notes for Linux

Name _____
Company _____
Address(1) _____
Address(2) _____
City/State/Zip _____
Country _____
Phone (Day) _____
email _____
Amex Visa Mastercard Check/Money Order
CC # _____ exp. ____/____
Signature _____

Offer Price $89

Add MA State Tax of $4.45 ☐

Shipping & Handling
International $25 ☐
Domestic US $8 ☐

Total $_____

Please fax or post this order to:
Red Hat for Small Business Offer
Applix Inc
112 Turnpike Road
Westborough, MA, 01581
Fax (508) 366 4873

my2cents.idgbooks.com

Register This Book — And Win!

Visit **http://my2cents.idgbooks.com** to register this book and we'll automatically enter you in our fantastic monthly prize giveaway. It's also your opportunity to give us feedback: let us know what you thought of this book and how you would like to see other topics covered.

Discover IDG Books Online!

The IDG Books Online Web site is your online resource for tackling technology — at home and at the office. Frequently updated, the IDG Books Online Web site features exclusive software, insider information, online books, and live events!

10 Productive & Career-Enhancing Things You Can Do at www.idgbooks.com

- Nab source code for your own programming projects.
- Download software.
- Read Web exclusives: special articles and book excerpts by IDG Books Worldwide authors.
- Take advantage of resources to help you advance your career as a Novell or Microsoft professional.
- Buy IDG Books Worldwide titles or find a convenient bookstore that carries them.
- Register your book and win a prize.
- Chat live online with authors.
- Sign up for regular e-mail updates about our latest books.
- Suggest a book you'd like to read or write.
- Give us your 2¢ about our books and about our Web site.

You say you're not on the Web yet? It's easy to get started with IDG Books' *Discover the Internet,* available at local retailers everywhere.

CD-ROM Installation Instructions

CD-ROM #1 contains a complete distribution of Red Hat Linux 6.0 from Red Hat Software. See Chapter 1 for complete instructions on how to install Red Hat Linux. CD-ROM #2 contains a demo of Applixware office suite, a demo of the Arkeia backup software, and custom scripts from the author. For information on how to install these items, see Appendix B.

This book includes a copy of the Publisher's Edition of Red Hat Linux from Red Hat Software, Inc., which you may use in accordance with the GNU General Public License. The Official Red Hat Linux, which you may purchase from Red Hat Software, includes the complete Official Red Hat Linux distribution, Red Hat Software's documentation, and 90 days of free e-mail technical support regarding installation of Official Red Hat Linux. You also may purchase technical support from Red Hat Software on issues other than installation. You may purchase Official Red Hat Linux and technical support from Red Hat Software through the company's web site (www.redhat.com) or its toll-free number 1.888.REDHAT1.